ATLAS OF THE
ROMAN WORLD

ATLAS OF THE
ROMAN WORLD

by Tim Cornell and John Matthews

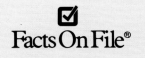

Facts On File®

AN INFOBASE HOLDINGS COMPANY

CONTENTS

Editor Graham Speake
Art editor Andrew Lawson
Map editors Liz Orrock,
Zoë Goodwin
Text editor and index
Jennifer Drake-Brockman
Design Adrian Hodgkins
Production Clive Sparling

Published in North America by
Facts on File, Inc.,
460 Park Avenue South,
New York, N.Y. 10016

Planned and produced by
Andromeda Oxford Limited,
11-15 The Vineyard, Abingdon,
Oxfordshire, England OX14 3PX

Copyright © 1982 Andromeda
Oxford Ltd
Text © Timothy Cornell and
John Matthews 1982
Reprinted 1986, 1987, 1990, 1992,
1994, 1995

Library of Congress Cataloging in
Publication Date

**Library of Congress Cataloging
in Publication Data**

Cornell, Tim.
  Atlas of the Roman world.

  Bibliography : p.
  Includes index.
  1. Rome—Civilization.
  2. Rome—Maps. I. Matthews,
John Frederick. II. Title.
DG77.C597 937′.02 81–19591
                           AACR2

ISBN 0–87196–652–2

Origination by MBA Ltd,
Chalfont St Peter, Bucks,
England, and David Brin Ltd,
London

Filmset by Keyspools Ltd,
Golborne, Lancs, England

Maps drawn and originated by
Lovell Johns Ltd, Oxford

Printed in Spain by
Fournier A. Gráficas SA, Vitoria

Frontispiece Mosaic of a Nile
landscape, from Pompeii.

Special Features

List of Maps

Abbreviations of praenomina

A.	Aulus	P.	Publius
C.	Gaius	Q.	Quintus
Cn.	Gnaeus	Sex.	Sextus
D.	Decimus	Ser.	Servius
L.	Lucius	Sp.	Spurius
M.	Marcus	T.	Titus
M'.	Manius	Ti.	Tiberius

CHRONOLOGICAL TABLE

This table is supplemented by the list of emperors that appears on pp. 98–99.

	800 BC	600 BC	500 BC	400 BC	300 BC	200 BC
ROME AND ITALY	Foundation of Rome trad. 753 Tarquin I 616–579 Growth of the city	Servius Tullius 579–534 Reorganization of the tribes, army and civic constitution Tarquin II 534–509 Beginning of the Republic 509 Rome dominant in Latium	Latins defeated at Lake Regillus 499 Incursions of Sabines, Aequi and Volsci Domination of the patricians Campania overrun by Samnites 420 Siege and capture of Veii 405–396	Rome sacked by Gauls Patricians and plebeians share the consulship Latin War 340 Latin League dissolved, Campania incorporated in Roman state 338 Roman colonization and conquest of Italy 334–264 Second Samnite War 327–304	Third Samnite War 298–290 Pyrrhus' invasion 280–275 Early Roman coinage (from c. 280) First Punic War 264–241 Gauls invade Italy 225 Second Punic War 218–202	Trials of the Scipios 187 Censorship of the Elder Cato 184 Direct taxation on Roman citizens abolished 167 Tribunates of Ti. and C. Gracchus 133, 123–122 Marius consul 7 times: 107, 104–100, 86 Defeat of Cimbri and Teutones 102–101

Villanovan hut urn, c. 800 BC

Head of Apollo from Veii, c. 500 BC

Coin of Hannibal c. 210 BC

The Capitoline wolf, early 5th century BC

	800 BC	600 BC	500 BC	400 BC	300 BC	200 BC
ART AND ARCHITECTURE	Primitive huts on the Palatine Rich orientalizing tombs at Caere, Praeneste etc. Roman Forum laid out; first permanent stone buildings in Rome	Temples of Diana, Fortuna and Mater Matuta c. 560 Walls of Servius Tullius (?) Temple of Jupiter Capitolinus 509 Etruscan tomb paintings →	Temple of Saturn 497 Temple of Ceres 493 Temple of Castor 484 Temple of Apollo 431	Walls around Rome rebuilt 378 Temple C in Largo Argentina c. 350 Via Appia, Aqua Appia built 312 François Tomb at Vulci c. 320–310	Program of temple building in Rome 302–272 Roman fine pottery industry flourishes Tomb of the Scipios c. 280 Circus Flaminius 221	Greek art brought to Rome 200– Basilica Porcia built in the Roman Forum 184 Basilica Aemilia and Aemilian bridge 179 Temple of Fortuna at Praeneste c. 120
LATIN LITERATURE		Earliest Latin inscriptions c. 600	Laws of the Twelve Tables 451–450		Appius Claudius Caecus, orator Livius Andronicus, Naevius, Plautus, Ennius, Statius Caecilius and Pacuvius, playwrights and poets Cato, orator, historian, scholar	Terence and Accius, playwrights Lucilius, satirist L. Calpurnius Piso and Caelius Antipater, historians C. Gracchus, L. Crassus and Q. Hortensius, orators
AFRICA, SPAIN AND THE WESTERN MEDITERRANEAN	Foundation of Carthage trad. 814 Phoenician settlements in the western Mediterranean Greek colonization of Sicily and S Italy begins c. 750 Greek colony of Massilia (Marseilles) founded c. 600	Phocaean Greeks defeated at Alalia (Corsica) by the Etruscans and Carthaginians 535 First treaty between Rome and Carthage 509	Carthaginians defeated at Himera 480 Hieron defeats Etruscans at Cumae 474 Athenians defeated at Syracuse 413	Second treaty between Rome and Carthage 348 Timoleon drives Carthaginians from Sicily 344 Agathocles tyrant of Syracuse 317–289; invades Africa 310–307	Sicily becomes Roman province 241 Sardinia and Corsica overrun and formed into a province 238 Carthaginians build an empire in Spain 237–218 Romans occupy Carthaginian dominion in Spain and form two new provinces 206	Celtiberian and Lusitanian wars 197–133 Third Punic War 149–146; Carthage destroyed 146 First Sicilian Slave War 136–132 Jugurthine War 112–105 Second Sicilian Slave War 104–102
GAUL, BRITAIN AND CENTRAL EUROPE	Halstatt Culture		La Tène Culture Celtic invasion of northern Italy (and sack of Rome 390)		Gauls invade Macedonia, Greece and Asia Minor 279 Gallic invasion of Italy halted at Battle of Telamon 225	Roman conquest of Cisalpine Gaul 202–191 Gallia Narbonensis made a Roman province 121(?) Migration of Cimbri and Teutones c. 120–100 Roman campaigns in Dalmatia 118–117
GREECE AND THE EAST	First Olympiad 776 Homer, Hesiod c. 700	Cyrus the Great establishes the Persian Empire c. 550–530 Sparta dominates the Peloponnese from c. 560 Pisistratus tyrant at Athens 546–528	Ionian Revolt 499–494 Persian invasions of Greece 490 and 481–479 Athenian Empire in the Aegean 478–404 Parthenon built 447–432 Peloponnesian War 431–404	Battle of Leuctra 371 Philip II makes Macedon the dominant power in Greece 359–336 Alexander the Great conquers the Persian Empire 333–323	Athens occupied by Macedonians 261 Romano-Illyrian wars 229–219	Second Macedonian War 200–197 Syrian War 191–188 Third Macedonian War 172–168 Corinth destroyed 146

Age of Greek colonization (beginning c. 750)
Age of Greek tyrants c. 655–510 →

Attalid dynasty in western Asia Minor 281–133
Antigonid dynasty in Macedonia 277–167

Seleucid dynasty in Syria and Mesopotamia →
Ptolemaic dynasty in Egypt ·

100 BC	AD	100 AD	200 AD	300 AD	400 AD	500 AD
Social War 91–89 Civil War: Sulla dictator 83–82 Revolt of Spartacus 73–71 First Triumvirate 60 Civil War: Caesar dictator 49–44 Murder of Caesar 44 Second Triumvirate 43 Reign of Octavian/ Augustus 31 BC–14 AD	Julio-Claudian dynasty 27 BC–68 AD Fire of Rome 64 Flavio-Trajanic dynasty 69–117 Eruption of Vesuvius 79	Antonine emperors 117–93	Severan emperors 193–235 Roman citizenship extended to all free inhabitants of the provinces 212 Usurpations and fragmentation of the imperial office 235–84 Tetrarchy established by Diocletian 293	"Great Persecution" of Christians 303–05 Freedom of worship restored 313 Constantine sole ruler of the Empire 324–37 Failed pagan revival of Julian 361–63 "Disestablishment" of paganism 382 Division of the Empire 395	Imperial court shifted to Ravenna 402 Visigoths under Alaric sack Rome 410 Rome pillaged by Vandals 455 Deposition of last Roman emperor of the west 476 Barbarian kings at Ravenna 476–540	Byzantine reconquest of Italy 540

Augustus as Pontifex, late 1st century BC

The Colosseum, 79 AD

Diocletian and Maximian, c. 300 AD

Mosaic of Justinian at Ravenna, c. 560 AD

100 BC	AD	100 AD	200 AD	300 AD	400 AD	500 AD
Tabularium 78 Theater of Pompey 55 Forum of Caesar 46 Arch of Augustus 21 Baths of Agrippa 19 Theater of Marcellus 17 Ara Pacis Augustae 9 Forum of Augustus 2	Augustan building program at Rome Colosseum dedicated 79	Trajan's Forum dedicated 112 Pantheon rebuilt 118–28 Hadrian's Villa at Tivoli 126–34	Severan building at Leptis Magna Baths of Caracalla built at Rome 216 Aurelian builds walls around Rome 271	Arch of Constantine Church-building programs at Rome, Jerusalem and Constantinople	Mosaics in churches at Ravenna	St Sophia rebuilt at Constantinople 537
Cicero, orator, philosopher Caesar, orator, historian Lucretius, poet and philosopher Sallust and Livy, historians Catullus, Virgil, Horace, Tibullus, Propertius, Ovid, poets	The "Silver Age" of Latin literature Seneca the Elder, orator Persius, Lucan, Martial, poets Pliny the Elder, natural historian Pliny the Younger, letter writer Tacitus, historian	Juvenal, poet Suetonius, historian Apuleius, novelist	Ulpian, Papinian, jurists Tertullian, Christian apologist	Ausonius and Claudian, poets Lactantius, Christian apologist Ambrose, Jerome and Augustine, Christian writers Symmachus, orator Ammianus Marcellinus, historian	Jerome's Vulgate completed c. 404 Orosius, historian Servius and Macrobius, scholars Theodosian code compiled 429/37 Sidonius Apollinaris, poet	Boethius, philosopher Cassiodorus, historian and administrator
Sertorius' "revolt" in Spain 80–72 Defeat of Pompeian forces in Spain (49) and Africa (46) Battle of Munda 45 Sextus Pompey controls W Mediterranean 40–36 Conquest of NW Spain by Agrippa 27–19	Annexation of Mauretania 42		Expansion of Roman settlement in North Africa	Origins of Donatist schism 311/12	Vandals enter Spain Vandal kingdom at Carthage 439	Byzantine conquest of Vandal kingdom in Africa 533 Byzantine conquest of southern Spain 554
Caesar's conquest of continental Gaul 58–51; expeditions to Britain 55–54 Noricum and Raetia become provinces 16–15 Tiberius conquers Pannonia 12–9	Rebellion of Vindex 68 Roman occupation of Britain 43 Frontier in Germany advanced Danube frontier of Illyricum consolidated Dacian wars 86–92	Province of Dacia formed 107 Marcomannic wars of M. Aurelius Barbarian invasion of Dacia 167	Breakaway Gallic "empire" 259–73 Britain in rebellion (Carausius and Allectus 287–96) Rise of Trier as Gallic capital Dacia ceded to the Goths 272	Goths allowed to settle within the Empire's boundaries 376 Battle of Hadrianople fought 378	Gothic regime in southern Gaul Britain abandoned by Romans and colonized by Saxons Burgundians occupy middle Rhône valley Hunnish "empire" under Attila	Franks drive Visigoths from Gaul 507 Slav, Bulgar and Avar incursions
Mithridatic Wars 88–84, 83–82, 74–63 Pompey's conquest of the east 66–63 Pompey defeated at Pharsalus 48 Brutus and Cassius defeated at Philippi 42 Antony defeated at Actium 31	First Jewish revolt 66–73 Temple in Jerusalem destroyed 70 Josephus, Jewish historian	Second Jewish (Bar-Kochba) revolt 132–35 Province of Meso-potamia formed 165 Plutarch, Pausanias, Greek writers "2nd Sophistic" work in Greek literature	Rise of Sasanian dynasty in Persia Palmyrene rebellion 266–72 Heruli invade Attica and Peloponnese 267 Cassius Dio, Herodian, Greek historians Eusebius, Christian apologist	Council of Nicaea 325 Constantinople consecrated as new imperial capital 330 Visigothic invasion of Greece 395 Eunapius, Greek historian	Hunnish invasions Council of Chalcedon convened 451 Olympiodorus, Priscus, Malchus, Greek historians	Persian attacks on Asia Minor Slav raids in the Balkans Nika riots 532 Zosimus, Procopius, Greek historians

INTRODUCTION

The purpose of this Atlas is to give a comprehensive general view of the Roman world in its physical and cultural setting. It covers the period from the foundation and early development of the city of Rome, through its expansion and conquest of Italy and the Mediterranean, the establishment of imperial rule by Augustus and the subsequent emergence of a new political and religious order, to the collapse of the west and the recovery of Italy from Germanic kings by a Christian Byzantine emperor. Our survey is built upon a historical narrative, for which a broadly chronological structure seemed appropriate, given the sheer length of the period (over 1300 years) described and the scale of the changes in question. We hope, however, that the manner in which we have written, and our choice and presentation of illustrations, maps and special features, have resulted in an integrated and balanced picture in which thematic interpretation is at least as prominent as historical narrative.

For the same reason – the length and variety of the period covered – joint authorship seemed a necessity, at least if the Atlas were to possess across more than a fraction of its range any of that sense of immediacy which comes from direct acquaintance with the latest research. While we have tried constantly to write for the general reader, we have indicated areas of specialist controversy and made our position clear.

Our own research interests, respectively in the earlier republican and later imperial periods, should mean that our book is not biased, as many are, in favor of the "central," but rather of the "outer," periods of Roman history. The section on the provinces of the Roman Empire is directed to the Empire of the 2nd century AD (though here too tracing change and development in the choice and description of individual sites); but in general we have found ourselves writing with greater relish of those periods which lie at the beginning and the end of the history of the Roman world. We have given perhaps greater attention to the problems of the nature of archaic Roman society and to the Christianization of the Empire after Constantine than to the civil wars of the late Republic and the dynastic politics of

the Julio-Claudians, and we make no apology for this.

The historian Ammianus Marcellinus criticized those philosophers who wrote books on the vanity of human ambition and put their names to them. As historians ourselves, however, and sharing Ammianus' regard for the true recollection of facts, we think that it will be helpful to indicate which of us is responsible for which part of the book. Tim Cornell has composed the survey of the Roman Republic and of the Empire until the death of Augustus, and has chosen the material and written the captions for the maps, illustrations and special features that go with it, and in addition for the features on Pompeii, Ostia and Roman religion. John Matthews is responsible in the same terms for the description of and illustrative material for the Empire after Augustus and for Part Three, on the provinces of the Empire. We have worked independently, though with firmly agreed guidelines and with every effort to achieve compatibility.

We have learned much from each other, and also acknowledge with pleasure the collaboration of members of the editorial team, especially Andrew Lawson, with whom we have discussed the choice and presentation of illustrations with a mutual understanding of historical and artistic aims which has delighted us; Liz Orrock and Zoe Goodwin for their preparation of cartographic material from briefs which were probably the more obscure and confusing, the fuller we tried to make them; and Graham Speake, whose editorial suggestions have much influenced the design of the book. In addition, Ray Davis compiled the material for the map on the distribution of estates listed in the *Liber Pontificalis*, Michael Whitby for the map on the eastern frontier in the time of Justinian, and Margaret Roxan has advised us on matters connected with the distribution of the Roman army. Other scholars have helped us in a variety of ways, notably Benjamin Isaac, Kenan Erim and Brian Croke, and many others who may not always have been aware of the purpose of the inquiries addressed to them by authors who have, in the course of writing, become more sharply aware how little they themselves know.

PART ONE
EARLY ITALY AND THE ROMAN REPUBLIC

SWITZERLAND
Berne
Rhein
AUSTRIA
Graz
Mur
Lausanne
L. Léman
Klagenfurt
Rhône
Geneva
Ortles
3899
DOLOMITES
Friuli—
Venezia—
Giulia
Ljubljana
Zagreb
Matterhorn
4477
ALPS
Trentino—
Alto Adige
Mt Blanc
4807
L. di Como
L. Maggiore
Valle d'Aosta
Venezia—
Euganea
Trieste
Rijeka
Grenoble
Bergamo
L. d'Iseo
Vicenza
Piave
Krk
FRANCE
Lombardia
Brescia
L. di Garda
Verona
Padua
Venice
Gulf of
Venice
Cres
Turin
Milan
Adda
Oglio
Mincio
Adige
Piemonte
Po
Trebbia
Piacenza
Parma
Panaro
Po
Ferrara
Reno
Reggio
nell'Emilia
Modena
Bologna
Ravenna
YUGOSLAVIA
LIGURIAN ALPS
Liguria
Genoa
Emilia—
Romagna
Ronco
Forlì
Rimini
Zadar
La Spezia
Nice
MONACO
Split
Toulon
LIGURIAN SEA
Pisa
Arno
Florence
SAN
MARINO
Ancona
Brac
Hvar
Leghorn
ITALY
Arezzo
Marche
Toscana
Cecina
Val di Chiana
APENNINES
Chienti
Elba
Amiata
1738
Perugia
L Trasimeno
Umbria
ADRIATIC SEA
Tuscan
Archipelago
Ombrone
Terni
Corno
2914
Pescara
Bastia
L di
Bolsena
Tiber
GRAN SASSO
D'ITALIA
Pescara
Golo
L di
Vico
Salto
Amaro
2795
Corsica
(Fr)
L di
Bracciano
MONTAGNA
DELLA MAIELLA
Ajaccio
Rome
Abruzzo
L di
Varano
Strait of
Bonifacio
Sacco
PROM. DEL
GARGANO
Lazio
Molise
TAVOLIERE DELLA PUGLIA
Foggia
Sassari
Campania
Ofanto
Puglia
Naples
Vesuvius
1277
Sardinia
Sardegna
Ischia
Salerno
Basilicata
Capri
Bradano
TYRRHENIAN SEA
Basento
Agri
Tirso
Cagliari
Crati
Calabria
2000m
1000m
200m
0
Ustica
Lipari Is
▲3899 mountain peak (meters)
━·━·━ international boundary
─ ─ ─ regional boundary
MEDITERRANEAN SEA
Palermo
Messina
Reggio di
Calabria
scale 1:4 250 000
Egadi
Strait of
Messina
0   150 km
Sicily
Sicilia
Etna
3323
0   100mi
Catania
Sicilian Channel
ALGERIA
TUNISIA
Tunis
Pantelleria

A CITY DESTINED TO GROW GREAT

The geography of Italy

The most important feature of the historical geography of Italy is the close interaction of plain, hill and mountain. Only about one-fifth of the total land surface of Italy is officially classified as plain (that is, land below 300 meters), and of this lowland area more than 70 per cent is accounted for by the valley of the Po. Of the rest, about two-fifths is classified as mountain (land over 1000 meters), and the remaining two-fifths as hill (land between 300 and 1000 meters). The alternation of these types of relief and their distribution throughout the country create a great diversity of climatic conditions and sharp contrasts in the physical appearance of the landscape from one region to another.

Italy is separated from central Europe by the great barrier of the Alps. In spite of their altitude these mountains have not kept Italy isolated from the rest of the continent. Although the winter snows make them impenetrable for more than half the year, most of the passes have been known since the earliest times; movements of people across the Alps have taken place throughout history, sometimes on a very large scale, for example during the incursions of the Celts and the Cimbri in the republican period and the barbarian invasions in the 5th and 6th centuries of our era.

Although there can be no doubt about the basic geographical unity of the Italian mainland to the south of the Alps, it is convenient to draw a distinction between "continental Italy," which consists of the valley of the Po and its surrounding mountain fringes — the Alps in the north, the Apennines in the south — and "peninsular Italy," which comprises the rest of the country apart from the islands. The two areas are different in climate and physical topography, as well as in cultural and economic development.

Peninsular Italy enjoys a typically "Mediterranean" climate, which is characterized by mild winters, hot summers and a moderate annual rainfall; this rainfall is however concentrated in heavy precipitations during the winter months, so that fierce drought occurs in June, July and August. Continental Italy on the other hand belongs climatically to central Europe. It has much greater extremes of temperature; the severe cold of the winter is matched by the intense heat of the summer, when temperatures are as high as those of the peninsula. Annual rainfall is no heavier than in some parts of peninsular Italy, but it is more evenly distributed through the seasons. The most telling sign of the climatic distinction between the two areas is that the olive tree, which is grown almost everywhere in peninsular Italy and along the Ligurian riviera, is not to be found north of the Apennines.

Today the Po plain is the most productive agricultural district in Italy. Its economic predominance certainly goes back to ancient times, and writers such as Strabo dwell on its fertility, the size of its population and the prosperity of its towns. Communications are made easy by the Po river itself, then as now navigable as far as Turin. In antiquity the region was well wooded, and its abundant acorns fed the herds of swine that supplied most of the meat consumed in the city of Rome. However in the lower part of its course the Po runs through a wide flood plain, and widespread inundations are prevented only by means of canals and dikes. It is clear that in pre-Roman times the lower part of the Po valley was marshy and subject to flooding, especially in Emilia and the Veneto; the marshes on the south side of the river formed a serious obstacle to Hannibal's invading army in 218 BC. But after the Roman conquest the land was reclaimed by a system of canals and dikes which the censor M. Aemilius Scaurus had constructed in the area between Parma and Modena in 109 BC. Further schemes were carried out by the emperor Augustus and his successors, and during the 1st century of our era northern Italy was one of the most prosperous areas of the Empire.

Continental Italy is bounded on its southern side by the Apennines, a system of massifs which runs the whole length of the peninsula from the Ligurian Alps to the straits of Messina, and continues beyond the straits along the north coast of Sicily. In doing so the mountains adopt a serpentine course. In the north they extend in a straight line which cuts obliquely across the peninsula from the Ligurian riviera in the west almost as far as Rimini in the east; at this point they curve gently round towards the south and run parallel with the Adriatic coast,

Right The Gran Sasso d'Italia. At nearly 3000 meters the Gran Sasso (the "Great Crag") dominates the central Apennine range and is the highest point in the Italian peninsula.

reaching their highest peaks in the Abruzzi region at the Gran Sasso d'Italia (2914 meters) and the Montagna della Maiella (2795 meters). From there they once again cut diagonally across the peninsula to reach the Tyrrhenian coast in Lucania, and thence they extend into Calabria and on into Sicily.

In terms of physical features, then, the difference between continental Italy and peninsular Italy can be summed up in the observation that the former is essentially a large lowland plain surrounded by mountains, while the latter consists of a central mountain chain surrounded by small coastal plains.

As far as peninsular Italy is concerned, the coastal plains have a historical importance out of all proportion to their relative area. Broadly speaking the Apennines divide the peninsula into two separate lowland zones. The main central chain of the Apennines is much closer to the eastern than the western seaboard, and for a distance of about 350 kilometers from Rimini to the Biferno river there is only a very narrow lowland strip, about 30 kilometers wide, between the coast and the mountains of the interior. On the western side, however, the Apennines descend gently and irregularly into the lowland plains of Latium and Campania and the hilly but fertile land of Etruria.

In the south of the peninsula, from Molise and the northern edge of the Gargano promontory, the Apennines run almost due south into Lucania and Calabria (the "toe"). To the east of this line lies the second main lowland area of peninsular Italy, the region of Apulia, which stretches from the plain of the Tavoliere around Foggia to the tip of the Salentine peninsula (the "heel").

In general the Tyrrhenian side of Italy enjoys certain natural advantages over the Adriatic side; as a consequence the northwestern lowland area (Campania-Latium-Etruria) has been culturally favored by comparison with the southeastern district of Apulia. These differences relate largely to climate and to the nature of the soil. The main climatic difference lies in the general distribution of rainfall. Taking the country as a whole it can be said that the north is wetter than the south, and, except in the Alpine regions, the west is wetter than the east. This general pattern is complicated by the fact that more rain falls on the high ground than on the plains; but for the present purpose it is sufficient to note the general trend, which can be illustrated by comparing the average annual rainfall of La Spezia on the northwest coast (115 centimeters) with that of Ancona on the Adriatic (64 centimeters), or that of Naples (79 centimeters) with that of Bari (60 centimeters).

The Tyrrhenian coast is moreover fortunate in being served by relatively large rivers, at least two of which, the Tiber and the Arno, were navigable waterways in classical antiquity. The streams which flow into the Adriatic on the other hand are mostly dried up in the summer, and in winter become raging torrents which erode the thin soil from the upland slopes. The Adriatic coast is at a further disadvantage in having no good harbors.

The consequence of this natural imbalance has been that the western side of Italy has played a more prominent part in the history of civilization than the east, ever since the earliest Greek colonists rejected the desolate Adriatic coast and chose to make their homes on the Ionian and Tyrrhenian shores.

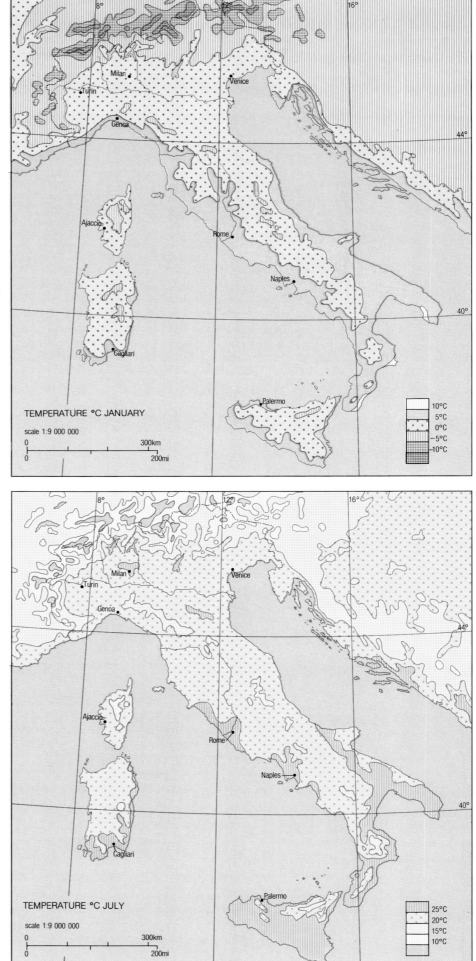

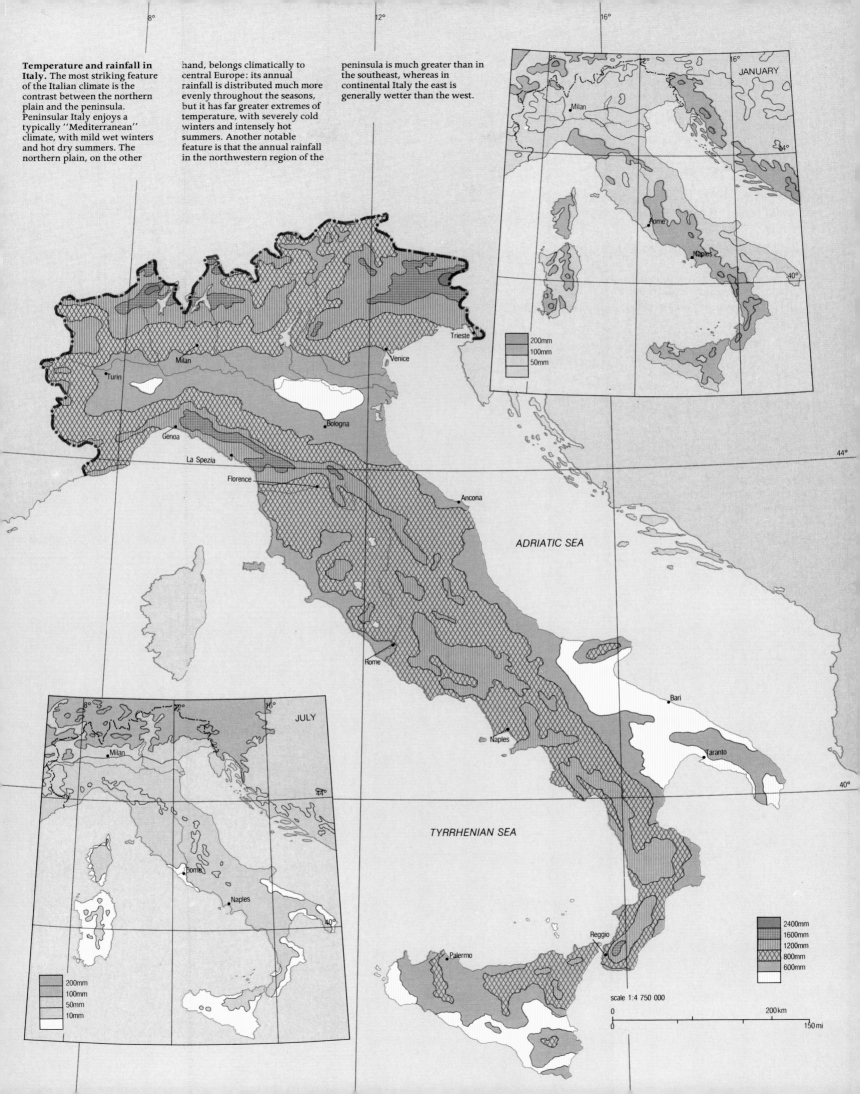

Temperature and rainfall in Italy. The most striking feature of the Italian climate is the contrast between the northern plain and the peninsula. Peninsular Italy enjoys a typically "Mediterranean" climate, with mild wet winters and hot dry summers. The northern plain, on the other hand, belongs climatically to central Europe: its annual rainfall is distributed much more evenly throughout the seasons, but it has far greater extremes of temperature, with severely cold winters and intensely hot summers. Another notable feature is that the annual rainfall in the northwestern region of the peninsula is much greater than in the southeast, whereas in continental Italy the east is generally wetter than the west.

JANUARY

- 200mm
- 100mm
- 50mm

Milan

Rome

Naples

Turin

Milan

Venice

Trieste

Genoa

Bologna

La Spezia

Florence

Ancona

ADRIATIC SEA

Rome

Bari

Naples

Taranto

TYRRHENIAN SEA

JULY

Milan

Rome

Naples

- 200mm
- 100mm
- 50mm
- 10mm

Reggio

Palermo

- 2400mm
- 1600mm
- 1200mm
- 800mm
- 600mm

scale 1:4 750 000

0   200km

0   150mi

The earliest traces of human activity on the site of Rome were found near the Tiber island, which marks an ancient crossing place. The first bridge, the Pons Sublicius, which was situated downstream, was traditionally ascribed to King Ancus Marcius. The ruins of a republican bridge, the Pons Aemilius (2nd century BC), can still be seen (in the foreground). The island itself has long been connected with the art of healing. A temple to Aesculapius, the Greek god of healing, was established there after a plague in 293 BC; and a famous hospital (16th century) still stands on the island.

Apulia has always been a backward region. It has the lowest rainfall of all the regions of peninsular Italy (an annual average ranging between 57 and 67 centimeters), and suffers badly from drought, especially in the barren and riverless uplands of the Murge, the limestone plateau between Bari and Taranto. In Cicero's day (the 1st century BC) Apulia was the ''most sparsely populated part of Italy'' (*Letters to Atticus* 13.4), and throughout antiquity it remained culturally isolated and politically unimportant.

The other main lowland area of peninsular Italy lies to the west of the central Apennines and occupies the regions of Campania, Latium and Tuscany. These regions exhibit a variety of physical features. A network of volcanic hills and mountains runs down the western side of Italy from Mount Amiata in southern Tuscany to the still active Vesuvius on the bay of Naples. The greater part of this system consists of extinct volcanoes surrounded by volcanic tuff plateaus and interspersed with a series of crater lakes, the main examples being lakes Bolsena, Vico and Bracciano in south Etruria, Albano and Nemi to the south of Rome in the Alban hills, and Lake Averno in the Campi Flegrei to the west of Naples. The volcanic soil of this central region contains essential natural fertilizers (phosphates and potash) and is extremely productive. Along the Tyrrhenian coast is a series of small alluvial plains, while the interior of the region is traversed by an interconnected chain of elevated basins which borders the eastern side; the most important of these alluvial valleys are the upper Arno between Florence and Arezzo, the Val di Chiana, the middle Tiber, and the Liri, Sacco and Volturno valleys which connect Latium and Campania.

These river valleys are also natural corridors of communication, and together they form the main longitudinal route along the western side of Italy which is followed today by the main railroad track and the Autostrada del Sole between Florence and Naples. The chief natural lines of communication from the coast to the interior also run along the river valleys, and above all along the Tiber. The lower Tiber valley is the nodal point of the network of natural communications of central Italy, and it was inevitable that the lowest available crossing of the Tiber, which occurs at Rome, should become an important center. A defensible position with a good supply of fresh water, it dominated the crossing point at the Tiber island, where the first bridge, the Pons Sublicius, was constructed in the reign of King Ancus Marcius. In historical times this part of the city comprised the commercial harbor (the Portus) and the cattle market (the Forum Boarium). It was also the site of the ''Great Altar'' of Hercules, which was supposedly founded by the natives of the region in gratitude to Hercules, who had slain Cacus, the giant of the Palatine. The legend implies that the Forum Boarium was an important meeting

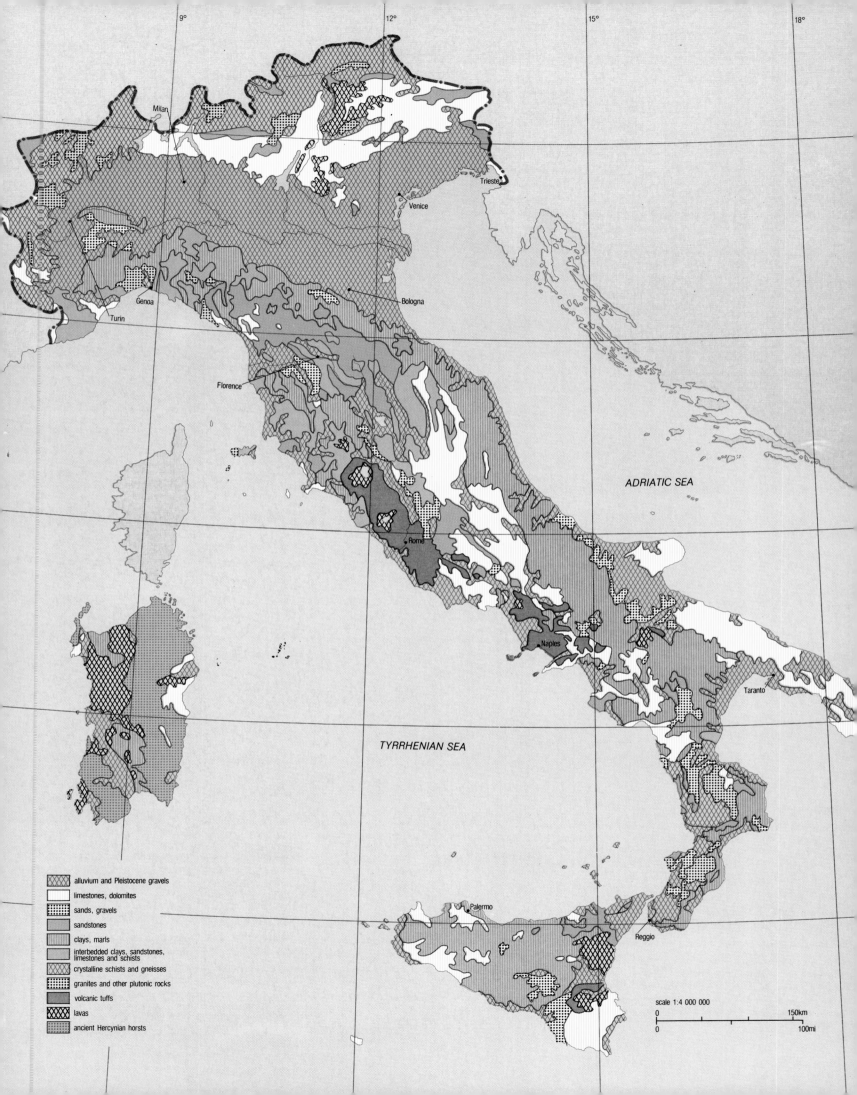

ADRIATIC SEA

TYRRHENIAN SEA

Milan

Trieste

Venice

Genoa

Turin

Bologna

Florence

Rome

Naples

Taranto

Palermo

Reggio

	alluvium and Pleistocene gravels
	limestones, dolomites
	sands, gravels
	sandstones
	clays, marls
	interbedded clays, sandstones, limestones and schists
	crystalline schists and gneisses
	granites and other plutonic rocks
	volcanic tuffs
	lavas
	ancient Hercynian horsts

scale 1:4 000 000

0   150km

0   100mi

place which was frequented before the city of Rome was founded.

The natural advantages of the site were clearly recognized by the Romans themselves. Thus Livy, in a speech which he puts into the mouth of Camillus: ''Not without reason did gods and men choose this spot for the site of our city — the salubrious hills, the river to bring us produce from the inland regions and sea-borne commerce from abroad, the sea itself, near enough for convenience yet not so near as to bring danger from foreign fleets, our situation in the very heart of Italy — all these advantages make it of all places in the world the best for a city destined to grow great'' (Livy 5. 54. 4).

The foundation of Rome

The beginnings of Rome have been the object of inquiry, speculation and controversy since historical writing first began. As early as the 5th century BC Greek historians included Rome among the foundations of the Trojan hero Aeneas, who was thought to have fled to Italy after the sack of Troy. Aeneas was in fact only one of several mythical adventurers who were said to have wandered around the western Mediterranean and to have founded settlements along its shores. Whether any historical reality lies behind these legends is doubtful, but they were popular with the Greek reading public and eventually took root also in Rome.

The Romans themselves produced no historical literature until about 200 BC when a senator of illustrious family, Q. Fabius Pictor, wrote the first history of Rome. The work, written in Greek, does not survive, apart from a few quotations. Fabius Pictor probably consulted priestly archives, the records of the leading aristocratic families and the accounts of Greek historians; these sources, together with the evidence of popular oral tradition and of archaic inscriptions, monuments and relics, are likely to have formed the basis of his account of Rome's earliest history. Fabius Pictor attributed the foundation of the city to Romulus. According to the traditional story, Romulus was abandoned as a child on the banks of the Tiber, together with his twin brother Remus. The infants were saved when they were suckled by a she-wolf, and then rescued by shepherds among whom they spent their early years in the hills overlooking the left bank of the river. It was here that Romulus later founded the city that bore his name, after killing his brother in a petty quarrel.

This famous story was part of the oldest native tradition, and was well established as part of the city's heritage many years before the time of Fabius Pictor. But at a certain point (the dating is uncertain) the story of Aeneas was accepted locally and grafted onto the native tradition. The result was a version which eventually became canonical: Aeneas arrived in Latium where he founded the city of Lavinium; after his death his son Ascanius founded Alba Longa, where his descendants ruled as kings for over 400 years. Romulus and Remus belonged to this line, being the sons of the god Mars and the daughter of one of the kings of Alba.

This contrived assemblage of folk tale and conjecture was put together in the course of the 3rd century BC. A version of it certainly appeared in Fabius Pictor, and it was handed down and developed in later historical works until it received definitive treatment in the hands of Virgil, Ovid and Livy. Historical elements in the story are hard to discern. As has been said, the part played by Aeneas and the Trojans is almost certainly pure fiction, although some scholars see in it a dim memory of contacts between the Aegean world and Italy in the Mycenaean age. The prominence of Lavinium and Alba Longa does however reflect the importance which these places had as religious centers in early times; it is striking that some of the earliest archaeological traces of permanent settlement in Latium have been found precisely at Lavinium and in the area of the Alban hills. It should be noted, however, that the very earliest Latin sites also include Rome, which cannot at present be shown to be later than either Lavinium or the Alban hills sites. The developed tradition held that all the historic centers of Latium were colonies of Alba Longa and that Rome was the latest; but the supposed chronological interval between the foundations of Alba and Rome is a purely artificial construction based on the discrepancy between the conventional Greek date (1182 BC) for the Trojan War, in which Aeneas took part, and the firmly held belief of the Romans that their city was founded in the 8th century BC. The consequence was that a dynasty of kings of Alba had to be fabricated in order to fill the gap of more than 400 years between Aeneas and Romulus.

Most Roman writers believed that the city was founded in the 8th century BC, although there was disagreement about the exact year. Fabius Pictor placed it in 748 BC, but other alternatives (753, 751, 728) were canvassed by his successors. The date which finally became standard (753) was proposed by the scholar M. Terentius Varro at the end of the Republic. Traces of primitive huts have been found on the Palatine hill, traditionally the site of Romulus' settlement, dating from the 8th century BC; but other finds, mostly from tombs in the valley of the Forum, seem to indicate that the site had been occupied from at least the 10th century. The archaeological evidence does however seem to confirm that the Palatine was the first part of the city to be permanently settled. Thus it can be said that some of the elements of the foundation story may be based on fact, although Romulus himself cannot be considered historical. But the belief that the city came into being through a deliberate act of ''foundation'' made it necessary to postulate a founder; the same mechanical process required that Romulus must have created some of the basic institutions of the city. Thus the senate, the tribes, the *curiae* and so on are attributed to him by our sources, which are effectively saying that these institutions were as old as the city itself. In this they were probably correct.

Since the work of Theodor Mommsen in the last century it has been recognized that our tradition is basically sound on the history of the constitution, but is less reliable when dealing with political and military events. But even the most sensational and romantic parts of the traditional story may contain elements of historical fact, as an extreme example will illustrate. A few months after the founding of the city, so we are told, there occurred the rape of the Sabine women, a notorious escapade that led to a

Above The story of the miraculous rescue of Romulus and Remus became a favorite theme in Roman art. This relief on a stone altar of the 2nd century AD shows the shepherd Faustulus discovering the twins and the she-wolf near the Palatine.

Left: The geology of Italy. The geology of Italy is mainly determined by that of the Apennines, the great chain of mountains that forms the backbone of the peninsula. The Apennines consist largely of limestone, sandstone and clay in the northern and central districts, and of granite in Calabria. The western foothills of the Apennines in Tuscany are rich in mineral deposits; while further south along the shores of the Tyrrhenian Sea there is a series of volcanic zones, extinct in the region of Lazio from Mt Amiata to the Alban hills south of Rome, but still active in the area of Mt Vesuvius, which has erupted on several occasions since the great explosion of 24 August 79 AD.

war between the Romans and the Sabines and then to a reconciliation between them and the joint rule of their respective leaders, Romulus and Titus Tatius. This story, fantastic though its details are, forms part of a considerable body of evidence which suggests that the population of early Rome contained a significant Sabine element; for example the Latin language exhibits many signs of Sabine influence, most strikingly in certain basic domestic words such as *bos* ("ox"), *scrofa* ("sow") and *popina* ("kitchen").

Secondly, the union of Romans and Sabines under the joint rule of Romulus and Titus Tatius must be considered in the light of the many indications that Rome came into existence as the result of a fusion of two communities, the one on the Palatine, the other on the Quirinal – or perhaps rather through the incorporation of the latter by the former. That Rome was originally a double community is the view of our sources (Livy (1.13.4) writes of the *geminata urbs*, "the two-fold city"), and is confirmed by the dualism of certain archaic institutions. Thus for example the Salii, the "dancing priests" of Mars, were divided into two groups – the Salii of the Palatine and the Salii of the Quirinal. This primitive dualism may also be reflected in the fact that the Roman citizens were also called "Quirites."

The early kings

After Romulus' death the kingship was held in turn by men of Sabine and Latin extraction. The Sabine Numa Pompilius, Rome's second king, is presented in the tradition as a pious man whose peaceful reign saw the creation of the major priesthoods and religious institutions of Rome, and in particular of the calendar. He was succeeded by the Latin Tullus Hostilius, a fierce warrior who fought an epic struggle against Alba Longa, Rome's mother-city, and finally destroyed it. The next king was Ancus Marcius, a Sabine, who was remembered by tradition for extending Roman territory as far as the coast and for the foundation of Ostia at the mouth of the Tiber.

With the exception of the shadowy Romulus these early kings are probably historical. Admittedly they no longer emerge from the legends as real flesh-and-blood personalities – it is obvious for instance that the pacific Numa and the bellicose Tullus are little more than contrasting stereotypes – but we need not doubt that the kings of Rome did include men named Numa Pompilius, Tullus Hostilius and Ancus Marcius. The traditions that linked their names with particular institutions and military achievements may well be correct in essentials. Above all the stories are set against a background of authentic constitutional practice, and it is possible to piece together a coherent and plausible reconstruction of the political and social organization of Rome under the early kings.

Political and social organization

We are told that Romulus chose a hundred "fathers" to advise him; these men formed the first senate, and their descendants were known as patricians. He also divided the people into three tribes, called Ramnes, Tities and Luceres, which were in their turn subdivided into 30 smaller units (ten in each tribe) called *curiae*. The *curiae* were local

divisions, but membership was also determined by kinship. This means, probably, that in origin the *curiae* consisted of groups of neighboring families. They also functioned as constituent units of a primitive assembly, the *comitia curiata*. Romulus is also said to have organized an army of 3000 infantry (*milites*) and 300 cavalry (*celeres*), each tribe contributing 1000 and 100 men respectively. The tribal contingents were commanded by tribunes (*tribuni militum, tribuni celerum*).

At the head of the state was the king. Kingship in early Rome was not hereditary. On the death of a king the functions of government were carried on by the senators, each one in turn holding office for a period of five days, with the title *interrex* ("between-king"), until a suitable successor could be found. The essential test of his suitability was religious. According to Livy, the normal procedure was for the augurs (experts in divination) to ask the gods to give their assent by sending suitable signs (auspices). Thus the king was "inaugurated," a word that has passed into our language. Finally, the king's position was confirmed by a vote of the *comitia curiata*.

The king had political, military, judicial and religious functions, and the powers he exercised in these spheres can be summed up in the concept of *imperium*. This *imperium* was a kind of divine or magical authority which could only be conferred by inauguration and the taking of auspices. As for the senate, its role seems to have been confined during the monarchic period to that of advising the king. It was said however to possess *auctoritas*, a kind of religious prestige which the fathers exercised in approving and ratifying the decisions of the *comitia curiata*; and they played a fundamental role in nominating the king through the *interrex*, who was one of their number. When the king died (or if, during the Republic, both consuls happened to die before any replacement could be inaugurated) it was said that "the auspices returned to the fathers."

The fathers represented groups of great social importance called *gentes*. The *gens* was essentially a kinship group consisting of families which traced their descent back to a common ancestor and expressed their relationship in the use of a common name. The individual members of the *gentes* in fact had two names: a personal name or *praenomen* (e.g. Marcus, Gnaeus, Titus) and a gentile name or *nomen* in the form of a patronymic (hence Marcius, Naevius, Titius). We may compare the names of the Scottish clans – MacDonald, MacGregor, etc. The two-name system is found also among other Italic peoples, and must imply that they too had *gentes*.

In the historical period the *gentes* practiced their own religious rites and festivals, and had their own distinctive customs in matters such as burial of the dead. Their origin and their character in early times are however matters of dispute. Some scholars have argued that the *gens* was a primordial unit which existed before the emergence of the state; on this view it functioned as an autonomous political and economic organization, possessing its own territory and its own recognized leader. Some residual traces of this hypothetical "gentile organization" survived into the republican period, and can be seen for example in the exploit of the Fabian *gens*, which in 479 BC fought a private war against the town of Veii. The notion of the *gentes* existing "before the

This terracotta head of Hermes is from a 6th-century statue group which stood on the roof of a temple at Veii. The sculptures are popularly attributed to Vulca, a famous Veientine artist of the time who was summoned to Rome by King Tarquin to make the cult statue of Jupiter for the temple on the Capitol.

The *fasces* (bundles of rods and axes) symbolized the powers of the chief magistrates, and were carried by their attendants (lictors). According to tradition the *fasces* were among the royal insignia borrowed from the Etruscans, a tradition confirmed by the discovery of an iron model of *fasces* in the Etruscan town of Vetulonia.

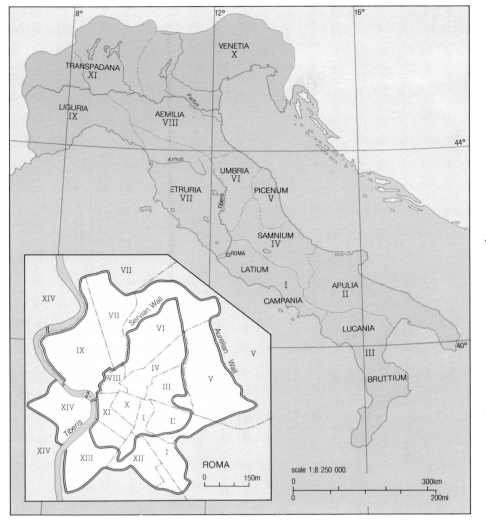

The Regions of Rome

I	Porta Capena
II	Caelimontium
III	Isis et Serapis
IV	Templum Pacis
V	Esquiliae
VI	Alta Semita
VII	Via Lata
VIII	Forum Romanum
IX	Circus Flaminius
X	Palatium
XI	Circus Maximus
XII	Piscina Publica
XIII	Aventinus
XIV	Trans Tiberim

Augustan regions of Italy and regions of Rome. In early times, Italy was a country of great linguistic, ethnic and cultural diversity. With the unification of the country under Roman rule this primitive disunity was largely, but not entirely, submerged; traces of it were, and still are, preserved in the names of the Italian regions. The first formal division of Italy into regions was made by the emperor Augustus, who divided the country into 11 administrative districts. The city of Rome was similarly divided into 14 regions for administrative purposes.

state'' is however very speculative, and their position in relation to the tribes and *curiae* is uncertain.

In historical times the family, not the *gens*, was the basic unit of Roman society. The Roman *familia* comprised the whole household, including property as well as persons, and was under the control of the head of the household, the *paterfamilias*. The *paterfamilias* exercised a virtually unrestrained authority over all members of the household, who were said to be in his power (*in potestate*). His sons, even though they might be mature adults with children of their own, had no independent legal status or rights of property, and were not released from their father's authority until his death, whereupon they became *patres familiarum* in their own right. The father's power (*patria potestas*) included the right to kill members of his family or to sell them into slavery. He was subject only to moral constraints and the limits of custom; for example on important matters he was traditionally expected to consult the advice of senior relatives and friends, although he was under no obligation to follow it. He represented the family in its relations with other families and with the community as a whole; and he performed, on behalf of the family, the necessary rituals and sacrifices to his departed ancestors and to the gods. The family was thus a kind of miniature state, with the *paterfamilias* as priest, judge and source of law.

Private ownership of property, and its concen-

tration in the hands of the *paterfamilias*, are taken for granted as original features of Roman society by our historical tradition, and are presupposed in the earliest surviving legal texts. Nevertheless it is still possible that this represents a secondary development from a time when property, especially land, was held in common by the *gens*. There may be a shadowy reflection of this in the provision of the Twelve Tables (450 BC) that if a *paterfamilias* died intestate and without heirs, his property should go back to the *gens*. In any case nothing prevents us from assuming that in the archaic period there was much greater solidarity among the constituent families of a *gens*, that they occupied neighboring properties and that the most influential of the *patres* exercised some sort of *de facto* leadership over the *gens* as a whole.

The power and influence of the leading aristocratic *gentes* derived partly from the support of large numbers of dependants called clients (*clientes*). *Clientela* was one of the oldest Roman institutions and was traditionally ascribed to Romulus. The relationship between patron and client was based on moral, rather than legal, constraints, the client having been accepted into the "good faith" (*fides*) of the patron. A client can be defined as a free man who entrusted himself to the protection of another man and in return paid him respect and performed certain services. In the late Republic these services consisted of political support and personal attendance, but in earlier times the obligations of clients were apparently much more extensive.

The status of both patron and client was hereditary and passed on from one generation to another. It is possible moreover that at first clients belonged within the structure of the *gens* alongside the *gentiles* properly so called, and that they too bore the gentile name. There is some evidence that in the archaic period clients were assigned portions of land which they cultivated on behalf of their patrons and were also obliged to perform military service; it was among their clients that the great *gentes* of the early republican period recruited their private armies.

The development of the city

In the earliest period Rome was a small village or collection of villages on the Palatine and neighboring hills. Similar settlements existed at other sites in Latium Vetus, and excavations have recently begun to give us some idea of their character. The villages consisted of small groups of thatched huts clustered together in defensible positions on the hills overlooking the Roman campagna.

The daily life of these hut villages, which probably consisted of no more than a few hundred persons at most, was very basic. Subsistence was provided by primitive agriculture (the chief crops being emmer wheat, barley, peas and beans) supplemented by raising stock (chiefly goats and pigs), fishing, hunting and gathering. Domestic production saw to the provision of pottery, textiles and other household necessities. Sharp differences of wealth or status are not apparent in the evidence.

From about 770 BC onwards the volume of evidence (still mainly from cemeteries) begins to increase, indicating a rise in the population. Secondly there are signs of more intensive contacts with the outside world, especially with the Greek

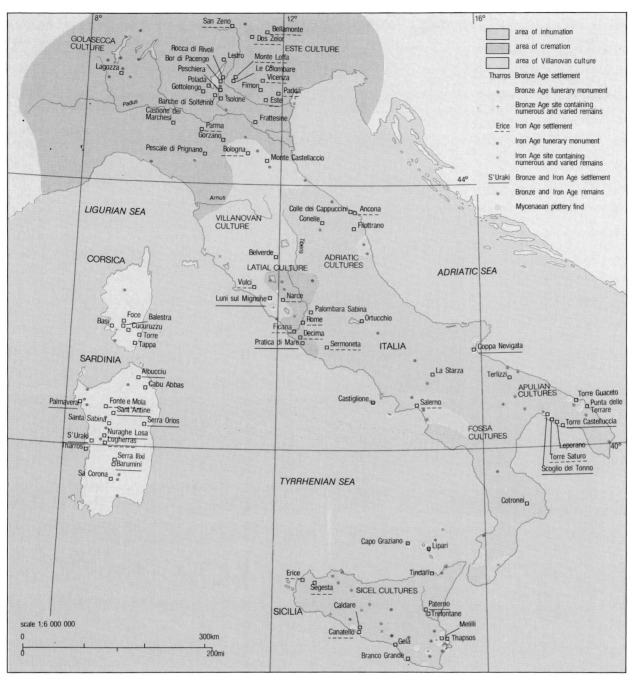

Legend:
- area of inhumation
- area of cremation
- area of Villanovan culture

Tharros — Bronze Age settlement
- Bronze Age funerary monument
+ Bronze Age site containing numerous and varied remains

Erice — Iron Age settlement
- Iron Age funerary monument
× Iron Age site containing numerous and varied remains

S'Uraki — Bronze and Iron Age settlement
* Bronze and Iron Age remains
Mycenaean pottery find

Bronze and Iron Age sites in Italy. Italy during the Bronze Age shows a remarkable uniformity in its material culture. The large number of mountain sites has led to the use of the term "Apennine culture" to describe the civilization of the Italian Bronze Age, which seems to have been based largely on a transhumant pastoral economy. With the beginning of the Iron Age in the first millennium BC the evidence becomes more abundant, indicating a general increase in the size and number of settlements, and the emergence of locally differentiated cultures. These can be broadly divided into two groups, according to the type of burial rites used. Inhumation (the "Fossa cultures") was generally practiced in southern Italy and in the Adriatic regions, while cremation (the "urnfield cultures") was the rule in northern Italy, Etruria and Umbria west of the Tiber.

Coin of 54 BC issued by Marcus Brutus, the future murderer of Caesar. The reverse type shows his ancestor L. Junius Brutus, consul in 509 BC and one of the founding fathers of the Republic. The obverse celebrates the aristocratic ideal of *libertas*, here portrayed as a goddess.

colonies of Campania. Other features of the period include increasing specialization of craft production (for example the use of the potter's wheel), and the emergence of economically differentiated social classes. The latter phenomenon begins to appear in the second half of the 8th century and becomes increasingly evident in the 7th. The evidence comes from tombs of exceptional richness which have been unearthed in many sites in Latium, especially during the last few years. These tombs contain extraordinarily rich personal ornaments and show the progressive formation of a dominant aristocracy which had succeeded in concentrating the economic surplus of the community into its own hands and perpetuating its domination through inheritance.

During this period the villages on the hill tops became large nucleated settlements, and in a number of cases received the protection of artificially constructed fortifications in the form of terraces, earthworks and ditches. This development no doubt occurred also at Rome, which had

expanded considerably from the original Palatine village, and by the middle of the 7th century included the valley of the Forum, the Quirinal, parts of the Esquiline and probably also the Caelian.

Towards the end of the 7th century BC there is evidence of a major change in the physical aspect of the settlement, which now began to take on the appearance of a fully urbanized community. In various parts of the city the huts were replaced by more substantial houses with stone foundations, timber frames and tiled roofs. In the area of the Forum the huts were demolished and in their place a formal public square was laid out. Traces of the foundations of temples, public buildings and sanctuaries have been unearthed, together with fragments of roof-tiles, terracotta antefixes and decorated architectural friezes.

The later kings
The first appearance of these changes coincides in date with the accession of Tarquinius Priscus, or

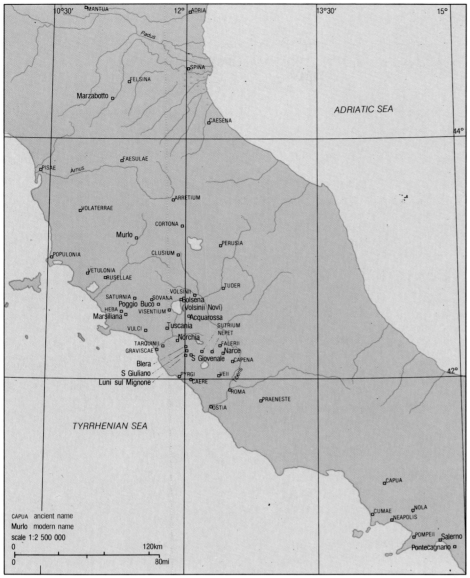

may have been more complex. For example the emperor Claudius unearthed some information about a king of Rome called Mastarna, who did not appear in the traditional list of seven kings enshrined in the writings of the historians. His evidence suggests that there may have been more than three kings of Rome in the 6th century BC, and that the dynastic history of the period was more confused than the tradition alleges.

The same is true of the downfall of the monarchy. This event is said to have occurred as a result of the outrage caused by the rape of Lucretia by one of Tarquin's sons. Tarquin was expelled but tried to return to Rome with the aid of Lars Porsenna of Clusium. Although the conventional histories maintained that Porsenna's attack was repelled by the Romans, thanks largely to Horatius and his two companions who held the bridge, there was a variant tradition which asserted that Porsenna actually succeeded in capturing Rome. The unpalatable version is less likely to have been invented than the more patriotic (and romantic) one, and it may even be that the overthrow of the monarchy was occasioned not by the fate of Lucretia but by the invading army of Lars Porsenna. However that may be, the anecdotal details of the story are only of secondary importance. What matters is that the main structural elements are sound, and permit us to make generalizations about the character of Roman society in the late regal period.

The first point to note is that a perceptible change takes place in the character of the monarchy itself. The later kings based their position on popular support and challenged the power and privileges of the aristocrats. Thus Tarquin I obtained the throne by canvassing among the masses, and enrolled new men in the senate. Servius Tullius and Tarquin II went further by openly flouting traditional procedures and launching an all-out assault on the aristocracy. Both seized power by illegal means and ruled without bothering to obtain the assent of the gods or the vote of the *comitia curiata*. Tarquin II completely ignored the advice of the senate, put to death its most prominent members and generally behaved like a typical tyrant. The most obvious comparison is in fact with the tyrants who were ruling in many of the Greek cities during this same period.

Like the Greek tyrants, the last three kings of Rome pursued an ambitious foreign policy, patronized the arts and embarked on extensive and grandiose building projects. The Greek tyrants also attempted to legitimize their position by claiming the special personal favor of the gods; for example, Pisistratus of Athens presented himself as a protégé of Athena. In the same way, it seems, Servius Tullius claimed a special relationship with the goddess Fortuna, to whom he built a temple in the Forum Boarium (excavations have in fact revealed part of the foundations of an archaic temple in this part of the city, dating precisely from the mid-6th century BC).

But the most important element of tyranny was its populist character. The tyrants expropriated the wealth of their aristocratic opponents and distributed it among their friends and supporters; at the same time they attacked oligarchic privileges and extended the franchise to wider groups. It is against this general background that Servius Tullius'

Etruria and Etruscan cities, 6th century BC. The Etruscan civilization grew up in the region bounded by the Tyrrhenian Sea in the west, the Arno in the north, and the Apennines and the Tiber in the east and south. Politically speaking, the region was divided into powerful independent city-states which reached the height of their power during the 6th century BC. Etruscan settlements were also established in the Po valley, including Felsina (Bologna), Mantua and Ravenna, and in Campania, where the main centers were Capua, Nola and Pompeii, and a number of sites near Salerno.

Tarquin I (traditional dates 616–579 BC), who according to our sources transformed the appearance of the civic center of Rome. The archaeological evidence thus provides a general confirmation of the historical tradition, which can in fact be shown to contain much genuine information about the last century of the monarchy. The last kings undoubtedly belong to history, although it should be noted that the personal history of the kings themselves contains many uncertain elements.

Tarquinius Priscus was an Etruscan who migrated to Rome where he was accepted in the most influential circles, and was at length chosen as king on the death of Ancus Marcius. He ruled for more than 35 years, and was eventually succeeded by Servius Tullius, a man of obscure origin who seized power in a palace revolution following the assassination of Tarquin. The long and successful reign of Servius was brought to a violent end when he too was murdered, in a coup engineered by his son-in-law and successor, Tarquin II, who was either the son or grandson of Tarquin I. Known to posterity as Tarquin the Proud, the second Tarquin was a brutal and despotic ruler who was finally overthrown in 509 BC by a group of aristocrats who established a republican government.

This is a fairly straightforward story; the reality

"constitutional reforms" should be viewed. Servius is said to have created the *comitia centuriata*, a new assembly in which citizens were distributed in voting units called centuries and classified according to the amount of property they owned and for military purposes according to the weapons and armor they were able to afford.

The sources attribute to Servius an elaborate system which comprised five classes of infantry graded according to ascending levels of wealth and bearing different types of arms; in this form it certainly reflects later conditions, and cannot date back to the 6th century. But there is no reason to doubt that Servius introduced the centuriate organization. It is probably to him that we should attribute a simpler system, of which some traces survive in antiquarian sources, in which there was only one class of infantry; this was composed of men who owned a minimum amount of property and were called *adsidui*, to distinguish them from the poor, who were *infra classem* ("beneath the class") and excluded from the army. The poor were called *proletarii*, since they produced only offspring (*proles*).

According to the most widely accepted interpretation of the meager evidence, the class of infantry originally comprised 60 centuries (in later times this was the standard complement of a Roman legion), and the cavalry formed an additional six centuries. It is logical to assume that at the time of its introduction the century was a body of 100 men; this means that at the time of Servius Tullius Rome had a potential fighting force of 6000 infantry and 600 cavalry.

The reform was probably connected with the introduction of improved military techniques and a disciplined method of fighting in close formation. The Romans are said to have learned these new tactics from the Etruscans, who had themselves adopted the methods of the Greek heavy infantry, the so-called hoplites. The hoplites, like Servius' *adsidui*, were men who had sufficient property to equip themselves with arms. The introduction of the new techniques gave these men the means to bring about political changes, and it is often, and rightly, suggested that the tyrants were able to seize power and challenge the aristocrats because they were supported by the hoplites.

Servius is also said to have changed the basis of citizenship by creating new local tribes to which the citizens were assigned on the basis of residence. This had the effect of enfranchising large numbers of immigrants and others who were not members of the *curiae* and had hitherto been excluded from the citizen body. From this time onwards the old "Romulean" tribes and the *curiae* became increasingly obsolete.

The popular and anti-aristocratic character of the regime of the last kings is confirmed by the Romans' later attitude to the institution of kingship. In the republican period the very idea of a king was viewed with an almost pathological dislike. It is hard to believe that this was due solely to the popular memory of the second Tarquin's misdeeds; it is much more likely to be an element of the powerful aristocratic ideology of the ruling class of the Republic. This class was dominated by a narrow oligarchy of "nobles" who claimed the exclusive right to compete for positions of power and

influence, and dignified this state of affairs with the name of "liberty" (*libertas*). The Romans were always conscious of the basic incompatibility of monarchy and *libertas*, and by taking precautions against the incidence of the former they hoped to defend and preserve the latter. The tradition is very likely correct when it states that two of the first acts of the new leaders of the Republic were to make the people swear an oath never to allow any man to be king in Rome and to legislate against anyone aspiring to a monarchical position in the future. But what was truly repugnant to the nobles was the thought of one of their number attempting to elevate himself above his peers by attending to the needs of the lower classes and winning their support by taking up their cause.

This explains why all the serious charges of monarchism (*regnum*) in the Republic were leveled against mavericks from the ruling elite whose only offense, as far as we can see, was to direct their personal efforts and resources to the relief of the poor. This was the case with the unfortunate Sp. Cassius, put to death in 486 BC, with Sp. Maelius, executed in 440, and with M. Manlius, who suffered a similar fate in 382. Later the murders of the

The "Lapis Niger," Rome's oldest public document. The fragmentary stone inscription, which was found under an area of black marble paving in the Forum, dates probably from the early 6th century BC. The text is in very archaic Latin and cannot be fully understood; but it seems to be some sort of ritual prescription for the performance of a cult or the maintenance of a sanctuary.

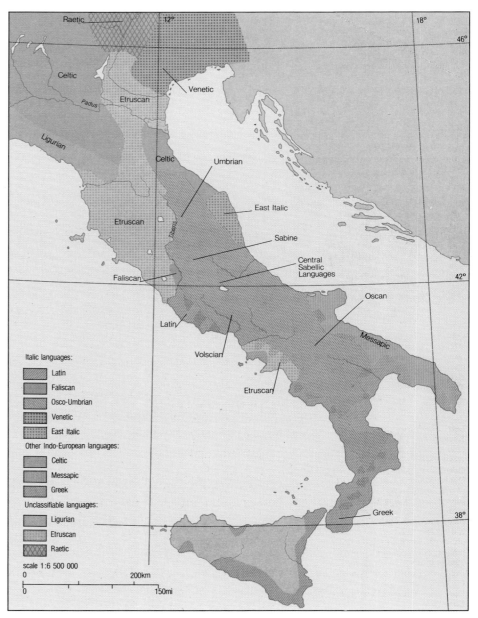

Italic languages:
- Latin
- Faliscan
- Osco-Umbrian
- Venetic
- East Italic

Other Indo-European languages:
- Celtic
- Messapic
- Greek

Unclassifiable languages:
- Ligurian
- Etruscan
- Raetic

scale 1:6 500 000

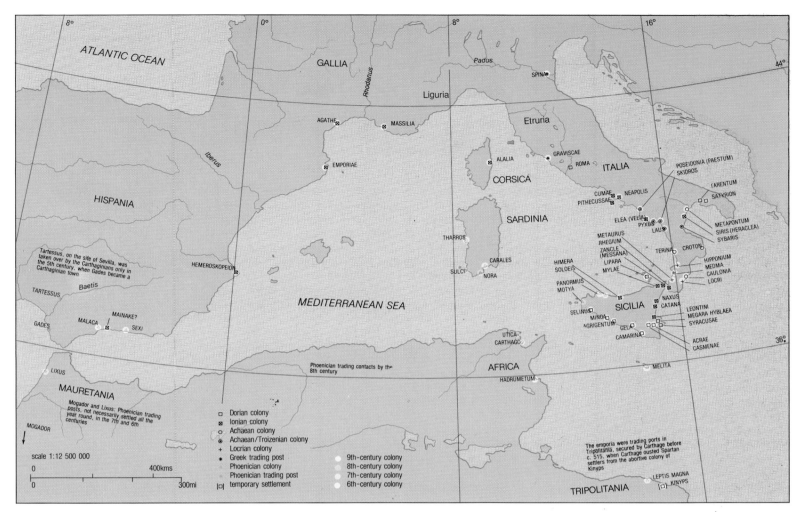

Greek and Phoenician colonies in the western Mediterranean.

Coin of P. Porcius Laeca, 110 or 109 BC. *Provocatio*, the right of appeal to the people, was considered a fundamental element of Roman citizenship. The coin shows *provocatio* in action, and bears the legend *"provoco"* ("I appeal").

Left: The languages of pre-Roman Italy, 450–400 BC. Before the Roman conquest, Italy was a country of great ethnic, cultural and linguistic diversity. Our knowledge of the languages of pre-Roman Italy is very limited, but by examining the meager evidence of inscriptions, place-names and other indications, scholars have been able to divide the early Italian languages into distinct groups. The main division is between Indo-European and non-Indo-European languages (the chief example of the latter being Etruscan).

Gracchi were justified also on the grounds that the brothers had aimed at kingship. However absurd this charge may have been in actuality, it was not made simply for rhetorical effect. At the time it was no doubt genuinely believed by those whose openly expressed hatred of kingship concealed a profound subconscious fear of the lower classes.

Early Rome and the Etruscans

The traditional view, which sees the end of the monarchy as an aristocratic reaction against a tyrannical regime, is undoubtedly more convincing than a modern theory which regards the expulsion of the Tarquins as a moment of national liberation, and the end of a period of Etruscan domination in Rome. It is true that the Tarquins were of Etruscan origin, but this does not mean that they were the puppets of some Etruscan power that had subordinated Rome to its rule. Tradition maintains that Rome was an independent city under the kings, and there is absolutely no evidence to suggest the contrary (apart from the brief episode of Lars Porsenna).

On the other hand it is clear that the cultural life of Rome was strongly influenced by the civilization of Etruria, a fact which is fully admitted by the tradition. For example the royal insignia, particularly the *fasces*, the bundles of rods and axes which symbolized the awesome powers of the holder of *imperium*, were borrowed from Etruria, as were the games, the ceremony of the triumph and certain religious cults and practices. Etruscan goods were imported into Rome; large quantities of *bucchero*

pottery have been found in excavations, and there is evidence that local wares began to be produced in imitation. Etruscan influence is also evident in architecture and the decorative arts, and the presence of Etruscan craftsmen is indicated by the story that Tarquin II summoned a Veientine sculptor named Vulca to make the cult statue for the great temple of Jupiter.

A few Etruscan inscriptions have been found in Rome, but the majority of the inhabitants were Latin-speaking. The Latin language shows very few traces of Etruscan influence, which would be surprising if the city had been under Etruscan rule for any length of time. Moreover, Latin was the language of public documents, for example the inscription from beneath the so-called Lapis Niger, which dates from the early 6th century BC. That a number of Etruscan families took up residence in Rome is demonstrated by the presence of Etruscan names among the consuls of the early years of the Republic. This proves incidentally that the end of the monarchy did not entail the wholesale expulsion of Etruscans from the city.

The evidence shows that the Romans were apparently willing to accept immigrants into their society. This curious feature of archaic Rome, which is fully recognized by the historical tradition, seems also to have been characteristic of some of the Etruscan cities, where inscriptions have revealed the presence of families of Greek, Latin and Italic origin. The evidence seems to imply a kind of horizontal social mobility, by which individuals and groups could move freely from one community

An important archaic inscription was discovered in 1977 during excavations at the temple of Mater Matuta at Satricum in southern Latium. The preserved part of the text reads: "the comrades of Publius Valerius dedicated this to Mars." The P. Valerius in question may be the great P. Valerius Publicola, one of the first consuls of the Republic; but the real importance of the text is that it confirms the picture of a society dominated by bands of warriors owing their allegiance to aristocratic leaders and clans.

to another and expect to be accepted and integrated into the social structure even at the highest levels. Thus the simple story of how the elder Tarquin made a purely personal decision to leave Tarquinia and seek his fortune in Rome is another case in which the ancient tradition turns out to be more credible than the modern theories which aim to replace it.

The origins of the Roman Republic

In 509 BC a group of aristocrats expelled Tarquin and put an end to the monarchy. In its place they devised the curious institution of a collegiate magistracy, in which two men shared the supreme power. The consuls, as they later came to be called (originally they were known simply as "praetors," but the term consul will be used here to avoid confusion), were elected by the *comitia centuriata* and held office for a year. Reelection for consecutive terms was not permitted. The consuls held *imperium* (they were still obliged to submit to the formality of a vote of the *comitia curiata*) and they inherited from the kings all the outward marks of sovereignty, although in order to avoid the appearance of having merely substituted two kings for one, the Republic's founders arranged that the consuls should take it in turns to hold the *fasces*.

But the power of the consuls was limited in other, more substantial, ways. According to the tradition, in the very first year of the Republic a law was passed which gave citizens the right of appeal (*provocatio*) to the people against a decision of a magistrate. Some scholars doubt the authenticity of this law, treating it as a fictitious anticipation of similar laws passed in 449 and 300 BC; but there is no proof of this, and the tradition is certainly not unbelievable as it stands. The consul's freedom of action was restricted by the fact that his office was both collegiate and annual. The twin principles of "collegiality" and "annuality" became basic elements of Roman constitutional practice, and were applied to all subsequent magistracies, the only (partial) exception being the dictatorship. The collegiate principle meant that the intentions of any one consul could be frustrated by the intervention of his colleague, since it was agreed that in any dispute the negative view should prevail. The limitation of the consul's term to one year also reduced his chances of making mischief, and ensured that continuity of government and the direction of policy rested with the senate, from which the consuls were chosen and to which they afterwards returned. Strictly speaking the senate could do no more than advise the consuls, but since its most influential members were men who had themselves been consuls its advice effectively bound those who held the office for the time being.

The senate was a living embodiment of the Roman tradition and a repository of political wisdom and experience. In practice it was the governing body of Rome, the magistrates being merely its executive officers.

The exception to these basic rules was the dictatorship, instituted in about 500 BC. In cases of extreme emergency a dictator could be appointed by the consuls to act on his own as supreme commander and head of state. He had an assistant, the Master of the Horse, who commanded the cavalry but was strictly subordinate to the dictator. There was no appeal against a dictator, and he was not hampered by colleagues; on the other hand his term of office lasted for only six months.

Among other magistrates were the quaestors, who assisted the consuls and were chosen by popular election from 447 BC onwards, and the censors, first elected in 443. The censors performed tasks which had formerly been carried out by the consuls; the most important of these duties was to conduct a census of the community, to assess the rights and obligations of the citizens and to assign them to their appropriate tribes and centuries. The censors were elected at intervals of four to five years, and held office for 18 months.

The new system was a very sophisticated set of political institutions which, as far as we know, had no obvious parallels in the Greek world or in Etruria. For this reason a number of scholars have doubted whether a unique institution like the consulship could have been simply invented out of nothing at the start of the Republic; they have argued instead that the consulship developed gradually out of a more primitive system in which the state was governed by an annual dictator or a single chief magistrate (*praetor maximus*). But there is no convincing evidence to support these theories.

In fact there are good grounds for thinking that the founding fathers of the Republic were far from being political illiterates. One of their most daring innovations was the appointment of an official who would take care of the former king's religious responsibilities. This official was called the *rex sacrorum* ("king of the sacrifices"). His functions were purely religious and he was not allowed to hold any other office. This ban was no doubt designed to prevent any possibility of the title "king" being associated with a position of political power. In the words of A. Momigliano, whose view of the matter is followed here, "the double consulate was not a usual form of government and implies a certain maturity. It is the maturity of the men who created the *rex sacrorum* in order to isolate and therefore sterilize the sacral power of the kings. We see an alert and ruthless aristocracy at work at the beginning of the Roman Republic."

Coin of L. Cassius Caecianus (102 BC). The bust of Ceres on the obverse recalls the dedication of the plebeian temple of Ceres on the Aventine by Sp. Cassius in 493 BC.

Yet for all its sophistication the new system was not able, and indeed was not primarily intended, to guarantee well-ordered and stable government. On the contrary, the political and military history of Rome in the first half-century of the Republic is a confused picture of turmoil and disorder. It seems that the strong centralized authority which had been established by the kings disintegrated with the fall of Tarquin, and gave way to a revival of disorderly competition between powerful individuals and groups, who were able to resume their activities independently of the control of the state and to operate with private armies of dependants and clients.

The best illustration of this situation is the story of the Sabine leader Attius Clausus, who migrated to Rome in 504 BC with 5000 clients and dependants; taking the name Appius Claudius he was admitted to the senate, and became the ancestor of the Claudian *gens*. Other examples of the same phenomenon include the attempted coup d'etat of Appius Herdonius, who in 460 BC occupied the Capitol with a band of 4000 clients, and the private war of the Fabii and their clients, who in 477 BC were massacred by the Etruscans at the battle of the Cremera river. The political importance of the Fabii at this period is confirmed by the fact that for seven consecutive years down to 479 BC (when the Cremera campaign began) one of the consuls was always a Fabius; after the disaster no Fabii held the chief magistracy until 467.

The general picture of a society dominated by closed groups or bands under aristocratic leadership can now be confirmed by a recently discovered inscription from Satricum which records a dedication to Mars by "the comrades of Publius Valerius." The inscription dates from around 500 BC, which raises the interesting possibility that the Publius Valerius referred to might be the celebrated P. Valerius Publicola, one of the founding fathers of the Republic. The important point however is that we have here a group of men who define themselves not as citizens of a state or as members of an ethnic group, but as comrades of an individual leader. The Latin word *sodales*, here translated "comrades," implies a group bound together by a strong sense of solidarity and devoted to the service of a leader or leaders. The same word is also used by Livy to describe the followers of the Fabii at the Cremera. Such groupings are found in many aristocratic societies: we may compare for instance the Celtic *ambacti* ("surrounders") who accompanied the Gallic chieftains, and were regarded as equivalent to clients by Caesar (*Gallic War* 6. 15).

It seems that this kind of society flourished for a brief period following the disintegration of the centralized and ordered regime of the kings. Many of the civic institutions established under the later kings must have fallen into abeyance when the aristocrats took over in 509 BC. One is bound to assume, for instance, that the centuriate system of Servius Tullius had become rather shadowy and ineffectual in the days when the Fabii marched out to the Cremera with their clients. But the aristocratic fling came to an end in the second quarter of the 5th century. This must have happened partly as a result of the catastrophe at the Cremera, which was in fact only one of a series of military reverses. But the main challenge to the aristocratic order came from a completely new factor which began to make itself felt in these years: this factor was the newly organized strength of the *plebs*.

The rise of the *plebs*

The domestic history of Rome during the first two centuries of the Republic is entirely dominated by the conflict between the patricians and the plebeians. Although the surviving sources have a good deal to tell us about this epic struggle, conventionally known as the "struggle between the orders," the unfortunate fact is that we are not really in a position to understand it. The explanation of this paradox is that the main issues of the conflict were resolved long before the first historians of Rome were even born, so that they themselves had only a very hazy idea of the nature of the events they were attempting to describe. The surviving narratives are full of misleading anachronisms and distortions; there are very few certain facts, and any modern reconstruction is bound to be largely hypothetical.

We should be able to understand the history of the conflict much better if we knew how to define patricians and plebeians. What the sources have to say about the origins of the distinction is certainly inadequate and at least partly wrong. They tell us that the patricians were the descendants of the original senators chosen by Romulus. There is a certain element of truth in this, in as much as the patricians were a group of senatorial families with certain hereditary privileges, one of which was probably the right to a place in the senate. The senate in fact was composed of two groups, the "fathers" and the "conscripts" (*patres et conscripti*), of whom only the former were patricians. If the patrician "fathers" were hereditary senators, the *conscripti* were probably the equivalent of life-peers.

The patrician senators had certain prerogatives in the historical period of the Republic. For example, they chose the *interrex*, whenever one was needed, and he was himself always a patrician. They monopolized the priesthoods and had the exclusive right to take the auspices, and it was they who possessed the *auctoritas* by which decisions of the *comitia* were approved. From this it seems that the original definition of patrician status was the hereditary possession of certain religious privileges; these must have been granted to a particular group of families during the monarchy, when the *interregnum* was a regular and important institution.

It does not however follow that the Roman ruling class was exclusively patrician from the earliest times. This possibility seems to be excluded by the fact that four of the kings, and some of the early consuls, including Brutus himself, were plebeians – or, at least, bore names which were later considered plebeian. The most probable reconstruction is that the priestly families of the patriciate took a leading part in establishing the Republic, and gradually extended their influence during its first years, no doubt making full use of their religious prerogatives, until they acquired a virtual monopoly of political power. In the period down to 486 BC 77 per cent of the consuls were patricians; the proportion increased to over 90 per cent in the years between 485 and 445. The disgrace and execution of Spurius Cassius, the plebeian consul of 486 BC, may have been a part of this process, which has been called the "closing of the patriciate." The final stage came in 450 with the ban on intermarriage between the orders.

The rise of the *plebs* was a parallel development, but its origins are even more obscure. The term *plebs* is sometimes used in our sources to designate all Roman citizens who were not patricians, but that was almost certainly not its original meaning. In classical Latin the word also has the more specific sense of "the masses" or the "common people," for example in such phrases as *plebs urbana* ("city mob"). It is probable that the *plebs* was in origin a particular group of underprivileged persons. It is perfectly possible, indeed likely, that the original *plebs* was not a well-defined group at all, but rather a heterogeneous body of poor, weak and vulnerable men of diverse origins and backgrounds. They probably included peasants, craftsmen, shop-keepers, traders and the like. To search for the remote "origins" of the *plebs* is almost certainly the wrong approach to the problem. The important point is that the plebeians enter history in the early years of the Republic, when they emerge as an organized movement; and it is by describing this organization and investigating its aims that we can best hope to understand the Roman *plebs*.

In 494 BC the plebeians, weighed down by debt and arbitrary oppression, withdrew in a body from the city and occupied the Sacred Mount (or, according to an alternative tradition, the Aventine). There they formed themselves into what amounted to a self-contained state, or "state within a state." They created an assembly, the *concilium plebis*, and chose their own officials, known as tribunes. There were probably only two tribunes at first, but their number was later increased to ten. The tribunate came into being through what the Romans called a *lex sacrata*. This was a collective resolution reinforced by a solemn oath of those who made it. The plebeians swore to protect their tribunes and invoked curses on anyone who should harm them. The tribunes thus became "sacrosanct."

The *lex sacrata* is otherwise known as a feature of primitive military organization among the Italic peoples. Among the Samnites, for example, we find bands of warriors who were sworn to obey their leaders and to follow them to the death. There are also clear affinities with the bands of comrades or *sodales* who, as we saw, attended the aristocratic leaders of the early Republic. It is probably not fanciful to suggest that the plebeians, who were excluded from these groups and enjoyed no special aristocratic protection, resolved to form a rival organization which would counterbalance the tightly knit groupings on which the patricians' power rested.

The patricians themselves constituted a small minority of the total population of the city (Roman antiquarians reckoned that there were 136 patrician families in existence in 509 BC), and they were only able to control the state because of the support they received from their clients. The latter seem in many cases to have been fairly well off and owed their position to the patrons on whom they were dependent; they thus had a vested interest in preserving the status quo. The clients of the patricians could afford arms and were enrolled in the Servian *classis*, which they were probably able

to dominate. This explains how the patricians retained their privileged position and survived with their throats uncut for over 200 years.

The organization of the *plebs* was an immensely powerful and potentially revolutionary instrument of change. Its strength derived ultimately from its collective solidarity, not from any statutory authorization, although the patricians were eventually compelled to recognize the plebeian institutions by a series of enactments such as the *lex Publilia* of 471 BC and the Valerio-Horatian laws of 449. The final stage of this process occurred in 287, when the resolutions of the plebeian assembly (*plebiscita*) were given the full force of law. The ultimate weapon of the *plebs* was "secession," an extreme form of civil disobedience which was resorted to no less than five times between 494 and 287 BC. On these occasions the *plebs* withdrew en masse from the city to the Aventine, which became a center of plebeian activity.

In 493 BC, following the first secession, a temple to Ceres, Liber and Libera was dedicated at the foot of the Aventine by Spurius Cassius, who was consul in that year. The temple became an important plebeian cult center, and was also used as a treasury and archive. At the same time the *plebs* created two officials, called aediles, whose job it was to look after the upkeep and administration of the temple (*aedes*).

The tribunes of the *plebs* became extremely important. Although they were not magistrates in the strict sense, and had no *imperium*, they did possess an effective power (*potestas*) which allowed them to act as if they were magistrates. They were able to enforce their will by coercion (*coercitio*); they could impose fines, imprisonment and perhaps even the death penalty. Because of their personal inviolability they were able to protect individual plebeians against ill-treatment by the consuls by giving them "assistance" (*auxilium*). Moreover, they were able to "intercede" in the general legislative, deliberative and executive procedures of the official organs of the state, and thus in effect bring its business to a standstill. This was the famous tribunician "veto" (*intercessio*).

The chief aims of the plebeians' agitation in the early years were to obtain relief from debt and a more equitable distribution of economic resources, especially land. In the matter of debt the plebeians seem to have been particularly concerned with a form of debt-bondage called *nexum*. This practice is not clearly defined by our sources, who do not seem to have understood it very well themselves. The most likely interpretation is that *nexum* was a contract whereby a free man offered his services as security for a loan; if he failed to repay the loan (at an agreed rate of interest) he could be made to work off the debt. The *nexus* was not a slave, in that he remained a citizen and, at least in theory, retained his legal rights. But the condition of *nexum* became very widespread and was the source of intense bitterness, perhaps because the *nexi* were in practice subjected to all kinds of abuse and found it almost impossible to obtain release from the situation of bondage once it had been established. Plebeian agitation against *nexum* continued until it was finally abolished by a *lex Poetilia* in either 326 or 313 BC.

The second major grievance of the *plebs* was land-

Rome and its neighbors during the monarchy. The extent of Rome's territory in the early regal period (say around 700 BC) was commemorated in the festival of the *Ambarvalia*, a kind of "beating the bounds" ceremony held every year in May, in which Roman priests (the "Arval Brethren") traced a boundary which extended for a few kilometers around the city. According to our sources conquests under the kings took the confines of Roman territory as far as the Alban hills to the south, and westwards as far as the Tiber mouth, where a fort was established at Ostia by Ancus Marcius. The map shows the approximate extent of the territories of the various Latin communities at the end of the monarchy. The boundaries as shown are conjectural, and follow the lines suggested by K. J. Beloch, who estimated their respective areas as follows (in square kilometers): Rome 822, Tibur 351, Praeneste 262·5, Ardea 198·5, Lavinium 164, Lanuvium 84, Labici 72, Nomentum 72, Gabii 54, Fidenae 50·5, Tusculum 50, Aricia 44·5, Pedum 42·5, Crustumerium 39·5, Ficulea 37. These figures are accepted here as being of the correct order of magnitude. Rome thus occupied more than one third of the territory of Latium Vetus, and was the leading power in the region. This general picture is confirmed by archaeological evidence, which suggests that Rome was a rich and powerful state at the end of the 6th century, and by the text of the treaty with Carthage (509 BC), in which Rome's hegemony in Latium is explicitly recognized.

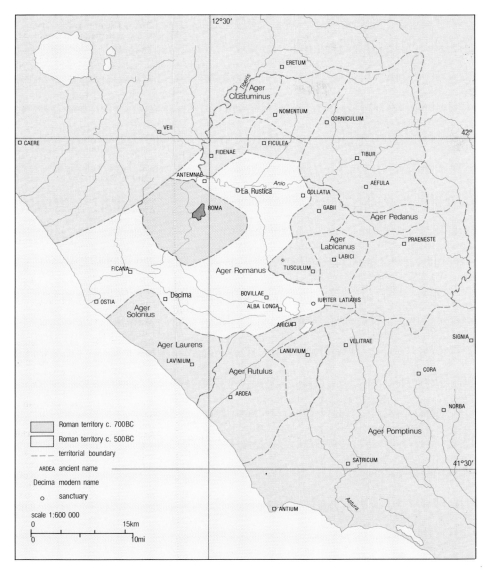

Roman territory c. 700BC
Roman territory c. 500BC
--- territorial boundary
ARDEA ancient name
Decima modern name
o sanctuary

scale 1:600 000
0   15km
0   10mi

publication of the law. Agitation for this measure led in 451 to the suspension of the constitution and the appointment of ten legislators (the "Decemvirs"). The Decemvirs were in power for two years, in which they published 12 "tables" of laws. In 450 however they began to abuse their position and were themselves overthrown. In 449 the consuls L. Valerius and M. Horatius passed a series of laws which reaffirmed the rights of the citizens and recognized the plebeian institutions.

The Twelve Tables were the foundation of Roman law. The full text does not survive, but can mostly be reconstructed from quotations. These take the form of terse injunctions and prohibitions in archaic language. For example: "If he summons him to court, let him go. If he does not go, summon a witness. Then he shall seize him" (1.1). "If he has maimed another's limb, unless he settles with him, let there be retaliation" (8.2). The Twelve Tables were not a systematic code in a modern sense. The main topics dealt with are: the family, marriage and divorce; inheritance, ownership and transfer of property; torts and delicts; debt, slavery and *nexum*. On the other hand the whole subject of public law was omitted.

The Twelve Tables are a mixture of codification and innovation. The chief innovation was the prohibition of intermarriage between patricians and plebeians. This enactment aroused a storm of protest, and was soon repealed by the tribune C. Canuleius (445 BC). Apart from this clearly exceptional clause, the Tables gave equality of rights to all free citizens, which is what the plebeians had demanded. But it was still left to the individual to get his opponent to court, and to execute judgment himself. Moreover the appropriate forms of action were not set out in the code, and remained mysterious to the majority of Romans. In these circumstances weak and vulnerable citizens would have found little protection in the law, and must have continued to depend on the patronage of the rich and powerful.

Rome and its neighbors

Under the early kings Rome was a small, primitive settlement whose external relations were confined to local wars and petty disputes with immediate neighbors. Tradition records campaigns against Etruscan Veii, whose territory lay across the Tiber from Rome, and against the settlements of the "Ancient Latins" to the northeast of Rome in the region between the Tiber and the Anio. These settlements (such as Antemnae, Corniculum, Ficulea, etc.) are repeatedly named in accounts of the wars of the early kings, but they disappear from the record as Rome's horizons become wider in the 6th century.

In very early times Rome's territory extended for about 7 kilometers in each direction and measured about 150 square kilometers altogether. But this area was considerably enlarged during the regal period. Tullus Hostilius overran Alba Longa and added its territory to that of Rome, while Ancus Marcius carried the boundaries of the Roman state as far as the coast, incorporating as he went the settlements of Tellenae, Politorium and Ficana. In the 6th century BC Rome extended its influence over a wide area, and began to have dealings not only with the historic centers of Latium, such as Tibur,

hunger. According to tradition the amounts of land held by peasants in early Rome were extremely small. Romulus is said to have given to each of his followers a plot of land measuring two *iugera* (1 *iugerum* = 0·25 hectares = 0·625 acres) as a *heredium* (hereditary estate). Other sources imply that the normal size of a peasant farm in early times was seven *iugera*. But since even this larger figure is less than half the minimum that would be required to provide subsistence for a family, we must assume that the peasants had access to some other land. The most likely explanation is that the peasants depended on access to public land, the *ager publicus*. This was land belonging to the state, originally acquired by conquest, which could be occupied for farming and grazing by individuals. But it seems that in the early period the public land was occupied by the wealthy patricians, who simply annexed it to their estates and reduced the poor to dependence by extracting from them a payment in kind for the use of the land. Agitation for the redistribution of *ager publicus* is recorded on many occasions during the 5th century BC. These reports should not be dismissed as anachronistic retrojections of conditions in the age of the Gracchi. Land-hunger, poverty and debt were enduring features of Roman society which were present from the earliest times.

The *plebs* also demanded the codification and

Lavinium and Ardea, but also with the cities of Etruria and Magna Graecia. It had commercial links with Carthage, and in the reign of one of the Tarquins established friendly relations with the Greek colony of Massilia (Marseille) which persisted down to imperial times.

Servius Tullius is said to have founded a sanctuary of Diana on the Aventine which was to be a common cult center for a federation of Latin states under Roman leadership. The foundation of this cult, together with the names of the Latin cities that took part, was recorded on an archaic inscription which could apparently still be seen on the Aventine in the time of Augustus.

The precinct of Diana was only one of several cult places which were shared in common by some or all of the Latin peoples. The most venerable of these sanctuaries was that on the Alban Mount (Monte Cavo), where every year representatives of the Latin states would assemble to celebrate a common festival in honor of Jupiter Latiaris. Other common cults of a similar kind were celebrated at Lavinium, at Ardea and at Mount Corne near Tusculum. These festivals gave expression to a sense of kinship among the Latins, who shared the same language and culture and a belief in a common racial origin. It is likely that Servius Tullius was attempting to exploit this ancient religious union for political purposes and to enhance the position of Rome by making it the new religious center of Latium. Our sources believe that under Servius Tullius Rome was the leading military power in Latium, and that his successor Tarquin II managed to achieve a formal hegemony over the other Latins. He is said to have established a political league or federation of Latin states with a central meeting place at the Grove of Ferentina (*Lucus Ferentinae*) near Aricia; he used this league to organize joint military enterprises under Roman leadership.

The view that Rome was already the chief city in Latium in the 6th century BC is almost certainly well founded. It is confirmed in the first place by what we know of the size of the city and its territory. Under Servius Tullius the *pomerium*, the sacred boundary of the city, was extended to include the Quirinal, the Viminal and the Esquiline. The resulting "city of the four regions" comprised a total area of about 285 hectares. Servius Tullius is also said to have surrounded Rome with a defensive wall. As yet there is no definite archaeological confirmation of this tradition. The so-called "Servian" wall, of which impressive remains are still visible, is of republican date, but may well follow the line of earlier fortifications. It is extremely unlikely that Rome was without any defenses in the monarchic period, since we know that other Latin settlements, such as Lavinium, had walls in the 6th century. The area enclosed by the circuit of the Servian walls is 427 hectares. Even allowing for the possibility that there were large open spaces within the walls which were not built up, there can be no doubt that Rome in the archaic period was a very large city indeed. A further indication of the size and prosperity of the city under Servius Tullius is the reformed military organization, which presupposed a force of 6000 infantry and 600 cavalry. Since these troops were recruited from the propertied classes and could afford to provide their own arms, we must assume

that the total population, including women, children, old men, proletarians, slaves and resident aliens, was very considerable, perhaps over 30 000.

It has been estimated that by 500 BC Rome's territory embraced an area of some 822 square kilometers, which was included in the new tribal districts established by Servius Tullius. At the most probable level of productivity such an area ought to have been able to support a population of between 30 000 and 40 000 (at an average density of 40–50 per square kilometer), which is consistent with the figure already postulated in connection with the Servian army, and must be of the correct order of magnitude. The other Latin communities were very small by comparison. The largest of them, Tibur, possessed a territory which was less than half the size of Rome's. The Roman state in fact incorporated more than one-third of the total land surface of Latium Vetus in about 500 BC.

Further confirmation of Rome's power and standing at this time comes from a document preserved by the Greek historian Polybius (c. 200–118 BC). This is the text of a treaty between Rome and Carthage, which dates from the first year of the Republic. The treaty (which is almost certainly an authentic document) assumes that a number of Latin cities are subject to the Romans, who also claim to be able to speak on behalf of the Latins in general: "The Carthaginians shall not injure the people of Ardea, Antium, Lavinium, Circeii, Terracina or any other city of the Latins who are subjects of Rome. As for the Latins who are not subjects, they shall keep their hands off their cities, and if they take any such city they shall hand it over to the Romans unharmed. They shall build no fort in Latin territory. If they enter the territory in arms, they shall not spend a night there."

The treaty probably represents an attempt by the new republican regime to secure international recognition and to reaffirm Rome's hegemony in Latium. But it seems that the Republic's leaders were nevertheless unable to prevent the Latins taking advantage of Rome's temporary weakness and organizing a united resistance. This resistance was based on the existing league of states which met at the Grove of Ferentina, from which the Romans were now excluded. The anti-Roman alliance may well be connected with a document which records the dedication of a common shrine of Diana at Aricia by Egerius Baebius of Tusculum, who is styled "dictator of the Latins." This act could be seen as an attempt to establish a common cult of Diana which would replace the Aventine sanctuary at Rome and provide a religious focus for the coalition.

The ensuing struggle between Rome and the Latins culminated in an epic battle at Lake Regillus in 499 BC, where the Romans won a narrow victory. Five years later a treaty was drawn up by the Roman consul Spurius Cassius. The treaty was inscribed on a bronze pillar and set up in the Forum, where it remained until the time of Sulla. The two parties to the treaty were the Romans on the one side and all the Latin cities on the other. It stipulated peace between them, military cooperation against the attacks of third parties and an agreement to share the booty and other profits of successful wars. The treaty also gave legal backing to the community of private rights which had existed among the Latins since time immemorial. The traditional arrangement

Coins of c. 96 BC, recalling the victory of A. Postumius Albinus at Lake Regillus (499 BC). The types show a cavalry charge, and the divine twins Castor and Pollux, who were said to have fought on the Roman side, and later appeared watering their horses at a fountain in the Forum.

This inscribed gold tablet from the Etruscan port of Pyrgi records a dedication by the ruler of Caere, probably during the early 5th century BC. The text is in Etruscan, accompanied by a shorter version in Phoenician. This fact seems to indicate close relations between the Etruscans and the Phoenician-speaking Carthaginians; the Carthaginians had also made a treaty with Rome at the beginning of the Republic.

Northern Italy under Celtic occupation. A tradition much overlaid with legend informs us that the Celts were tempted to invade Italy by its rich agricultural products, and particularly wine. According to Livy the Gauls crossed the Alps before 500 BC, while Polybius dates the invasion to around 400. The truth lies somewhere in between, and it seems that in the course of the 5th century the main tribal groupings of what later became Cisalpine Gaul were established – the Insubres with their capital at Milan, the Boii around Bologna, the Cenomani with their centers at Brescia and Verona, and the Lingones and Senones along the Adriatic, in a region which came to be known as the *ager Gallicus*. The Celtic presence is confirmed archaeologically by finds that are widely distributed in small sites throughout northern Italy, but the principal concentrations are in Lombardy, Romagna and the valley of the upper Adige.

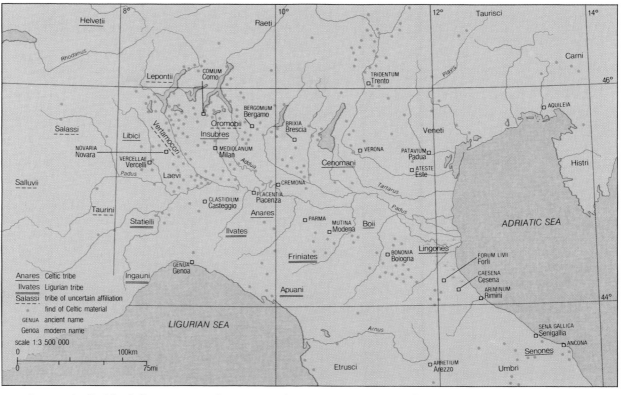

A Lucanian hunter from a 4th-century BC tomb painting near Paestum. The Lucanians were an Italic people related to the Samnites, who descended from the mountains of the interior into the coastal plains of southern Italy during the 5th century BC. By 400 most of the Greek cities on the Tyrrhenian coast (including Paestum) had been overwhelmed.

This coin of 43 BC shows the archaic cult statue of Diana in the grove at Aricia, which was a common shrine of the Latin peoples in early times. The goddess is represented in her three forms: Diana, Hecate and Selene.

was that an individual from one Latin community who happened to find himself in another could enjoy all the rights and privileges possessed by its inhabitants, and could become a full member of that community simply by taking up residence there. In later times these reciprocal rights were summed up in the juridical concepts of *conubium* (the right to contract a legal marriage with a partner from another state), *commercium* (the right to engage in commercial activity with full legal protection) and *migratio* (the right to become a citizen of another state by changing one's domicile). These rights were probably defined in the treaty of Sp. Cassius.

The treaty provided the basis for a new Latin league in which the Romans played the dominant part. It was administered jointly by representatives of Rome and the other Latins who continued to meet every year at the Grove of Ferentina to discuss matters of common interest and to organize joint military enterprises. The allied army probably consisted half of Romans and half of Latins, with the Romans supplying the commander. The evidence on this point is not however very clear, and it is in fact equally possible that the command alternated between Romans and Latins.

The military strength of the reorganized Latin League was soon put to the test. During the early years of the 5th century Latium was increasingly threatened by the incursions of enemies from beyond its borders, and in particular by the Sabines, the Aequi and the Volsci. The movement of these peoples into the plain of Latium was the consequence of a general expansion of the populations of the central and southern Apennines which had widespread repercussions. The Greek and Etruscan cities of Campania and the Greeks of the far south were also troubled at this time by increased pressure from the native peoples of the interior.

The infiltration of Sabines into Latium began in the monarchic period, and incursions are intermittently recorded down to the middle of the 5th

century. A much more serious menace came from the Aequi and Volsci, whose appearance on the borders of Latium at the end of the 6th century caused a dramatic change in the fortunes of Rome and her Latin allies. The Volsci were an Italic people who spoke a dialect similar to Umbrian. Shortly before 500 BC they migrated from their Apennine homeland towards the coast and occupied the territory on the southern borders of Latium. The Volscian wars of this period form the setting for the romantic tale of Coriolanus, the proud Roman who left his homeland in disgust at the treatment he received from the plebeians, and went to join the Volsci, who recognized his worth and elected him as their leader. Coriolanus led the Volscian army on a victorious march through Latin territory to within eight kilometers of Rome, where only the entreaties of his mother persuaded him to spare his native city. The reality behind this famous episode is the memory of a Volscian invasion which threatened the existence of Rome. Subsequent Volscian incursions are recorded throughout the 5th century and beyond, but the high point of their activities was reached in the 490s and 480s BC.

The second major threat came from the Aequi, an Oscan-speaking people who lived in the upper Anio valley and the hills above Praeneste, from where they repeatedly descended into the plain. In 486 BC a tripartite alliance was formed on equal terms between Rome, the Latins and the Hernici, which was of decisive importance since the territory of the Hernici effectively separated the Aequi and the Volsci. During the later years of the 5th century the allies were gradually able to gain the upper hand against the Aequi and Volsci, allowing the Romans to concentrate their efforts in another direction.

Rome's great adversary on her northern border was the Etruscan city of Veii, situated on a rocky plateau some 15 kilometers to the north. Veii's territory stretched along the right bank of the Tiber as far as the coast, and the quarrel with Rome perhaps arose from the attempts of each to control the salt beds at the mouth of the river and the trade routes to the interior which ran along either side of the Tiber valley. During the 5th century a series of major wars is recorded, the first of which saw the massacre of the Fabii at the Cremera (477 BC) and ended in 475 with an inconclusive peace; the second ended in 426 when the Romans captured Fidenae, a Veientine outpost on the left bank of the Tiber about nine kilometers upstream from Rome. The decisive struggle soon followed, and culminated in the great siege of Veii, which in the Roman tradition is made to last for 10 years (405–396) and is associated with many legends and stories, some of which are borrowed from the Greek legend of the Trojan War. The final result was one of the crucial turning points in Roman history: Veii was captured and destroyed by the Roman general M. Furius Camillus, and her territory was annexed to that of Rome. The effect of the conquest was that the size of Rome's territory was doubled at a stroke. Rome was in a very strong position at the beginning of the 4th century BC. But only a few years after the capture of Veii, Rome itself was overtaken by a sudden and unexpected calamity.

The Gallic invasion

The movement of Celtic peoples across the Alps into northern Italy may have begun as early as the 6th century BC. This is Livy's view, although as yet there is no definite evidence of a Celtic presence in the Po plain before the 5th century. By 400 BC, however, the main tribal groupings (Insubres, Cenomani, Boii, Lingones, Senones) had established themselves in what later came to be known as Cisalpine Gaul, and were threatening the Etruscan settlements there. By about 350 BC most of the Etruscan cities in the Po valley, including Felsina (Bologna), had been overwhelmed by the Gauls, who had also begun to make occasional raids across the Apennines into peninsular Italy. One such raid took place in the summer of 390 BC, when a horde of Senones swept into Etruria, passed down the Tiber valley by way of Clusium and made for Rome.

On 18 July, which ever after was marked as an unlucky day in the Roman calendar, the Roman army which was sent to face the Gauls was routed at the Allia river. Three days later the Gauls arrived at the defenseless city and sacked it. Only the Capitol resisted capture and held out for some months; later generations of Romans told the story that a night attack by the Gauls was foiled when the cackling of the sacred geese aroused the garrison in the nick of time. Eventually the Gauls decided to leave, encouraged, so it is said, by the offer of a large payment of gold. A patriotic tale maintained that, just as the gold was being weighed out, a Roman army appeared on the scene and drove the Gauls away. This scratch force had been assembled by Camillus, who had been in exile at the time of the Allia, following accusations of dishonestly handling the spoils of Veii. The truth of the matter is probably that the Gauls were looking for plunder and had no intention of staying anyway. The story of Camillus' face-saving victory can be safely rejected; it may have been suggested by the fact that the Gauls were caught on their way back by an Etrucan army and soundly beaten. In any case, the Gauls went away, leaving the Romans to pick up the pieces.

Early Latium

Most of the communities of Latium Vetus seem to have originated in small hut villages on the low hills overlooking the plain. But very few of the habitation sites have so far been systematically investigated, and our knowledge is largely based on the finds from their cemeteries, which have been more intensively studied. These finds provide evidence for the development of the so-called "Latial culture" from the 10th to the 6th century BC. The typological classification of the grave-goods from these cemeteries has allowed scholars to divide the Latial culture into six archaeologically defined "phases": phase I, c. 1000–c.900 BC; phase IIA, c.900–c.830 BC; phase IIB, c.830–c.770 BC; phase III, c.770–730/720 BC; phase IVA, 730/720–640/630 BC; phase IVB, 640/630–580 BC. In the earliest phases (I–II) the settlements were no more than collections of thatched huts. But during phases III–IV they grew in size and sophistication, with the development of external contracts ("trade"), specialized craft production, and the emergence of a wealthy aristocracy. In the so-called "orientalizing" period (phases IVA and IVB) there is clear evidence of the development of fortified urban centers, which appear in our sources as the states of the Latin League.

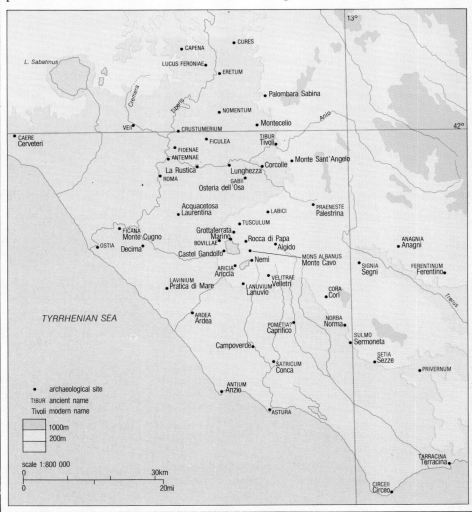

The "princely" tombs discovered in the 19th century at Palestrina contain an extraordinary amount of luxury prestige goods and testify to the wealth and power of the local aristocracy. This silver dish with Egyptian-style scenes from the Tomba Bernardini was perhaps manufactured in Cyprus. Early 7th century BC (phase IVA).

Below right The earliest tombs were cremations. The ashes of the dead were placed in hut urns together with miniaturized grave goods, including weapons, handmade pots and, in a few instances, terracotta figurines crudely modeled in the posture of making an offering. These examples are taken from tombs of phase IIA at Osteria dell'Osa.

Bottom left Carved ivory forearm from the Tomba Barberini at Palestrina, probably of Syrian manufacture and dating from the 7th century BC (phase IVA).

Bottom right In the later phases, cremation is replaced by inhumation, and the tomb furnishings become more elaborate. In phase III they begin to include metal vases and fine pottery, some of it imported from Greece and Etruria. Personal ornaments include brooches, pendants, silver spiral hair rings and glass and amber beads. The lady buried in the tomb shown here (La Rustica, end of phase III) was wearing a belt of sheet bronze.

Below Figurines of sheet bronze found in the votive deposit on the Capitol in Rome, where there was an open-air shrine long before the construction of the temple of Jupiter. Such votive deposits furnish important evidence of cult activity during the Iron Age.

Right Cylindrical "cist" (container) from the Castellani Tomb at Palestrina (Phase IVA, mid-7th century BC). The cist, which is made of wood (restored) overlaid with strips of silver laminate, is a fine orientalizing piece, probably of Phoenician manufacture.

The Etruscans

Etruscan civilization is an enigma because of the paucity of our information. Etruscan literature, which once existed, has long since perished, and we have to rely on the statements of Greek and Roman writers (who were often ignorant or prejudiced) and the uncertain indications of archaeology. Most of the archaeological evidence comes from the elaborate cemeteries which lay outside the walls of the great Etruscan cities. The tombs of the noble families were richly furnished, and provide vivid testimony of the life-style of the upper classes. But the picture is one-sided: Etruscan society was based on the dependent labor of a class of rural serfs, of whom we know almost nothing; equally little is known about the character of the urban settlements, which have never been systematically investigated.

Below Aerial view of the Banditaccia cemetery outside Cerveteri (Caere). The cemetery was formally laid out like a city, with the tombs representing houses.

Bottom Tarquinia: Tomb of the Leopards. Painting of the early 5th century BC showing an aristocratic banquet.

Bottom right Tarquinia: Tomba dell'Orco I, early 4th century BC. Detail showing the head of a lady named Velia. The tomb probably belonged to the great noble clan of the Spurinnae.

Left The interior of the tombs at Caere contained features of standard domestic architecture, as can be seen in the Tomb of the Shields and Chairs (6th or 5th century BC).

Our knowledge of Etruscan art is enriched by the thousands of artifacts that have been found in the tombs. The Etruscans are especially noted for the high quality of their bronze sculptures. Examples are the warrior from Cagli (*below*) and the Chimaera from Arezzo (*bottom left*).

THE CONQUEST OF ITALY
AND OF THE MEDITERRANEAN

The recovery of Rome

The effects of the Gallic sack are difficult to assess. The physical destruction of the city has, perhaps surprisingly, left little trace in the archaeological record, and may only have been superficial. The manpower losses at the Allia were probably not great, and would in any case have been made up within a few years. As early as 378 BC the Roman state was able to organize the building of a massive city wall, parts of which still survive. The wall, which was 10 kilometers long and enclosed the whole of the city, was made of squared stone blocks from the Grotta Oscura quarries in the territory of Veii. This region was still in Roman hands, and soon after the departure of the Gauls it was colonized by Roman settlers who were enrolled in four new tribes. At this date Roman territory measured some 1510 square kilometers. The city was well placed for a rapid recovery.

To the north of the former *ager Veientanus* lay the territory of the Etruscan city of Caere, which befriended the Romans at this time and aided their recovery. Rome's northern border was thus secured. In 383 BC it was able to found colonies to the north of Veii at Sutrium and Nepet, two strongholds which came to be known as the "gateways of Etruria."

On the other hand the Romans were confronted with serious difficulties in Latium. The Volsci and Aequi returned to the offensive, and the traditional accounts of the years following the Gallic sack make it clear that the alliance with the Latins and Hernici had ceased to function. But the Romans were able to hold their own, and won some important victories under the leadership of Camillus, whom later tradition regarded as the "second founder" of the city. A few events stand out. A Roman colony was established at Satricum in 385 and another at Setia in 382; in 381 Tusculum was given citizenship and its territory incorporated in that of Rome. But the circumstances of these events are unknown; the years following the Gallic sack constitute one of the most obscure periods in Roman history. It seems however that Rome had fully recovered its position by 358 BC, when the alliance with the Latins and the Hernici was renewed.

The recovery of Rome by the mid-4th century is indicated by the fact that it was able to conclude a second treaty with Carthage in 348. To the south Rome's horizon now extended beyond the borders of Latium. In 354 it made an alliance with the Samnites, an Oscan-speaking people who formed a powerful confederation of tribes in the region of the southern Apennines. The treaty probably defined the respective spheres of influence of the two sides and provided for cooperation against hostile third parties, such as the Gauls. Relations between the two powers became strained in 343, but it seems that after a brief period of hostilities (the so-called "First Samnite War," 343–341 BC) the Romans and Samnites renewed their alliance; they were then

confronted in 340 by a hostile coalition of Latins, Campanians, Sidicini, Volsci and Aurunci. A bitter war ensued, which the Romans eventually won, with Samnite help, in 338 BC.

The settlement which was imposed on the losers was of crucial importance in that it established a pattern for the future development of Roman expansion in Italy. Some of the defeated Latin cities were incorporated in the Roman state, and their inhabitants made Roman citizens. Others retained their status as independent communities, although some were deprived of part of their territory. They remained allies of Rome, which effectively meant that they were obliged to provide military assistance in time of war, and they continued to possess the rights of *conubium* and *commercium* with Roman citizens; however they were no longer permitted to exercise such rights among themselves and were forbidden to have political relations with one another. Thus the old Latin League was finally dissolved, although the common religious festivals continued to take place under Roman supervision. The non-Latin peoples who had joined the struggle against Rome (the Volsci, Campanians and others) were incorporated in the Roman state, but were given only limited citizen rights. This half-citizenship, or "citizenship without suffrage" (*civitas sine suffragio*), meant that they had to fulfill all the military and financial obligations of citizens, but that they could not vote in the assemblies or hold office at Rome. By extending this form of limited citizenship to whole communities the Romans were able to enlarge their territory and to increase their manpower while maintaining the essential character of Rome as a city-state and conserving the integrity of her traditional political institutions. The incorporated communities also retained their own identity, and continued in

Above The republican city wall, of which large portions still remain, was constructed in 378 BC following the Gallic sack. The arches were probably added during the civil wars of the 80s BC.

Right: Wars of conquest and colonization in Italy 334–241 BC and (inset) central Italy in 338 BC. Rome's conquest of Italy involved incorporating defeated enemies as Roman citizens or compelling them to become allies. Large areas of territory were annexed from the allies and colonized by the Romans. Colonies had been founded since very early times at strategic points near the borders of Latium; after 338 BC Rome began to found colonies as military outposts in enemy territory. The colonists were drawn mainly from the Roman proletariat (although some allies also took part). They forfeited their citizenship in exchange for allotments of land in the new colony, which became an independent community. Colonies possessed the rights of *conubium* and *commercium*, and their status was equivalent to that of the old Latin communities; for this reason they were called "Latin colonies." The needs of coastal defense were met by the planting of small forts around the shores of Italy, each manned by a few hundred Roman citizens. In 311 BC they were backed up by a squadron of small ships under two commodores (*duoviri navales*). The coastal garrisons are misleadingly termed "colonies" in the sources; they are conventionally called "Roman" colonies, to distinguish them from the (much more important) "Latin" colonies.

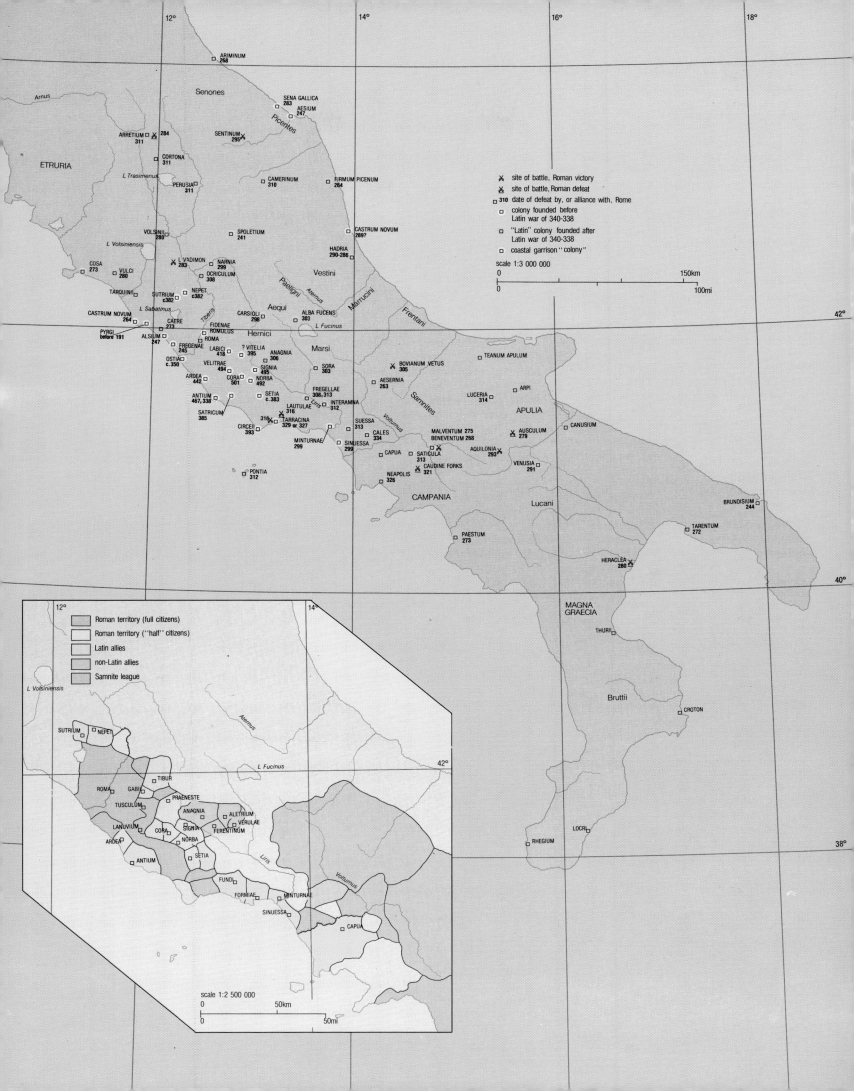

ARIMINUM 268

Senones

Arnus

Picentes

SENA GALLICA 283

AESIUM 247

ARRETIUM 284 311

SENTINUM 295?

ETRURIA

CORTONA 311

L Trasimenus

CAMERINUM 310

FIRMUM PICENUM 264

PERUSIA 311

Vestini

VOLSINII 280

SPOLETIUM 241

CASTRUM NOVUM 289?

L Volsiniensis

HADRIA 290-286

COSA 273

VULCI 280

L VADIMON 283

NARNIA 299

OCRICULUM 308

Paeligni

Aternus

Marrucini

TARQUINII

SUTRIUM c382

NEPET c382

Aequi

CARSIOLI 298

ALBA FUCENS 303

Frentani

CASTRUM NOVUM 264

CAERE 273

FIDENAE

ROMULUS

ROMA

L Fucinus

Hernici

Marsi

BOVIANUM VETUS 305

TEANUM APULUM

PYRGI before 191

ALSIUM 247

FREGENAE 245

LABICI 418

?VITELIA 395

ANAGNIA 306

OSTIA c.350

VELITRAE 494

SIGNIA 495

SORA 303

AESERNIA 263

LUCERIA 314

ARPI

ARDEA 442

CORA 501

NORBA 492

FREGELLAE 308,313

APULIA

ANTIUM 467,338

SETIA c.383

INTERAMNA 312

Samnites

SATRICUM 385

LAUTULAE 316

Liris

Voltumus

CANUSIUM

CIRCEII 393

316 TARRACINA 329 or 327

SUESSA 313

MALVENTUM 275 BENEVENTUM 268

AUSCULUM 279

MINTURNAE 299

SINUESSA 299

CALES 334

SATICULA 313

AQUILONIA 293

VENUSIA 291

PONTIA 312

CAPUA

CAUDINE FORKS 321

NEAPOLIS 326

BRUNDISIUM 244

CAMPANIA

Lucani

PAESTUM 273

TARENTUM 272

MAGNA GRAECIA

HERACLEA 280

✕ site of battle, Roman victory

✕ site of battle, Roman defeat

310 date of defeat by, or alliance with, Rome

□ colony founded before Latin war of 340-338

□ "Latin" colony founded after Latin war of 340-338

□ coastal garrison "colony"

scale 1:3 000 000

0 _____ 150km

0 _____ 100mi

THURII

Bruttii

CROTON

LOCRI

RHEGIUM

Inset map

12°   14°

Roman territory (full citizens)

Roman territory ("half" citizens)

Latin allies

non-Latin allies

Samnite league

L Volsiniensis

Aternus

L Fucinus   42°

SUTRIUM   NEPET

TIBUR

ROMA   GABII

PRAENESTE

TUSCULUM

ANAGNIA   ALETRIUM

VERULAE

LANUVIUM   CORA   SIGNIA   FERENTINUM

ARDEA   NORBA

ANTIUM   SETIA

Liris

Voltumus

FUNDI

FORMIAE   MINTURNAE

SINUESSA

CAPUA

scale 1:2 500 000

0 _____ 50km

0 _____ 50mi

practice to govern themselves. These self-governing communities of Roman citizens were known as municipalities (*municipia*), and were the most important innovation of the settlement of 338 BC.

Domestic conflicts and political reforms

Although the Gallic sack proved in the long term to be only a minor setback, the immediate effects of wholesale destruction of property and economic disruption were severe, especially for the poor, and it is no surprise to read in Livy that in the aftermath of the catastrophe there was a renewed crisis of indebtedness among the *plebs*. Complaints against debt are frequently recorded during these years, and provide the setting for the story of M. Manlius, who was executed in 382 for attempting to make himself king. Although a patrician, Manlius had sided with the plebeians and had helped them by paying their debts from his personal fortune.

Plebeian agitation for the relief of debt led to riots in 378 BC, and in the later 370s to a period of political anarchy in which no magistrates were elected for at least a year. The Licinio-Sextian laws (367) provided for the short-term relief of debt; subsequent measures in 357, 352 and 347 attempted to regulate and to reduce interest rates. In 342 the *lex Genucia* made it illegal to lend at interest, but this law was doubtless impossible to enforce. Finally the system of debt-bondage (*nexum*) was abolished in 326.

In the event, however, what did most to alleviate the economic distress of the *plebs* was the acquisition by the state of new territory through military conquest, and its distribution in allotments to Roman citizens. On many occasions Livy records the agitation of the *plebs* for the distribution of such land, which was otherwise left as *ager publicus* and occupied by the rich. According to tradition the Licinio-Sextian laws of 367 BC imposed a limit on the amount of public land any one *paterfamilias* might occupy, and on the number of sheep or cattle he might graze on it.

Licinius and his colleague, L. Sextius, were celebrated in the Roman tradition for a whole series of laws, the most famous of which is supposed to have admitted plebeians to the consulship. The background to this reform is puzzling. In 445 BC it was apparently decided that in certain years the consulship should be suspended and that three or more "military tribunes with consular power" should be elected instead. We do not know why this new magistracy was introduced, or what determined the choice between the two types of magistracy in any given year. Livy suggests that the new office was to be open to plebeians, but in fact only patricians were elected as military tribunes in the first decades of the experiment. Moreover it is not certain that plebeians were ever legally ineligible for the consulship. The only certain facts are that military tribunes came to be elected more frequently than consuls towards the end of the 5th century (and invariably after 390), and that in the years after 400 they began to include increasing numbers of plebeians.

Licinius and Sextius seem in fact to have agitated for the restoration of the consulship as the regular chief magistracy, and to have demanded not only that it be open to plebeians, but that one of the two annual consulships should be reserved for plebeians. In other words they sought positive discrimination in favor of plebeian candidates. This amounted to an experiment in what we should call statutory power sharing.

The Licinio-Sextian proposals were finally enacted in 367 BC, and L. Sextius himself became the first plebeian consul under the new arrangement in 366. At this date the consuls were still known as praetors, or "consul-praetors." But in 367 a third praetor was created, junior to the two existing ones, who from now on were known simply as consuls. The praetorship thus became a separate magistracy, which in 337 BC was for the first time held by a plebeian. A plebeian dictator was elected in 356, and in 351 one of the censors was a plebeian. By the Licinio-Sextian laws two curule aediles were created, to work as civic officials alongside the plebeian aediles. The new aedileship was to be held in alternate years by patricians and plebeians. The principle of statutory power sharing was extended in 339 to the censorship and in 300 to the major colleges of priests, the augurs and the pontiffs. The equalization of the orders was finally accomplished in 287 BC, when plebiscites, the resolutions of the plebeian assembly, were given the force of law and made binding on the whole community.

One of the most important results of the legislation of 367 BC was the gradual formation of a new ruling elite which included the leading plebeian families. These families achieved distinction through the tenure of the senior "curule" magistracies (praetorship, consulship, dictatorship); the descendants of the holders of these offices were known as *nobiles* ("nobles"). The new patricio-plebeian nobility (as it is called) became a dominant group within the senate, and tended to regard the senior magistracies as its own preserve. But the exclusiveness of the nobility should not be exaggerated. One of the features that characterized it and distinguished it from the old patriciate was precisely the fact that new families were being continually admitted to its ranks.

The senate was also open to new blood; a significant percentage of senators will therefore always have been "new men" (i.e. first-generation senators). For a new man to reach the consulship was, naturally, a rare event; this fact should not however be taken as a sign that the consulship was a "hereditary" office. On the contrary, for the whole of the "classical" period of Roman history, say from c. 300 BC to 200 AD, only a minority of the consuls had consular fathers. In other words the nobility included a far greater number of families than would have been the case if office holding had been a hereditary privilege. The result was that the senior magistracies were extremely competitive, and the competition became more intense as time went on.

The patriciate survived as a prestigious and influential group of families within the nobility. Certain archaic priesthoods and offices (*rex sacrorum, interrex* and others) continued to be reserved exclusively for patricians, and it is to be noted that until 172 BC one of the consuls was always a patrician. As for the *plebs*, the organization that succeeded in obtaining equality of civil rights in the 4th century soon afterwards lost its revolutionary character. Its institutions were gradually integrated with those of the community as a whole, and its leaders, who before 367 BC had made common cause with the poor in their effort to gain access to the

chief magistracies, now became part of the nobility. The office of tribune became equivalent to a junior magistracy, and was regarded as a stage in the career of an aspiring young plebeian noble. By about 300 most of the tribunes were probably members of the senate, and no doubt shared the outlook and interests of the senatorial class as a whole.

The conquest of Italy

The emergence of the nobility is one of the symptoms of a wholesale transformation of Roman society which occurred in the period between the settlement of the Latin War in 338 BC and the outbreak of the First Punic War in 264. This process of change coincided with, and was partly caused by, a remarkable, although poorly documented, series of military conquests which in the space of little more than half a century brought all of Italy under Rome's control.

In the years after 338 BC the Romans set about consolidating the gains they had acquired in the Latin War. Colonies were founded at Cales (334) and Fregellae (328) in the strategically vital region of the middle Liris valley. The settlers who took part in these colonies were drawn mainly from the Roman proletariat. They forfeited their Roman citizenship in exchange for an allotment of land in the new colony, which became an independent community. The colonies possessed the rights of *commercium* and *conubium*, and their status was equivalent to that of the old Latin cities; for this reason they were called "Latin colonies." Cales and Fregellae were the first of a long series of such Latin colonies, which contributed more than any other single factor to the consolidation and eventual unification of Italy under Rome.

The foundation of Fregellae in 328 immediately provoked a hostile reaction from the Samnites, and within a year a war had broken out which was to last intermittently for nearly 40 years. The conflict is conventionally divided into two parts: the Second and Third Samnite Wars (respectively 327–304 BC and 298–290 BC).

The Romans scored an early success in 326, when the government of the Greek city of Naples decided to expel a Samnite garrison and to call in the Romans. The result of this episode, the first formal contact Rome had had with a Greek community in Italy, was an extremely valuable alliance. It was followed by several years of inconclusive border warfare, until in 321 the consuls rashly embarked on a full-scale invasion of Samnite territory. The attempt ended in disaster when the Roman army was ambushed at the Caudine Forks and ignominiously forced to surrender. The patriotic Roman tradition attempted to compensate for this humiliation by fabricating a series of brilliant Roman victories in the following years. In fact it seems that peace was made on terms that clearly favored the Samnites, who gained possession of Fregellae, and that hostilities ceased until 316 BC.

The Romans used the lull to strengthen their position in Campania and to forge alliances with communities in northern Apulia (these included Arpi, Teanum Apulum and Canusium). The war was resumed in 316 with the Samnites taking the initiative. In 315 they invaded Latium and won a victory in a pitched battle at Lautulae near Terracina; but in the following year, after devastat-

ing Latin territory and advancing as far as Ardea, they were themselves defeated by the Romans. Fregellae was retaken in 313, and further Latin colonies were founded at Suessa Aurunca and Saticula (in 313), and at Interamna on the Liris and the island of Pontia (in 312). In 312 the censor Appius Claudius Caecus began the construction of the coast road from Rome to Capua which bears his name to this day (the Appian Way). From now on the Romans pressed ahead with a policy of encirclement, and were no longer in any serious danger of defeat, despite the intervention in 311 of some Etruscan and Umbrian cities. The Romans drove them back and retaliated with a vigorous advance up the Tiber valley into Etruria and Umbria. On the southern front a period of indecisive warfare against the Samnites was ended in 305 when the Romans captured the stronghold of Bovianum. Peace was made in the following year.

In the last years of the Second Samnite War the Romans began to strengthen their hold on the mountainous region of central Italy. In 306 a revolt of the Hernici was crushed, and their leading town, Anagnia, was incorporated with *civitas sine suffragio*; in the following years the peoples of the Abruzzi region were subdued, and one after another the Marsi, Paeligni, Marrucini, Frentani and Vestini were made allies of Rome. Particularly harsh treatment was reserved for the Aequi, whom the Romans overwhelmed in a lightning campaign in 304. Their territory was annexed and they ceased to exist as a separate people.

These conquests were reinforced by the construction of a military road from Rome to the Adriatic through the central Apennines (the Via Valeria, 306 BC), and by the foundation of Latin colonies at Sora (303), Alba Fucens (303) and Carseoli (298). An expedition into Umbria in 299 led to the foundation of another Latin colony at Narnia.

By 298 the Romans were once again fighting on two fronts. Annual campaigns in Etruria and Umbria are recorded from 302 onwards, and in 298 hostilities between Rome and the Samnites were resumed. One of the first actions of this war is recorded in the epitaph of L. Cornelius Scipio Barbatus, the consul of 298. The text, which was composed in the 2nd century BC, reads: "Lucius Cornelius Scipio Barbatus, begotten by his father Gnaeus, a brave and wise man, whose good looks matched his gallantry, who served you as consul, censor and aedile, captured Taurasia and Cisauna in Samnium, overran all Lucania and brought back hostages." The epitaph no doubt exaggerates the extent of Scipio's achievements, but it is to be preferred to the version of Livy (who makes him campaign in northern Etruria) and reflects the ever-widening scope of Roman operations.

The events of the Third Samnite War came to a head in 295 BC when the Samnites managed to get an army into northern Italy and to combine with the Etruscans and Umbrians who were still at war with Rome. At the same time they were able to take advantage of the presence of the Gauls, who had been making incursions across the Apennines since 299 BC. A grand anti-Roman coalition was formed, and its combined forces met a Roman army in a great battle at Sentinum in Umbria in the summer of 295. Victory went to the Romans, perhaps largely because of the absence of the Etruscans and

Left Bronze statuette of a Samnite warrior, 6th or 5th century BC. He is clad in full armor – greaves, helmet, cuirass and belt – and a short leather tunic. He originally must have carried a shield and spear, but these are now lost, as is the crest of his helmet.

Below The best evidence for the appearance of Roman soldiers at this period is provided by these ivory plaques from Palestrina, dating probably from the first half of the 3rd century BC.

Umbrians, who had been drawn away by a diversionary maneuver; later tradition preferred to dwell on the heroic act of self-sacrifice by the consul P. Decius Mus, who "devoted" himself and the enemy forces to the infernal gods. After this the result of the war was no longer in doubt. The Samnites' territory was overrun and in 290 they came to terms. They were compelled to become allies of Rome and thus lost their independence; and they were deprived of all their territory that lay beyond the Volturnus river, which became the new frontier. This was in addition to the loss of a large area of land in southeast Samnium on which the Latin colony of Venusia had been founded in 291.

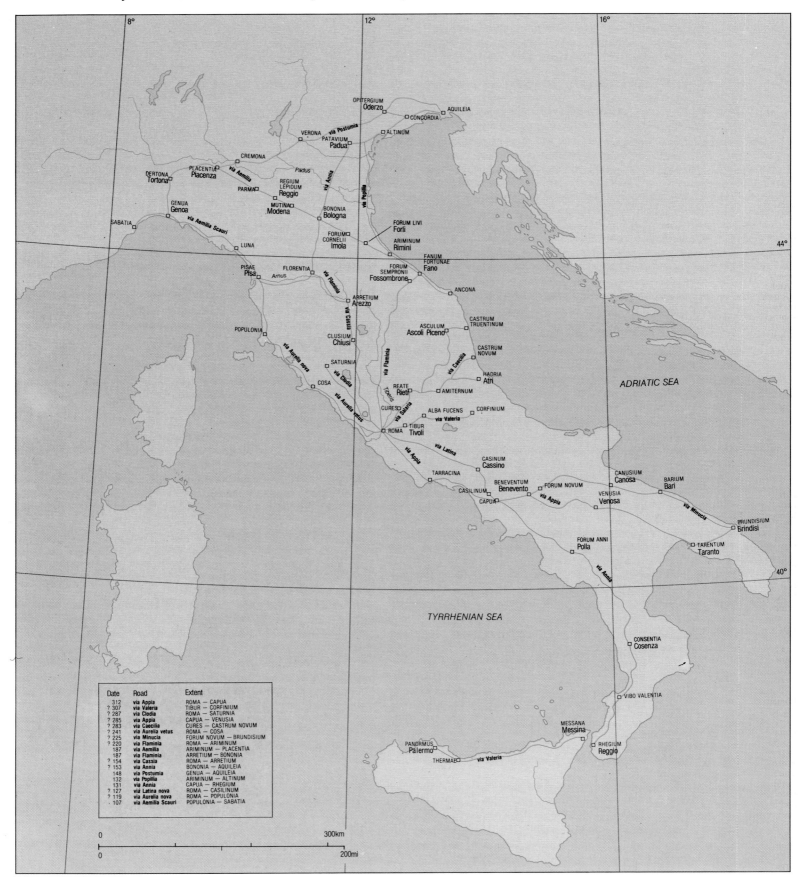

Date	Road	Extent
312	via Appia	ROMA — CAPUA
? 307	via Valeria	TIBUR — CORFINIUM
? 287	via Clodia	ROMA — SATURNIA
? 285	via Appia	CAPUA — VENUSIA
? 283	via Caecilia	CURES — CASTRUM NOVUM
? 241	via Aurelia vetus	ROMA — COSA
? 225	via Minucia	FORUM NOVUM — BRUNDISIUM
? 220	via Flaminia	ROMA — ARIMINUM
187	via Aemilia	ARIMINUM — PLACENTIA
187	via Flaminia	ARRETIUM — BONONIA
? 154	via Cassia	ROMA — ARRETIUM
? 153	via Annia	BONONIA — AQUILEIA
148	via Postumia	GENUA — AQUILEIA
132	via Popillia	ARIMINUM — ALTINUM
131	via Annia	CAPUA — RHEGIUM
? 127	via Latina nova	ROMA — CASILINUM
? 119	via Aurelia nova	ROMA — POPULONIA
· 107	via Aemilia Scauri	POPULONIA — SABATIA

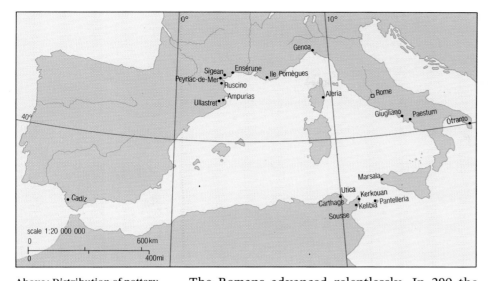

Above: Distribution of pottery made in Rome in the 3rd century BC. By the middle Republic Rome had become a major trading and manufacturing center. Among its products was fine pottery, which was exported throughout the western Mediterranean. One characteristic type of pottery, from a workshop known as the ''Atelier des petites estampilles,'' has been found at numerous sites in central Italy, along the southern coast of France, in southern Spain, Corsica, Sicily and North Africa.

Left: Roman roads in the republican period. The earliest Roman roads were no doubt little more than tracks or strips of land along which a public right of way was recognized. Some, like the old Via Latina, which ran down the Sacco valley, followed natural lines of communication that had been used since time immemorial. The great Roman achievement was in the construction of straight, paved roads carried on bridges and viaducts, and through cuttings and tunnels. In this they were to some extent preceded by the Etruscans, whose settlements were linked by a network of well-built roads. The first great Roman highways were built in the age of the conquest, and had a strategic function, linking Rome to the Latin colonies. The roads and colonies together were the most important factor in the consolidation of the conquest. The second great age of road building in Italy came in the latter part of the 2nd century BC, and to some extent represents an investment of the profits of empire in public works, which provided employment for the proletariat as well as improved amenities for the community at large.

The Romans advanced relentlessly. In 290 the consul M'. Curius Dentatus conquered the Sabines and the Praetuttii, who were made Roman citizens *sine suffragio*; some of their land was seized and distributed to poor Romans. As a result of this episode Roman territory was extended right across the center of the peninsula to the Adriatic coast, where the Latin colony of Hadria was founded (between 290 and 286). In the poorly documented period that followed the Romans recorded victories against the Gauls and subdued the Etruscans and Umbrians, who were compelled to become allies.

Conflict with Magna Graecia
At the beginning of the 3rd century BC the Greek cities of southern Italy were in a state of advanced decline, resulting from the continuous pressure of hostile natives and centuries of internecine strife. The Romans became involved in the affairs of Magna Graecia in the 280s when the city of Thurii appealed to them for aid against the Lucanians; within a few years Locri, Rhegium and Croton had also placed themselves under Rome's protection. These developments were viewed with alarm in Tarentum, the most powerful of the Greek cities, which had for some time been suspicious of the growing power of Rome. In the face of this threat the Tarentines appealed for aid to King Pyrrhus of Epirus, an ambitious ruler who was himself on the lookout for an opportunity to increase his power.

Pyrrhus landed in 280 with a force of 25000 men and 20 elephants. This was the first time that the Romans had had to face a fully trained Hellenistic army, and in the first engagement at Heraclea (280 BC) they were driven from the field, but not before they had inflicted heavy losses on their opponents. Pyrrhus then offered to make peace, but his terms were rejected by the Romans, who were persuaded by the aged Appius Claudius not to treat with him as long as he remained on Italian soil. Pyrrhus then attempted to march on Rome, and penetrated as far as Anagnia before turning back; Capua and Naples had closed their gates, and none of Rome's allies joined him. He must have begun to realize the size of the task he had set himself; Rome was a well-organized state with access to resources he could not hope to match. In 279 he won a second victory at Ausculum, but his losses were even greater than at Heraclea, and the battle had cost him more than the Romans.

In 278 he decided to abandon Italy for the time being and to try his hand in Sicily, where the Greek cities had requested his help against the Carthaginians. The result was a renewed alliance between Rome and Carthage. In Sicily Pyrrhus promised much but again achieved little, and when he returned to Italy in 275 he was met and defeated by a Roman army at Malventum (which was renamed Beneventum after the battle). Pyrrhus then sailed back to Greece where he continued to waste his talents in fruitless enterprises; his brilliant but ultimately worthless career came to an end a few years later when he was struck on the head and killed by a roof-tile during a street battle in Argos.

The unification of Italy
Following Pyrrhus' departure from Italy, the Romans pressed home their victory. Tarentum was besieged, and its fall (272 BC) marks the end of Italian independence. From this time on the whole peninsula, from the straits of Messina in the south to a line running from Pisa to Rimini in the north, was under Rome's control. Lucania and Samnium were secured by the foundation of colonies at Paestum (273), Beneventum (268) and Aesernia (263); two further colonies were founded at Brundisium (244) and Spoletium (241). The latter foundation occurred following a revolt by the city of Falerii, an isolated gesture of defiance which the Romans put down, with overwhelming force, in a campaign of only six days.

The general policy of the Romans during the Italian wars was a paradoxical blend of brutality and calculated generosity. Their victories entailed full-scale massacres (for example of the Aurunci in 314 BC or the Aequi in 304), extensive confiscations of territory and the mass enslavement of captives. For example on Livy's figures alone it is possible to calculate that over 60000 individuals were enslaved during just five years of the Third Samnite War (297–293).

But the final settlement which Rome imposed on her vanquished enemies was enlightened and ultimately of considerable benefit to both sides. Those communities which were not incorporated in the Roman state with either full or half-citizenship were bound to Rome by treaties of alliance. As one might expect, many other states in Italy voluntarily entered into alliances with the Romans rather than suffer the consequences of a military defeat. In either case the allies were obliged to give military aid to Rome whenever it was required; in effect this meant that they lost their independence in the conduct of foreign policy and became vassal states, although they were left free to run their own internal affairs. On the other hand Rome imposed no taxes or tribute on them. The situation was in fact a kind of partnership in which the allies helped Rome to make further conquests and obtained a share of the profits. These profits included movable booty (including slaves) and land. Admittedly the land which was confiscated from defeated communities passed entirely into the possession of the Roman state, whereupon it was either sold, leased out as *ager publicus* or resettled by means of colonization or individual assignation, but it should be noted that the settlers who took part in these schemes included men from Latin and Italian allied states as well as Roman citizens. Thus it can be said that by being enrolled in the gang and invited to share the loot Rome's victims were in a way compensated for the losses they had originally suffered.

An important feature of the Roman organization in Italy was the senate's support for local aristocracies in the allied states. In their turn the propertied classes of the Italian communities turned naturally to Rome whenever their own interests were threatened. On several recorded occasions Roman military force actually intervened on behalf of the local ruling class to put down popular insurrections (for example at Arretium in 302 BC, in Lucania in 296 and at Volsinii in 264). In return the Romans expected, and usually received, the active cooperation of the ruling aristocracies in the allied communities. This convenient arrangement ensured the continuing loyalty of the allies to Rome. Even in the darkest days of the Second Punic War the majority of the allies remained faithful, in spite of Hannibal's repeated efforts to win them over to his side.

The most significant long-term result of the Roman conquest of the Italian peninsula was the gradual disappearance of its ethnic, linguistic and cultural differences. The progressive romanization of the indigenous peoples of Italy took place in the course of the following three centuries, and was more or less complete by the 1st century AD, apart from a few quaint survivals in remote areas. The first parts of Italy to be thus assimilated were the central districts whose inhabitants had been granted half-citizenship; they were gradually incorporated in the Roman body politic with full citizen rights, beginning with the Sabines in 268 BC.

The process of assimilation also affected the allies. It was not brought about by a deliberate or conscious policy of the Roman government; rather it was a natural result of the fact that men from the allied communities performed military service alongside Roman citizens, and under Roman commanders, sometimes for years on end. Moreover the dissemination of the Latin language and of Roman ways of life was promoted by the Latin colonies, which were distributed throughout allied territory. These colonies were founded as self-governing political units, but since the majority of the settlers were of Roman or Latin origin they in fact constituted romanized enclaves in which Latin was spoken and the Roman way of life was practiced.

The system of Latin colonies was linked to the network of military roads which were constructed in the wake of the conquest. These great roads, whose names (Appia, Aurelia, Flaminia, etc.) preserve the memory of the men who ordered them to be built, were primarily strategic in function, but had the secondary effect of improving communications generally and facilitating other forms of intercourse between the various regions of Italy. The inevitable result was the further spread of Roman ideas and practices.

Roman society in the age of the Italian wars

During the period of the wars of conquest Rome itself was transformed, and the characteristic political, social and economic structures of the middle Republic began to take shape. Political power was in the hands of an elite of patrician and plebeian nobles, who dominated the senate and the senior magistracies. These men included forceful political leaders who guided Rome's foreign policy and who worked to improve the lot of the lower classes. Examples are the plebeians Q. Publilius Philo and M'. Curius Dentatus, and the patrician Appius Claudius Caecus. Of the latter it has been said that he is "the earliest Roman to appear in our sources as a personality." His achievements, which are conveniently listed in an inscription dating from

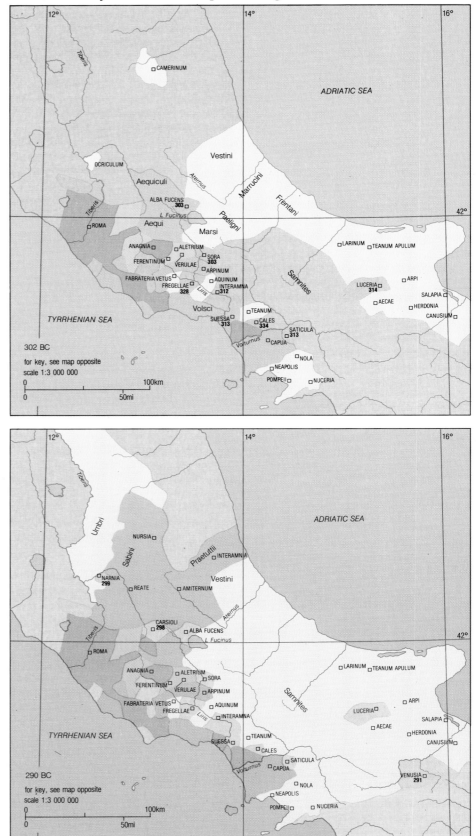

King Pyrrhus of Epirus (319–272 BC). Of all the Greek kings who ruled in the generations following Alexander the Great, Pyrrhus was the one who by general consent most closely resembled the legendary conqueror, not only in appearance and temperament, but also in ability. His defeat by the Romans in 275 created a sensation in the Greek world.

the reign of Augustus, are indeed impressive: "Appius Claudius Caecus, son of Gaius, censor, consul twice, dictator, interrex three times, praetor twice, curule aedile twice, quaestor, tribune of the soldiers three times. He captured several towns from the Samnites, and routed an army of Sabines and Etruscans. He prevented peace being made with King Pyrrhus. In his censorship he paved the Appian Way and built an aqueduct for Rome. He built the temple of Bellona."

The nobility was an elite within a wider ruling class, whose wealth and power were based on ownership of land. Its dominance was ensured by the peculiar structure of Roman political institutions. Rome was ruled by annual magistrates and a senate of ex-magistrates. The magistrates were chosen by popular election in voting assemblies in which all full citizens could participate. The voting assemblies (the various *comitia*) also had the power of decision on matters such as peace and war, on legislative proposals and in serious criminal cases. In theory the assembled Roman people was sovereign, but in practice the system was far from democratic. The *comitia* could only be summoned by magistrates, who alone had the right to address the people and to submit proposals. The assembled

citizens had no right either to debate or to amend the proposals put to them. There was no freedom of speech.

But the most undemocratic aspect of the Roman assemblies was that the voting took place by groups. In the *comitia tributa* and the plebeian assembly, the *concilium plebis*, the constituent groups or voting units were the local tribes. The number of local tribes gradually increased as Rome acquired new territory, until in 241 BC the definitive figure of 35 was reached. This total was made up of four so-called "urban" tribes, and 31 "rural" tribes. The significance of this division is that only landowners were able to register in the rural tribes, while the landless inhabitants of the city were confined to the four urban tribes and thus had only minimal voting power, even though they probably formed a majority of those who attended the assemblies, which were held only in Rome. In this way the system artificially favored the wealthy landowners and discriminated equally against the urban proletariat and the far-flung peasant smallholders who for practical reasons were unable to attend the *comitia* in person. The voting units of the *comitia centuriata* were the 193 centuries, which were distributed among five economically defined

The growth of the Roman Confederacy. The "Roman Confederacy" is a label conventionally attached to the system of alliances and dependencies which the Romans built up during their conquest of the peninsula in the years 338–264 BC. Defeated enemies were either compelled to become allies, which meant that they had to contribute troops to Rome's armies, or incorporated in the Roman state as citizens. Newly incorporated citizens were given either full citizenship (*civitas optimo iure*) or "half citizenship" (*civitas sine suffragio*), which meant that they performed all the duties of citizens, such as tax paying and military service, but had only limited civil rights; for example they could not vote in the Roman assemblies. In the course of time the half citizens were given full citizen rights; this happened for example to the lowland Sabines in 268 BC, and to the people of Arpinum in 188 BC. It is probable that all communities of half citizens had been upgraded by the end of the 2nd century BC. With the extension of full citizenship the Romans created a series of new local tribes, in which they enrolled the new citizens as well as any existing citizens who were settled on areas of newly annexed territory. The local tribes functioned as constituent voting units in Roman political assemblies.

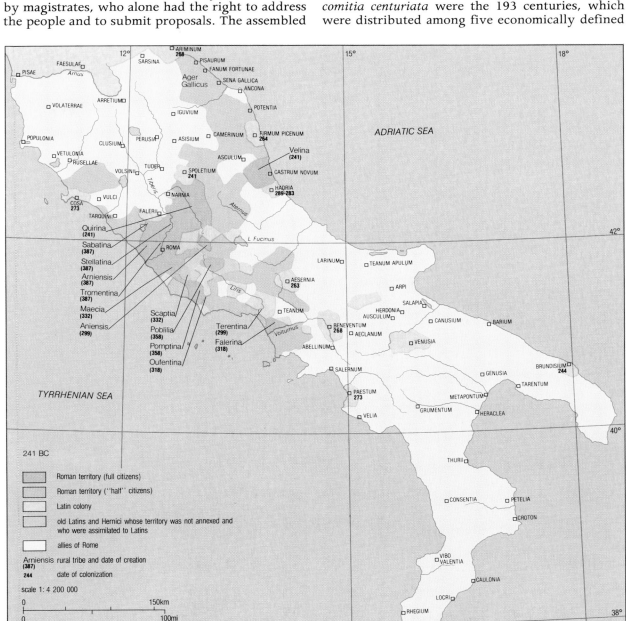

241 BC

▨	Roman territory (full citizens)
▨	Roman territory ("half" citizens)
▨	Latin colony
▨	old Latins and Hernici whose territory was not annexed and who were assimilated to Latins
□	allies of Rome

Arniensis **(387)** rural tribe and date of creation

244 date of colonization

scale 1: 4 200 000

0 — 150km
0 — 100mi

classes; but the distribution was so arranged that the wealthiest class comprised the largest number of centuries, and thus dominated the assembly.

The division of property-owning citizens (*adsidui*) into five distinct classes is attributed by our sources to Servius Tullius (see above, p. 22), but in fact it was probably a later refinement connected with the institution of the *tributum*, a direct tax on the capital wealth of Roman citizens. The revenue which this tax yielded was used to provide pay for the army. The soldiers' pay, the *stipendium*, was traditionally introduced in 406 BC during the siege of Veii, in order to compensate the men for the loss of their normal income during the 10-year siege. This tradition reflects the fact that the Roman army was a part-time militia recruited from peasants who owned sufficient property to equip themselves, and who were registered for political and fiscal purposes in the five property classes.

It is important to understand that in many ancient city-states military service was regarded not as a burden but as a privilege and a mark of status. At the same time it was felt that a man's political rights should be commensurate with his contribution to the state. Thus the proletarian, who owned no wealth and was therefore necessarily free from the burden of taxation, was relieved of the obligation of military service and excluded from effective participation in political life. This kind of system, which was known in antiquity as timocracy, was based on the principle that "the higher one's census qualification, the greater one's military obligations and the wider one's political rights" (E. Gabba).

Wealth based on land was therefore the key to political power in republican Rome. This statement is not inconsistent with the fact that the political leaders of the late 4th and early 3rd centuries BC were looked upon in later times as models of parsimonious frugality and honest virtue. This they may have been, if the standard of comparison is the luxury and extravagance of the late Republic; but such men were in no sense poor. To that extent the stories about M'. Curius Dentatus, whose humble rustic dwelling was later to make a great impression on Cato, or C. Fabricius Luscinus, who contemptuously refused bribes offered by Samnite envoys who had found him cooking turnips for his supper, are misleading. In fact the later tradition was more concerned with the moral example which these men set than with their real economic status. An equally revealing story is the fate of P. Cornelius Rufinus, who was expelled from the senate in 276 BC because he owned 10 pounds of silver plate. Here the point is surely that the establishment disapproved not of Rufinus' wealth as such, but of the way he chose to display it.

In fact the decades on either side of 300 BC saw an unparalleled increase in the public and private wealth of the Romans. Their most obvious gain was in land. Roman territory, which after the conclusion of the Latin War in 338 BC had comprised 5525 square kilometers, had expanded by 264 BC to some 26 805 square kilometers, more than 20 per cent of the total land surface of peninsular Italy. Roman citizens also benefited directly from the foundation of Latin colonies, which by 241 BC occupied a further 10 000 square kilometers of confiscated land (according to the most probable modern estimates).

The population of Roman citizens grew accordingly. The recorded census figures, which first become plausible at the beginning of the 3rd century, suggest a total population of free Romans of between 750 000 and one million. At this date Rome itself was one of the largest cities of the Mediterranean, with a probable population of more than 150 000 persons. In order to provide for the needs of the inhabitants of the city it became necessary to construct aqueducts, the first of which was the Aqua Appia, built by Appius Claudius in 312, followed by the Anio Vetus, which M'. Curius Dentatus began in 272.

These public works were financed by the profits of war, which flowed into the city in the form of booty and indemnities, and gave rise to a program of public building on a scale which had not been seen since the great days of the Tarquins. The spoils of victory paid for the construction of at least 11 major temples between 302 and 272 BC, including those of Bellona (296), Jupiter Victor (295) and Victoria (294), which reveal the Romans' growing obsession with militaristic cults. Two of the temples which can now be seen in the Largo Argentina in Rome can be dated to around 300 BC and clearly belong to this series. The influx of wealth into the city must also have created a prosperous service sector, as well as generating a demand for luxury goods which was at least partly met by local production. This can be deduced from the survival of particular artifacts such as the Ficoroni *cista*, and of large quantities of Roman fine pottery, which has been found at many sites throughout the western Mediterranean.

This very fine bronze *cista* from Praeneste dates from the last decades of the 4th century BC. It bears two inscriptions: "Dindia Macolnia gave this to her daughter," and "Novios Plautios made me in Rome." The "made in Rome" label proves that Rome was at this date a major center for the production of high-quality goods.

The increasing economic prosperity and cultural sophistication of Rome in the early 3rd century BC can be illustrated by a number of important developments. The first is the growth of slavery. The mass enslavement of prisoners of war has already been mentioned, and demonstrates that the institution was well established and was being practiced on a large scale. By tradition freed slaves in Rome were admitted to the citizenship, though with limited civil rights; their offspring had full rights and were completely assimilated. An indication of the extent to which the citizen body was permeated by persons of servile origin is provided by the fact that in 312 Appius Claudius admitted sons of freedmen to the senate. At this date the majority of slaves were probably employed in domestic service in the houses of the rich and in trading and manufacturing enterprises in the city; but there is some evidence that slave labor was already being used on the land, to work the estates of the wealthy.

Secondly, during this period the Roman state began for the first time to issue coined money. The origin of Roman coinage is a difficult and controversial subject, but the most authoritative modern opinion seems to be that the earliest Roman coins appeared in about 280 BC. Before that date monetary transactions had taken place using uncoined metal which was measured by weight according to a fixed scale of units; the introduction of coinage simplified the system, so that it became possible to make payments, for example to soldiers or workmen, merely by counting out the required number of coins. An equally important aspect of coinage was that the circulation of money entailed the propagation of the legends and types which the

minting authority chose to put on its coins. Coinage in other words provided a medium through which the state could advertise itself to the world at large. In 269 BC an issue of Roman silver coins bore as its reverse type a representation of the twins Romulus and Remus being suckled by the she-wolf. A slightly later series had the helmeted head of a female personification of Roma on the obverse, and a Victory on the reverse. Such types are signs of Rome's growing self-confidence and awareness of her enormous power.

Coinage was a Greek device, and Rome's adoption of it indicates the increasing influence of Greek culture on Roman life. This also manifests itself in monuments and artifacts which show that Roman craftsmen were imitating Greek styles and techniques, and in the direct importation of Greek religious cults, such as that of the healing god Aesculapius, to whom a temple was dedicated in 291 on the Tiber island. The cults of Victory were also based on Greek models. It is during this period that Hellenism began to become fashionable among the Roman elite. It is significant for example that some leading aristocratic families began to adopt Greek surnames such as Sophus, Philippus and Philo.

News of the sensational defeat of Pyrrhus by a hitherto little-known Italian republic made a tremendous impact on the Greek world. In 273 BC the king of Egypt, Ptolemy II Philadelphus, sent an embassy to Rome, no doubt as a fact-finding mission as well as a gesture of goodwill. The Romans replied with an embassy of their own to Alexandria; the three senators, unaccustomed to diplomatic protocol, were embarrassed when Ptolemy offered them gifts. At the court of Alexandria Rome and the Romans became a fashionable topic in intellectual and literary circles. Callimachus wrote a poem about a Roman called Gaius; Lycophron wrote an epic poem about a new Troy founded by the descendants of Aeneas; and the scientist Eratosthenes wrote about the "wonderful" system of government of the Romans. Meanwhile in Athens the historian Timaeus, a Sicilian exile, gave an important place to Rome in his monumental study of the peoples of the western Mediterranean, and also composed a separate monograph on the war between Rome and Pyrrhus (these works no longer survive). It was Timaeus more than anyone else who made Rome familiar to the Greeks. His realization of the importance of the new power in Italy derives from his knowledge of Sicilian affairs and from his perception of an impending conflict between Rome and Carthage, in which the fate of his native island would be decided.

The struggle between Rome and Carthage
In 264 BC the Romans and their Italian allies became involved in a war with Carthage which arose from a petty incident in northeastern Sicily. This situation rapidly escalated into the first of a series of major wars which resulted in a dramatic change in the power politics of the Mediterranean world. Within less than 100 years the Romans had not only reduced Carthage to impotence; they had also humiliated all the major powers of the Greek east, and by 167 BC they were the effective rulers of the Mediterranean.

None of this was consciously planned. The crisis of 264 BC must have seemed at first sight a relatively

minor affair. It arose when the Romans answered an appeal from the city of Messana (Messina). Originally a Greek city, Messana was at this date in the hands of some Oscan-speaking Italian mercenaries who had occupied it some 20 years earlier in a bloodthirsty coup. Not surprisingly the Mamertines, as these Italian adventurers called themselves, found few friends among the Greeks of Sicily, and when they were attacked by the Syracusans under King Hiero II, they were obliged to cast about for allies. Some of their leaders resolved to appeal to Carthage, the traditional enemy of the Sicilian Greeks; others argued in favor of calling in the Romans, whose sympathy they hoped to win by stressing the fact of their own Italian origin. The Carthaginians had every reason to be alarmed at the growing power of Rome, and when their small garrison in Messana was expelled by the Mamertines, they decided to form an alliance with Hiero, whose army was by now investing the city.

Hostilities began when a Roman army arrived at Messana and attacked the besieging forces. Initial Roman successes soon caused Hiero to change his mind; in 263 he abandoned his Carthaginian allies and went over to the Romans. Further Roman successes followed, and in 261 they captured the Carthaginian base at Agrigentum. By now both sides were fully committed to all-out war. Polybius tells us that after the fall of Agrigentum the Romans began for the first time to contemplate the possibility of driving out the Carthaginians and gaining complete control of Sicily. But they soon realized that they would be unable to carry out this plan as long as Carthage ruled the seas, and so with characteristic determination they resolved to build a fleet. By the beginning of 260 a fleet of 100 large warships (quinqueremes) was manned and ready for action, a remarkable achievement considering that hitherto the Romans had not possessed any naval forces to speak of.

In their first major naval engagement, at Mylae in 260 BC, the Romans under the consul C. Duilius won a memorable victory. This was followed by further victories, particularly at the battle of Ecnomus in 256, where the Carthaginian fleet was decisively beaten. But Rome's good fortune did not continue. An attempt to strike directly at Carthage by sending an invasion force to Africa under M. Atilius Regulus ended in failure, and turned into a complete disaster when the fleet sent to evacuate the army was wrecked in a storm on the return voyage (255). In Sicily itself the Romans managed to capture Panormus (Palermo) in 253, and two years later L. Caecilius Metellus won a decisive battle there, capturing over 100 elephants. But at sea they suffered further reverses, culminating in a disastrous battle at Drepana (249). Later in the same year the remainder of the fleet was almost entirely destroyed in a storm. The war dragged on inconclusively for the next few years, although the Carthaginians began to make some headway in Sicily under Hamilcar Barca, the father of Hannibal. But by the winter of 243–242 the Romans had recovered sufficiently to be able to resume the war at sea. A new fleet was built, and in 241 an overwhelming victory at the Aegates islands, off the western coast of Sicily, at last brought the war to an end. Under the peace terms offered by the victor C.

Coin of T. Veturius (137 BC) recalling the agreement with the Samnites made by his ancestor T. Veturius Calvinus (consul 321 BC) after the surrender of his army at the Caudine Forks. The scene shows two warriors taking an oath by touching a pig (held by the kneeling figure in the center) with their swords.

Early Roman silver coins. The reverse of a silver didrachm of 269 BC (below) shows the she-wolf suckling the twins Romulus and Remus; a later issue, dating from the period of the First Punic War, shows the head of Roma, personified as an armed goddess (cf. Britannia), on the obverse (left), and a Victory with a palm branch and wreath on the reverse (left below). These types are signs of Rome's growing self-confidence and military power.

Lutatius Catulus, the Carthaginians agreed to evacuate Sicily, to return all Italian prisoners of war and to pay a large indemnity (the figure finally arrived at was 3200 talents, to be paid in 10 annual instalments).

Thus ended one of the most destructive wars in ancient history. The losses on both sides were enormous; at a conservative estimate the Romans and their allies lost over 100 000 men and more than 500 warships, and Carthaginian losses were probably nearly as great. The sufferings of the native Sicilians were undoubtedly appalling. Several major cities were sacked (Panormus, Agrigentum, Camarina, Selinus), and their populations enslaved. At Agrigentum in 261 the number of persons enslaved is said to have reached 25 000. In the opinion of Polybius the First Punic War was, "in terms of its duration, intensity and scale of operations, the greatest war in history."

The terms of Lutatius' treaty left the Carthaginians in an extremely weak position. They were shortly to suffer further as a result of a mutiny of their own mercenaries, which turned into a disastrous and bloody war (241–238). In 238 the Romans took advantage of this state of affairs and seized Sardinia, formerly a Carthaginian possession (an act for which there was not the slightest justification, according to Polybius). At the same time they began to reduce Corsica. After some fighting, these islands became Roman possessions, with the same status as Sicily.

Sicily had been the Romans' principal gain from their victory in 241. Apart from certain privileged cases, such as Messana and the kingdom of Syracuse, the various communities of Sicily became subjects and paid tribute to Rome in the form of a tithe. From 227 BC the administration of these overseas possessions was made the responsibility of magistrates with *imperium*, and two new praetorships were created for the purpose, one for Sicily and one for Corsica and Sardinia. The sphere in which a magistrate exercised his *imperium* was known as his "province" (*provincia*), a term which thus came to be used to describe Rome's overseas possessions. The praetor's job was to organize the defense of the province, to maintain law and order, and to supervise the collection of taxes.

While these matters were being settled the Romans turned their attention to northern Italy, where the Gauls had once again become restless. Their hostility was at least partly caused by an enactment of the tribune C. Flaminius (232 BC), which provided for the distribution of allotments of land in the *ager Gallicus* to Roman citizens and probably involved the eviction of Gauls who had occupied it as squatters since 283. In 225 an invading army of Gauls was heavily defeated at Telamon in Etruria and driven back across the Apennines. The Romans followed up their victory by advancing into the Po plain. Mediolanum (Milan) was captured in 222, and the process of integrating Cisalpine Gaul with the rest of Roman Italy was begun. In 218 two large Latin colonies were dispatched to Placentia (Piacenza) and Cremona. These had hardly been established, however, when Hannibal's army descended into Italy.

Following the two-fold disaster of the mercenaries' revolt and the loss of Sardinia, the Carthaginians had begun to create a new overseas

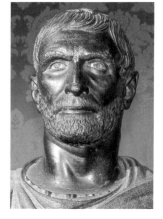

Top The old Phoenician city of Carthage, traditionally founded in 814 BC, was completely obliterated by Scipio Aemilianus in 146 BC. The standing remains date from the Roman period, when a new town was founded by Caesar. Recent excavations have however begun to reveal some traces of the old Punic city and its harbor installations.

Above Bronze bust of a Roman aristocrat (popularly known as "Brutus"), probably dating from the late 4th century BC.

Right: The First Punic War. The first great war between Rome and Carthage began when Rome intervened in a minor incident in Sicily in 264 BC. Since neither side was prepared to allow the island to fall into the possession of the other, the dispute rapidly escalated into a full-scale conflict. The Romans built a fleet and took to the seas in 260 BC; the war was then waged by land and sea for a further 20 years, with enormous losses on both sides. In the end Rome's resources proved greater than those of Carthage, and after the Roman victory at the Aegates islands in 241 BC the Carthaginians surrendered. The Romans occupied Sicily, which became their first province.

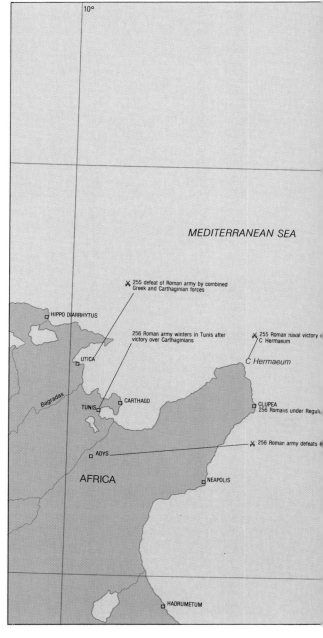

Coin of C. Metellus (125 BC) showing Jupiter in a chariot drawn by elephants. The type recalls the victory of L. Metellus at Panormus (Palermo) in 251 and the capture of over 100 Carthaginian war elephants.

empire in Spain. This enterprise was started in 237 by Hamilcar Barca, and was continued after his death by his son-in-law Hasdrubal. Rome kept a close watch on these developments, and in 226 it demanded, and received, assurances from Hasdrubal that the Carthaginians would confine their activities to the area south of the Ebro river. The real problems began when Hannibal, who succeeded Hasdrubal in 221, moved against the town of Saguntum (219). Saguntum was well to the south of the Ebro, but was nonetheless an ally of Rome. Hannibal ignored Rome's demands that he should not harm Saguntum, and when the city fell an embassy was sent to Carthage with an ultimatum demanding his surrender. Livy describes the dramatic scene in the Carthaginian senate. ''Fabius [leader of the Roman delegation] laid his hand on the fold of his toga, where he had gathered it at the breast: 'Here,' he said, 'we bring you peace and war. Take which you will.' Scarcely had he spoken, when the answer no less proudly rang out: 'Whichever you please – we do not care.' Fabius let the gathered folds fall, and cried: 'We give you war.' The Carthaginian senators replied, as one man: 'We accept it; and in the same spirit we will fight it to the end.'''

The Romans probably hoped to fight Hannibal in Spain, and at the same time to put pressure on Carthage by sending an expeditionary force to Africa. But these plans were thwarted by Hannibal, who promptly marched his forces out of Spain and proceeded towards the frontiers of Italy. In the autumn of 218 BC he crossed the Alps with 20 000 infantry and 6000 cavalry, and was immediately joined by the Gallic tribes of the northern plain, who had revolted from Rome on hearing news of his approach. With their help he won the first major engagements of the war, at the rivers Ticinus and Trebia, before the end of 218.

The attitude of the Gauls must have encouraged Hannibal, whose chief hope was that the Italian allies would rise up in rebellion against Rome. In 217 he advanced into Etruria and won a crushing victory at Lake Trasimene, but although he made a great show of the fact that his quarrel was solely with Rome, and freed all his non-Roman Italian

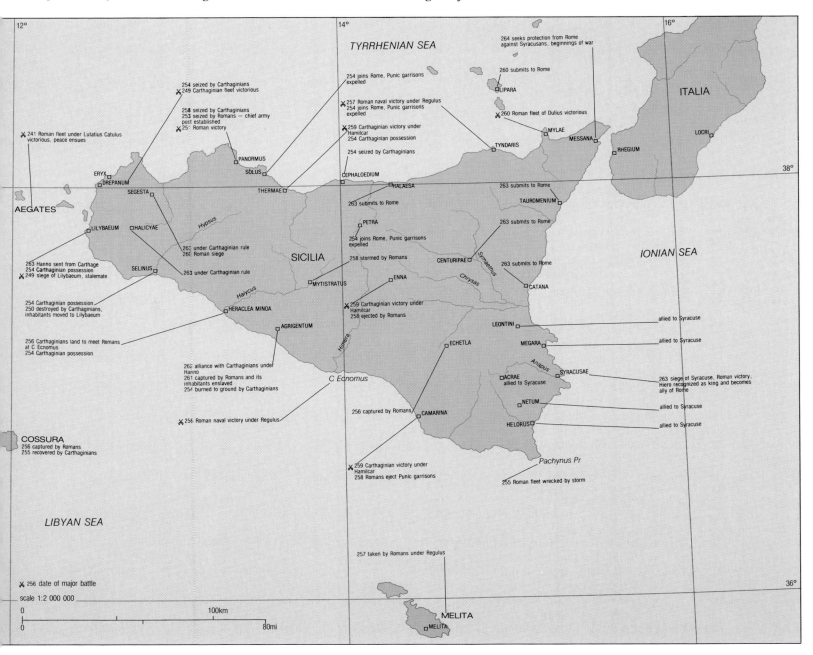

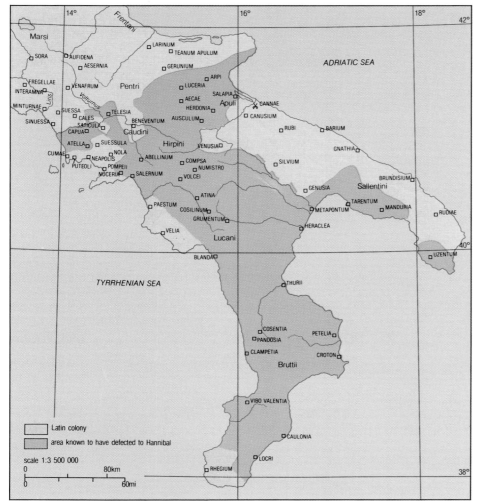

their side and all the circumstances favored them. They still had large reserves of manpower and supplies; Hannibal was cut off from his home base, and as yet none of the major ports had fallen into his hands. Rome's allies in Etruria, Umbria, Picenum and central Italy gave her solid support, and she was able to present a united front to the enemy, whereas the area controlled by Hannibal in the south was dotted with fortified loyalist enclaves, including most of the large towns and all of the Latin colonies. Hannibal could not afford to move too far from his base of operations in the south, whereas the Romans could ravage the territory of his allies almost at will, and reconquer them one by one. As Polybius noted, the Romans could divide their forces, but Hannibal could be in only one place at a time.

As the years went by the initiative gradually passed to Rome. In 211 Hannibal suffered a serious blow when Capua fell after a long siege. His attempt to relieve the city by a sudden march on Rome was a

Italy during the war with Hannibal. During the early years of the war, Rome's Italian allies remained loyal, in spite of Hannibal's efforts to win them over. But the disaster of Cannae changed everything. Livy writes: "How much more serious was the defeat at Cannae than those which had preceded it can be seen by the behavior of Rome's allies: before that fatal day their loyalty had remained unshaken; now it began to waver, for the simple reason that they despaired of the survival of Roman power. The following peoples went over to the Carthaginian cause: the Atellani, Calatini, Hirpini, some of the Apulians, all the Samnites except the Pentri, the Bruttii, the Lucanians, the Uzentini, and nearly all the Greek settlements on the coast, namely Tarentum, Metapontum, Croton and Locri, and all the Gauls on the Italian side of the Alps." One should add that the greatest prize of all, the Campanian town of Capua, went over in 215. However the Romans began to recover lost ground almost immediately: by the time the Greek cities went over (212 BC), Rome had regained control of Samnium and northern Apulia; Capua fell in 211, Tarentum and Thurii in 209. By 206 Hannibal had been forced to retire to the extreme south, where he was confined to Bruttium.

prisoners, the allies still remained firmly loyal to the Romans. Hannibal had clearly miscalculated if he had been expecting a general revolt; in fact the upper classes of the allied communities felt that their interests lay with Rome, and at this stage they could see no advantage in joining an alien invader, especially one who had allied himself with the Gauls.

In 216 Hannibal won his greatest victory at Cannae in Apulia, one of Rome's worst military disasters, in which perhaps as many as 30 000 lost their lives (the ancient sources give much higher figures). After Cannae some defections did take place among the allies, and large areas of the south, including much of Samnium, Lucania and Bruttium, went over to Hannibal. Some towns in Apulia and, most important of all, Capua in Campania also seceded. At this point Hannibal might reasonably have expected that the Romans would sue for peace, and that he would be able to end the war with a settlement favorable to Carthage.

The Romans' blind refusal to admit defeat in any circumstances meant that Hannibal's enterprise was doomed, however much appearances might have suggested the contrary. He was able to win over more of Rome's allies (Tarentum and other Greek cities joined him in 212), and in 215 he received the support of Philip V of Macedon and of the kingdom of Syracuse, following the death of the aged Hiero II. But in spite of these successes, his general position became steadily weaker. This was because the Romans adopted a policy (devised by Q. Fabius Maximus, "the Delayer") of avoiding pitched battles and fighting a war of attrition. Time was on

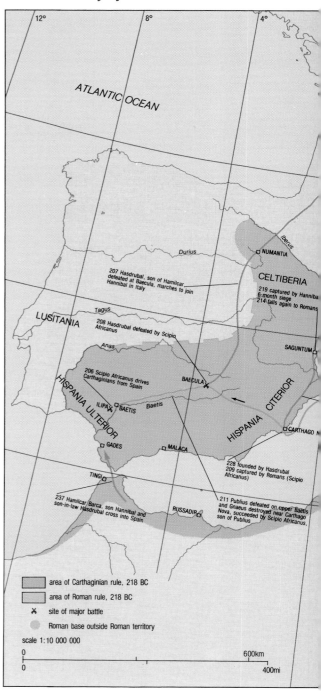

hopeless failure, although his appearance outside the walls caused consternation for a few days. Meanwhile the Romans were operating successfully against the Carthaginians in Sicily, where Syracuse was taken and sacked by M. Claudius Marcellus in 211, and a general revolt was crushed in 210. In Spain the Carthaginians had been held in check since 218 by a Roman expeditionary force under Publius and Gnaeus Scipio. In 215 they defeated Hasdrubal, Hannibal's brother, at Ibera, and in 214 they recaptured Saguntum. There was a serious setback in 211 when the Scipio brothers were defeated and killed, but the Romans immediately sent reinforcements to Spain and in 210 appointed as commander the young son and namesake of Publius Scipio, who at once embarked on a bold offensive strategy. In 209 he made a surprise attack on Carthago Nova (Cartagena) and captured it. In the following year he defeated Hasdrubal in a pitched battle at Baecula, but was unable to prevent him

from taking his army out of Spain and setting off to join his brother in Italy. Hasdrubal crossed the Alps in the spring of 207 and advanced rapidly to the Adriatic, intending to rendezvous with Hannibal in Umbria. But before the two brothers and their forces could meet, Hasdrubal was caught by a Roman army under C. Claudius Nero at the Metaurus and was decisively defeated. By now there was no hope left for Hannibal, who retired to Bruttium. In 203 he yielded to the inevitable and, still undefeated, shipped his army back to Africa. His return was necessitated by the fact that the young Scipio, after driving the Carthaginians out of Spain in 206, had persuaded the senate to allow him to lead an invasion of Africa, which began in 204.

Hannibal returned to defend Carthage, which he had last seen in 237 BC at the age of nine. The final showdown occurred at Zama in 202, where in a closely contested battle Scipio's forces were finally victorious. Hannibal himself negotiated a peace

The Second Punic War. Hannibal's invasion of Italy in 218 BC took the Romans by surprise and foiled their plan of a direct attack on Carthage. But by waging a war of attrition against Hannibal in Italy, and adopting a bold offensive strategy in Spain and Sicily, culminating in the invasion of Africa in 204, the Romans gradually gained the upper hand. The Carthaginians failed to send reinforcements to Hannibal, and their allies (the Gauls of north Italy, Philip V of Macedon) proved ineffectual. Hannibal was eventually forced to abandon Italy in order to defend Carthage, and was finally defeated by Scipio Africanus near Zama in 202.

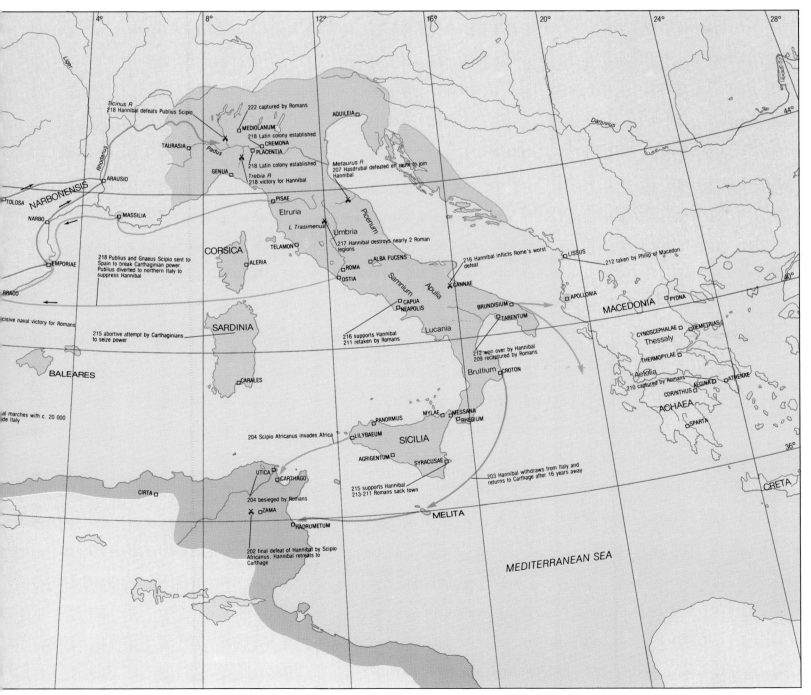

settlement, which confined Carthage to a restricted area of territory, deprived her of her fleet and imposed an indemnity of 10000 talents to be paid over a period of 50 years.

The growth of Roman imperialism

The peace settlement removed the threat of Carthage and brought relief to Italy, which had suffered extensive devastation and pillage during the 16 years of Hannibal's occupation. However, the victory over Carthage did not result in an immediate or drastic reduction in the scale of Rome's military commitments; in fact in the decades after 200 there were major wars in northern Italy, Spain, Sardinia and the eastern Mediterranean, in which large Roman armies were engaged, often for years on end. P.A. Brunt has pointed out that plausible estimates of the numbers of Italians in military service during this period ''seem to show that the requirements for manpower were still enormous after the Hannibalic war had ended, and that in 191–190 they rose to much the same peak as in the gravest crisis of that struggle.''

In 203 BC the Romans resumed the systematic conquest of Cisalpine Gaul, which had begun in 224 but was interrupted by Hannibal's invasion. Successive fierce campaigns in the Po valley ended in 191 with the defeat of the most powerful of the Cisalpine Gallic tribes, the Boii. Cremona and Placentia were reinforced and other colonies established, and in 187 the Via Aemilia (from which the present-day region of Emilia takes its name) was constructed from Placentia to Ariminum (Rimini). The Romans then turned to the task of conquering the warlike tribes of Liguria and the northern Apennines. This process was largely completed by 175, although resistance continued sporadically in some areas for a further 20 years. In 178–177 the Istrian peninsula was also overrun, following the establishment of a colony at the strategic site of Aquileia in 181.

In Spain Rome inherited from Carthage a substantial dominion in the southeast of the peninsula which required the presence of a permanent standing army, normally of two legions. This area was formed into two provinces, Hispania Ulterior and Hispania Citerior (Further and Hither Spain), after the Carthaginian withdrawal in 206. In 197 the number of annual praetors was raised from four to six, in order to provide regular magistrates to govern the new provinces. During these early years Spain was systematically looted by the Romans, who inevitably aroused the hatred of the native population. In 197 a revolt broke out in Further Spain which spread rapidly through both provinces and also involved the tribes of the interior. In spite of some energetic campaigning by Cato in 195, the war did not end until 179, when T. Sempronius Gracchus pacified the provinces and made an alliance with the Celtiberians. Twenty-five years of comparative peace ensued, until a new round of fighting began against the Lusitanians under their leader Viriathus (154–138), and a second war was fought against the Celtiberians (153–151). These wars proved immensely difficult and costly for the Romans, and disastrous for the Spaniards, who suffered countless atrocities. A final rebellion of the Celtiberians in 143 led to another lengthy and brutal war. One of the most unedifying chapters of Roman

history was brought to a close in 133 BC when Scipio Aemilianus (the adoptive grandson of the victor of Zama) captured and destroyed Numantia, the chief stronghold of the Celtiberians. A permanent military presence continued to be necessary, however, and the northwestern corner of Spain remained unconquered until the time of Augustus.

It is clear that in the western Mediterranean the Romans had committed themselves to an aggressive policy aimed at enlarging their existing possessions at the expense of the native ''barbarians.'' This led to an almost literally endless series of Gallic and Spanish wars. Mention should also be made of serious revolts among the natives of Sardinia (181–176 and 126 BC) and Corsica (181 and 166–163 BC). The conquest of Gallia Narbonensis (Provence) between 125 and 121 BC was a continuation of this policy, which led in the end to the occupation of all continental Gaul by Caesar (58–50 BC) and the invasion of Germany under Augustus. The Romans do not seem to have had any moral qualms about this activity, and the senate was evidently prepared to condone the harsh and often highly questionable methods of its commanders. In 151 BC Ser. Sulpicius Galba, who had massacred thousands of Lusitanians after they had surrendered to him, was acquitted at his trial although his guilt was palpable. Very few people in Rome cared much about what happened to the barbarians.

A rather more complex pattern of events developed in the eastern Mediterranean, where the Romans had further unfinished business at the end of the Hannibalic war. Here they were dealing with a culturally advanced world of established political communities which had emerged from the disintegration of the empire of Alexander the Great (356–323 BC). By the end of the 3rd century BC a relatively stable balance of power existed between the major kingdoms – the Antigonids of Macedon, the Attalids of Pergamum in Asia Minor, the Seleucids in Syria and Mesopotamia and the Ptolemies in Egypt. In the middle were the states of Greece and the Aegean, the most important of which were Athens, Sparta, Rhodes, the Achaean League (which comprised the cities of the northern Peloponnese) and the Aetolian League of northwest Greece.

Above Alba Fucens, founded as a colony in 303 BC in the territory of the Aequi, occupies a commanding position at the foot of Mt Velino (2487 meters). Belgian excavations since 1949 have revealed substantial remains of the city, which like most Roman colonies was built on a grid plan within a very impressive circuit of defensive walls. King Perseus of Macedonia was interned here after his surrender in 167 BC.

Below The *groma* was a Roman surveying instrument which allowed the surveyor to mark out lines at right angles to one another by taking sights from a central point.

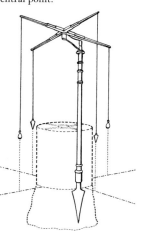

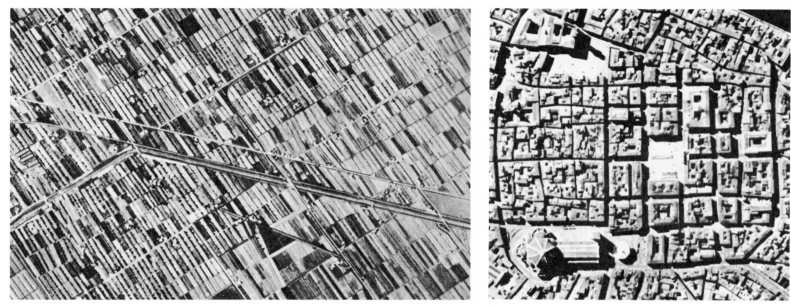

Above The distribution of land to Roman colonists was based on a process of survey and division known as centuriation, whereby the land was marked out in large squares of 200 *iugera* (50 hectares) called *centuriae* (that is, areas embracing 100 2-*iugera* units). Traces of centuriation have been revealed by aerial photography in many parts of Italy and the provinces. This photograph shows centuriated land in Emilia.

Above right The grid plan of Roman colonies is reflected in the street plans of many Italian cities of colonial origin. One example is Florence, where the colony of Florentia was founded in the time of Augustus.

Right: Colonization in Italy, 2nd century BC. Rome's traditional policy of colonization continued after the Hannibalic war with the reinforcement of some existing Latin colonies and the founding of new ones at Vibo and Thurii in southern Italy. Notice the Roman habit of giving colonies optimistic names such as *Valentia* ("strength") and *Copia* ("plenty"). During the 190s a number of coastal garrison colonies were founded around the shores of south Italy to guard against the possibility of an invasion by the Seleucid King Antiochus III, who was thought to be capable of anything and was being advised by the hated Hannibal. The Roman occupation of Cisalpine Gaul and Liguria was consolidated in the usual way by the foundation of colonies; but because it was apparently becoming increasingly difficult to persuade Romans to give up their citizenship, the government stopped founding Latin colonies and began instead to found large colonies of Roman citizens. Parma and Mutina (183) were the first colonies of the new type, and Aquileia (181) was the last of the old. After the founding of Luna in 177 Roman colonization came to an abrupt end and was not resumed until the end of the century. The only exception was Auximum (157), whose date is doubted by some scholars.

EPOREDIA 100
PLACENTIA 218, reinforced 190
CREMONA 218, reinforced 190
AQUILEIA 181, reinforced 169
Padus
PARMA 183
MUTINA 183
BONONIA 189
LUNA 177
LUCA 178
Arnus
PISAURUM 184
AUXIMUM 157
POTENTIA 184
SATURNIA 183
COSA reinforced 197
GRAVISCAE 181
Tiberis
ROMA
SIPONTUM 194, refounded 186
FABRATERIA NOVA 125
VENUSIA reinforced 200
VOLTURNUM 194
LITERNUM 194
PUTEOLI 194
NEPTUNIA (TARENTUM) 122
SALERNUM 194
BUXENTUM 194, refounded 186
THURII COPIA 193
CROTON 194
TEMPSA 194
CASTRUM HANNIBALIS 199
VIBO VALENTIA 192
MINERVIUM (SCOLACIUM) 122

☐ Latin colony
▣ Roman citizen colony
◉ coastal garrison colony
194 date of colonization

scale 1:6 000 000

0 ———————— 300km
0 ———————— 200mi

Rome's first venture east of the Adriatic had occurred in 229 BC, when it declared war on Queen Teuta of Illyria, whose subjects had been engaging in piracy and molesting Italian traders. In two brief campaigns (the First and Second Illyrian Wars, 229–228 and 221–219 BC) Rome humbled the Illyrians and gained effective control of a number of Greek cities on the Illyrian coast. These developments aroused the suspicions of Philip V of Macedon, who in 215 took advantage of Rome's weakness after Cannae to form an alliance with Hannibal. The Romans responded in 211 by making an alliance with the Aetolians, old enemies of Philip, who undertook to prosecute the war on land with Roman naval support. Other Greek states soon joined the alliance, and the Romans found that they had successfully contained the threat of Philip without having to commit any large forces of their own. The Aetolians however felt that they were bearing the brunt of the war and were not receiving enough support from Rome; in 206 they decided to cut their losses and make their own peace with Philip. The Romans, still preoccupied with the problem of Hannibal, followed suit a year later.

Once Hannibal had been dealt with the Romans were free to turn their attention once again to the Balkans, where Philip had begun to build up his power in the Aegean and was making threatening moves in Illyria. In 200 the Second Macedonian War began. During two years of indecisive military action, the Romans were remarkably successful on the diplomatic front, winning the support of most of the states of central and southern Greece by making it known that their aim was to drive Philip out of Greece and to confine him to Macedonia. They were soon in a position to enforce this policy when they decisively defeated Philip at the battle of Cynoscephalae in 197 BC. At the Isthmian games of 196 the Roman commander T. Quinctius Flamininus dramatically proclaimed to an enthusiastic audience that the Romans intended to leave the Greek states free and independent. Two years were spent in implementing the settlement, and in 194 all Roman troops were withdrawn from the Balkans.

By this date considerable tension had built up between Rome and the Seleucid king Antiochus III, who had been operating in Asia Minor and in 196 had invaded Thrace. The two powers watched one another's movements with considerable anxiety; complex negotiations took place, accompanied by a propaganda campaign which modern observers have compared to the Cold War. In 192 the Aetolians, resentful because Flamininus had not permitted them to reoccupy some of their former territories evacuated by Philip, seized the fortress town of Demetrias and summoned Antiochus to free the Greeks from Rome. Antiochus saw his chance and responded by taking a small expeditionary force to Greece. Within a year he had been driven out of Greece by a Roman army which defeated him at Thermopylae. The Romans then invaded Asia under the command of L. Scipio (brother of Africanus, who accompanied the army), and defeated Antiochus in a pitched battle at Magnesia (190 BC). Antiochus was forced to withdraw beyond the Taurus mountains, to pay a huge indemnity and to surrender his elephants and fleet. In the following year the consul Cn. Manlius Vulso invaded the territory of the Galatians, killed large

numbers of them and acquired enormous booty. In 188 a final settlement was reached with Antiochus, and a treaty signed, at Apamea. His former territories in Asia Minor were divided between Rhodes and Eumenes II of Pergamum, who had succeeded Attalus in 197. The Romans then withdrew entirely from Greece and Asia.

This remarkable sequence of events inevitably raises questions about the nature and purpose of Roman policy in the eastern Mediterranean, and more generally about the origins and growth of Roman imperialism. Broadly speaking, modern discussions of this subject fall into two categories. Some historians argue that the growth of the Roman empire was the accidental result of a predominantly defensive policy: the Romans made war in order to defend their interests, and those of their allies, against real or imagined threats. This view coincides to a certain extent with the Romans' own claim that they only fought "just wars." Other scholars however prefer to believe that imperialism was a bad habit which the Romans fell into because of their love of war and military glory, and their desire for land and booty. On this view their policy was consciously aggressive, and all the pious talk of "just wars" was either a cynical exercise in public relations or a naive fabrication of patriotic historians.

The trouble with these two lines of interpretation is that they are solely concerned with the conscious aims and motives of the actors, who did not necessarily either understand or control the events in which they took part. Even on a conscious level such explanations are probably too schematic and elaborate. For example, it is unlikely that the Romans declared war on Macedon in 200 because they thought that Philip represented a threat to their interests, or because they were seeking a new outlet for aggressive action. A much simpler and more convincing motive is suggested by Livy: Philip's alliance with Hannibal in 215 was a "stab in the back" which could not be overlooked, and as soon as the Romans had dealt with Hannibal they crossed over to Greece and gave Philip the thrashing he deserved.

The most significant fact about the growth of the Roman empire is that it was the product of a continuous series of successful wars. We need to ask, therefore, not only why the Romans fought so many wars, but also why they were so successful. In the final analysis the answer to both questions is the same: the Romans had at their disposal a very efficient military machine and enormous reserves of manpower which could not be matched by their opponents. They had an almost infinite capacity for replacement, and could absorb huge losses, as the events of the Second Punic War demonstrated. Livy was absolutely right when he declared (with reference to Trasimene and Cannae): "No other nation in the world could have suffered so tremendous a series of disasters and not been overwhelmed."

Rome's military power depended ultimately on the system of alliances that resulted from its conquest of Italy. By making the allies active military partners rather than passive tribute-paying subjects the Romans committed themselves in advance to a career of militarism and conquest. They had built up a military organization which had

The ancient Greek city of Corinth was destroyed by Rome in 146 BC as an example to the rest of the empire. Roman Corinth, of which impressive remains survive, including the theater shown here, was founded as a colony by Julius Caesar. See below, p. 149.

to be used if they were to derive any benefit from it; war and conquest thus became a logical necessity. In practice this meant that the Roman government could afford to use war as an instrument of policy in circumstances where other states might have been deterred by the risks or unable to sustain the losses that might be incurred. The constant practice of warfare on an ever-increasing scale led to even greater military effectiveness and expertise, and created a militaristic ethos that pervaded Roman society at every level.

The results of military success were an increase in territory, wealth (in the form of taxes, booty and indemnities), security and power. The Romans believed themselves entitled to these rewards, which compensated them for the expense and effort of the military operations that they had been compelled to undertake. The conquests were further justified by the benefits which Roman rule gave to the subjects of the empire: civilization to the barbarians, stability and order to the unruly Greeks. Everyone gained except those who were foolish or arrogant enough to resist.

tu regere imperio populos, Romane, memento
(hae tibi erunt artes), pacisque imponere morem,
parcere subiectis et debellare superbos.

("Remember, Roman, that it is for you to rule the nations. This shall be your task: to impose the ways of peace, to spare the vanquished and to tame the proud by war." Virgil, *Aeneid* 6. 851–53.)

Roman rule took different forms, according to circumstances. In the western Mediterranean, as we have seen, the Romans favored a policy of annexation, direct rule and a permanent military presence; in the Greek east, on the other hand, they tended to avoid annexation and preferred to rule indirectly through local governments which were left theoretically independent but were expected to act in the Roman interest. In fact the nominally free states of Greece were dependent on Rome in much the same way as clients were dependent on their patron (see above, p. 19); whether or not the Romans themselves used the terminology of *clientela* to describe their relations with other states, there is no doubt that the term "client states" accurately defines the position of the "free" allies controlled by Rome.

Nearly 20 years passed before the Romans felt any need for military intervention in the Greek world. Then in 171 a Roman army was sent across the Adriatic to deal with Perseus, who had in 179 succeeded his father Philip V in Macedon. The Romans are said to have been alarmed by the revival of Macedonian power, which had begun before Philip's death, and they became especially concerned when Perseus attempted to effect a reconciliation between himself and the Greek states. The allegation that his ultimate aim was to make war on Rome may be unfounded, although the Romans are unlikely to have been pleased by his appeal to the lower classes in the Greek cities; as in Italy, so too in Greece the Romans naturally tended to support the interests of the properted classes (although there are some exceptions to this general pattern). Perseus had some initial successes, and was victorious in a pitched battle at Callinicus in 171, but in 168 he was decisively defeated at the battle of Pydna by L. Aemilius Paullus. The Macedonian army was almost totally destroyed, and Perseus himself surrendered shortly afterwards.

The settlement after the battle of Pydna was harsh and illustrates the extent to which Roman attitudes had changed since the 190s. Macedonia was divided up into four separate republics, and its population forced to pay tribute to Rome at half the rate that had been levied by Perseus. In this way the Romans obtained the benefits of direct rule without having to shoulder the burdens of administration and defense. A cruel fate was reserved for the Molossians of Epirus, who had joined Perseus after his victory at Callinicus. Their territory was systematically pillaged by Paullus' army, and the population was enslaved. A general purge of anti-Roman elements in the Greek states was then carried out. In particular, 1000 members of the upper class of the Achaean League were deported to Italy, where they were interned without trial. The most famous of these detainees was the historian Polybius. In Asia, Pergamum and Rhodes were punished with loss of territory. They had not taken part in the war, but they had been loitering with intent. Rome thus demonstrated that it would tolerate nothing less than complete obedience from its subjects.

By these methods the Romans were able to rule the Greeks indirectly for a further 18 years. Then in about 150 BC an uprising in Macedon under the leadership of a pretender named Andriscus prompted the Romans to intervene once more. Andriscus was defeated in 148, and Macedonia became a regular province. Two years later the Achaean League was crushed following a futile revolt, and its territory incorporated in the province. Corinth was sacked as an example to the rest of the world, and timocratic constitutions (see above, p. 42) were established instead of democracies in the Greek cities.

This was a crucial period in the growth of the Roman empire. In 150 BC the Third Punic War broke out when Rome intervened in a dispute between Carthage and Rome's friend and ally, King Masinissa of Numidia. At the insistence of the aged Cato, the Romans resolved to destroy the city. The Carthaginians put up a desperate resistance, but in the end the city fell to the Roman commander Scipio Aemilianus and was obliterated (146 BC). Its territory became the new province of Africa.

Archaic Rome

The earliest traces of habitation on the site of Rome consist of cremation graves in the Forum, which from the 10th century BC served as a burial ground for settlements on the surrounding hills. An early settlement on the Palatine is indicated by Iron Age hut foundations that have been found there, and by the tradition that Romulus founded his city on the Palatine. Later the Palatine settlement expanded to include the Forum, and from the 8th century the Esquiline became the chief cemetery. At the end of the 7th century the huts in the Forum were demolished, and a formal public square was laid out; the surrounding settlement also took on a more "urban" aspect, with the construction of permanent stone houses, temples and other public buildings. Tradition associated this development with the reign of Tarquin I (616–579 BC); according to Livy, Tarquin "made grants of land around the Forum to be used as private building sites, and built shops and porticoes." His successor Servius Tullius further enlarged the city, incorporating the Esquiline, Quirinal and Viminal hills, surrounded it with a wall and divided it into four regions. The archaeological record confirms the general picture of urban growth in the 6th century.

The "Capitoline Wolf." This archaic bronze masterpiece dates from around 500 BC and is possibly of Etruscan workmanship. The figures of the twins were added in the Renaissance, but there is good reason to think that the restoration is justified. If so, it follows that the legend of Romulus and Remus was already well established in Rome at the end of the regal period.

Reconstruction (after Gjerstad) of the frontal elevation of the great temple of Jupiter, Juno and Minerva, which was built by the Tarquins and dedicated by the first consuls in 509 BC. The building, which is some 64 meters long, 55 meters wide, and an estimated 40 meters high, was one of the largest archaic temples of the Mediterranean world. It survived intact until 83 BC, when it was destroyed by fire.

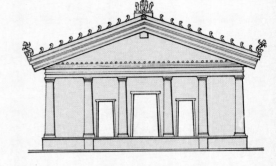

Left Traces of crude huts dating from the 8th century BC have been found on the Palatine, traditionally the site of Romulus' settlement. The Romans retained a memory of this primitive stage in the Casa Romuli (House of Romulus), a simple shepherd's hut lovingly preserved until the time of the Empire.

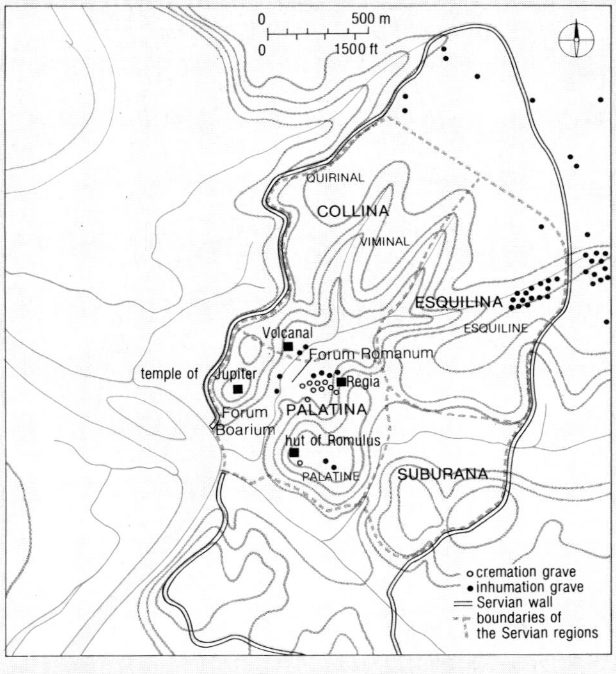

Above Two-handled impasto jar from an inhumation grave on the Esquiline – probably late 8th century BC.
Above right Hut urn from a cremation burial in the Roman Forum. Urns of this type are clearly meant to represent human dwellings: foundations of oval-shaped huts have been found on the Palatine.
Right Forum Tomb Y: a typical cremation grave. The hut urn and surrounding grave goods were placed in a large jar and buried in a pit; 10th-9th century BC.

Map legend:
- QUIRINAL
- COLLINA
- VIMINAL
- ESQUILINA
- ESQUILINE
- Volcanal
- Forum Romanum
- temple of Jupiter
- Regia
- Forum Boarium
- PALATINA
- hut of Romulus
- PALATINE
- SUBURANA

- ○ cremation grave
- ● inhumation grave
- Servian wall
- boundaries of the Servian regions

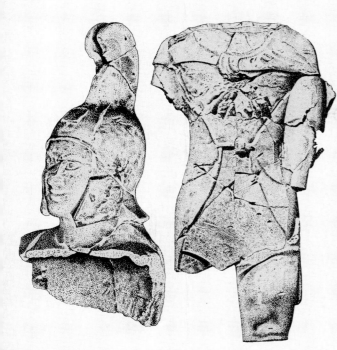

Right Terracotta architectonic frieze from the Regia, a sacred building in the Forum where the king (and in the Republic the *rex sacrorum*) carried out his religious functions. The first Regia was constructed around the end of the 7th century BC; the frieze belongs to a later reconstruction, probably in the second half of the 6th century.

Left Fragments of an archaic statue group portraying Hercules and (probably) Minerva, found near the archaic temple in the Forum Boarium. The statues were probably part of the acroterium – that is, they stood on the roof of the temple and formed part of its decoration. The iconography and style of sculpture are East Greek, and suggest that the statues were made by craftsmen from Ionia, probably around 530 BC.

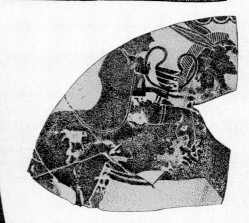

Top Miniature ivory plaque in the form of a lion couchant, from a votive deposit associated with the archaic temple in the Forum Boarium (second half of the 6th century BC). On the back of the lion is an Etruscan inscription – "araz silqetenas spurianas" – which is probably the name of the person who made the offering in the sanctuary. This is one of several Etruscan inscriptions from archaic Rome (see p. 23).

Above Fragment of an Attic black-figure crater (c. 570–560 BC) showing Hephaestus returning to Olympus. The fragment was found in the votive deposit of the sanctuary of the Lapis Niger, a sanctuary which can be independently identified as the shrine of Vulcan (Volcanal). The presence of this fragment in this context can hardly be a coincidence, and proves that the Romans had identified Vulcan with Hephaestus as early as the 6th century BC.

CRISIS AND REFORM

The consequences of empire

Rome's conquest of the Mediterranean inevitably brought about profound changes in the political, social and economic life of Rome and Italy. At a political level, the senate's conduct of the war effort against Hannibal and its successful handling of subsequent foreign entanglements in the Greek east led to a general acceptance by the people of senatorial government; popular legislation and attacks on the established order were very infrequent in the century following the tribunate of C. Flaminius in 232 BC (see above, p. 44). The period was one of apparent political calm and stability, which Cicero was later to look back on as a kind of golden age of senatorial rule.

The senate itself was dominated by the nobles, who were divided up into competing factions. These groups took the form of *ad hoc* alliances of friends and kinsmen who united to promote particular policies and mobilized their clients and supporters to vote for favored candidates at the elections. The factions were certainly not permanent political parties, and although some "friendships" undoubtedly lasted longer than others, there is no good reason to suppose that Roman politics were dominated by permanent and hereditary alliances of noble families or *gentes*. Rivalry between individuals and groups was traditional and ensured a kind of equilibrium, but tensions within the senatorial oligarchy arose as the rewards for office increased and the competition for the senior magistracies intensified.

In the course of the Hannibalic war military necessity had given rise to the practice of prolonging the commands of successful generals beyond the statutory limit of one year. While this innovation may have been justified from a practical point of view, it clearly had dangerous political implications in that it allowed ambitious individuals like Scipio and Flamininus to break away from the constraints of the system of annual collegiate magistracies. These men also set themselves apart from their peers by affecting an ostentatious and luxurious life-style and parading their knowledge of Greek culture. Other nobles hastened to follow suit, and the results were intensified competition for office, self-enrichment, corruption and an indiscriminate cult of Hellenism. Opposition to these trends was led by Cato the Censor (234-149 BC), who deliberately adopted a simple and austere way of life in imitation of the great men of the past such as M'. Curius Dentatus (see above, p.42). Cato made fun of the frivolous exhibitionism of the Hellenists, advocated homespun virtues and showed a profound respect for native Italic traditions. His efforts to maintain the traditional cohesion of the oligarchy led him to mount a political attack on Scipio, who was eventually forced to retire from public life in 184 BC. Cato supported sumptuary laws and frequently spoke out against bribery, corruption and abuse of power.

Cato's opposition to Hellenism was not based on mere prejudice. He himself spoke Greek and understood Greek culture better than many of those whom he attacked; he actually favored the borrowing of Greek ideas, provided that they could be adapted to Roman needs. It was Cato who ordered the construction of Rome's first basilica, a building of Greek type, during his censorship in 184. This is one of many examples of public buildings in the Greek style which were erected during this period.

But the most striking example of the adaptation of Greek ideas to Roman needs is the growth of Latin literature, to which Cato himself made a decisive contribution. The earliest writer of literary Latin was Livius Andronicus, a Greek who was brought to Rome as a captive after the fall of Tarentum in 272 BC. Andronicus produced a Latin translation of the *Odyssey* and composed tragedies based on Greek originals. His example was followed by Cn. Naevius (c. 275–200 BC) and Q. Ennius (239–169), both of whom wrote epic poems as well as plays. It is noteworthy that these men were not native Latin speakers: Naevius was an Oscan-speaking Campanian and Ennius a Messapian from Rudiae. The same is true of the Umbrian T. Maccius Plautus, the Celtic Caecilius Statius, and the African P. Terentius Afer (Terence), all of whom produced Latin comedies in the Greek style during the early part of the 2nd century BC (those of Plautus and Terence are still extant). Other prominent figures of early Latin literature were the tragedians M. Pacuvius (220–c. 130 BC) and C. Accius (170–c. 90 BC) and the satirist C. Lucilius (c. 180–102 BC). Cato's achievement was the creation of Latin prose literature. His works included speeches, 142 of which were known to Cicero who greatly admired them, a work on agriculture which still survives and a historical work on Rome and Italy entitled *Origines*. Earlier Roman histories (for example, that by Fabius Pictor) had been written in Greek. A unique feature of the *Origines* was that it included the history of the Italian peoples as well as Rome.

Cato's efforts were thus directed towards a constructive exploitation of Greek cultural borrowings, and resistance to the corrupting influence of wealth, luxury and the pursuit of power, which he associated with Hellenism as the indirect products of military conquest. But Cato did not, as far as we can see, have any perception of a deeper and more serious consequence of Roman imperialism. During his lifetime the rural economy of Italy was being transformed by a process which eventually led to a major agrarian crisis. The most obvious symptoms of this development were the impoverishment and displacement of the Italian peasantry which resulted from more than half a century of continuous war.

Warfare affected the political economy of Italy in two distinct ways. First there were the direct effects of Hannibal's invasion, which resulted in extensive devastation of the countryside, especially in

Above This fine torso of Apollo from a temple at Falerii (late 4th or early 3rd century BC) is probably the work of a Greek sculptor from Magna Graecia. The piece illustrates the way in which central Italy was being influenced by Greek culture at this date, and is an excellent example of "Italo-Hellenic" art.

Above right The circular temple in the Forum Boarium (usually called, quite erroneously, the temple of Vesta) dates probably from the late 2nd century BC and is the earliest surviving example of a marble temple in Rome. The style is pure Greek.

southern Italy, and the annihilation of whole communities. For example, when Tarentum was captured by the Romans in 209 BC, the whole population was enslaved and a once flourishing city became a remote village. While devastation would not necessarily affect the productive capacity of agricultural land, the mere destruction of standing crops, buildings and livestock will have been sufficient in itself to ruin many peasant families and to depopulate large areas of territory. The indirect effects of continuous warfare were even more serious for the peasants, who had to bear the burden of prolonged military service. The traditional Roman army was a peasant militia which had proved adequate and efficient at a time when wars were local, seasonal conflicts against neighboring communities; but it was quite unsuited to Roman military needs during and after the Hannibalic war, when enormous numbers of soldiers were required to serve for years on end in distant areas of the Mediterranean.

It is estimated that the average size of the combined Roman and Italian army during the 35 years following the defeat of Hannibal was over 130000 men; this represents a very high proportion of the total adult male population of Italy. Of Roman citizens the average proportion of adult males in service at any one time during the last two centuries of the Republic is reckoned to have been around 13 per cent; this means that over half the adult males regularly served in the legions for at least seven years of their lives. Such a level of involvement in warfare was disastrous for the class of peasant smallholders. Many peasant families were thus deprived of essential manpower for long periods, or permanently, if their menfolk were killed in battle. Farms were neglected, debts were incurred and dispossession followed through sale or eviction. The process was hastened by the fact that the rich sought to invest the profits of successful war in Italian land. This led to the growth of large estates

(*latifundia*) through the accumulation, by a few, of land which had formerly been worked by peasant smallholders.

Peasant families were driven out in large numbers by rich investors and were replaced on the land by slave labor. Slaves were in plentiful supply thanks to military victories and the resulting mass enslavement of defeated populations; they could be organized in gangs to provide the necessary labor for large-scale agricultural enterprises, they were relatively cheap and had the additional advantage of being exempt from conscription. Thus the development of the *latifundia* was facilitated by the influx of wealth and slaves, the products of victories which had been won by the efforts and sacrifice of Italian peasants who served in the army. As Keith Hopkins puts it, "Roman peasant soldiers were fighting for their own displacement."

The growth of the *latifundia* in the 2nd century BC was accompanied by new methods of farming, which were designed to provide absentee landlords with a cash income from the sale of surplus produce. The new regime is exemplified in Cato's work *On Agriculture,* a handbook aimed at proprietors of medium-sized estates (he specifies holdings of 25 and 60 hectares) worked by slaves and supervised by resident slave managers (*vilici*). Cato deals especially with the cultivation of vines and olives, which produce a good cash return but which require both a large initial capital outlay and relatively extensive holdings of land to allow economies of scale to be achieved. Equally profitable was the practice of cattle ranching and sheep grazing, which also required capital and large areas of land. Extensive pastures were available in southern Italy, where whole regions had been depopulated in the Second Punic War. Much of this land was technically *ager publicus*, having been confiscated by Rome from the allied states that had joined Hannibal, but the Roman government turned a blind eye to the expropriation of such land and did not enforce the legal restrictions on the size of holdings. It seems likely that the same thing happened to *ager publicus* in other parts of Italy.

Many of the displaced peasants migrated to the towns and cities of Italy, and especially to Rome, where opportunities for employment were being created by the lavish expenditure of the rich on luxuries, services, political bribes and entertainments. Public spending also contributed to the development of an urbanized market economy. The state's income, in the form of booty, indemnities and taxes, was immense; after the settlement of Macedon in 167 BC the *tributum* was abolished and direct taxes were not thereafter levied on the property of Roman citizens in Italy. A high proportion of public revenue was reinvested in further conquest, that is, spent on pay and supplies for the army. The rest was spent on the extensive public building projects which were undertaken in Rome and the towns of Italy throughout the 2nd century BC (there is no evidence for a decline in building activity in the 130s, as is sometimes supposed). The growth of the towns created a market for the produce of the estates of the rich, while the needs of the army accounted for much of the wool and leather produced on the ranch lands of southern Italy.

The towns and cities were also centers of craft production and small-scale industrial activity, which were probably based on slave labor. The principal market for manufactured goods was undoubtedly the army, which needed regular supplies of clothing, equipment and weapons. The organization of supplies was undertaken by private individuals and companies who competed for government contracts. These private contractors were known as "publicans" (*publicani*). They contracted for the construction and repair of public buildings, roads and other utilities, and it was they who bought the rights to exploit state-owned mines and to collect indirect taxes (such as tolls and harbor dues) and rents on public land. The contracts, which were let out every five years by the censors, were immensely lucrative and of great economic importance. Polybius tells us that there was hardly anyone in Rome who was not involved either in the sale of these contracts or in the kinds of business to which they gave rise. They brought wealth and power to the leading *publicani*, who formed an influential pressure group outside the senate (senators were not allowed to participate in public contracts).

The challenge of the Gracchi
The process of urbanization and the growth of a market economy produced a number of disturbing side effects which did not escape the notice of contemporaries. The continual displacement of peasant smallholders was worrying not only because of the human misery it caused but also because it led to a gradual decline in the numbers of potential recruits for the army, who were traditionally drawn from the class of *adsidui*; dispossessed peasants were reduced to the status of proletarians and were no longer qualified for army service. Difficulties in recruiting men for the legions are recorded on a number of occasions in the years after 150 BC. Secondly there was growing concern at the numbers of slaves who were being imported into

Italy to work the land in place of the free peasants. In 136 BC a major uprising of slaves occurred in Sicily which involved tens of thousands of runaways and was only put down with extreme difficulty. Similar disturbances occurred in Italy at the same time, and Rome was faced with the threat of a general breakdown of law and order.

The problem of internal security, the increasing difficulties of recruitment and the wretched condition of the rural proletariat were the problems which Tiberius Gracchus set out to tackle during his tribunate in 133 BC. His carefully planned solution, a single agrarian law, was simple in conception, ostensibly moderate in form and potentially revolutionary in effect. Gracchus proposed to resettle the dispossessed peasants on allotments of public land. The necessary land was to be made available by enforcing the statutory limit (500 *iugera*) on the size of individual holdings of *ager*

Above Coin of P. Licinius Nerva (113/12 BC) showing citizens in an assembly passing along the gangway (*pons*) to cast their votes. The coin celebrates the system of secret ballot, which was introduced by a series of laws in the second half of the 2nd century BC.

Left The circular temple at Tivoli (Tibur) closely resembles that in the Forum Boarium in Rome (see p. 55), and dates from the same period. It shows that monumental buildings in the Greek style were being erected in the towns of Italy as well as in Rome.

Below The sanctuary of Fortuna Primigenia at Palestrina (Praeneste) was more impressive than any contemporary structure in Rome. The huge complex of buildings, dating probably from the last part of the 2nd century BC, is modeled on similar Hellenistic sanctuaries at Pergamum and Rhodes.

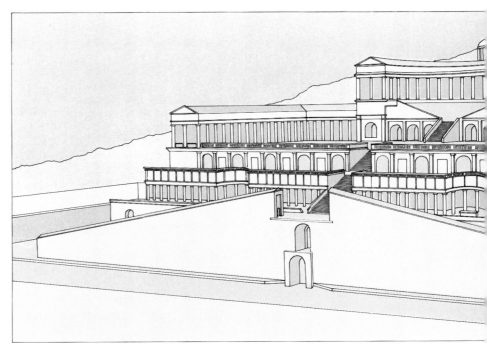

The land reforms of the Gracchi. The agrarian reforms of the Gracchi took place against a background of military crisis, rural impoverishment and mounting urban unrest. The free peasants of Italy were being driven from their land and replaced by slave labor on large estates; the results of this process were seen by Tiberius Gracchus on a journey through Etruria in 137 BC. A few years later a major slave revolt had broken out in Sicily, accompanied by minor uprisings in Rome and Italy.

Tiberius' solution was to reconstitute the free peasantry by distributing state-owned "public" land in small allotments to poor citizens. His agrarian law led to a political upheaval and his own death, but the land commission he set up was able to carry out its task, and has left evidence of its activities in the inscribed *termini* (boundary stones) which have been found in various parts of Italy. His brother Gaius continued his work, and also revived the tradition of founding colonies, at least two of which are known – at Scolacium (Minervium) and Tarentum (Neptunia).

Overleaf The Roman Forum, seen through the arch of Septimius Severus, looking towards the temple of Vesta.

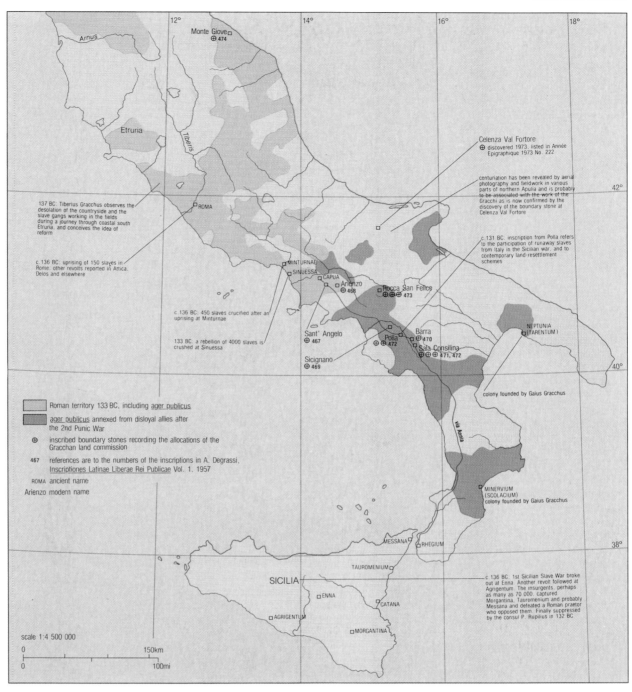

137 BC: Tiberius Gracchus observes the desolation of the countryside and the slave gangs working in the fields during a journey through coastal south Etruria, and conceives the idea of reform

c. 136 BC: uprising of 150 slaves in Rome; other revolts reported in Attica, Delos and elsewhere

c. 136 BC: 450 slaves crucified after an uprising at Minturnae

133 BC: a rebellion of 4000 slaves is crushed at Sinuessa

Celenza Val Fortore
⊕ discovered 1973, listed in Année Epigraphique 1973 No. 222

centuriation has been revealed by aerial photography and fieldwork in various parts of northern Apulia and is probably to be associated with the work of the Gracchi as is now confirmed by the discovery of the boundary stone at Celenza Val Fortore

c. 131 BC: inscription from Polla refers to the participation of runaway slaves from Italy in the Sicilian war, and to contemporary land-resettlement schemes

colony founded by Gaius Gracchus

c. 136 BC: 1st Sicilian Slave War broke out at Enna. Another revolt followed at Agrigentum. The insurgents, perhaps as many as 70,000, captured Morgantina, Tauromenium and probably Messana and defeated a Roman praetor who opposed them. Finally suppressed by the consul P. Rupilius in 132 BC

Roman territory 133 BC, including ager publicus

ager publicus annexed from disloyal allies after the 2nd Punic War

⊕ inscribed boundary stones recording the allocations of the Gracchan land commission

467 references are to the numbers of the inscriptions in A. Degrassi, Inscriptiones Latinae Liberae Rei Publicae Vol. 1, 1957

ROMA ancient name

Arienzo modern name

scale 1:4 500 000

0 ——— 150km
0 ——— 100mi

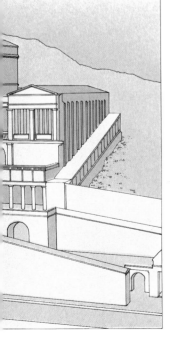

publicus and by reclaiming in the name of the state land held in excess of the limit. The task of reclamation was to be carried out by a commission of three men, who would then distribute small allotments to the poor. The beauty of the scheme was that it did not offend traditional rights of private property; on the contrary, it would only affect those who were already outside the law. In practice, however, Gracchus' bill was a major threat to the vested interests of many wealthy landowners, and intense opposition was aroused. On the other hand popular support was assured, especially among the rural poor, who flocked to Rome to vote for the bill. An attempt to veto the bill was foiled when Gracchus had the offending tribune voted out of office; the law was passed, and the land commission, consisting of Tiberius Gracchus himself, his brother Gaius and his father-in-law Appius Claudius, was duly set up.

But the opposition became alarmed at the political implications of what was happening. Gracchus had proposed his law without consulting the senate, as was customary; he had brushed aside the veto of a colleague by means that were possibly illegal; and he was now serving on his own land commission. Moreover he had not hesitated to make use of an unexpected windfall that occurred when Attalus III of Pergamum died, leaving his kingdom to the Romans. Gracchus immediately enacted that the bequest should be accepted, and the royal treasures distributed to the recipients of land allotments, to assist them in stocking their farms. The opposition was outraged by this unprecedented interference with the senate's traditional control of public finance. Finally, when Gracchus announced his intention to stand for a second tribunate for the following year, and to hint at further legislation, there was consternation and talk of *regnum* (see above, pp. 22–23). On the day of the election some leading senators and their attendants tried to break up the assembly, and in the ensuing riot Tiberius Gracchus and 300 of his supporters were killed. A general witch-hunt followed, in which many more Gracchan sympathizers were condemned by a special senatorial court of inquiry.

The sacrosanctity of the tribunate had been violated, and political conflict had ended in bloodshed for the first time in the history of the Roman Republic. Even so, it is unlikely that the full significance of the event was realized at the time. The land commission remained in being and continued its work (although not without difficulty), but in other respects the life of Rome appeared to return to normal. But the example of Tiberius Gracchus lived on, and soon began to be imitated by other tribunes. Within a few years an even more radical attack on the established order was mounted by Gaius Gracchus, Tiberius' younger brother. Gaius Gracchus held two successive tribunates (123 and 122 BC), in which he introduced a wide range of reforming legislation.

Gaius Gracchus' laws can be summarized under four main headings. First, a series of important measures aimed to promote the general welfare of the people. He passed an agrarian law which superseded that of his brother and provided in addition for the founding of colonies in Italy, at least two of which were actually established (at Minervium and Neptunia). A more radical step was the attempt to found a colony (Iunonia) on the site of Carthage. Other measures provided for a program of public works, the improvement of conditions of service in the army, the organization by the state of the corn supply of the city of Rome and the distribution of grain to the citizens at a fixed price, subsidized by the government. Secondly Gracchus attempted to increase the state's revenue, by imposing new customs tariffs and by enacting that the taxes of the immensely rich province of Asia (assessed as a tithe of its produce) should be collected by the *publicani*. Contracts were to be auctioned by the censors at Rome; in this way the state would receive a guaranteed income for five years, while the risks of fluctuations in the yield and the burden of administrative costs would be borne by the *publicani*. Gracchus' concern for public revenues arose from the need to finance his welfare schemes; his actions were guided by the principle that Rome's overseas possessions should be exploited to the full, and the proceeds used for the benefit of the people as a whole.

Thirdly Gaius attacked senatorial corruption and attempted to curb abuses of magisterial authority. He outlawed judicial conspiracy and enacted that special tribunals like that which had carried out the purge after his brother's death could not be constituted without popular authorization. Above all he reorganized the procedure for dealing with cases of peculation and maladministration by senatorial officials. In 149 BC a special standing committee of senators had been set up to deal with such offenses (prompted perhaps by the scandal of Ser. Galba: see above, p. 48). But experience had shown that senators were more concerned to cover up the nefarious activities of their peers than to see justice done, and the committee proved an inadequate safeguard against abuse. Gaius scrapped this convenient system of "internal inquiry," and replaced it with a regular criminal court manned by a jury from which senators were rigorously excluded. The jury was to be chosen from the equestrian order, that is from the propertied class. It was later asserted that Gracchus had split the ruling class, and given the state two heads. An unfortunate aspect of the new system was that the *publicani* became influential within the equestrian order, with the result that provincial governors who colluded with the *publicani* in robbing the provincials might hope to be acquitted if brought to trial in Rome. The reverse was also true; in 92 BC P. Rutilius Rufus was condemned for extortion by an equestrian jury after he had tried to check the abuses of the *publicani* in the province of Asia. The case was notorious and apparently the first of its kind; it is unlikely that such consequences could have been foreseen at the time of Gaius Gracchus.

Lastly, Gracchus attempted to widen the franchise by giving Roman citizenship to the Latins, and Latin rights to the other Italian allies. The proposal, which was not the first of its kind (an associate of Gracchus had proposed a similar bill in 125), was perhaps a response to expressions of discontent among the ruling class of the allied states, which had objected strongly to the activities of the Gracchan land commission. In any case the bill was rejected by the *plebs*, who did not wish to share their privileges. At this time (late in 122 BC) Gracchus was gradually losing support, and he failed to win a third tribunate for 121 BC. As soon as his tenure expired, an attempt was made to repeal some of his laws, beginning with the colony at Carthage. Gracchus and his supporters attempted to protest with a show of strength. The senate chose to view this as a threat to the state and ordered the consuls to see to it that the Republic suffered no harm. Gracchus and his friends fled to the Aventine, the old plebeian refuge (see above, p. 26), where they were rounded up and put to death; 3000 persons are said to have lost their lives in this grisly massacre.

The historical importance of Gaius Gracchus lies partly in the sheer volume and range of his legislation. Nothing like it had ever been seen before in Rome, and it was not to be repeated until the dictatorship of Julius Caesar. The whole Roman establishment had been shaken to its foundations, and there was no longer any doubt that the period of unchallenged oligarchic government that went back to the Hannibalic war was definitely at an end. The Gracchi had revived the traditional role of the tribunes as protectors of the *plebs*, and had asserted the people's right to legislate in its own interest on any matter whatsoever. Gaius Gracchus did not intend to remove the conduct of policy and administration from the senate and magistrates, but he hoped to make them more accountable to the people through the assemblies and by means of an independent judiciary which would be drawn from a class that was by definition outside politics.

The age of Marius and Sulla
Gaius Gracchus' miserable end was a victory for the most reactionary elements in the state. But their triumph was shortlived. Agitation by tribunes began again almost immediately, and the *populares* (political leaders who adopted the aims and methods of the Gracchi) were provided with an opportunity for a major assault in the years after 114 BC when

Rome was unexpectedly faced with a desperate military crisis. In that year the consul M. Porcius Cato (grandson of the famous censor) was disastrously defeated in Macedonia by the Scordisci, a Thracian tribe who had invaded the Roman province. At the same time news was received of a folk migration involving two Germanic tribes, the Cimbri and Teutones, who were reported to be approaching the borders of Italy. This created panic in the city, where attempts were made to appease the gods through archaic rituals, including that of human sacrifice. The same thing had happened at the time of the battle of Cannae, and the Romans clearly sensed that they were once again in extreme peril.

The senatorial oligarchy had acquired a position of unquestioned authority during the Hannibalic war, when it demonstrated competence in military leadership and organization, and skill in the conduct of foreign affairs. But these qualities were conspicuously lacking in the post-Gracchan senate. In 113 the consul Cn. Papirius Carbo risked a battle against the Cimbri at Noreia and suffered a calamitous defeat. Italy survived only because the Germans, for reasons of their own, decided to move westwards towards Gaul; but they returned a few years later, and defeated Roman armies in southern Gaul on three separate occasions (109, 107, 105). The last of these defeats, the battle of Arausio, was a

massacre, and left Italy at the mercy of the Germans.

Meanwhile popular indignation had been aroused at Rome by the senate's handling of a crisis in North Africa, where a Numidian prince called Jugurtha had been making a nuisance of himself. The senate's role in this affair was a mixture of indecision, corruption and incompetence. When a Roman army was humiliatingly defeated by Jugurtha in 110, a tribune proposed that a special court of inquiry be set up, with equestrian jurors, to investigate the senate's conduct of foreign policy. As a result a number of leading nobles were exiled, including L. Opimius, the murderer of Gaius Gracchus. This event, which would have been unthinkable a generation earlier, was followed in 108 by the election of C. Marius to the consulship.

Marius was a "new man" (see above, p. 36) from the Volscian town of Arpinum. His election to the consulship was the result of a skillful campaign in which he attacked the nobility and made a positive virtue of his own lack of ancestry. Marius obtained a huge following and was not only elected to the consulship, but also appointed by plebiscite to take charge of the war against Jugurtha in place of the senate's nominee Q. Metellus, whom he had accused of incompetence (in this case probably unjustly). After some setbacks Marius defeated Jugurtha in 105, and was elected, in his absence, to a second consulship for 104. Since his departure from Rome

Rome and the Mediterranean world, c. 146–70 BC. Rome's triumphant march of imperial expansion came to an end with the destruction of Corinth and Carthage in 146 BC. The following generations saw the collapse of the political equilibrium that had prevailed since the end of the Hannibalic war, and at the same time witnessed an unprecedented series of military reverses. In the years 146–70 BC the Romans were faced with unrest and hostility in every part of the empire, and in attempting to respond, the ruling aristocracy showed itself corrupt and incompetent. The lowest point was reached in 105 BC when a Roman army was annihilated at Arausio by the German barbarians; at that moment Rome was faced with complete extinction. Almost equally serious was the revolt of the eastern provinces during Mithridates' advance in 88; this was a reaction to a generation of criminal exploitation and oppression by the Romans. These crises were resolved only by allowing able and ambitious individuals to reach positions of supreme power in the Roman state.

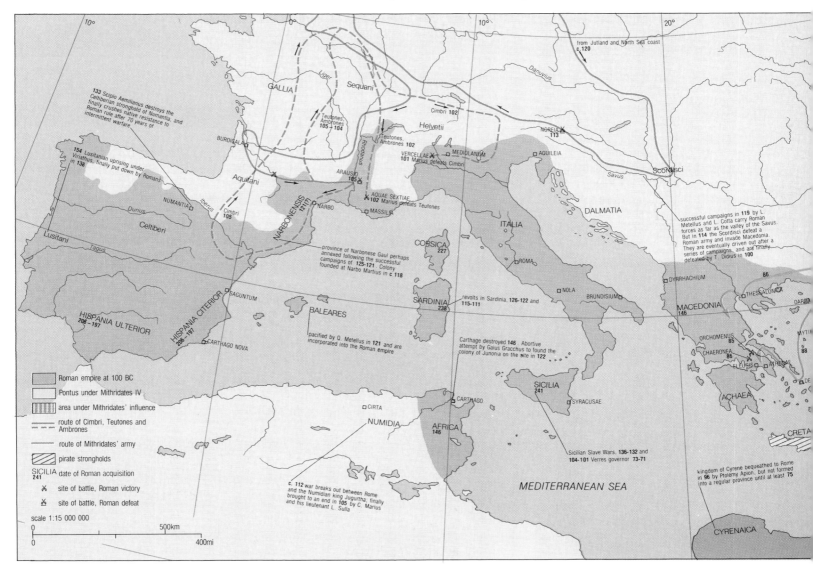

there had been a brief conservative reaction led by Q. Servilius Caepio, the consul of 106. But when Caepio was defeated in the following year at Arausio the oligarchy lost its nerve completely. Caepio became the first man since King Tarquin to have his *imperium* abrogated, and Marius, the people's hero, was appointed to save Italy from the Germans. The barbarian threat temporarily receded, however, and Marius was given the opportunity to carry out a systematic reform of the organization, training and equipment of the Roman army (104–102 BC). During this period he was reelected consul every year, contrary to all law and precedent, until finally he defeated the Teutones at Aquae Sextiae (102) and the Cimbri at Vercellae (101). Marius returned in triumph to Rome, and to a sixth consulship, in 100 BC.

Marius' victories were won by an army which he had turned into an efficient and disciplined fighting force. His military reforms had imposed professional standards on men who were already professionalized in a socio-economic sense. For his campaign against Jugurtha in 107 Marius had abandoned the traditional practice of raising troops from the class of *adsidui* and had simply enlisted volunteers from the proletariat. As we have seen, the numbers of *adsidui* had declined in the course of the 2nd century and had given rise to the agrarian reforms of the Gracchi. The Gracchi had attempted

to revive the class of peasant smallholders, but they had not tackled the root cause of the problem. As P.A. Brunt points out, "There was an inherent contradiction in the Gracchan objective of increasing the number of Rome's peasant soldiers, when it was soldiering that did so much to destroy the peasantry." In any case the Gracchan scheme was repealed by a series of laws in the years following Gaius' death, and must be regarded, in the long term, as a failure. With a steadily declining peasantry the only way to solve the problem of recruitment was either to reduce the property qualification for military service, which indeed happened on a number of occasions before the 120s, or to ignore it altogether, as Marius did in 107. The evidence suggests that the army was already "proletarianized" by this date, and that Marius' action was merely the final stage in the formation of a professional army which was no longer based on the part-time service of the peasantry. The connection between ownership of property and military service was now completely broken, and soldiering became a form of employment for men who owned no land. The consequence however was that the proletarian armies began to demand some permanent reward for their services, and since the state was not prepared to institute a regular system of granting land allotments to discharged veterans, the men looked instead to their commanders to make provision for them. Thus the armies became instruments of political conflict in the hands of unscrupulous commanders, of whom there was no shortage in the late Republic.

These consequences were certainly not foreseen by Marius, but some elements of the new situation became apparent immediately. In 103 a tribune, L. Appuleius Saturninus, had enacted that large allotments of land in Africa should be distributed to veterans of the Jugurthan war. During a second tribunate in 100 he proposed further distributions, and the foundation of colonies in the provinces, for veterans of the German wars and of a recent campaign in Sicily where a second slave revolt had taken place (104–101). These and other proposals received strong support from the veterans and were forced through the assembly with the help of mob violence. Later in the year matters got so bad that Marius was compelled to intervene to restore order. Saturninus and his associates surrendered, but Marius was unable to save them from a lynch mob. Saturninus' laws were then revoked by the senate. The end result was that Marius was discredited and his veterans never received their hoped-for rewards.

The profound shock of the German invasions exposed underlying tensions and divisions within Roman society and hastened the process of political breakdown. One such problem, which became critical in the decade following the battle of Vercellae, was a deterioration in relations between Rome and the Italian allies. In the Hannibalic war Rome had stood at the head of an alliance of free Italian communities and had led them to victory against the foreign invader. But during the far-flung wars of the 2nd century, in Spain, Greece, Asia and Africa, the notion of a defensive alliance began to fade. The allies gradually came to feel that they were no longer free partners, but subjects who carried the burden of wars in which they had no interest,

Coin of C. Fundanius (101 BC). The type shows C. Marius in a chariot celebrating his triumph over the Cimbri and Teutones.

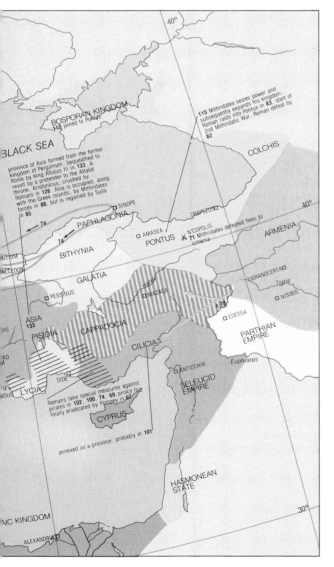

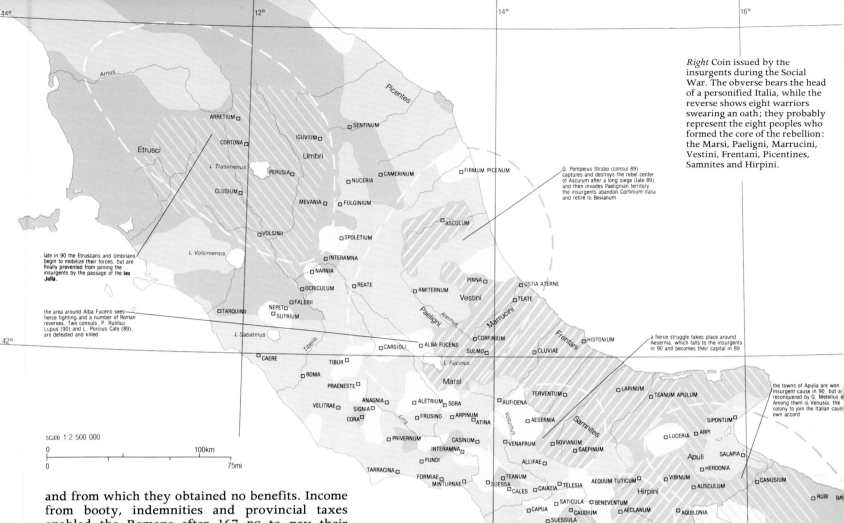

Map labels:

44° 12° 14° 16°

Arnus

Picentes

Etrusci

ARRETIUM

CORTONA

IGUVIUM

SENTINUM

Umbri

PERUSIA

CAMERINUM

FIRMUM PICENUM

NUCERIA

CLUSIUM

MEVANIA

FULGINIUM

late in 90 the Etruscans and Umbrians begin to mobilize their forces, but are finally prevented from joining the insurgents by the passage of the **lex Julia**.

VOLSINII

SPOLETIUM

ASCULUM

Q. Pompeius Strabo (consul 89) captures and destroys the rebel center of Asculum after a long siege (late 89), and then invades Paelignian territory: the insurgents abandon Corfinium-Italia and retire to Bovianum

L. Trasimenus

L. Volsiniensis

INTERAMNA

NARNIA

PINNA

OSTIA ATERNE

42°

the area around Alba Fucens sees fierce fighting and a number of Roman reverses. Two consuls, P. Rutilius Lupus (90) and L. Porcius Cato (89), are defeated and killed

OCRICULUM

REATE

AMITERNUM

Vestini

TEATE

FALERII

NEPET

SUTRIUM

Paeligni

Aternus

Marrucini

TARQUINII

CARSIOLI

ALBA FUCENS

CORFINIUM

Frentani

HISTONIUM

a fierce struggle takes place around Aesernia, which falls to the insurgents in 90 and becomes their capital in 89

CAERE

L. Sabatinus

Tiber

SULMO

CLUVIAE

TIBUR

ROMA

L. Fucinus

Marsi

LARINUM

TEANUM APULUM

PRAENESTE

TERVENTUM

the towns of Apulia are won insurgent cause in 90, but a reconquered by Q. Metellus Among them is Venusia, the colony to join the Italian caus own accord

VELITRAE

ANAGNIA

SIGNIA

ALETRIUM

SORA

AUFIDENA

AESERNIA

Samnites

SIPONTUM

CORA

FRUSINO

ARPINUM

ATINA

Liris

Volturnus

VENAFRUM

PRIVERNUM

CASINUM

BOVIANUM

LUCERIA

ARPI

INTERAMNA

SAEPINUM

Apuli

SALAPIA

FUNDI

ALLIFAE

AEQUUM TUTICUM

VIBINUM

AUSCULUM

HERDONIA

TARRACINA

TEANUM

scale 1:2 500 000

0   100km

0   75mi

FORMIAE

MINTURNAE

SUESSA

CALES

CAIATIA

TELESIA

SATICULA

BENEVENTUM

AECLANUM

Hirpini

AQUILONIA

CANUSIUM

RUBI

BA

CAPUA

CAUDIUM

SUESSULA

VENUSIA

Venusini

SILVIUM

Campania is overrun by insurgent forces in 90, but is largely regained in 89 by Sulla, who puts Nola under siege and leads a victorious march into Samnium

ATELLA

ACERRAE

NOLA

ABELLINUM

FORENTUM

BANTIA

CUMAE

Campani

NEAPOLIS

HERCULANEUM

NUCERIA

COMPSA

Lucani

POMPEII

SALERNUM

Lucani

POTENTIA

SURRENTUM

STABIAE

PICENTIA

EBURUM

"theater" of war

Roman territory at the time of the Social War, 91–89 BC

PAESTUM

Latin territory at the time of the Social War

allied territory at the time of the Social War

territory of the insurgents, 91 BC

GRUMENTUM

allies who later joined the insurgents

P. Licinius Grassus fails to overrun Lucania, which joins the insurgents (90)

HERACLEA

Apuli tribal name

40°

THURII

Bruttii

---

and from which they obtained no benefits. Income from booty, indemnities and provincial taxes enabled the Romans after 167 BC to pay their soldiers without having to impose direct taxes on their own citizens (see above, p. 56); this did not apply to the allies, who were obliged to fall back on their own resources. Moreover it seems likely that as the Romans found it increasingly difficult to raise recruits among their own citizens they attempted to shift the burden onto the allies, who were obliged to contribute an increasingly large proportion of Rome's total forces. The allies were also directly affected by political decisions taken at Rome, over which they had no control. The agrarian law of Tiberius Gracchus is a case in point; it is not clear exactly how the allied communities were affected, but our sources imply that many Italian landowners had been occupying *ager publicus* and were evicted by the land commission. Gaius Gracchus attempted, as we have seen, to compensate them by giving them Roman citizenship; his efforts were abortive, but it seems that the idea of obtaining Roman citizenship gradually caught on among the allies, for whom it became an increasingly attractive political goal. As citizens the Italians would gain the right of appeal against Roman magistrates, a say in the political process, direct access to the profits of empire (in particular the right to bid for public contracts) and the chance to enter the senate and the magistracies.

A general sense of resentment was no doubt accentuated by the German wars, which brought Romans and Italians together in a fight for survival and exposed the flagrant injustice of the allies' inferior status. It is probable that Marius appreciated this fact and was sympathetic to the allies' cause; it is also likely that Saturninus had intended to include them in his colonial settlements.

If so, the annulment of Saturninus' laws will have been a bitter disappointment to the allies, who were alienated still further when the consuls of 95 BC cracked down on Italians who had unlawfully registered as Roman citizens. Finally in 91 the cause of Italian enfranchisement was taken up by the tribune M. Livius Drusus as part of a wider program, which included proposals for agrarian settlement in Italy and the provinces and a reform of the jury courts.

Unfortunately Drusus' attempts to win widespread support were inept, and succeeded only in arousing general hostility. The proposal to extend the citizenship had no chance and was probably never put to the vote. The death of his most influential supporter, the orator L. Crassus, left Drusus politically isolated; his laws were annulled by the senate on a legal technicality, and late in the year he was murdered in mysterious circumstances. For the allies, who had pinned all their hopes on Drusus, this was the last straw. Before the end of 91 an armed revolt had broken out.

The conflict which followed (it became known as

Right The Tabularium, one of the finest surviving republican buildings, stands at the western end of the Forum, backing on to the Capitol. The building, which was used as a record office and housed the state archives, was built in 78 BC by Q. Lutatius Catulus, and replaced an earlier structure that was destroyed by fire in 83 BC.

Italy and the Social War, 91–89 BC. The Social War (the War of the Allies) began in 91 BC following the persistent refusal of the Romans to grant the right of citizenship to their Italian allies. The insurgents formed themselves into an independent state called Italia, with its capital at Corfinium. The revolt was centered in the southern and central regions of the peninsula, and involved the Oscan-speaking peoples of the central Apennines (especially the Marsi), the Samnites and Lucanians, and the town of Asculum in Picenum. With the exception of Venusia, the Latin colonies remained loyal to Rome, as did the Greek cities; the Etruscans and Umbrians held back until the final stages of the war, and were the first to accept the Roman citizenship under the terms of the *lex Julia*.

the Social or Marsic War) was fiercely contested, and the Romans achieved a military victory only by conceding political defeat. In 90 BC the consul L. Julius Caesar passed a law granting Roman citizenship to all loyal communities and to any others which laid down their arms. By 89 the war was mostly over except for pockets of resistance in the south which were mopped up in the following years.

The Italian crisis had scarcely been resolved when news came of a disaster in the eastern provinces. For some years Rome had been keeping a watchful eye on the rise of the kingdom of Pontus under its powerful ruler Mithridates VI (121–63 BC). In 89 a Roman praetor had rashly provoked an attack on Mithridates, who retaliated by invading the province of Asia and ordering the massacre of all Romans resident there (88 BC). Our sources claim that 80 000 persons were killed in a single day. This is a wild exaggeration: the actual number was probably in four figures, although even this is a conjecture.

By this date Romans and Italians were scattered throughout the Roman provinces as tax collectors, traders, moneylenders and landowners. They were very numerous in Sicily, which had been open to Roman exploitation since the 3rd century BC: at the time of the First Slave War (136 BC) many of the slave-owning landlords were Roman citizens of the equestrian class, and there were many Italian residents in the cities in the time of Verres, who governed Sicily in the late 70s. Their presence in North Africa is indicated by the story of the massacre of a group of Italian "businessmen" (*negotiatores*) at Cirta in 112 BC, which gave rise to the Jugurthan war. Soldiers often chose to settle in the provinces where they had served, especially in Spain, where there were a number of Italian communities. As for southern Gaul, Cicero tells us (in 74 BC) that "Gaul is packed with traders, crammed with Roman citizens. No Gaul does

business independently of a citizen of Rome; not a penny changes hands without the transaction being recorded in the books of Roman citizens." Cicero classifies the Romans in Gaul as "publicans, farmers, ranchers and other businessmen." Italian businessmen were very numerous in the east, especially in Greece, the Aegean islands and western Asia Minor. For example in Greece an inscription of c. 103 BC shows that as much as 10 per cent of the land of the city of Messene was owned by Romans and Italians. An important center was the island of Delos, which the Romans had declared a free port in 167 BC as part of their policy of harming the trade of Rhodes (see above, p. 51). Delos became the center of the slave trade, and according to Strabo was able to handle more than ten thousand transactions in a single day. In the province of Asia itself many of the Italian residents would have been employed by the companies of *publicani*, who had been given the right to collect direct taxes there by the law of Gaius Gracchus. Their depredations were notorious (compare the case of the unfortunate Rutilius Rufus, above p. 58) and aroused the hatred of the native population, who willingly cooperated with Mithridates in the slaughter of 88. Mithridates was able to pose as a liberator of the Greeks against the hated Romans, "the common enemies of all mankind." By the end of 88 his forces had overrun the Aegean and invaded Greece.

The task of leading a Roman army against Mithridates was assigned to one of the consuls of 88, L. Cornelius Sulla. Sulla was an unprincipled and dissolute noble from an old patrician family (one of his ancestors was the notorious Rufinus – above p. 42). He had shown his ability as one of Marius' trusted lieutenants in the African and German campaigns, and had made a reputation for himself as a commander in the Social War. He was therefore well qualified for the task of dealing with Mithridates. However the decision came as a disappointment to Marius, who was still influential and had hoped that the command would be conferred on him. It was generally assumed that victory over Mithridates would be both easy and profitable, and Marius was especially annoyed that the prize should have gone to Sulla, with whom he had quarreled a few years previously.

In order to rectify this state of affairs Marius employed the services of a tribune, P. Sulpicius, who had entered office as a supporter of the *optimates* (the conservative elements in the senate) but for some reason had become embittered. Sulpicius proposed a series of laws, including one to give equal voting rights to the newly enfranchised Italians (they had been cheated of this by being confined to a restricted number of tribes) and another to appoint Marius in place of Sulla as commander in the forthcoming eastern campaign. Events then moved swiftly. Sulpicius' laws were passed amid violent scenes of street fighting. Sulla left to join his army at Nola in Campania, where he made a personal appeal to the troops. On receiving a favorable response he at once marched on Rome, which fell without a blow. Marius was taken completely by surprise, but managed to escape to Africa; Sulpicius was killed, and his laws were canceled. After enacting some constitutional measures which foreshadowed those of his dictatorship, Sulla left for the east.

As soon as his back was turned fresh dissensions broke out. One of the consuls of 87, L. Cornelius Cinna, attempted to revive Sulpicius' law on the new citizens, but was obstructed by his colleague Cn. Octavius, a supporter of Sulla. Rioting ensued and Cinna was forced to flee, but he found a willing ally in Marius, who had returned from Africa and was mobilizing his supporters. Cinna and Marius then marched on Rome in their turn, captured the city and massacred their opponents in a new reign of terror. Marius then entered his seventh consulship, but died after a few days (86 BC). His colleague Cinna attempted to restore some sort of normality: a fair deal was arranged for the new citizens, Sulla was declared an outlaw and an "official" army was sent to Asia under the command of L. Valerius Flaccus.

The events of the next few years are difficult to evaluate because the sources are heavily slanted in favor of Sulla. Part of the bias is due to Sulla's own memoirs, which do not survive but which clearly had a strong influence on the historical tradition. In Rome the government was controlled by Cinna, who was consul for four years in succession (87–84) and evidently had strong support. The upper classes seem at least to have acquiesced; at this stage few of the leading senators were prepared to go over to Sulla, and as far as we know none of them did so.

In the east Sulla succeeded in driving Mithridates' forces out of Greece after a victory at Chaeronea in 86 BC; in the same year Valerius Flaccus appeared with his army and began to campaign against Mithridates in Asia Minor. Flaccus was soon murdered by his own legate, C. Flavius Fimbria, but the war continued and Fimbria scored some notable successes. Sulla however made a peace treaty with Mithridates in 85 – on fairly generous terms – and then turned on Fimbria, whose troops deserted him. Sulla's settlement of Asia was extremely harsh; he allowed his troops to plunder almost at will and billeted them on the cities.

In 83 he returned to Italy, where he was joined by young opportunists such as M. Crassus and Q. Metellus Pius, and in particular by the young Pompey, who had raised three legions on his own initiative. The opposition was disorganized and poorly led (Cinna had been murdered in a mutiny in 84), and Sulla's support grew as it became increasingly clear that he was going to win. Even so there was bitter fighting in Italy, where the "Marians" were joined by the Samnites, and in the provinces, where they had a considerable following. But by the end of 82 Sulla was established in Rome after defeating the Samnites at the battle of the Colline Gate, and after the son of Marius had been defeated and killed at Praeneste. Resistance in Sicily and Africa was rapidly put down by Pompey, who was awarded a triumph (probably in 81) and greeted by Sulla with the title *Magnus* ("the Great").

In Rome Sulla carried out a purge of his opponents, who were hunted down and put to death without trial. The condemned persons were "proscribed," that is, their names were listed on public notices which declared them outlaws with a price on their heads. Thousands are said to have died, including over 40 senators and 1600 knights (*equites*); their property was confiscated and handed over to Sulla's supporters, many of whom made fortunes (an infamous example is Crassus). Sulla punished communities in Italy that had opposed him by confiscating their land and assigning it in allotments to his soldiers; 120 000 men are said to have been settled in colonies, mostly in Etruria and Campania.

In an attempt to regularize his position Sulla assumed the dictatorship, an office that had been in abeyance since the Second Punic War. Under its authority he introduced a series of laws (81 BC) which he hoped would create stability and prevent a recurrence of the disorders that had afflicted Rome since the time of Tiberius Gracchus. In particular he sought to defuse the tribunate, by severely limiting its powers of veto and legislation, and by not allowing tribunes to proceed to further offices. He drafted several hundred men from the equestrian order into the senate, and he gave the enlarged body (of about 600 members) the task of providing juries for the permanent courts, which were themselves thoroughly reorganized. A whole series of regular tribunals was set up to deal with particular public crimes: extortion, treason, bribery, embezzlement, fraud, assault, murder etc. Some of these were in existence before Sulla (for example the extortion court; see above, p. 58), but others were probably instituted by him.

Sulla established a regular order for the chief magistracies, and prescribed minimum ages for the quaestorship (30), praetorship (39) and consulship (42). Those who obtained the quaestorship were automatically admitted to the senate, and in order to maintain the number of senators at around 600 Sulla raised the number of annual quaestors to 20 (assuming therefore an average age at death of over 60). The number of praetors was raised from six to eight in order to provide governors for the increased number of provinces. Finally, he abolished the state-subsidized grain rations.

Sulla laid down the dictatorship at the end of 81, held the consulship in 80, retired into private life in 79 and died at the beginning of 78. His extraordinary career left a legacy of bitterness and hatred that overshadowed the last generation of the Roman Republic. It is remarkable that a man who in his own actions showed nothing but contempt for legality, human life and rights of property should have made such a determined effort to create order and stability. The result was undoubtedly a failure. In his efforts to cure the ills of the Republic Sulla attacked the symptoms but not the cause. Tribunician agitation during the previous half-century was the product of underlying discontent which could not be simply legislated out of existence. The enforced settlement of his veterans, so far from providing an armed guarantee of stability, merely created further unrest in the Italian countryside and furnished recruits for future revolutionary attempts. Sulla had established a governmental structure in which the senatorial oligarchy had more power than ever before, but it had originated in violence and bloodshed, and it was not borne up by any general consensus. Sulla's chief supporters were trimmers and opportunists who were among the first to exploit the weaknesses of his system as soon as he was gone; while the chief beneficiaries of his new order, the *optimates*, had neither the will nor the moral authority to make it work. In the words of E. Badian, "The Sullan oligarchy had a fatal flaw: it governed with a guilty conscience."

L. Cornelius Sulla (c. 138–78 BC) came from an old but not recently distinguished patrician family. He first rose to prominence as an associate of Marius, and served under him in the Jugurthine and Cimbric wars. His quarrel with Marius dates from the late 90s, and came to a head in 88 during his consulship, when Marius was appointed by a plebiscite to take over the command against Mithridates which had previously been conferred on him. Sulla responded by marching on Rome and forcing his enemies to give way. After four years' campaigning in the east he returned to a second civil war; his victory in 82 enabled him to establish a ruthless dictatorship.

Mithridates VI of Pontus (132–63 BC) succeeded his father while still a child in 120 BC. His career of expansion began when he overran most of the north coast of the Black Sea; he then occupied part of Armenia and turned his eyes towards Asia Minor. His chance came in 88, when he was able to advance into the province of Asia and to occupy the Aegean islands by posing as a liberator and exploiting the Greeks' hatred of the Romans. Defeated in successive campaigns by Sulla, Lucullus and Pompey, he was eventually driven to suicide in 63 BC.

PART TWO

FROM REPUBLIC TO EMPIRE

THE ROMAN REVOLUTION

The aftermath of Sulla and the rise of Pompey
Almost all effective opposition to Sulla had been wiped out by the end of 81 BC, with one significant exception. This was Q. Sertorius, a former confidant of Marius and Cinna, who had withdrawn from Italy in 83 at the approach of Sulla's armies and gone to his province in Spain. Temporarily driven out in 81, he returned in 80 and began a general revolt with the support both of the native Spaniards and of the Roman and Italian residents. Q. Metellus Pius, sent against him in 79, was unable to make any headway; in 77 the senate realized that reinforcements would have to be sent.

Meanwhile in Italy the government had had to deal with an uprising led by the consul of 78, M. Aemilius Lepidus, who had attempted to overthrow Sulla's arrangements and had found support among the dispossessed peasants in Etruria. Lepidus was fairly easily crushed by Pompey, who had been given a special command by the senate (77 BC), but Pompey then offered to take his army to Spain to help Metellus. Since he had a loyal army at his back the senate found his offer hard to refuse; late in 77 Pompey was appointed as "proconsul" to share the command against Sertorius.

Pompey's departure was followed by an uneasy period of oligarchic rule, interrupted by occasional agitation. In the east Rome annexed the provinces of Bithynia and Cyrene in 74, but was faced with another war against Mithridates, the conduct of which was assigned to L. Licinius Lucullus, formerly one of Sulla's henchmen. During this period the Roman world was also suffering from the depredations of pirates. But the most serious problem for the Roman government during the late 70s was the revolt of Spartacus, the last and greatest of the slave wars of classical antiquity. Spartacus was a Thracian gladiator who escaped in 73 and assembled a force of fugitive slaves on Mount Vesuvius. Within a short time he had an army of tens of thousands of slaves (our sources allege as many as 120 000), who roamed Italy for two years, pillaging as they went and inflicting defeat on the Roman forces that were sent against them (including two consular armies in 72). Finally the slaves were defeated in Bruttium by Crassus, who marched against them in 71 with an enormous army (eight or ten legions). Spartacus was killed, and over 6000 captured slaves were crucified along the Appian Way. The lines of crosses stretched from Rome to Capua. It should be noted that neither the revolt of Spartacus, nor the two uprisings in Sicily that preceded it (see above, pp. 56, 61), were genuine revolutionary movements, but rather pathetic attempts by the slaves to escape from their wretched condition and to take revenge on their masters. There is no sign of a conscious revolutionary ideology or of an articulate movement for the abolition of slavery as such.

In Spain Pompey and Metellus made slow progress until 72, when Sertorius was murdered by one of his own officers. Pompey rapidly concluded the war and took his army back to Italy, where he arrived in time to finish off some remnants of Spartacus' army. He and Crassus then joined forces and, although suspicious of one another, decided to stand together for the consulships of 70 BC. Pompey was not legally qualified for the office, as he was only 36 years old and had not held any other magistracy (indeed, he was not yet even a member of the senate). But the government, with the prudence of a man who hands over his wallet to a thief without waiting to be asked, waived the constitution in his favor.

Pompey was by now an immensely powerful figure. He was popular, gifted and handsome, and was already being compared to Alexander the Great. He had a loyal following not only among the

Above Pompey the Great (106–48 BC). "In his youth," writes his biographer Plutarch, "Pompey had a very engaging countenance, which spoke for him before he opened his lips. Yet that grace of aspect was not unattended with dignity, and amid his youthful bloom there was a venerable and princely air. His hair naturally curled a little before; which, together with the shining moisture and quick turn of his eye, produced a stronger likeness of Alexander the Great than that which appeared in the statues of that prince. So that some seriously gave him the name of Alexander, and he did not refuse it."

Below Monument of the early 1st century BC, known conventionally as the "Altar of Domitius Ahenobarbus." The frieze along one side shows scenes from a Roman census. On the left a citizen is being registered, while in the center the *lustrum* (purification) is being performed, with the sacrifice of a bull, sheep and pig. Possibly a monument of L. Gellius Publicola, censor in 70 BC.

Right: Colonization in Italy, 1st century BC. In the late Republic colonization became a device by which revolutionary leaders could reward the mass of their supporters. Sulla founded colonies for his veterans on land expropriated from his enemies; many of his colonies were established alongside existing cities, which became double communities (e.g. Pompeii). Sulla's example was followed by Caesar, Antony and Augustus.

Below M. Tullius Cicero (106–43 BC) came from a well-to-do family of Arpinum. Largely because of his extraordinary powers as an orator Cicero made his way to the consulship in 63 BC and became a prominent member of the senate. The leading intellectual figure of his generation, Cicero wrote not only speeches but also rhetorical and philosophical treatises; his voluminous correspondence survives as an invaluable record of the political life and high society of the period. A staunch upholder of the Republic, Cicero was brutally murdered in the proscriptions of 43 BC.

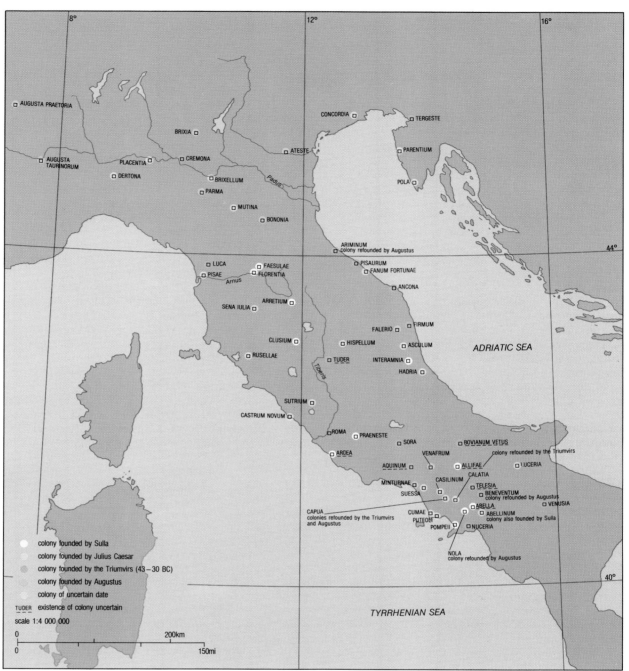

soldiers and the people, but also in the provinces, where he had shown moderation and respect for the native populations. He made it clear that he intended to reform Sulla's system, and that he wanted Crassus to be his colleague. After that, their election was a formality.

As consuls Pompey and Crassus restored the powers of the tribunate and supported a law which ended the senate's monopoly of the jury courts. Juries were to contain a mixture of senators (one-third) and equestrians (two-thirds). This move came in response to continuing evidence of the senate's unwillingness to check abuses by its own members. The conviction of C. Verres in 70 BC after three years of misgovernment in Sicily occurred in spite of obstruction by the *optimates*. In this infamous case the prosecution was led by Cicero, whose speech against Verres still stands as one of the most damaging indictments of official malpractice ever delivered.

After the defeat of Spartacus the problem of piracy became acute; by the early 60s the pirates had taken to making raids on the Italian coast, sacking villas and kidnapping travelers on the Appian Way. When the city's corn supply began to suffer, public opinion demanded action which led in 67 to the appointment of Pompey to a special command against the pirates. Pompey was granted wide-ranging powers and immense resources of men, money and supplies. Within three months he had completely cleared the seas of pirates, a truly astonishing feat of organization and tactics.

In the following year the tribune C. Manilius proposed that Pompey's command should be extended to allow him to finish the war against Mithridates. Mithridates was still at large, in spite of being driven out of the province of Asia by Lucullus in 70 BC. Lucullus had made himself unpopular with his troops by preventing them from looting the cities of the eastern provinces; he had also curbed the activities of the *publicani* who determined to ruin him. Manilius' proposal, which was supported by Cicero (now praetor), was overwhelmingly carried, and the unfortunate Lucullus was forced to make way for Pompey.

Pompey remained in the east for four more years. During this time he made short work of Mithridates, conquered all Anatolia and Syria and advanced as far south as Jerusalem, which he captured in 63. He annexed Syria, enlarged Cilicia, added Pontus to Bithynia and surrounded the new provinces with a ring of client kingdoms, which paid tribute to Rome. By this single campaign Pompey claimed to have raised the provincial revenues of the Roman state by 70 per cent. He brought back enormous quantities of booty, and was able to reward his soldiers by giving each of them a donative of 1500 denarii, equivalent to $12\frac{1}{2}$ years' pay. In all of this he acted largely on his own initiative, without consulting the senate, and generally behaved like an absolute monarch – which, in effect, is exactly what he was.

The political atmosphere in Rome during these years was dominated by thoughts of the absent Pompey, by fears of what he might do on his return and by the memory of Sulla. Tension was heightened by a monetary crisis (the reasons for which are unclear — we know merely that the amount of money in circulation had been declining since the

70s); there was a consequent squeeze on credit, widespread indebtedness and discontent among the poor. Social unrest and economic deprivation fostered complex political intrigue, in which Pompey's rivals attempted to build up their own positions during his absence. The most prominent of these men was Crassus, who was aided and abetted by the young Caesar.

In 63 Crassus and Caesar backed the proposal of a tribune to purchase land in Italy and the provinces for the settlement of the poor and of the veterans of Pompey's campaigns, which were now coming to an end. But the bill was successfully opposed by Cicero, on the rather perverse grounds that it was a threat to Pompey's interests, of which he was the self-appointed custodian. The activities of Crassus and Caesar aroused deep suspicion in conservative circles, and there was much sinister talk of conspiracies and threats to public order. The principal object of these fears, however, was a disreputable patrician named L. Sergius Catilina (Catiline), who stood for the consulship of 63 with a promise of agrarian reform and cancellation of debts. This threat united the propertied classes behind a rival candidate, Cicero, who was triumphantly elected in spite of being a "new man." When Catiline failed again at the elections for 62, he attempted to stage a coup d'etat, but the attempt was foiled by Cicero, who managed to arrest the ringleaders before they could strike. Catiline himself fled to Etruria where a general revolt had broken out; it was easily crushed and Catiline was killed. His associates in Rome were summarily executed on Cicero's orders. This act later aroused a storm of controversy, since as citizens the conspirators were entitled to a trial. Pompey was horrified when he heard the news and wrote a very frosty reply to Cicero's fulsome account of the affair.

The Catilinarian conspiracy reveals the extent of the problem of debt and poverty. Discontented groups included the victims of Sulla's expropriations, the families of the proscribed, Sulla's own veterans who had themselves fallen into debt, and the urban *plebs*, who were oppressed by high rents and appalling living conditions. The countryside of Italy had been extensively ravaged by war in the 20 years preceding the defeat of Spartacus. The high levels of conscription in the 70s and 60s hastened the continuing process of displacement, which agrarian legislation had done little to curb. Violence became endemic as desperate men turned to a life of crime. Gangsters and terrorists were active in the city of Rome, where there was no police force to maintain order. Indebtedness had also become a problem among the upper class, as increasing amounts of money were invested in the competition for high office, which promised huge rewards for the few who succeeded and ruin for the majority who failed. The careers of Catiline and his crew of frustrated nobles epitomize this unhealthy state of affairs.

At the end of 62 Pompey landed at Brundisium. There he disbanded his army, to everyone's relief, and returned to Rome for his triumph and what he probably hoped would be a life of ease and dignity as Rome's most respected statesman. If so, he was disappointed. He had hoped that the senate would ratify without question his settlement of the east, and would provide land allotments for his veterans.

Right Reconstruction of the great villa at Settefinestre in the territory of Cosa. Impressive standing ruins mark the site of this great establishment, which grew up in the 1st century BC as the center of a large estate. Since 1976 the villa has been the subject of a major program of excavation by a joint Anglo-Italian team. Preliminary results confirm that the villa was the center of an enterprise devoted to large-scale agricultural production (particularly wine production) using slave labor.

Gaius Julius Caesar (100–44 BC) belonged to a patrician family which traced its descent back to Aeneas. More recent political connections included Marius, his uncle by marriage, and Cinna, his father-in-law. As a young man Caesar incurred the enmity of Sulla, but managed to escape the proscriptions. In the post-Sullan period Caesar eagerly sought popularity: he associated himself with Pompey by supporting his cause, and he attached himself to Crassus, to whom he became heavily indebted. In 60 BC he formed an agreement with Pompey and Crassus which enabled him to obtain the consulship with their support, and to use the office to promote their interests. But the chief beneficiary of the "First Triumvirate" was Caesar, who engineered for himself a special command in Gaul, where his military successes ultimately provided him with a means to achieve absolute power. Caesar proved himself immensely gifted as an orator, writer, soldier, politician and administrator. He was completely unscrupulous in the pursuit of his own interests, and had nothing but contempt for the republican system of government, which he quite deliberately sought to destroy.

Fresco from Pompeii of a *villa marittima* (seaside villa), a type of luxury dwelling which became common in the last years of the Republic, when it became fashionable for wealthy Romans to spend time in relaxation away from the city. The great majority of these coastal villas were built around the Bay of Naples.

together with large numbers of destitute families, were settled on the land by laws which resembled the abortive measure of 63. Another enactment provided for a reduction of the contract price for the taxes of Asia that had been agreed by the *publicani* in 61. The concession favored Crassus, who was probably financially involved. Finally, Caesar rewarded himself with a special command in Gaul and Illyricum for five years. During the year the triumvirate was strengthened by Pompey's marriage to Caesar's daughter, Julia; the triumvirs also secured the election of friendly consuls for the following year.

In 58 Caesar left for his province, where he embarked on the conquest of continental Gaul. In Rome the year 58 was dominated by the activities of the tribune P. Clodius (a member of the proud Claudian *gens*, who had had himself adopted into a plebeian family so that he could stand for the tribunate). Clodius built up a following among the urban *plebs*, in whose interest he passed several enactments, beginning with a radical corn law. The subsidized grain ration, introduced by C. Gracchus and subsequently abolished by Sulla, had been reinstated in a limited form in 73 and extended by Cato in 62. Now Clodius abolished the charge and transformed it into a regular dole. He legalized the formation of *collegia* (guilds or associations), which enabled him to mobilize the urban proletariat for political purposes. Other laws led to the exile of Cicero (for the murder of the Catilinarians) and the removal of Cato, who was sent on a mission to annex Cyprus. At first Clodius worked as an ally of the triumvirs, but he was in no sense their agent; towards the end of the year he launched a series of attacks on Pompey. In 57 Pompey enlisted the aid of another tribune, T. Annius Milo, who formed a rival band of ruffians and openly campaigned against Clodius' gangs on the streets. Clodius was thus held in check, and Pompey was able to arrange the recall of Cicero. In the same year (57) Pompey was given a special "command" for five years to organize the city's corn supply, a task which he undertook with characteristic efficiency, although shortages continued to occur from time to time.

In 56 Caesar summoned Crassus and Pompey to a meeting at Luca in Cisalpine Gaul, where their alliance was renewed. Pompey and Crassus became consuls in 55 and by a plebiscite received special commands for five years each. Crassus obtained Syria and the opportunity to lead a campaign against the Parthian empire. Pompey was awarded the Spanish provinces, which he decided to govern indirectly through legates (deputies appointed directly by himself), while he remained in Rome, continuing to administer the corn supply and able to watch over events in the city. Caesar's command in Gaul was prolonged for a second five-year term.

The renewed alliance soon began to show signs of strain. In 54 Pompey's wife, Julia, died, and the personal tie that linked him with Caesar was severed. A year later the triumvirate ceased to exist with Crassus' defeat and death at the battle of Carrhae (Harran), which ended his rash attempt to invade the Parthian empire. Increased tension between Pompey and Caesar was the inevitable result. Meanwhile violence and disorder prevailed at Rome, impeding the normal machinery of government; both 53 and 52 began without consuls.

But his requests were met with obstruction and resistance from the *optimates,* led by Lucullus. Lucullus was aided by M. Porcius Cato, a posturing diehard whose principal distinction was his descent from Cato the Censor, whom he attempted to impersonate. These men and their friends managed to frustrate Pompey's wishes for a considerable time; in so doing they unwittingly contrived their own downfall and the destruction of the Republic.

The end of the Republic

The *optimates'* tactics eventually drove the frustrated Pompey into an informal alliance with Crassus and Caesar. This pact, now known as the First Triumvirate, was an informal arrangement of the traditional kind (see above, p. 24), but the particular combination of Pompey's immense popularity, Crassus' wealth and connections and Caesar's political acumen proved irresistible. Caesar gained the consulship of 59, and when in office introduced a legislative package which satisfied the wishes of all three partners. Pompey's eastern settlement was confirmed, and his veterans,

Early in 52 Clodius and Milo met on the Appian Way and in the ensuing scrap Clodius was killed. The event provoked riots in which the senate-house was burned down. Finally the senate appointed Pompey sole consul, and order was eventually restored.

By this time Caesar's conquest of Gaul was almost complete, and his second five-year term was nearing its end. Fear of Caesar began to drive Pompey and the *optimates* closer together, as they tried to frustrate Caesar's aim of passing directly from his present command to a second consulship and thence (presumably) to a further long-term appointment. The senate sought instead to terminate his command, but its deliberations were vetoed by tribunes friendly to Caesar. Negotiations were prolonged but futile; it was clear that neither side was prepared to give way. Finally on 7 January 49 BC the senate passed the "Ultimate Decree," instructing the magistrates to see that the Republic suffered no harm. The Caesarian tribunes (one of whom was Mark Antony) fled from the city, and three days later Caesar crossed the Rubicon with his army and invaded Italy.

With the beginning of the Civil Wars the Republic, defined as the rule of magistrates, senate and people of Rome, was already dead. Since 60 BC control of affairs had passed from the oligarchy to the dynasts, who were supported by their private armies and vast *clientelae*, and were constitutionally provided for by special commands which freed them from the restrictions of the system of annual collegiate magistracies. The oligarchy that Sulla restored had shown itself to be irresponsible, corrupt, self-seeking and indifferent, and no longer commanded the respect or loyalty of any significant group in society. The propertied classes of Italy had no confidence in a regime which excluded their leading men from senior positions and was unable to guarantee order and stability; the poor happily surrendered their spurious freedoms and ineffectual political rights in favor of individual leaders who depended on them for support and who consequently took care to supply their material needs. The position of Pompey in the mid-50s, with his control of the corn supply, his sole consulship in 52 and his *imperium* in Spain (which in 52 was renewed for a further five years), already foreshadowed that of the emperors.

The triumph of Caesar

Caesar's conquest of Gaul was a remarkable achievement. Its details are outlined in the seven books *On the Gallic War*, which Caesar published probably in 51 or 50 BC (an eighth book, on the events of 51–50, was published later by A. Hirtius). The work was no doubt intended to justify its author's actions and to increase his prestige in Rome, but it remains a masterly account of the progress of events. The campaign itself began in 58 when Caesar attacked the Helvetii, who, he thought, represented a danger to the Roman province. During the first three years he overran most of Gaul by proceeding in a roughly anti-clockwise direction and subduing the tribes in Franche Comté and Alsace (58), in Belgium and

Portrait of a Gaul (once wrongly thought to be Vercingetorix) on a coin of 48 BC celebrating Caesar's victories.

The rise of Julius Caesar: the events of the Gallic and civil wars (58–45 BC).

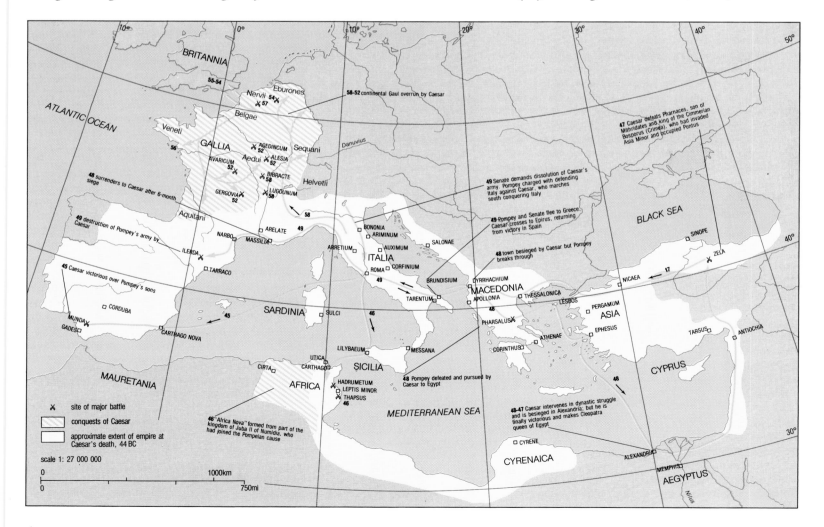

scale 1: 27 000 000

✕ site of major battle

▨ conquests of Caesar

☐ approximate extent of empire at Caesar's death, 44 BC

Normandy (57), and in Brittany and along the Atlantic seaboard (56). In 55 and 54 he ventured across the Rhine and also made two expeditions to southern England. On his return he was faced with a revolt among the Belgae which was put down after fierce fighting in 53. In 52 a serious revolt broke out in central Gaul under Vercingetorix, who was proclaimed supreme commander of the Gauls at Bibracte (near Autun); but later in the year Caesar managed to trap Vercingetorix in the fortress of Alesia in Burgundy, which the Romans captured after a month-long siege. In 51 the last remnants of Gallic resistance were dealt with, and Caesar was able to turn his attention to the political crisis. The Gauls were left for the time being as client states, subject to an annual tribute which amounted to ten million denarii.

When Caesar invaded Italy at the beginning of 49, Pompey chose not to face him, but instead staged a skillful withdrawal across the Adriatic and began to mobilize his forces in the Balkans. Thus Italy fell without a blow to Caesar, who entered Rome and seized the contents of the treasury. Then he made a rapid dash to Spain, where he defeated the Pompeian forces, before returning to Italy where he was appointed dictator. At the end of 49 he left for the east and the final showdown with Pompey. The decisive battle occurred in the summer of 48 at Pharsalus in northern Greece, where Caesar was victorious. Pompey fled to Egypt, where he was treacherously murdered. Caesar arrived shortly afterwards, to be greeted with the news of his rival's death. At Alexandria he intervened in a dynastic struggle, taking the side of Cleopatra who became his mistress. Despite fierce opposition he eventually succeeded in installing Cleopatra and her brother Ptolemy XIV on the throne of Egypt. Returning to Rome by way of Asia Minor, where he put down a revolt led by Pharnaces, a son of Mithridates, Caesar pardoned those (such as Cicero) who had joined Pompey, and settled affairs in the city. He then (late 47) left for Africa, where the Pompeians had established a base after defeating Caesar's lieutenants in 49. Caesar defeated the republicans at Thapsus and overran the province of Africa. The surviving Pompeians, including Pompey's two sons, escaped to Spain, but Cato, in a theatrical scene, committed suicide at Utica in order to deny Caesar the chance of pardoning him. On his return to Rome in 46 Caesar celebrated a magnificent triumph, but before the end of the year he was called away to Spain where Pompey's sons had raised an army. The republican cause finally came to grief on the field of Munda in 45; young Gnaeus Pompey was killed, but his brother Sextus lived to fight again. Caesar headed back to Rome, arriving early in October. Less than six months later he was assassinated.

During his brief sojourns in Rome Caesar launched a vast program of political, social and administrative reform, of which only a very brief summary can be given here. Urgent action was required to deal with poverty and debt. As early as 49 Caesar reduced debts by up to 25 per cent and decreed that for purposes of repayment property should be valued at prewar levels. A year's remission of rents was granted in 48, and probably again in 47. Large numbers of poor citizens and discharged veterans were to be settled on allotments and in colonies in Italy and especially in the provinces. Caesar's soldiers each received 5000 denarii at his triumph in 46, and the regular annual pay for legionary soldiers was raised from 120 to 225 denarii. Other measures regulated the corn dole, controlled the traffic in the city, banned the *collegia* (an exception was made for Jewish synagogues) and reformed the laws of extortion, treason and bribery. The system of contracting out the collection of direct taxes in Asia and other provinces was ended. The provinces were governed by legates appointed directly by Caesar himself. In 49 he granted Roman citizenship to all the inhabitants of Cisalpine Gaul (who had been excluded from the settlement after the Social War); he also enfranchised provincial communities, such as Gades in Spain, and he gave Latin rights to towns in southern Gaul and Sicily. He rewarded many of his supporters by admitting them to the senate, whose members rapidly increased to 900. He embarked on a series of grandiose building projects, the most impressive of which was a completely new Forum, centered around a temple of Venus Genetrix, the ancestress of the Julian house (the work on this project was begun in 54 and completed in 46). Western civilization owes to Julius Caesar the calendar of $365\frac{1}{4}$ days, which was introduced on 1 January 45 BC.

During his last years Caesar ruled as a king in all but name. In 46 he was made dictator for 10 years; in 44 he received the office in perpetuity. He was also consul in 48 and continuously from 46. Unprecedented and extravagant honors were heaped upon him by the senate. He was named "Superintendent of Manners" and "Father of the Fatherland"; the month in which he was born was renamed "Julius" (i.e. July). Although he eschewed the title *rex*, and rejected the "kingly crown" which Antony offered him at the Lupercalia in 44, he nonetheless adopted many of the trappings associated with kingship (such as a purple toga), had his statue placed among those of the old kings on the Capitol and issued coins bearing his portrait. He also began to institute cult honors for himself.

Caesar made no secret of his contempt for the Republic and its constitutional forms. He effectively nominated the magistrates, held the consular "elections" for several years in advance, summoned the senate merely in order to give notice of his decisions and silenced tribunes who attempted to oppose him. When a consul died on the last day of 45 BC, Caesar had another man elected for the remaining few hours. Such antics caused grave offense to men like Cicero who valued the traditions of the state. The murder of Caesar on the Ides of March 44 by a group of noble senators was a cruel and senseless act which unleashed a civil war even worse than the one that had just ended. But the deed was also very understandable. Caesar had it coming to him, and he probably knew it.

Antony and the new Caesar

Caesar's death was followed first by confusion and bewilderment, and then by a desperate struggle for power. The leading figures among Caesar's supporters were the surviving consul, Mark Antony, and the master of the horse, M. Aemilius Lepidus. Antony had the support of the army in Italy, which had been assembling for Caesar's projected Parthian expedition; he also won over the urban masses by

Coin issued in 43/2 BC by the liberators to celebrate the murder of Julius Caesar. It shows two daggers and a *pileus* (a kind of felt cap worn by freed slaves), and bears the legend *EID. MART.* ("the Ides of March").

Coin issued by Mark Antony in 39 BC. Antony's portrait on the obverse is matched on the reverse by that of Octavia, sister of Octavian, whom Antony married in 40 BC following the reconciliation of the two dynasts at Brundisium. The breakdown of the marriage in 36 led to a renewed breach between Antony and Octavian, and hastened the onset of civil war.

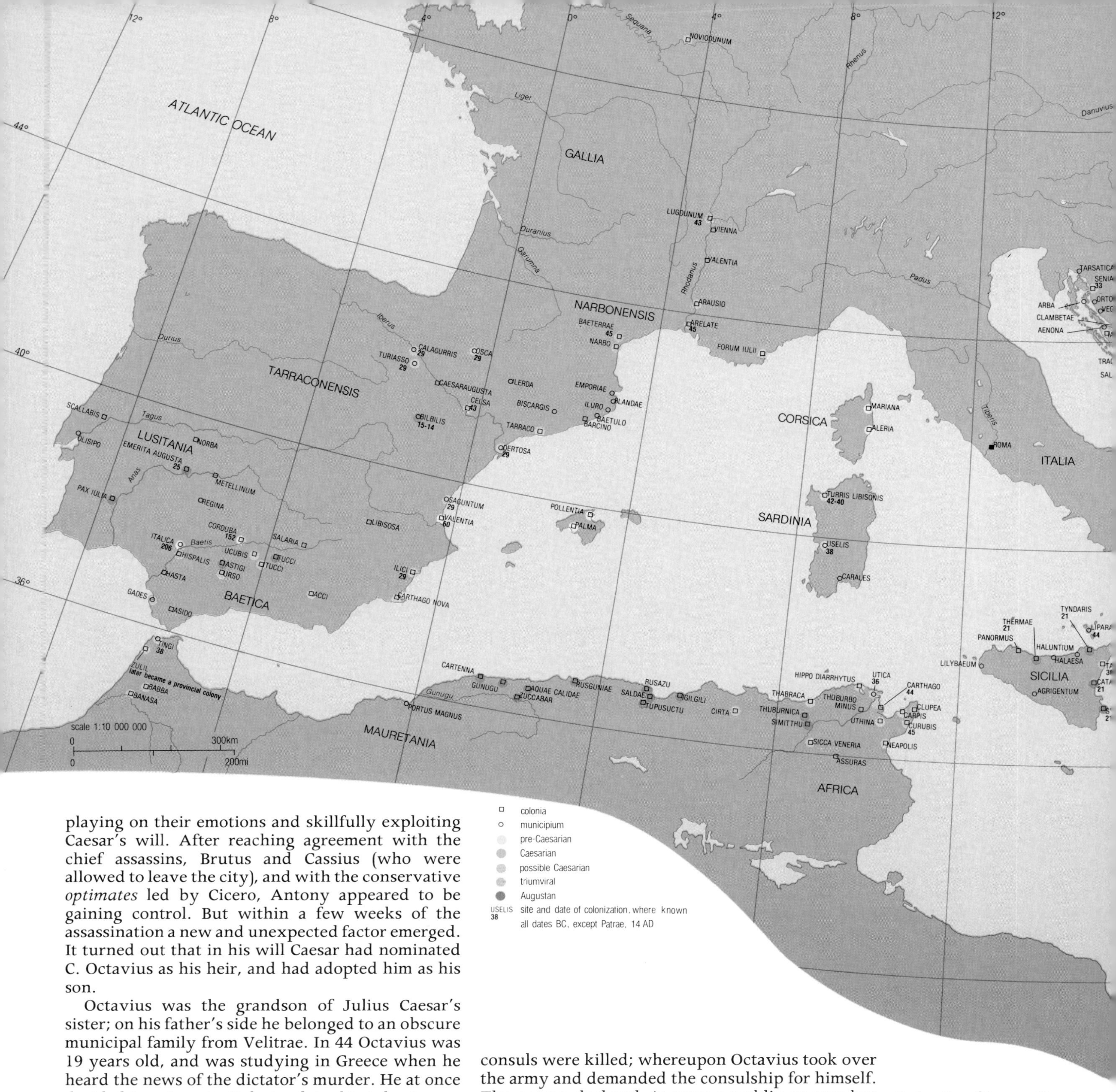

ATLANTIC OCEAN
GALLIA
NARBONENSIS
TARRACONENSIS
LUSITANIA
BAETICA
CORSICA
SARDINIA
ITALIA
SICILIA
MAURETANIA
AFRICA
Liger
Sequana
Rhenus
Danuvius
Duranius
Garumna
Rhodanus
Padus
Tiberis
Iberus
Durius
Tagus
Anas
Baetis
Gunugu
NOVIODUNUM
LUGDUNUM 43
VIENNA
VALENTIA
ARAUSIO
ARELATE 45
BAETERRAE 45
NARBO
FORUM IULII
CALAGURRIS 29
TURIASSO 29
OSCA 29
CAESARAUGUSTA
CELSA 43
ILERDA
BISCARGIS
EMPORIAE
BLANDAE
ILURO
BAETULO
BARCINO
TARRACO
DERTOSA 29
BILBILIS 15-14
SCALLABIS
OLISIPO
NORBA
EMERITA AUGUSTA 25
METELLINUM
PAX IULIA
REGINA
CORDUBA 152
SALARIA
ITALICA 206
HISPALIS
UCUBIS
ASTIGI
TUCCI
URSO
HASTA
GADES
ASIDO
ACCI
LIBISOSA
SAGUNTUM 29
VALENTIA 60
ILICI 29
CARTHAGO NOVA
POLLENTIA
PALMA
MARIANA
ALERIA
ROMA
TURRIS LIBISONIS 42-40
USELIS 38
CARALES
TARSATICA
SENIA 33
ARBA
CLAMBETAE
AENONA
TYNDARIS 21
THERMAE 21
PANORMUS
HALUNTIUM
HALAESA
LILYBAEUM
AGRIGENTUM
TINGI 38
ZULIL later became a provincial colony
BABBA
BANASA
CARTENNA
GUNUGU
AQUAE CALIDAE
ZUCCABAR
RUSGUNIAE
RUSAZU
SALDAE
IGILGILI
TUPUSUCTU
CIRTA
PORTUS MAGNUS
HIPPO DIARRHYTUS
UTICA 36
CARTHAGO 44
THABRACA
THUBURBO MINUS
THUBURNICA
SIMITTHU
UTHINA
CLUPEA
CARPIS
CURUBIS 45
SICCA VENERIA
NEAPOLIS
ASSURAS
scale 1:10 000 000
0 300km
0 200mi
colonia
municipium
pre-Caesarian
Caesarian
possible Caesarian
triumviral
Augustan
USELIS 38 site and date of colonization, where known
all dates BC, except Patrae, 14 AD

playing on their emotions and skillfully exploiting Caesar's will. After reaching agreement with the chief assassins, Brutus and Cassius (who were allowed to leave the city), and with the conservative *optimates* led by Cicero, Antony appeared to be gaining control. But within a few weeks of the assassination a new and unexpected factor emerged. It turned out that in his will Caesar had nominated C. Octavius as his heir, and had adopted him as his son.

Octavius was the grandson of Julius Caesar's sister; on his father's side he belonged to an obscure municipal family from Velitrae. In 44 Octavius was 19 years old, and was studying in Greece when he heard the news of the dictator's murder. He at once decided to return to Italy to claim his inheritance, ignoring his parents' advice to stay out of trouble. In Rome he was coolly received by Antony, who did not welcome his intrusion; this forced him into the arms of the *optimates*, who thought that they could use him in their struggle against Antony. Cicero wrote: "the boy is to be praised, honored, and kicked upstairs."

In 43 Antony went north to a provincial command in Gaul. In Rome Cicero launched a major attack on him (the so-called *Philippics*) and persuaded the senate to send an army against him under the consuls, together with Octavius. In two battles near Mutina Antony was defeated, but the consuls were killed; whereupon Octavius took over the army and demanded the consulship for himself. The senate declared Antony a public enemy but refused to accede to Octavius' demands; he therefore marched on Rome at the head of the army and obtained the consulship by force. At the same time he had his adoption ratified by the people, and formally became C. Julius Caesar Octavianus. Meanwhile other leading members of Caesar's party, such as Lepidus, aligned themselves with Antony. On his side Octavian had the support of the armies in Italy and of the *plebs*, who rallied to him as Caesar's heir.

Late in the year the Caesarian leaders decided to settle their differences and to present a united front against the senate and the liberators. Antony,

Emigration of Roman citizens to the provinces. The main social and economic problems that brought down the Republic were ultimately resolved by the enforced emigration of large numbers of free-born Italians to the provinces. Before Caesar's time overseas colonies (such as Narbo Martius, c. 118 BC) were few and controversial. Caesar however embarked on a policy of large-scale colonization in the provinces, and settled over 80 000 citizens and their families in over 30 colonies. These people included proletarians from the city as well as veterans. Caesar also granted Roman citizenship

Octavian and Lepidus were appointed as a trium-virate (a board of three for the organization of the state), whereupon they divided the empire among themselves, and purged their opponents by reviving Sulla's device of proscriptions. According to some sources as many as 300 senators (including Cicero) and 2000 knights met their deaths in the reign of terror that followed.

In 42 Octavian and Antony marched against Brutus and Cassius, who controlled the eastern provinces, and defeated them at Philippi. After the victory a new distribution of the empire occurred. Octavian received Italy and most of the western provinces, and the command against Sextus Pompey, who had occupied Sicily and had become a focus for resistance, while Antony took over the command against the Parthians in the east. Lepidus, "a slight unmeritable man," was fobbed off with Africa. In Italy Octavian attempted to settle the veterans of Philippi on land confiscated from certain specified towns. In this he was actively resisted by one of the consuls, Antony's brother Lucius, who eventually took up arms on behalf of the disgruntled Italians. After some months of fighting L. Antonius was besieged in Perusia (Perugia), which fell early in 40 BC; he himself was spared, but his

to many native communities, especially in the western provinces, which thus acquired the status of *municipia*. Caesar's policy was carried out on an even greater scale by Augustus, who founded around 75 provincial colonies. In the *Res Gestae* he writes: "I founded colonies of soldiers in Africa, Sicily, Macedonia, both Spanish provinces, Achaea, Asia, Syria, Gallia Narbonensis and Pisidia."

followers were killed. Mark Antony himself arrived at Brundisium later in the year, but a full-scale conflict was averted when the soldiers refused to fight and forced the two leaders to settle their differences. The triumvirate was re-established, and the division between east and west confirmed.

The following year Antony led a campaign against the Parthians, which ended in failure in 36, although he did manage to overrun Armenia in 34. After that he stayed in Alexandria with Cleopatra, with whom he had become increasingly infatuated. Meanwhile Octavian managed to finish off Sextus Pompey (36), and conducted a successful campaign in Illyricum (35–33). From 33 onwards he consolidated his position in Italy, and initiated a propaganda war against Antony, making capital out of his affair with Cleopatra and exploiting Roman prejudice against Orientals. In 32 the towns of Italy took a personal oath of allegiance to Octavian and demanded his leadership in a national crusade against Antony and Cleopatra. The campaign itself, which shortly followed, ended in total victory at Actium in 31 BC; Antony and Cleopatra escaped to Alexandria, where they committed suicide.

The principate of Augustus

The victory of Actium left Octavian in complete control of the Empire. After a number of experiments in the next few years he succeeded in regularizing his position within the constitution. He avoided the overt absolutism of Caesar and was able to rule in the guise of a constitutional *princeps* ("first citizen"). He restored peace and prosperity and reigned unchallenged for 45 years until his death in 14 AD, by which time he had secured the succession of one of his own family and the continuation of a monarchical regime that was to last for centuries.

With the return of peace Octavian set about the enormous task of reconstructing a society shattered by 20 years of civil war. From the start he made it clear that he intended to restore the traditional form of the constitution. The difficulty was his own position of arbitrary authority, which was backed by overwhelming force but probably had no legal warrant. In January 27 BC Octavian announced that he was handing over the state to the senate and people. It was then agreed that he should be appointed to a special command for 10 years, with a "province" which included Spain, Gaul, Syria and Cilicia, areas which contained the bulk of the army and which he would govern through legates. Thus his position was legalized by a grant of *imperium* that had clear republican precedents (for example, Pompey in 55). He also continued to hold the consulship, and received various honors, including the title Augustus. In 23 a plot against his life was discovered; he decided to resign the consulship, no doubt because his perpetual tenure of the office was causing offense and was restricting the consulships available to other nobles. But he continued to govern his large province as proconsul, and in addition his *imperium* was made "greater" than that of other proconsuls. In the same year (23 BC) he received the power of the tribunes for life. In 19 BC he was granted the insignia (and perhaps also the full powers) of the consuls; evidently the fact that he was no longer seen to be holding the supreme office had caused disquiet among the people, who urged him to become perpetual consul or dictator.

In such matters he was very restrained, and made a show of refusing extravagant honors. For example in the *Res Gestae* (his account of his own achievements which was published after his death) he writes that on three occasions "the senate and people of Rome agreed that I should be appointed supervisor of laws and morals without a colleague and with supreme power, but I would not accept any office inconsistent with the custom of our ancestors." Augustus claimed that he had no more legal power than the other magistrates, but that he was preeminent in *auctoritas*; what he presumably meant was that his personal authority enabled him to assert his will without reference to his legal powers. Elections continued to take place, but were gradually reduced to a formality; by the end of his reign Augustus was in practice appointing most of the chief magistrates. Serious political opposition to the emperor was out of the question. By virtue of his tribunician power he had an absolute right of veto, but as far as we know he never needed to exercise it. *Auctoritas* was enough.

As the principate was established, the *Res Publica* was restored. The notion of a restored republic was not meant to conceal the domination of Augustus, but rather to signify the return of normal conditions after the chaos of the preceding 20 years, and the revived working of the machinery of government. Augustus reduced the size of the senate by removing "unworthy" members, and he restored the regular sequence of offices. Unlike Julius Caesar he treated the senate and its traditions with great respect. Provincial governors and other administrators were chosen from its ranks. The so-called "public" provinces were assigned by lot to proconsuls who governed for a year, while the "imperial" provinces (those within the emperor's *provincia*) were governed by legates appointed directly by Augustus, usually for periods of several years. The proconsuls and legates were normally either ex-praetors or (in the more important or prestigious provinces) ex-consuls. Senators were also used to command individual legions, and for a range of other administrative posts in Rome and Italy, for example the praetorian curators of the roads and prefects of the treasury, and the consular curators (of public works, aqueducts etc.). During the Empire the traditional magistracies became honorific titles with no serious duties attached to them; their function was to confer status on members of the senate and to qualify them for important military and administrative posts in the emperor's gift. The imperial senate was less important as a deliberative assembly than as a body of administrators.

For a number of other administrative tasks Augustus employed men of the equestrian order, first of all as his personal agents (procurators), and then increasingly as officials in his own provinces, for example as financial administrators and governors of small provincial districts, such as the Alps. Equestrians were also appointed to a range of very senior military and administrative posts which required men of proven ability whose loyalty was beyond question. Such posts were those of Prefect of the Praetorian Guard (the elite corps of soldiers who formed the emperor's official escort and garrisoned Italy), the Prefect of the Corn Supply (*annona*) and the Prefect of Egypt (the Empire's

Silver denarius of c. 18 BC. The reverse type, two laurel branches and the legend "Caesar Augustus," commemorates the honors conferred on the emperor in 27 BC, when the senate decreed that the doorposts of his house should be decorated with laurel.

The government of the Roman Empire. Of the division of the Empire the geographer Strabo (c. 63 BC–c. 21 AD) writes as follows: "Augustus divided the whole of his empire into two parts, and assigned one portion to himself and the other to the Roman people ... and he divided each of the two portions into several provinces, of which some are called 'imperial provinces' and the others 'public provinces.' To the imperial provinces Caesar sends legates and procurators, ... whereas to the public provinces the people sends praetors or consuls." The governors of the public provinces (actually called "proconsuls") were senior senators, and were chosen by lot to serve for one year; the legates who governed the imperial provinces were also high-ranking senators, but were directly appointed by the emperor and served until they were recalled. The legates included all the senior army commanders, since the imperial provinces contained nearly all the legions. The most significant exception to the pattern is Egypt, which was governed by an equestrian prefect, appointed by the emperor.

richest province and an exception in that it was not governed by a senator).

The class to whom the restored republic most appealed, and who benefited most by it, was the propertied class of Roman citizens who had formerly been excluded from public life under the republican oligarchy, the people, that is, who are normally defined as *equites*. The majority of these well-to-do Roman citizens now came not from Rome but from the towns and cities of Italy. Augustus himself belonged to a municipal family, and it was among the Italian gentry that he found his strongest support. His leading henchmen were typical examples: his schoolfriend M. Vipsanius Agrippa, an Italian of uncertain origin; C. Maecenas, an Etruscan from Arretium; T. Statilius Taurus from Lucania in south Italy. New families of Italian origin rose to prominence under Augustus in the senate and in the range of public appointments created for men of equestrian rank. M. Salvius Otho, the son of an equestrian, belonged to an old Etruscan family and entered the senate under Augustus; his son became emperor in 69. Similarly Vitellius, another of the emperors of 69, was descended from P. Vitellius of Nuceria in Campania, who was an equestrian procurator of Augustus.

The interests and aspirations of the Italian middle class were fulfilled by a national program of moral and spiritual regeneration. Augustus presented himself as a defender of the Roman tradition, and set out to restore the old state religion, the moral standards of family life and the legalistic forms of republican government. He revived ancient religious festivals and cult practices that had fallen into disuse, filled vacancies in the archaic priesthoods and repaired the temples and sacred buildings in the city of Rome. In 18 and 17 BC he introduced laws against sexual offenses; divorce was curbed and adultery made a public crime. He also imposed penalties on unmarried persons and rewarded couples who produced children. These provisions were modified by a consular law of 9 AD; wags did not fail to notice that the consuls who passed the law were both bachelors. A further source of embarrassment was the fact that the emperor's only daughter, Julia, was notorious for sexual conduct so scandalous that in 2 BC she was banished to an island. It is unlikely that the marriage laws were

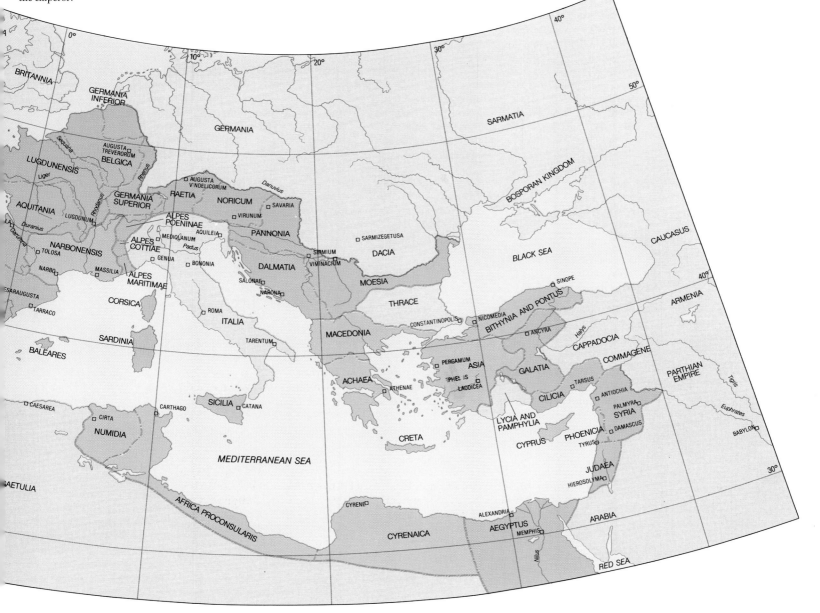

designed to increase the birth rate; the legislation should rather be seen as an attempt to regulate the life-style of the upper classes, whose decadence and pleasure-seeking were notorious in the late Republic. The old idea that it was the duty of all Roman citizens to marry and have children thus became official policy. Augustus also introduced sumptuary laws and restricted excessive and indiscriminate manumissions of slaves.

Writers and artists promoted the ideals of the regime, and were actively encouraged by the emperor's friend Maecenas. The poets in his circle included Propertius, who wrote mostly love poems, but also praised Augustus, and Horace, whose poems are full of favorable references to the emperor and his policies. In 17 BC Horace composed the *Secular Hymn* for the great festival held in that year to celebrate the dawning of a new age (*saeculum*). The Hymn outlines the achievements of Augustus and welcomes the return of ancient virtues. The greatest of the Augustan poets was Virgil, whose works include pastoral poems (*Eclogues*), a didactic poem on farming (*Georgics*), and the *Aeneid*, an epic on the legend of Aeneas, the ancestor of the Julian *gens* and the legendary hero of the Roman tradition; the poem expounds the greatness of Rome and foreshadows the achievements of Augustus. These men were undoubtedly sincere in their praise of the new order. On the other hand the erotic poet Ovid earned the emperor's displeasure (especially with his poem on the *Art of Love*), and was banished from Rome in 8 AD. One of the most important literary figures of the age was the historian Livy, whose magnificent account of the story of Rome occupied 142 books. The narrative contained examples of great men and noble deeds, and brought out the sobering lessons of moral decline. The visual arts also flourished under Augustus, as painters, sculptors and architects were commissioned to beautify the city and give concrete expression to the ideals of the new age. Important examples of "official" art are the Altar of Peace and the statue of Augustus from Prima Porta, which are classical pieces of stylistic and technical perfection, but which have been criticized for their lack of warmth and vitality.

In Rome Augustus continued the work of Julius Caesar and carried out a vast program of public building. Temples, theaters, porticoes and triumphal arches were erected everywhere and justified the emperor's claim to have transformed Rome from a city of brick to one of marble. He constructed a new Forum (inaugurated in 2 BC), and developed the area of the Campus Martius; here the principal monuments were the Portico of Octavia, the Theater of Marcellus and his own Mausoleum. In the same district Agrippa constructed the Pantheon and the first of the great imperial baths. Agrippa also built two new aqueducts and supervised the city's water supply. At this time the population of the city was probably around one million persons, most of whom lived in appalling squalor. The great majority were housed in high-rise slum tenements which were poorly constructed and badly lit; they had no heating and were liable to collapse or catch fire at any moment. The living quarters of the poor were similar to lodging houses, with short-term tenancies, no security of tenure and exorbitant rents. The drainage system was rudimentary; the sewers

(*cloacae*) ran beneath the streets, but only the houses of the rich were directly connected to them. Epidemics were frequent and destructive; excavations have unearthed mass graves containing thousands of corpses. There were no public hospitals or medical services. At night the streets were dark and dangerous; murder, housebreaking and mugging were frequent.

Augustus also followed Julius Caesar in taking responsibility for the city and its administration. He imposed a limit of 21 meters on the height of tenement blocks, and organized a fire brigade of 7000 *vigiles* ("watchmen") under an equestrian prefect. For administrative purposes the city was divided into 14 regions and 265 wards, which elected their own local officials. The task of policing the streets was given to a force of three "urban cohorts," under the command of the Prefect of the City, normally a senior ex-consul. Periodic flooding of the Tiber caused many deaths by drowning and undermined the foundations of the tenements; accordingly Augustus set up a conservancy board of senatorial "curators of the river banks." The corn supply was reorganized and eventually made the

responsibility of a senior equestrian prefect. Free rations of corn were distributed to a group of registered male citizens, whose numbers were restricted to 200 000 in 2 BC. The *plebs* also received cash donations from time to time, and were kept entertained by games and shows. Their enthusiasm for the new regime was unbounded.

By the end of his reign Augustus had established strong and efficient government and had won the loyalty and respect of all classes at home and abroad. The provinces had been ruthlessly exploited under the Republic by governors and tax farmers who were not subject to any effective controls. The principate changed all that. The provincials were now offered peace, security, a focus for their loyalty and the prospect of strong government which could control its own officials and agents. Standards of provincial government were still far from ideal, but there is no reason to doubt that the new dispensation was universally welcomed in the provinces.

In 2 BC Augustus received the title *Pater Patriae* ("Father of the Fatherland"), a title which inevitably suggested the firm but kindly hand of a *paterfamilias* (above p. 19). The 19-year-old revolutionary leader who had seized power by force of arms was long forgotten. One of Augustus' greatest achievements was to neutralize the most potent forces of revolutionary change, and in particular the army. After Actium he drastically reduced the numbers of men under arms and settled discharged veterans in colonies in Italy and the provinces. The 28 legions (about 140 000 men) that were retained were stationed permanently on the frontiers together with a roughly equal number of auxiliaries (non-citizen troops, levied in the provinces). The army became a regular establishment, with a constant intake of new recruits, who served in the legions for a 20-year fixed term. On discharge they received grants of land or severance payments in cash. In 6 AD the system was institutionalized by the formation of a military treasury, which was funded in the first instance by a grant from the emperor himself, and subsequently replenished by the income from two new taxes levied on Roman citizens: a one per cent sales tax and a five per cent death duty. The new system took the army out of politics and made it loyal to the state and to the emperor, who remained its commander-in-chief and personally appointed its officers. The army maintained its allegiance to the heirs of Augustus, until the death of Nero in 68 when the civil wars were briefly renewed.

Augustus lived a simple, austere life; his character seems to have been somewhat cold and humorless. He was a good judge of character and was fortunate in his choice of friends and collaborators, most of whom remained faithful to him to the end. His family life was marked by tragedy and failure, although he retained the affection and trust of his third wife, Livia, throughout their 53 years of marriage. Although his health was generally poor, he lived to the age of 77; he died peacefully at Nola on 19 August 14 AD.

The Julio-Claudian dynasty, 14–68 AD

The accession of Tiberius was the first occasion on which the nature of the imperial office could be reviewed by a senate which, formally speaking, sanctioned its existence. The succession was from the beginning a matter of dynastic inheritance, cloaked in the legal forms provided by the senate. Augustus had first favored his nephew Marcellus, then his associate Marcus Agrippa, to whom he married his daughter Julia. When Agrippa also died (12 BC), Tiberius was induced reluctantly to take on Julia, divorcing his own wife to whom he was happily married, and it was the promotion of Julia's young sons by Agrippa, Gaius and Lucius, added to his dislike of Julia, which led to Tiberius' famed retirement in 6 BC to the island of Rhodes, where he devoted himself to leisure, and to the Greek culture which he loved. When Gaius and Lucius died, respectively in 2 and 4 AD, Tiberius, who had returned to Rome, was adopted by Augustus and in turn made to adopt Germanicus. On all these occasions, the senate was called upon to vote the legal powers, consisting of grants of *imperium* and the tribunician power, which secured the position of the chosen successors.

Tiberius, who lacked Augustus' ease of manner, was resentful at his treatment by Augustus and was known not to have been the first choice for the succession; he was also disliked for his proud aloofness and alleged capacity for dissimulation. The aspect of his principate for which he was most bitterly criticized was his conduct of the so-called law of *maiestas*. The republican *lex maiestatis* only very roughly corresponds to the modern concept of treason; it covered anything that might "diminish the majesty of the Roman people." Under the principate it was applied not only to rebellion and conspiracy but to disrespect for the emperor, and in some cases to libelous comments directed against senators. It could thus function as a very real curb on freedom of speech and the ability to criticize an emperor.

Accusations of *maiestas* were made in the senate, which by an assumed extension of its powers formed itself into a court of law and by a sort of quasi-judicial procedure conducted trials of those who were denounced. Tiberius himself attempted initially to restrain the use of *maiestas*. Only later, and especially after the fall of Tiberius' minister Sejanus in 31 AD, do we find the reign of terror for which his principate is notorious. Part of the difficulty was that Rome lacked a system of state prosecution, it being left to the initiative of the private citizen to bring an accusation. Further, the financial and, increasingly, the political inducements to prosecution were considerable. A successful accuser in a capital charge like *maiestas* received a share of the convicted man's estate and might hope to receive imperial favor for the elimination of opponents or critics of the regime. Yet it was the senate which conducted the "trials," often playing out its own enmities and feuds, and it was the senate, as much as the emperor, which deserves the discredit for the frequency of *maiestas* accusations under Tiberius.

Tiberius' death in 37 AD was greeted with jubilation both by the senate and by the people of Rome, for whom he had done little to make himself popular. Always remote in manner, for the last 10 years of his life he lived in seclusion on Capri in the company of intimate friends, mainly literary men and astrologers. The stories of his sexual habits on Capri may be set aside as the free invention of sources who knew that they could not be refuted, and that no one would wish to try.

The reign of Tiberius' successor Gaius (Caligula) began well but, apparently after an illness affecting the balance of his mind, degenerated into a capricious tyranny ended by his assassination in 41. Attempts have been made to view Gaius' principate in a rational light, to the extent of suggesting, for instance, that he proposed to transform the principate into a flamboyant Hellenistic monarchy of a type familiar from the east; such a project, if seriously entertained, would reflect flaws of political judgment scarcely more acceptable than insanity.

Claudius, unexpectedly made emperor after Gaius' murder, proved a serious and busy, even officious emperor who devoted himself to administrative improvements, public works – of which the most impressive was his development of the harbor at Ostia – and foreign conquest. His principate was criticized for the excessive power considered to be wielded by his personal freedmen, and for his encroachment on properly senatorial or "public" areas of activity, particularly judicial. The explanation for the prominence of freedmen may be that Claudius became emperor without possessing any sort of power base in senatorial or palace circles. At the moment of his proclamation by the Praetorian Guard, the senate was actually debating a restoration of the Republic, and viewed his intrusion with great resentment.

The businesslike and humane virtues of Claudius failed in popular estimation to outweigh his personal lack of dignity and the humiliating chaos of his private life. His second wife, Messalina, was executed after a conspiracy with a senator called Silius to replace Claudius; to the aftermath of this affair may be assigned many of the executions of senators and *equites* mentioned by contemporary sources. Claudius' third wife, his niece Agrippina, devoted herself to the advancement of her son by a previous marriage, Nero.

Nero's succession in 54 (Claudius having died, allegedly poisoned by a mushroom) was accompanied by promises to restore the Augustan principle of the division of powers between emperor and senate. For some time, especially during the ascendancy of his tutor, the Stoic philosopher Seneca, these promises were observed, but this was achieved largely by diverting Nero, unwisely as it turned out, to frivolous tastes. After Nero's vengeful murder of his mother in 59, the reign developed into an unhappy though colorful tyranny in which Nero indulged his passions for music and charioteering, and those senators and philosophers who opposed him were hounded to death. Through lavish expenditure, he retained his popularity with the people of Rome. The conclusion of peace with Parthia was commemorated by fantastic celebrations, during which the Armenian king Tiridates received his crown in person from the emperor. In 66 Nero undertook a successful tour of Greece, returning to Rome with more than 1600 crowns from theatrical and athletic victories. But his position was deteriorating. After the great fire of Rome in 64, he had ransacked Greece for works of art to embellish the restored city, and it was widely believed that Nero himself had some part in the burning of Rome in order to build himself a grandiose new capital in its ruins. Choosing the adherents of an unpopular new sect, the Christians, as plausible incendiaries (they believed in the imminent end of the world through fire), Nero found that the terrible punishments which he imposed, of death by burning in the arena, won them sympathy and more unpopularity for himself.

Throughout the Julio-Claudian period there was no real opposition to the institution of the principate as such, and no more than fleeting possibilities of a restoration of republican government. Stoic philosophy, of which the best-known proponent apart from Seneca was the senator Thrasea Paetus, encouraged participation in public life under the rule of a monarch. *Libertas*, the political ideal of this group, had evolved under the Empire from its republican sense of freedom from monarchical rule into the rights of free speech and criticism permitted under such rule. Involvement in

Claudius, found hiding in the palace after Caligula's murder in 41 AD, was taken to the praetorian barracks and proclaimed emperor. In the coin illustrated (*below*), one of several issues commemorating the episode, Claudius and a praetorian standard bearer clasp hands, with the legend "received by the praetorians."

The young Nero was in the early years of his reign guided by advisers including Seneca, the praetorian prefect Burrus, and by his mother Agrippina. The early coin issue (*below*) is remarkable for its explicit recognition of the position of Agrippina.

Right: The distribution of legions in the provinces. The table illustrates the location of Roman legions in the provinces at three different dates – 24, 74 and 150 AD. These dates have been chosen as representing periods of relative peace and stability. No account is taken of the temporary movement of legions at times of crisis, such as the civil wars of 68–69, or of short-term variations which distort the general pattern, for example the concentration of seven legions in Syria during the Jewish revolt of the 60s, and the build-up on the Danube frontier during the wars of 86–112. But the table nevertheless makes it clear that there was a long-term shift in the balance of forces between the western and eastern halves of the Empire, as the armies in Spain and Germany were reduced, and those in the Balkans and the east were increased. (The information for this table was kindly supplied by J. C. Mann and Margaret Roxan.)

Distribution of Legions in the Provinces

Provinces	24 AD	74 AD	150 AD
AFRICA	III Augusta	III Augusta	III Augusta
SPAIN	IV Macedonica VI Victrix X Gemina	VII Gemina	VII Gemina
BRITAIN	—	II Augusta II Adiutrix IX Hispana XX Valeria Victrix	II Augusta VI Victrix XX Valeria Victrix
GERMANIA INFERIOR	I Germana V Alaudae XX Valeria Victrix XXI Rapax	VI Victrix X Gemina XXI Rapax XXII Primigenia	I Minervia XXX Ulpia
GERMANIA SUPERIOR	II Augusta XII Gemina XIV Gemina XVI	I Adiutrix VIII Augusta XI Claudia Pia Fidelis XIV Gemina	VIII Augusta XXII Primigenia
PANNONIA	VIII Augusta IX Hispana XV Apollinaris	XIII Gemina XV Apollinaris	Superior: I Adiutrix X Gemina Inferior: XIV Gemina II Adiutrix
DALMATIA	VII XI	IV Flavia	XIII Gemina
MOESIA	IV Scythica V Macedonica	I Italica V Alaudae V Macedonica VII Claudia Pia Fidelis	Superior: IV Flavia VII Claudia Pia Fidelis Inferior: I Italica V Macedonica XI Claudia Pia Fidelis
CAPPADOCIA	—	XII Fulminata XVI Flavia	XII Fulminata XV Apollinaris
SYRIA	III Gallica VI Ferrata X Fretensis XII Fulminata	III Gallica IV Scythica	III Gallica IV Scythica XVI Flavia
JUDAEA	—	X Fretensis	VI Ferrata X Fretensis
EGYPT	III Cyrenaica XXII Deiotariana	III Cyrenaica XXII Deiotariana	II Traiana
ARABIA	—	—	III Cyrenaica

Legions	24 AD	74 AD	150 AD
I Adiutrix	(raised c. 68)	Germania Superior	Pannonia Superior
I Germana	Germania Inferior	(disappears c. 70)	
I Italica	(raised c. 66)	Moesia	Moesia Inferior
I Minervia		(raised c. 83)	Germania Inferior
II Adiutrix	(raised c. 70)	Britain	Pannonia Inferior
II Augusta	Germania Superior	Britain	Britain
II Traiana		(raised c. 104)	Egypt
III Augusta	Africa	Africa	Africa
III Cyrenaica	Egypt	Egypt	Arabia
III Gallica	Syria	Syria	Syria
IV Flavia	(raised c. 70)	Dalmatia	Moesia Superior
IV Macedonica	Spain	(disappears c. 70)	
IV Scythica	Moesia	Syria	Syria
V Alaudae	Germania Inferior	Moesia	(disappears c. 86)
V Macedonica	Moesia	Moesia	Moesia Inferior
VI Ferrata	Syria	Syria	Judaea
VI Victrix	Spain	Germania Inferior	Britain
VII	Dalmatia		
VII Claudia Pia Fidelis		Moesia	Moesia Superior
VII Gemina	(raised c. 68)	Spain	Spain
VIII Augusta	Pannonia	Germania Superior	Germania Superior
IX Hispana	Pannonia	Britain	(disappears c. 132?)
X Fretensis	Syria	Judaea	Judaea
X Gemina	Spain	Germania Inferior	Pannonia Superior
XI	Dalmatia		
XI Claudia Pia Fidelis		Germania Superior	Moesia Inferior
XII Fulminata	Syria	Cappadocia	Cappadocia
XIII Gemina	Germania Superior	Pannonia	Dalmatia
XIV Gemina	Germania Superior	Germania Superior	Pannonia Superior
XV Apollinaris	Pannonia	Pannonia	Cappadocia
XVI	Germania Superior	(disappears c. 70)	
XVI Flavia	(raised c. 70)	Cappadocia	Syria
XX Valeria Victrix	Germania Inferior	Britain	Britain
XXI Rapax	Germania Inferior	Germania Inferior	(disappears c. 92)
XXII Deiotariana	Egypt	Egypt	(disappears c. 125)
XXII Primigenia	(raised c. 40)	Germania Inferior	Germania Superior
XXX Ulpia		(raised c. 104)	Germania Inferior

political life became impermissible when a reign like Nero's declined into cruelty and tyranny, for it was impossible for a philosopher to serve such a tyrant without losing his fundamental integrity as a moral being. At this point it was his duty to withdraw from public life – a decision which, as in the case of Paetus, was tantamount to a declaration of dissent. His conspicuous absence from the senate was an important aspect of the denunciation which, in 66, led to his suicide. The death of Paetus closely followed the suicides of Seneca himself and his nephew, the poet Lucan. They had been suspected, with many others, of involvement in a plot to kill Nero and replace him with an obscure senator called Piso. This conspiracy, ruthlessly suppressed in 65, ushered in the decline of the last years of Nero and the end of the Julio-Claudian line.

In the spring of 68 a Gallic senator called Julius Vindex, who was then governing the province of Gallia Lugdunensis, circulated provincial commanders in an attempt to get them to revolt. His appeal was successful only with Galba, the elderly governor of Tarraconensian Spain, who allowed himself to be proclaimed emperor with the support of Vindex and the small garrison of Spain, to which he added a second legion, raised by himself. Vindex was suppressed near Vesontio (Besançon) by the governor of Upper Germany, Verginius Rufus, who was himself proclaimed emperor by his army but refused to accept. The most likely interpretation of Verginius Rufus' somewhat ambiguous conduct is that he was supporting Nero in a situation in which he did not know what was happening elsewhere. After Nero's suicide (9 June 68), Rufus gave his support to Galba, but was replaced as governor.

Vitellius, sent out by Galba as governor of Lower Germany, was proclaimed there at the beginning of 69. In the following month Otho, whom Galba had passed over for the succession, was put up at Rome by the Praetorian Guard, and Galba killed. His policies, however necessary, had been too strict and parsimonious to compensate for the unattractiveness of his character. After losing a preliminary skirmish to the advancing forces of Vitellius, Otho committed suicide (19 April), without waiting for the arrival in Italy of the Illyrian legions which might have saved him. Vitellius, however, soon found himself facing the carefully organized threat of Vespasian, who was proclaimed by the armies of the east at the beginning of July. Vespasian himself went to Alexandria, from where he controlled the corn supply to Rome, and won the west by a massive build-up of power in the Balkans, combined with a rapid strike into Italy itself. After his defeat at Bedriacum, Vitellius' resistance fell into ever-increasing disarray; he was killed when the forces of Vespasian entered Rome on 20 December 69. Domitian, Vespasian's son, was hailed as Caesar, and now Rome awaited its new Augustus, who arrived in October of the year 70. Last pockets of Vitellian resistance had been suppressed, and the rebellion in the Rhineland of a Batavian auxiliary commander, Julius Civilis, subdued. The armies had all had their say, and the civil wars were at an end.

Frontiers and the Roman army

The disbanding of the huge armies involved in the civil wars of the late Republic left Augustus with 26 legions, later increased to 28. With these relatively modest forces he embarked on a series of rationally planned campaigns to complete the pacification of provincial regions already partly won. Only after this was completed did Augustus divert his resources to expansion and conquest.

The first area to be pacified was northwestern Spain, with its mountain fastnesses and recalcitrant native tribes. On the completion of these difficult wars, in 19 BC, Augustus transferred part of his Spanish army to the German frontier and Illyricum, leaving Spain with a garrison of four legions. By the end of the Julio-Claudian period, this had dwindled to a single legion, stationed at León. Augustus next attended to Raetia and Noricum, regions posing a potential threat to the agriculture and settled communities of north Italy, as well as to communications with the crucial province of Illyricum. In the east, despite popular clamor for conquest, relations with Parthia were settled by diplomacy. The standards taken from Crassus at Carrhae were recovered (19 BC) and Roman interests were secured by client kings who were allowed effective independence in return for loyalty. The Herods of Judaea are the best-known example of Hellenistic kingdoms which enjoyed a late flowering under Roman patronage. After the death of Cleopatra, last of the Ptolemies, Egypt was ruled by prefects of equestrian rank, more or less as the personal domain of the emperors. Senators were not permitted even to enter it.

After his earlier campaigns, which Augustus sometimes attended in person, the armies were used to consolidate the Rhine frontier and push beyond it towards the Elbe river, and to pacify Illyricum. With this apparently achieved, a campaign was planned to annex the kingdom of Maroboduus, lying north of the Danube between Illyricum and the newly occupied parts of Germany. The entire northern frontier policy fell in ruins in 6 AD when Illyricum rose in revolt and the campaign against Maroboduus was abandoned. By 9 AD the revolt was suppressed, but in that year Quintilius Varus and his three legions were destroyed by the German chief Arminius at an unknown site in the Teutoburg forest. Varus has been charged with incompetence in allowing himself to be surprised. Little, however, is known of the circumstances, and it might be stated in mitigation that the revolt of Illyricum had left Varus isolated in a province which now protruded from the Rhine front as an exposed and vulnerable salient.

Julio-Claudian policy in the north was to consolidate the frontier through the establishment of legionary and auxiliary camps on the Roman bank and the tenure of bridgeheads across the river. The Danube frontier, after the recovery of Illyricum by Tiberius (6–9 AD), received the same treatment. The army in these and other newly conquered provinces became an effective agent for romanization, since the legionary camps generated informal settlements known as *canabae,* and in due course the foundation nearby of civilian towns (*municipia*); a particularly good example of this is Carnuntum on the Danube.

Augustus' recommendation not to extend the Empire was strictly observed by Tiberius, who nevertheless had to intervene in Thrace and to suppress a native rebellion in Numidian Africa led by a tribal leader, Tacfarinas. In the east, Tiberius

The arch of Titus at Rome was erected in commemoration of the triumph over the Jewish rebellion, achieved by Titus in 70 AD on behalf of his father Vespasian. Here are shown the spoils of the destroyed Temple being conveyed into Rome in the triumphal procession.

confirmed on the throne of Armenia a client king acceptable to Parthia. This was achieved by Germanicus, during an extensive tour of the east in which he also visited Palmyra and Petra, caravan cities with links in the Parthian empire.

The invasion of Britain undertaken by Claudius in 43 AD must have been planned very soon after he became emperor. Its motives have been much debated. It is unlikely, despite the high level of romanization achieved in Britain, that the province ever paid for its occupation, but this may not have been part of the Romans' calculations. It is possible that Claudius was eager for the glory of conquest to outweigh his other disadvantages as emperor. Certainly, he made much of the conquest, attending the campaign for a brief time (accompanied by elephants, which must have been an extraordinary sight to the Britons), naming his son Britannicus and in general receiving an unprecedented number of military salutations. Yet the most likely explanation is that Britain was linked more closely than seemed safe to the Belgic principalities of Gaul. There is evidence for much cross-Channel economic and political activity in the period before the conquest, and it may have seemed to Claudius and his advisers that Gaul would not be fully secure without the annexation also of Britain.

Claudius also reduced Mauretania to provincial status after disorders there following the death of a client king. This annexation, more significant than appears from the surviving sources, completed the pacification of the lands adjoining the western Mediterranean.

In the east, Nero inherited from Claudius involvement in renewed difficulties with Parthia and Armenia. After nearly a decade of military campaigns and complex shifts of diplomatic policy, the Parthian king Vologaeses agreed that his favored nominee Tiridates should visit Rome to receive his crown from Nero. By the agreement Armenia passed from the Roman into the Parthian sphere of influence, which is where it belonged by racial affinity.

Judaea, in the time of Augustus a client kingdom under Herod the Great, had after his death been made into a Roman province. It was given back by Claudius to his friend Herod Agrippa as a reward for his help during his accession as emperor, but after Agrippa's death in 44 Judaea once again became a Roman province. One of its governors was the Felix, brother of Claudius' freedman Pallas, before whom St Paul appeared (Acts 23:24ff). After some years of

The coin issue with the legend "IVD [aea] CAP [ta]," with its figures of disconsolate captives and a palm tree, celebrates the same event as the arch of Titus illustrated *opposite*. Similar types were issued by Hadrian after the suppression of the revolt of Bar-Kochba in 135 AD. For further description of Jerusalem, and of the fortress of Masada, captured in 73 AD, see pp. 162–63.

discontent Judaea rose in rebellion in 66, its suppression being committed to Vespasian and his son Titus. Interrupted by Vespasian's proclamation in 69, the defeat of the rebellion was completed by Titus with the destruction of the Temple in 70. The last stronghold, Masada, fell three years later after a long and bitter siege.

The subjugation of Britain was pursued with a severity which led to the rebellion of Boudicca in 60–61 AD, British anger being directed particularly against the veteran colony of Camulodunum (Colchester), which was seen as a symbol of Roman oppression, and the provincial capital, London. Subsequent, milder policy achieved the extension of Roman power to the line later taken by Hadrian's Wall. An attempt under the governorship of Agricola to achieve further annexations to the north was shortlived, since Domitian needed to recall a legion from Britain for service in Germany. The legionary fortress at Inchtuthill, built by Agricola, was occupied only very briefly, and in fact abandoned before its construction was finished.

These additions to the Empire were secured, as we have seen, by a trained professional army of less than 150 000 men with an approximately equal number of auxiliary troops recruited from various regions of the Empire and sometimes from client kingdoms, who often provided specialized fighting techniques. It was as small an army as could reasonably be employed, its size being controlled by economic and by political considerations. The economic factors relate to the problem of securing military pay from income from taxation and other sources. A soldier's pay did not increase between the times of Augustus and Domitian, who raised it by one-third, quite possibly at the cost of considerable financial strain (see below, p. 102). Throughout the first and more particularly the second and third centuries of the Empire, the army depended increasingly on additional payments received, for example, on the accessions of new emperors, and to a lesser extent from the spoils of active campaigning.

The dangers presented by an efficient but frequently inactive army were partly met by diverting its energies to works of construction, such as the building of roads and bridges, mining and digging canals, all of them useful in the economic development of the provinces, but not offering much in the way of excitement or financial reward. If Roman governors were sometimes impatient at the constraints imposed upon them, the soldiers were also very probably attracted when prospects of gain were offered by active campaigning, even in civil war.

The armies were established in legionary fortresses placed at intervals along the frontiers. No provincial legate had more than four legions at his disposal, which limited the chances of successful revolt against an established emperor who could be sure of the support of his other commanders. In settled times rebellions of provincial armies happened only occasionally and were easily suppressed. But when an emperor fell or was known to be insecure, as in 41, 68, 97, 193 and repeatedly in the 3rd century (see below, pp. 168–69), it was impossible to restrain the individual initiatives of provincial commanders and their armies. In 68–69 all the major army groupings except for that of

Britain actively participated in civil war. As Tacitus remarked in a famous phrase, the secret had escaped, that emperors could be made elsewhere than at Rome.

In an obvious sense, the Roman emperors depended on the support of the army, and the unstated threat of military force was the reality behind the niceties of their constitutional position. Yet, the emperors of the 1st century – with the exceptions of Tiberius and Trajan, and to a lesser extent Vespasian – were not in general men of extensive military experience. In the same way, senatorial careers of the early Empire, which mingled civilian and military posts, and service in the provinces and at Rome, did not encourage the formation of a professionally self-conscious military elite. Some imperial legates, like Agricola and the writer on martial stratagems, Frontinus, were men of considerable military experience, systematically accumulated and put into practice. Yet such men remained attached to the life-style of Roman senators. They were men of private means, educated in the traditional culture of the civilian upper classes. A typical example is Pomponius Secundus, who governed Germany under Claudius. He was famous, wrote Tacitus, for his military triumphs, but still more so for the poetry which he composed. The contrast between this situation and that of the 3rd and 4th centuries could not be more marked.

The romanization of the west
The process known as "romanization" was the joint expression of imperial incentives and provincial wealth. The Romans did not use coercion to achieve it, but provided an example for imitation, with encouragement to the natives of the provinces to adopt Roman dress, to learn the Latin language and, to the differing degrees possible in different environments, to develop their settlements as urban centers. In the newly pacified west, the strongholds of native communities became the capitals of administrative districts known as *civitates*, based on the territories of the former tribes. Sometimes new cities took the place of inconvenient older sites. The Gallic hill-town of Bibracte (Mont Beuvray), for instance, yielded to the new foundation of Augustodunum (Autun), built by the Arroux river on a site far better suited to commercial activity. Similarly, in Noricum the native stronghold on the Magdalensberg was superseded by the new provincial capital, Virunum.

The Romans could provide civic institutions resembling those of the *municipia* of Italy. The new cities were given councils (*curiae*) composed of the wealthier members of local society, who on holding public office received the Roman citizenship and were formally enrolled in the ancient voting districts of Rome. The municipal office of *duumvir* appears in Gaul as the Celtic *vergobret* and in Punic Africa as *sufes*.

The political organization of the developing provinces was achieved through the existing upper classes. Many instances can be found of the political functions and civic munificence undertaken by the older nobility of the provinces. At Leptis Magna in Tripolitania the early theater and almost all the other public building of the 1st century were provided by members of wealthy Punic families. At Saintes (Mediolanum Santonum) in southwestern

The triumphal arch of Saintes (*left*) bears on its frieze the commemorative inscription of C. Julius Rufus, whose family rises through C. Julius Otuaneunus, C. Julius Gedomo (the first citizen of the family, receiving this privilege from Julius Caesar) to Epotsorovidus, a chieftain of the Santones in the pre-Caesarian period. Rufus was also priest of Rome and Augustus at the altar of the Three Gauls at Lugdunum (see *opposite*) and is known to have contributed to the building of the amphitheater there.

Below A wooden votive offering preserved by the waterlogged conditions at the sanctuary of Sources-de-la-Seine near Dijon. The statue is an interesting example of the style of popular Celtic art in Roman Gaul, just as the vigor of the sanctuary itself is an expression of ancestral religious custom in the Roman Empire.

Gaul the triumphal arch erected in 18 AD was provided by the romanized grandson, C. Julius Rufus, of a Celtic notable who had acquired the citizenship from Julius Caesar.

The degree of urbanization achieved in the west differed greatly between those regions influenced by a Mediterranean and those influenced by a north European climate. In Africa urbanization proceeded rapidly, based in the province's eastern regions on the existing Punic communities and in Numidia on the development of native settlements, supplemented as always by Roman colonies. Spain too underwent rapid urban development, but in northern Gaul, the Belgic and German provinces and in Britain the process was slower. Many towns, such as Verulamium (near St Albans) in Britain, only produced extensive building in stone in the 2nd century. Nevertheless, Augustodunum, the capital of the Aedui, was already a center of Roman culture in the early 1st century; the sons of Gallic nobles were being educated there in the liberal arts when

in 21 AD they were taken as hostages during a rebellion.

In the north, villa culture played a relatively more significant role than in the Mediterranean areas, and romanization should not be measured only by the degree of urban development. We must also estimate the advancement of material culture achieved in the villas, which was in its own way quite as impressive as that of the cities.

Two more factors are relevant to an assessment of the economic basis of romanization. The role of the army has arisen already, both in the provision of physical amenities like roads and bridges, and in the establishment of legionary camps which served as bases for urban development. Apart from the camps, with their adjacent *canabae* and, in due course, *municipia*, veterans retiring from the provincial armies tended to settle nearby and often became local gentry, the owners of villas and members of urban communities. The army's role as an agent of romanization can be seen clearly in

The temple of the goddess Vesunna at Périgueux (*right*), a stunning example of a Celtic shrine constructed during the early Roman period. Its huge circular cella or sanctuary was surrounded by an elaborate sacred precinct, of which the foundations survive. The ground plans of similar temples can be reconstructed from several sites in the former Celtic provinces of the Roman Empire.

The altar of Rome and Augustus at Lugdunum, founded in 10 BC, in association with a provincial council of the Three Gauls. Romanized tribal leaders held office as priests of Rome and Augustus, and with its annual festivities, held on 1 August, the altar had an important role in the unification of Gaul, and in the encouragement of its loyalty to Rome. The altar does not survive, but its general appearance is known from coin issues of Augustus (*above*). The nearby amphitheater of the Three Gauls has in recent years been cleared by excavation.

previously undeveloped regions like Pannonia and the Rhineland, and the plains of southern Numidia. In already urbanized areas like the east, soldiers were more involved in the social lives of the existing cities.

The second factor is that of Italian emigration under the later Republic, especially to Spain, Africa and Asia Minor. Civilians who had sought their fortune abroad, and veterans settled after campaigns in the provinces, often became very prosperous; their descendants were among the earliest to appear in the enlargement of the Roman ruling class by the admission of provincials to the senate in the first century of the Empire. The philosopher Seneca, the poet Lucan, the emperor Trajan, the first consuls from Africa – the Pactumeii brothers of Cirta – and many others, can be shown on the basis of their nomenclature to be descended from Italian families who had emigrated in the time of the Republic.

More frequently, provincial senators were members of indigenous local families taking their opportunity to express their wealth and social status at Rome. Claudius, who was particularly conscious of the process of the expansion from early times of the Roman ruling class, offered to the Aedui special privileges in seeking advancement through senatorial careers at Rome. The admission of Gauls, as of Spaniards and Africans, and later of Greeks and Orientals, to the Roman governing order, was part of a broader process, reflecting the steady advancement of the provinces under Roman rule and their absorption, to different degrees, of the classical ideal of political and civic life.

The limits of romanization must be defined as carefully as its extension. The regions of the Empire retained their own cultures and languages behind an often solid facade of romanization. The Celtic and Punic languages remained in use; a legal text of the early 3rd century states that wills made in either of these languages were valid. There is excellent evidence, throughout North Africa, for the survival

also of a native language, described in modern discussions as Libyan or "Berber," though there is no way of judging how closely these native dialects resembled the modern Berber language. In the east, Celtic, according to the late evidence of St Jerome, was spoken in parts of Galatia, and in the time of Nero Paul and Barnabas were acclaimed by the inhabitants of the city of Lystra "in the Lycaonian language" (Acts 14:11). Beyond the Taurus mountains Syriac in its various forms was everywhere spoken throughout the time of the Roman Empire, from Antioch into Babylonia and southwards to Gaza, though it produced a written literature only with the rise of the Christian church in the later 3rd century.

The persistence of local art forms, especially in relief sculpture, is conspicuous, often contrasting strikingly with the more universalized forms of Roman imperial sculpture found in the provinces. The architecture of temples in the Celtic west retained a distinctive style quite unlike classical models, of a large central cella surrounded by an extensive precinct. The best surviving examples of this, at Autun and Périgueux, contrast dramatically with the classical temples at Nîmes and Vienne. The gods and goddesses of the west were often romanized native deities, as in the cases of the triple "mother-goddesses" and the "god with the hammer" of Roman Gaul, and the three hooded divinities of Britain. In Africa, Virgo Caelestis and Saturn were romanized versions of the Punic gods Tanit and Ba'al Hammon. The Gorgon-like face of the goddess Sulis-Minerva from the temple pediment at Aquae Sulis (Bath) is a particularly vivid expression of the persistence of Celtic decorative style in a romanized religious and civic context. Those aspects of native religious practice least compatible with Roman civilized ideals, such as druidism, were suppressed by government action, one of the few areas in which the Roman authorities forcibly intervened in the development of provincial life.

An influence in favor of unity was provided by the imperial cult, of which much is known from all parts of the Roman Empire. Based on regional capitals, such as Tarraco, Narbo, Ephesus (for Asia Minor) and Sardis (for Lydia), the imperial cult cleverly directed local patriotism into the channel of loyalty to Rome. The cult was administered by a provincial council, consisting of delegates from the cities, which met annually under the presidency of one of their number, the chief priest of the province for the year. The council was able not only to express its formal good wishes or condolences to the emperor as circumstances required, but also, as many inscriptions attest, to select and dispatch embassies to the emperor on matters of substantial interest to the communities of the province concerned.

The religious attitudes involved in the imperial cult differed between the western and eastern parts of the Empire. In the west, worship of the emperor was centered not directly on the emperor but on his *numen* or guardian spirit, and was coupled with reverence for the city (or the goddess) Roma. The emperor was regarded as divine (*divus*) only after his death, and then not invariably, since promotion of a dead emperor to the ranks of the gods depended on the attitude of his successor and the senate. In the

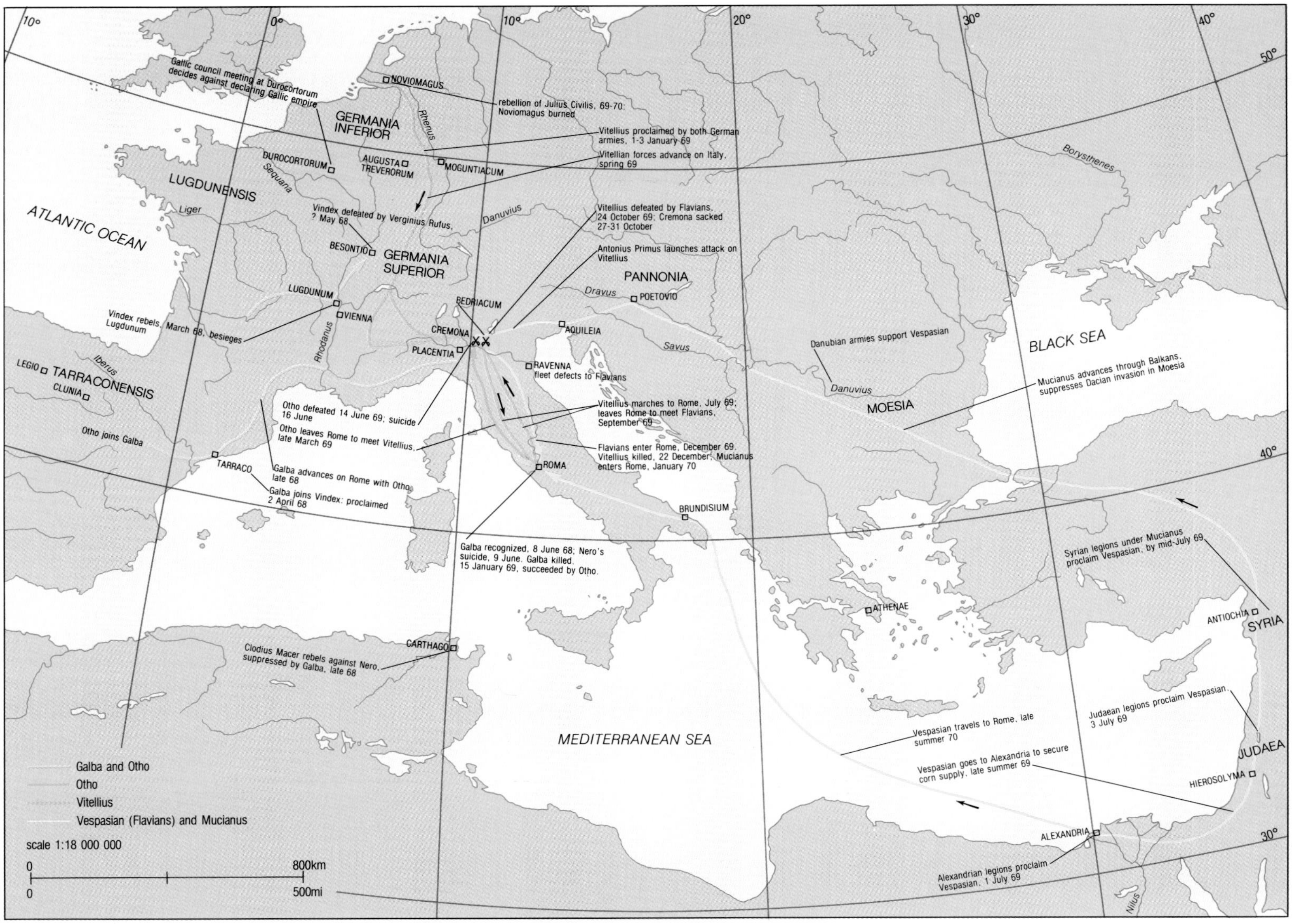
Gallic council meeting at Durocortorum decides against declaring Gallic empire
NOVIOMAGUS
rebellion of Julius Civilis, 69-70: Noviomagus burned
GERMANIA INFERIOR
Rhenus
Vitellius proclaimed by both German armies, 1-3 January 69
Vitellian forces advance on Italy, spring 69
DUROCORTORUM
AUGUSTA TREVERORUM
MOGUNTIACUM
LUGDUNENSIS
Sequana
Liger
ATLANTIC OCEAN
Vindex defeated by Verginius Rufus, ? May 68
Danuvius
BESONTIO
GERMANIA SUPERIOR
Vitellius defeated by Flavians, 24 October 69; Cremona sacked 27-31 October
Antonius Primus launches attack on Vitellius
PANNONIA
Dravus
POETOVIO
LUGDUNUM
VIENNA
BEDRIACUM
Vindex rebels, March 68, besieges Lugdunum
Rhodanus
CREMONA
AQUILEIA
PLACENTIA
Savus
Danubian armies support Vespasian
BLACK SEA
Iberus
LEGIO
TARRACONENSIS
CLUNIA
RAVENNA
fleet defects to Flavians
Mucianus advances through Balkans, suppresses Dacian invasion in Moesia
Otho defeated 14 June 69; suicide 16 June
Otho leaves Rome to meet Vitellius, late March 69
Vitellius marches to Rome, July 69; leaves Rome to meet Flavians, September 69
Danuvius
MOESIA
Otho joins Galba
TARRACO
Flavians enter Rome, December 69. Vitellius killed, 22 December; Mucianus enters Rome, January 70
ROMA
Galba advances on Rome with Otho, late 68
Galba joins Vindex: proclaimed 2 April 68
BRUNDISIUM
Borysthenes
Galba recognized, 8 June 68; Nero's suicide, 9 June. Galba killed, 15 January 69, succeeded by Otho.
Syrian legions under Mucianus proclaim Vespasian, by mid-July 69
ATHENAE
ANTIOCHIA
SYRIA
CARTHAGO
Clodius Macer rebels against Nero, suppressed by Galba, late 68
Judaean legions proclaim Vespasian, 3 July 69
MEDITERRANEAN SEA
Vespasian travels to Rome, late summer 70
JUDAEA
Vespasian goes to Alexandria to secure corn supply, late summer 69
HIEROSOLYMA
Galba and Otho
Otho
Vitellius
Vespasian (Flavians) and Mucianus
scale 1:18 000 000
0
800km
0
500mi
ALEXANDRIA
Alexandrian legions proclaim Vespasian, 1 July 69
Nilus
10°
0°
10°
20°
30°
40°
50°
40°
30°

east, accustomed as it was to divinized Hellenistic monarchs, imperial worship was more direct. The inscription, published in 1963, recording the governorship of Judaea of Pontius Pilate, attests the existence at Caesarea of a "Tiberieum," or temple of Tiberius; this was an emperor more strongly opposed than most to the natural tendency toward direct worship of the emperor.

The concept of romanization can hardly be applied to the Greek east. Roman attitudes to the Greeks combined admiration for their cultural achievement (an admiration taken to unnecessary lengths by Nero), with a sort of patronizing affection. For their part the Greeks were impervious to the influence of Latin culture. Roman colonies founded in the east were Latin-speaking enclaves gradually absorbed by their Greek environment. Yet Greeks flocked to Rome to seek advancement under Roman patrons – men such as the geographer Strabo, the astrologer Thrasyllus and many poets, historians and others whose names are known. Greek and Oriental cultural and religious ideas flowed to Rome along the pacified Mediterranean. The 2nd century witnessed a tremendous flourishing of this Greco-Roman culture in the literary movement known as the Second Sophistic, with its associated artistic developments (see below, pp. 110–12). At the same time, men from the Greek east progressively took a greater share in government, emerging by the early 2nd century to become senators, consuls and provincial governors. The transference of the Roman ideal of government to the Greek east, which is the essence of Byzantium, had been anticipated in the days of the high Roman Empire.

It has been argued that the civil wars of 68–70 AD which brought to an end the Julio-Claudian dynasty, were an expression of provincial dissension in the Roman Empire. The notion that Vindex was a "nationalist" leader aspiring to establish a separatist "empire of the Gauls" is disproved by his coinage and by what can be seen of his policies and attitudes, which were traditionally Roman. Yet, in gathering his forces from the peasantry of the Gallic countryside, Vindex clearly betrays his position as a tribal dynast as well as Roman senator, and to this extent his rebellion was an expression, if not of nationalistic sentiment, certainly of the particular social structure of the part of Gaul from which he came. Yet the more significant aspect of the civil wars of 68–70 may be that, given these circumstances and the general disorder, there was not any nationalistic secession in the Roman provinces. The wars were fought between Roman armies under the command of their generals, and there was no serious likelihood that the Empire would fall apart.

The wars of 68–70 AD. The wars of 68–70 AD involved in turn all the main military groupings of the Empire, victory going to the most coherently mobilized. The chief exception was Britain, with potentially formidable but isolated forces. The single African legion was inadequate for serious contention, and Galba's modest forces, inherited by Otho, were unequal to the combined armies of the Germanies, frustrated in their attempts to proclaim Verginius Rufus and transferring their support to Vitellius. In being able to combine the eastern legions and those of the Danube, Vespasian had irresistible advantages, and he could also use his Italian connections to spread disaffection. The soldiers behaved in general with an obedience to their officers which suggests that they had no revolutionary aims of their own. The only serious provincial unrest after the revolt of Vindex was in the extreme northeast of Gaul, in the rebellion of the Batavian Julius Civilis, but even this failed to provoke a general revolt.

Right A fanciful townscape from the cubiculum of the villa of Publius Fannius Sinister at Boscoreale.

Town Life at Pompeii

Pompeii was originally an Etruscan town, but was occupied in the 5th century BC by the Samnites. After this it remained a largely Oscan-speaking community until 80 BC when Sulla established a colony there. As a consequence it rapidly became romanized. Following its destruction in the eruption of 79 AD Pompeii lay buried (beneath a layer of ash and volcanic mud) until the 18th century.

The economy of Pompeii was principally based on the produce of its fertile hinterland, especially wine and olive oil. But it was also a flourishing industrial and trading center, the major industries being cloth manufacture and fulling. There is much evidence also of small-scale craft production, retailing and other service trades.

Like all Roman towns, Pompeii had a local government closely modeled on that of Rome. The ruling body was a town council (*ordo*) of 80–100 men (decurions), who were drawn from the propertied class and held office for life. The executive magistrates were two annually elected *duoviri* (equivalent to the Roman consuls), assisted by aediles who, like their Roman counterparts, administered public works. Slogans and graffiti survive to show that elections were lively affairs.

While the poor lived mostly in tiny apartments or in the *tabernae* (shops), which opened out on to the streets, the rich lived in luxurious town houses. The standard Pompeian house was centered on a large hall (*atrium*), opening out into a peristyle or colonnaded garden. The houses were richly decorated with murals, which provide the bulk of our knowledge of Roman painting. The paintings are divided into four chronological periods or "styles."

Right Still life with eggs and thrushes. Still-life paintings were very popular in the period of the Fourth Style (c. 55–79 AD).
Below The House of the Silver Wedding illustrates the standard design of an *atrium* house. The *atrium* was a central hall with an opening in the roof to let in light, and a rectangular pool in the floor to catch rain water.
Below right The peristyle (colonnaded garden) of the House of the Vettii.
Far right General view from the northern walls looking south towards the forum.
Opposite below left Street scene in Pompeii. Note the high sidewalks and stepping-stones for pedestrians.
Opposite below right View of the forum, looking north. The Capitolium (the temple of Jupiter, Juno and Minerva) stands to the left of the arch. Vesuvius can be seen in the background.

Republican Rome

The city of Rome underwent an extraordinary expansion during the Republic. Already a substantial settlement at the end of the 6th century, its population had risen to perhaps 100 000 by 300 BC, and was nearing the million mark in the time of Caesar. The squalid tenement blocks which dominated the imperial city were already making their appearance at the time of Hannibal. Public buildings – utilities, amenities, temples and decorative monuments – began to be constructed in large numbers in the time of Appius Claudius (who built the first aqueduct in 312), and continued on an ever-increasing scale, especially in the age of imperial expansion after the Second Punic War. Finally the dynasts of the 1st century BC, such as Sulla, Pompey and Caesar, embarked on building projects which changed the whole appearance of the city, in order to enhance their personal glory. But very few of the monuments of republican Rome survive to our time: they were mostly superseded in their turn by the even more grandiose building programs of the imperial age.

Top Marble relief from the Lacus Curtius ("Curtius' pond"). According to an ancient legend, a certain Curtius had once perished when he and his horse were swallowed by a chasm in the center of the Forum. One legend identified Curtius with a Sabine leader who fought in the war against Romulus; in another version of the story the event occurred in the 4th century BC and involved a Roman horseman. This relief illustrating the story, and dating from republican times, was found at the spot in the 16th century; it has since been moved to a museum and replaced by a replica.

Above The Forum Romanum was for centuries the center of Roman political and religious life. Its earliest monuments, such as the Lapis Niger (see p. 22), the temple of Vesta (*opposite*) and the Curia, date from the time of the kings. Here we see the Sacra Via, the oldest street in Rome, passing between the Lacus Curtius (left) and the Basilica Julia (right), built by Julius Caesar in 54 BC. Next to the basilica stand the three surviving columns of the republican temple of Castor, built on the site of an archaic temple which commemorated the victory at Lake Regillus in 499 BC. Dominating the skyline is the arch of Titus which belongs to the imperial period.

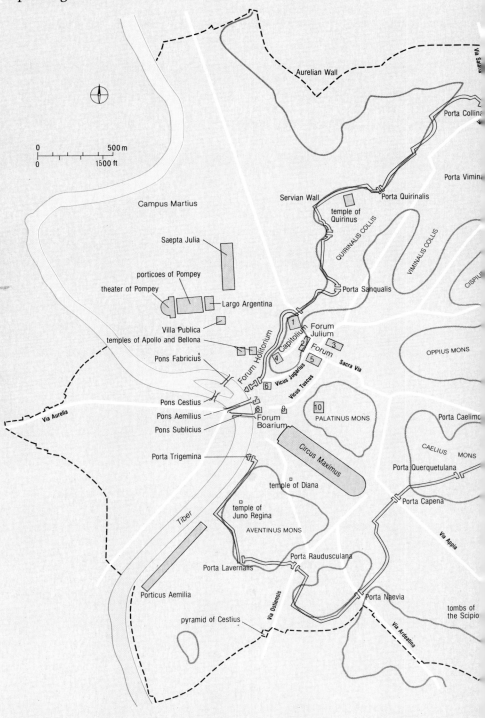

Right This well-preserved rectangular temple (early 1st century BC), commonly known as the temple of Fortuna Virilis, is more probably to be identified as the temple of Portunus, the deity associated with the nearby harbor.

Far right The forum of Caesar (dedicated in 46 BC) was dominated by a great temple of Venus, the mythical ancestor of the Julian house. An equestrian statue of the dictator stood in the center of the square.

Below right The monumental complex of the Largo Argentina came to light in the 1920s when excavations revealed four republican temples, ranging in date from the late 4th century to the end of the 2nd. The picture shows the remains of the 3rd-century temple A.

Far right The Pons Fabricius, connecting the left bank with the Tiber island, was built by L. Fabricius, supervisor of roads, in 62 BC.

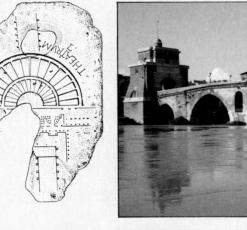

Porta Esquilina

Via Collatina

Via Labicana

Via Praenestina

Via Tusculana

Via Latina

1 temple of Juno Moneta
2 Tabularium
3 Basilica Aemilia
4 temple of Jupiter Capitolinus
5 Basilica Julia
6 temples of Fortuna and Mater Matuta
7 temple of Portunus
8 temple of Hercules Victor
9 Ara Maxima
10 temple of Cybele or Magna Mater

Above Rome's first stone theater was commissioned by Pompey and dedicated by him in 55 BC; little remains of the monument, but its layout can still be seen on a fragment of a 3rd-century marble plan of the city.

Above right The Milvian bridge (109 BC) stands to the north of Rome and carries the Via Flaminia towards Etruria and Umbria.

Right The Forum Romanum seen from the Palatine. Behind the columns of the temple of Castor stands the Curia or senate house begun by Sulla in 80 BC and rebuilt by Julius Caesar in 44.

Far right The temple of Vesta in the Forum. The site was associated with the cult of Vesta since the earliest times, although the surviving remains date from the imperial period.

Early Imperial Rome

Right This fine representation of Marcus Aurelius is the only bronze equestrian statue surviving from classical times.

Far right Trajan's market is the name given to the multistoried complex of buildings overlooking the forum of Trajan and occupying a space which was carved out of the SW slopes of the Quirinal. The market consists of a great vaulted hall surrounded by shops and commercial premises; these stand behind a grandiose brick exedra which forms the eastern side of Trajan's forum. Like the forum and baths of Trajan, the whole complex was designed by the architect Apollodorus of Damascus.

Imperial Rome was a huge conurbation with a probable population of over a million, most of whom lived in appalling conditions. The squalor of the slums contrasted with the magnificent public buildings erected by successive emperors, beginning with Augustus. According to Suetonius, "Augustus so embellished the city that his boast was justified: 'I left Rome a city of marble, though I found it a city of bricks.'" A further transformation occurred under Nero, following the disastrous fire of 64 AD. Tacitus tells us that "of the 14 regions into which Rome was divided [see map, p.19], only four remained intact [I, V, VI, XIV], three were destroyed to ground level [III, X, XI], and in the other seven a few houses survived, but half-burned and severely damaged." Nero began an energetic rebuilding program, which included a vast new palace, the Domus Aurea (the "Golden House"), which

stretched from the Palatine to the Servian walls on the Esquiline. This area was later occupied by the temple of Venus and Roma (135 AD), the Colosseum (80 AD), and the baths of Trajan, built out of the ruins of part of the Golden House, after its destruction by fire in 104. The baths of Trajan were the first of three great thermal complexes (the others being the baths of Caracalla and the baths of Diocletian) which mark the grandiose culmination of Roman monumental architecture.

The arch which dominates the western end of the Forum was built in 203 in honor of Septimius Severus and his sons Caracalla and Geta (whose name was erased from the inscription after his murder in 212). The reliefs show scenes from Severus' campaigns against the Parthians and Arabs.

INSET
1 column of Trajan
2 libraries
3 Atrium Libertatis
4 equestrian statue of Trajan
5 temple of Venus Genetrix
6 temple of Antoninus and Faustina
7 Regia
8 temple of Julius Caesar
9 arch of Augustus
10 temple of Vesta
11 Atrium Vestae
12 temple of Castor
13 Argiletum
14 temple of Saturn
15 Rostra
16 arch of Septimius Severus
17 portico of the Di Consentes
18 temple of Vespasian
19 temple of Concord
20 Forum Romanum

Above The temple of Antoninus and Faustina, built by Antoninus Pius in the Forum in 141, was converted into a church in the Middle Ages; the baroque facade was added in 1602.

Above right The Flavian amphitheater (the "Colosseum") was begun by Vespasian and completed by his sons Titus and Domitian. Over 50 meters high, it covered an elliptical area 188 by 156 meters. Officially opened in 80 AD, it could hold c. 70000 spectators.

Far right Trajan's column was erected in the emperor's new forum in 113 to commemorate his conquest of Dacia.

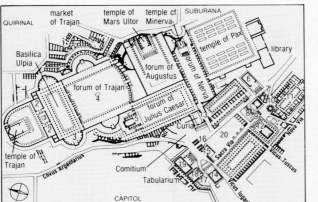

Above The Aqua Claudia, begun in 38 AD by Caligula and completed by Claudius in 52, brought water to the city from a source near Subiaco 68 kilometers away.

Right Detail of the model of ancient Rome in the Museo della Civiltà Romana, Rome. In the foreground is the Circus Maximus; beyond it are the imperial palaces on the Palatine. At the top of the picture, from left to right, are the Forum, the basilica of Maxentius, the temple of Venus and Roma, the Colosseum and the temple of the Divine Claudius.

Ostia: Port of Rome

Tradition ascribed the foundation of Ostia to King Ancus Marcius, but no trace of this early settlement has yet been found. The earliest remains belong to the coastal garrison "colony" (see p. 34) founded in the 4th century BC. Ostia was an important naval base in the Second Punic War, and expanded in the 2nd century as a commercial port serving the growing population of Rome. By the early Empire the river harbor could no longer cope with the volume of maritime traffic, so Claudius built a large artificial harbor some 3 kilometers to the north at Portus. This new harbor was itself enlarged under Trajan. Ostia flourished in the 2nd century, and its population almost doubled. High-rise tenement blocks appeared, and public buildings and amenities were constructed on a large scale. During the 3rd century, however, there was little new building, and some of the existing structures fell into disrepair. The population decreased, trade slumped, and the town gradually declined.

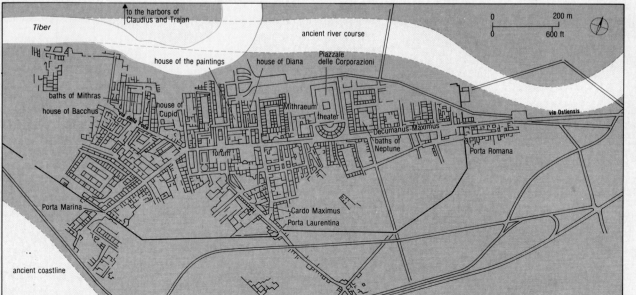

Top left The harbor at Portus in c. 350 AD, as shown on the medieval Peutinger map (see p. 116).

Above left Harbor scene on a marble relief of c. 200 AD, found near Trajan's harbor. The ship with furled sails on the right of the picture is being unloaded at the docks. On the left another ship sails into port while its crew sacrifice to celebrate their safe return. Note that the emblem of Rome, the wolf and twins, is twice depicted on the mainsail. A lighthouse (probably the one erected in the time of Claudius) can be seen in the background. The whole scene is dominated by the central figure of Neptune holding his trident.

Right Aerial view of Portus. The hexagonal plan of Trajan's inner basin can be clearly seen.

Below View of the Decumanus Maximus, the main street of Ostia.

Below Tomb painting from Ostia showing a river boat, the Isis Giminiana, being loaded with grain for the journey upstream to Rome. The captain, Farnaces, is shown holding the rudder in the stern. The representation of porters reminds us that many people in Rome and Ostia found employment in the docks.

Below center Mosaic (2nd century AD) in the Piazzale delle Corporazioni. This large colonnaded square in the town center was surrounded by shipping offices occupied by representatives of Roman and overseas trading companies. The offices are decorated with fine mosaics of nautical scenes.

An indication of the levels of maritime trade in the Mediterranean is given by the ancient wrecks discovered by underwater archaeology. The concentration in particular areas reflects the level of archaeological activity, and need not suggest that traffic was especially heavy in those waters or that they were particularly dangerous to ancient shipping! The chronological concentration of datable wrecks in the period 300 BC–300 AD illustrates the very high level of trade in classical times by comparison with earlier and later periods.

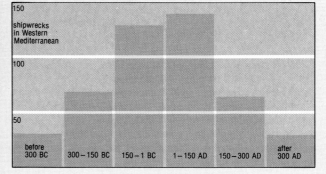

shipwrecks in Western Mediterranean

150

100

50

| before 300 BC | 300–150 BC | 150–1 BC | 1–150 AD | 150–300 AD | after 300 AD |

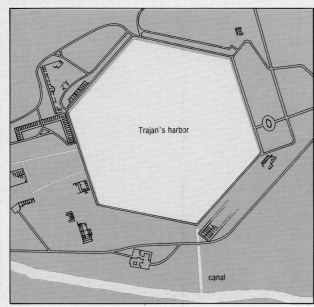

Trajan's harbor

canal

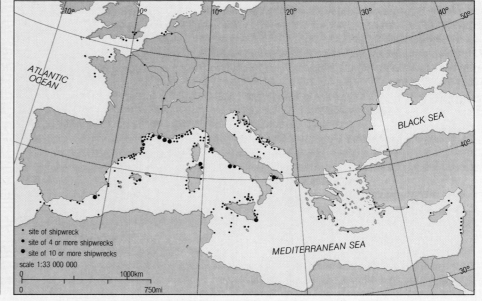

ATLANTIC OCEAN

BLACK SEA

MEDITERRANEAN SEA

• site of shipwreck
● site of 4 or more shipwrecks
● site of 10 or more shipwrecks
scale 1:33 000 000

0 ———— 1000km
0 ———— 750mi

Festivals of the State Religion

The traditional pagan religion of Rome appears to us as a confused jumble of archaic ceremonies and rituals which were performed repetitively and mechanically as a means of ensuring the goodwill of the gods – what the Romans called the *pax deorum*. It was the duty of the *paterfamilias* to perform the appropriate rituals to propitiate the gods of the household, such as Vesta (the hearth), the Penates (the store cupboard) and the Lares (departed ancestors). A similar function was exercised on behalf of the community by the chief priests and magistrates. In the course of time an elaborate set of public cults became established, located at the hundreds of shrines and temples in and around the city. The priests were not a professional class, but members of the ruling aristocracy who also held magistracies and commanded armies. The more important of these priests included the pontiffs, who supervised the state festivals and the calendar, the augurs, who were concerned with divination, and the Decemviri Sacris Faciundis, who looked after sacred books and foreign cults. Other priests included the Flamines, the Arval Brethren, the Fetiales, the Salii, the Rex Sacrorum and the Vestal Virgins. All came under the authority of the Pontifex Maximus, who was the head of the state religion.

From very early times the Romans adopted Greek cults and religious ideas. The first temple of Apollo was built in 431 BC during a plague. Apollo was especially favored by Augustus, who built a temple to him on the Palatine. Apollo is seen here (*below*), with his lyre, on a coin of c. 10 BC.

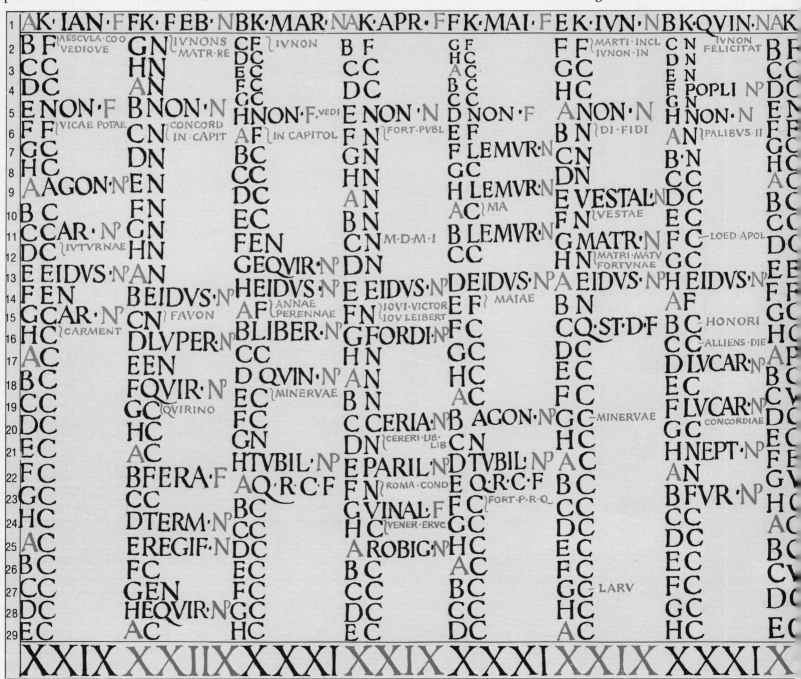

Divination based on the examination of entrails was an important part of both Roman and Etruscan religion. Etruscan diviners (*haruspices*) were considered especially expert and were regularly consulted by the Romans. This Etruscan mirror (*left*) shows the mythical seer Calchas in the guise of a *haruspex*.

Below Sacrifice of an ox, sheep and pig (*suovetaurilia*). From an early 4th-century monument of Diocletian, one of the last pagan emperors.

The six Vestal Virgins performed symbolic household tasks for the state. Above all they tended the sacred fire which burned continuously in a building in the Forum. Chosen between the ages of 6 and 10, the Vestals were bound to remain virgins for at least 30 years. Transgressors were buried alive.

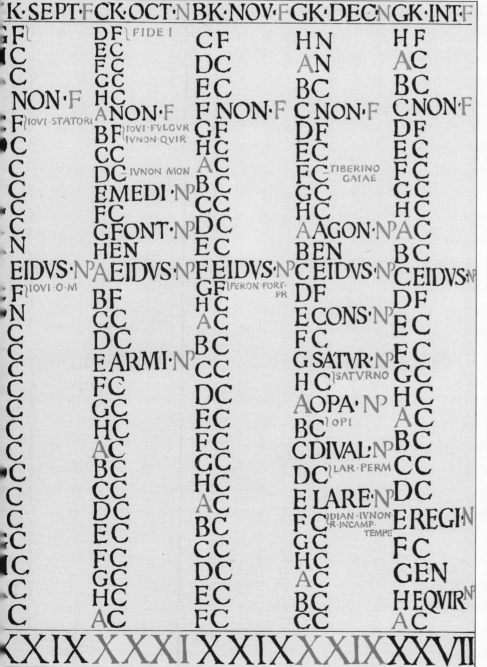

Before 46 BC, when Julius Caesar introduced the calendar we still use today, the Roman year consisted of 355 days, divided into 12 months: four of 31 days (March, May, Quintilis/July, October), one of 28 (February), and the rest of 29. In an attempt to keep the official calendar in line with the solar year the Romans used to insert an extra "intercalary" month of 22 or 23 days every other year. But this process was neither regularly nor competently carried out in practice, and the calendar was often seriously out of phase with the seasons. In order to make the necessary adjustment Caesar had to extend the year 46 BC by 90 days.

Our knowledge of the pre-Julian calendar is based partly on literary accounts and partly on an inscribed calendar from Antium, the *Fasti Antiates Maiores* (reconstructed *left*), the only pre-Julian calendar to survive.

Within each month there were three fixed points which originally corresponded with the phases of the moon. These were the Kalends, on the 1st day of the month, the Nones, on either the 5th or the 7th, and the Ides, on either the 13th or 15th. Days of the month were counted retrospectively (and inclusively) from these points. For example the battle of Cannae (2 August 216 BC) occurred on "the 4th day before the Nones of August" (for this reason the 4th day before the Nones was always considered unlucky). The months were also subdivided into "weeks" of eight days, with a market day (*nundinae*) every eighth day. On the calendars each day was marked with a letter from A to H, indicating its place in the nundinal cycle (see illustration). Besides the nundinal letter, each day was also marked with another letter or series of letters indicating whether it was a working day or a holiday. The letter F (*fastus*) marked an ordinary working day, the letter C (*comitialis*) one on which assemblies could be held. On days marked N (*nefastus*), however, certain types of public business were banned. Days marked EN (*endotercisus*) were split between the evening and morning, which were N, and the afternoon, which was F. The letters NP (probably *nefastus publicus*) usually designated the days of the great public festivals, the names of which were also included in abbreviated form – e.g. TERMI [*nalia*], AGON[*alia*], FORDI[*cidia*] etc. Apart from these fixed festivals (*feriae stativae*), there were a number of movable feasts (*feriae conceptivae*), such as the *Ambarvalia* (see above, p. 26), which did not appear in the calendar but were held on days which were determined each year by the pontiffs.

The festivals themselves were of very great antiquity, and most scholars would probably agree that the basic elements of the republican calendar date back at least as far as the 6th century BC. The festivals reflect the concerns of a simple agricultural community: to ensure the fertility of the soil and the health of the flocks, to promote childbirth, to placate the spirits of the dead, to avert disease and pestilence. A primitive warrior society is also implied in ceremonies such as the *Tubilustrium* (purification of the trumpets) on 23 March and 23 May, and the *Armilustrium* (purification of weapons) on 19 October. The rites performed at the various festivals were many and various; there was a good deal of mumbo jumbo, and by the late Republic the Romans themselves were unable to explain much of what they were doing or even to identify the gods who were being honored. Better-known festivals include the *Lupercalia* (15 February), a purification ceremony in which bands of naked youths ran around the Palatine, the site of the earliest settlement, striking any women they came across with strips of goatskin; and the *Saturnalia* (17 December), the forerunner of Christmas. At that time, according to Accius (see above, p. 54), "when people celebrate the day, they joyfully hold feasts throughout the countryside and towns, and each man waits upon his own slaves."

The Oriental Cults

The oriental religions which spread to Rome and the western provinces during the late Republic and early Empire belong to a world of ideas entirely different from the beliefs and practices of traditional Roman paganism. The traditional religions had fulfilled the needs of a simple agricultural society, and in their more advanced form gave sanction to the political activities and developing imperialism of the republican government of Rome; but they were increasingly found wanting in the cosmopolitan urban society of the Roman Empire. Oriental cults were first brought to the west by traders, merchants, and particularly slaves; it is significant that, for example, Eunus/Antiochus, the leader of the first Sicilian slave revolt (c. 136–132 BC), was a devotee of Atargatis, the "Syrian goddess," and derived much of his charisma from a claim to be her protégé. The large-scale manumission of slaves, and the spontaneous immigration occasioned by trade, led to the growth of sizable Greek and oriental communities in all the major cities of the western Empire, which became centers for the propagation of oriental cults, just as the Jewish communities of the Diaspora were centers for the spread of early Christianity. The movement of ideas was also facilitated by the ease of communication which Roman rule itself made possible.

The cult of the "Syrian goddess" was one of the most important of the increasingly popular mystery religions. Others include the Phrygian cults of Cybele and of Sabazios, the Egyptian Isis, and the Persian Mithras. One might add the Palestinian-Jewish cult of Christianity, which, although unique in certain respects, had much in common with the other oriental cults which were its rivals for a time.

The oriental cults differed from traditional paganism in that they made a direct appeal to the individual, offering him the chance of personal redemption through communion with the divine powers. The appeal to the personal convictions of the individual offered the possibility of conversion, which entailed ceremonies of initiation and the revelation of mysteries known only to a select and privileged group. There was a strong emphasis on ritual meals, on suffering as a means of atonement, and on ceremonies of purification. The most striking of the latter was the *taurobolium*, originally connected with the cult of Cybele, but later more generalized in usage; in a *taurobolium* the worshiper stood in a pit and was bathed in the blood of a bull sacrificed over him. He emerged from this rite in a state of purified innocence.

Part of the attraction of the mystery cults was that the initiate achieved an equality of status with his fellow believers which cut across existing social and ethnic barriers. Each of the mystery cults had elaborate rituals and liturgies, a complex theology and a doctrine of immortality; in short they were able to satisfy the aesthetic, intellectual and spiritual needs of all kinds of people in an often harsh and unjust world.

Mithraism originated in Persia and spread to the Roman Empire via Asia Minor in the 1st century AD. Mithras was a god of light, engaged in a permanent struggle with Ahriman, the evil prince of darkness. His role as creative god was symbolized in his slaying of the bull (*left*), whose flowing blood was the source of life and vegetation. The slaying took place in a cave, reflected in the underground location of Mithraic chapels, like the one beneath the church of St Clemente at Rome (*below*). Mithraism was an exclusively male cult, and was especially popular among soldiers, through whose agency it spread through the frontier provinces of the Empire. It possessed a rigid hierarchy of priesthoods and grades of initiation, and emphasized loyalty and discipline.

Right Relief showing an *archigallus*, or high priest of Cybele, with the robes and implements of his profession. The rites of the goddess were ecstatic and involved wild dancing, flagellation (notice the flail held by the *archigallus*) and self-mutilation. Those who went to the extreme of self-castration became her priests and were known as *galli*. From the first the Roman government suspected the strange new cult it had inadvertently admitted (see opposite). Originally Roman citizens were barred from the ceremonies and forbidden to join the ranks of fanatical eunuch priests, but this regulation was relaxed under the emperors.

The cult of Isis and her consort Osiris-Serapis, whose ceremonies are seen (*below*) in a wall painting from Herculaneum, was a hellenized version of an old Egyptian cult which spread through the Mediterranean world in the Hellenistic period. It was already established at Pompeii by 100 BC, and in Rome by the time of Sulla. The cult was repeatedly persecuted by the government until the time of Caligula, who officially recognized it and built a temple to Isis in the Campus Martius. The myth of Isis symbolized creation, in the death and resurrection of Osiris and Isis conception of Horus over his body.

The Phrygian deity Sabazios was variously identified with Jupiter and Dionysus, and often confused with Attis. Characteristic of his cult were votive offerings of hands, covered with magical symbols, in this case (*below*) the signs of the Zodiac. They make the liturgical sign of benediction, with thumb and first two fingers extended.

Below The jackal-headed figure of the Egyptian god Anubis, on a tombstone from the 1st- and 2nd-century catacombs at Kom el-Shuqafa at Alexandria. In ancient Egyptian belief, Anubis was connected with the rituals of death and the afterlife and is here seen in the dress and with the pose of a Roman soldier. ''Barking Anubis'' was among the monstrous oriental deities ranged by Virgil among the supporters of Antony and Cleopatra against the ancestral Roman gods on the side of Octavian.

The earliest oriental cult to be established in Rome was that of Magna Mater or Cybele, which originated in Phrygia in Asia Minor and was introduced into the Roman state religion in 204 BC as a result of a prophecy that she would help the Romans against Hannibal. A goddess of the earth, Cybele is often portrayed (*right*) riding a chariot drawn by lions, symbolizing her role as mistress of wild beasts. Her consort, who rides beside her, was the vegetation god Attis, whose death and resurrection were reflected by the seasons and celebrated with frenzied and ecstatic rites.

LCORNELIVS·SCIPIOOREITVS

The Emperors: Augustus to Justinian

The table expresses the changing nature of the imperial office: for its first two-and-a-half centuries, stable dynasties passing from one to another in a process accelerated by occasional civil war; in the 3rd century a rapid succession of short-lived emperors, their prospects of survival increasing towards the end of the century; and in the 4th and 5th centuries, after the flurry of the rise of Constantine, the restored stability of hereditary dynasties, based on the division of the Empire and collegiality of the imperial office.

The selected imperial portraits communicate the office as it was presented to successive contemporaries. The youthful paternalism of Augustus (here seen veiled as Pontifex Maximus) contrasts with the anxious thoughtfulness of Maximinus, an image picked up in more stylized form in the determined features of Diocletian and Maximian. The statue of Barletta in Italy has often been connected with Valentinian I, whom this tense, authoritarian character seems to fit; but the style is of the 5th rather than the 4th century, and the best candidate may be Marcian. Finally, the elderly Justinian, in an image of remote tranquillity.

Augustus

Maximinus

Diocletian
and Maximian

27 BC–14 AD	Augustus	
14–37	Tiberius	
37–41	Gaius	Julio-Claudian dynasty
41–54	Claudius	
54–68	Nero	
68–69	Galba	
69	Otho, Vitellius	
69–79	Vespasian	
79–81	Titus	
81–96	Domitian	
96–98	Nerva	
97–117	Trajan (97–98 with Nerva)	Flavian, Nervo-Trajanic, and Antonine dynasties
117–38	Hadrian	
138–61	Antoninus Pius	
161–80	Marcus Aurelius (161–69 with Lucius Verus)	
180–92	Commodus	
193	Pertinax	
193	Didius Julianus	
193–211	Septimius Severus	
211–17	Caracalla (211–12 with Geta)	Severan dynasty
217–18	Macrinus	
218–22	Elagabalus	
222–35	Alexander Severus	

Period of political anarchy and disorder

235–38	Maximinus
238	Gordian I and II (in Africa)
238	Balbinus and Pupienus (in Italy)
238–44	Gordian III
244–49	Philip
249–51	Decius
251–53	Trebonianus Gallus
253	Aemilianus
253–60	Valerian
253–68	Gallienus (253–60 with Valerian)

WEST		EAST	
259–74	Gallic empire of Postumus, Victorinus, Tetricus	260–72	Palmyrene empire of Odaenathus, Zenobia, Vaballath

268–70	Claudius
270	Quintillus
270–75	Aurelian
275–76	Tacitus
276–82	Probus
282–83	Carus
283–84	Carinus and Numerian

284–305 Diocletian and Tetrarchy

WEST		EAST	
287–305	Maximian Augustus	284–305	Diocletian Augustus
293–305	Constantius Caesar	293–305	Galerius Caesar
305–06	Constantius Augustus	305–11	Galerius Augustus
305–06	Severus Caesar (306–07 Augustus)	305–09	Maximinus Caesar (309–13 Augustus)

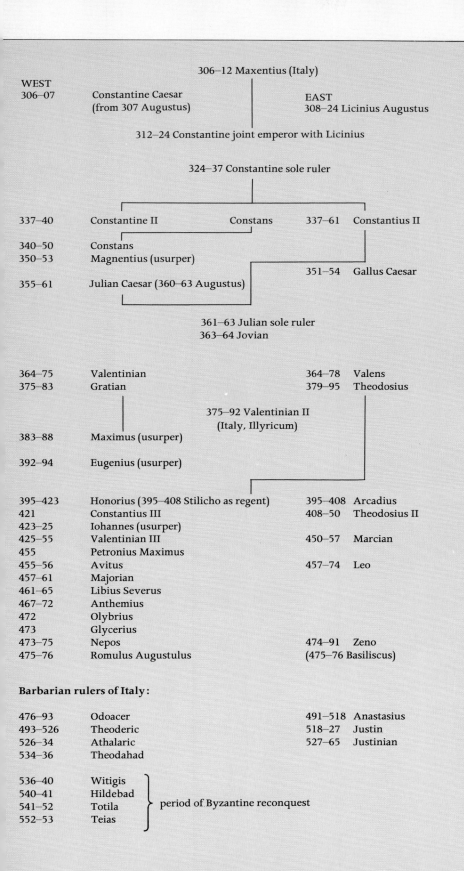

WEST		EAST	
	306–12 Maxentius (Italy)		
306–07	Constantine Caesar (from 307 Augustus)	308–24	Licinius Augustus

312–24 Constantine joint emperor with Licinius

324–37 Constantine sole ruler

337–40	Constantine II	Constans	337–61	Constantius II
340–50	Constans			
350–53	Magnentius (usurper)			
			351–54	Gallus Caesar
355–61	Julian Caesar (360–63 Augustus)			

361–63 Julian sole ruler
363–64 Jovian

364–75	Valentinian	364–78	Valens
375–83	Gratian	379–95	Theodosius

375–92 Valentinian II
(Italy, Illyricum)

383–88	Maximus (usurper)
392–94	Eugenius (usurper)

395–423	Honorius (395–408 Stilicho as regent)	395–408	Arcadius
421	Constantius III	408–50	Theodosius II
423–25	Iohannes (usurper)		
425–55	Valentinian III	450–57	Marcian
455	Petronius Maximus		
455–56	Avitus	457–74	Leo
457–61	Majorian		
461–65	Libius Severus		
467–72	Anthemius		
472	Olybrius		
473	Glycerius		
473–75	Nepos	474–91	Zeno
475–76	Romulus Augustulus		(475–76 Basiliscus)

Barbarian rulers of Italy:

476–93	Odoacer	491–518	Anastasius
493–526	Theoderic	518–27	Justin
526–34	Athalaric	527–65	Justinian
534–36	Theodahad		

536–40	Witigis	⎫	
540–41	Hildebad	⎬	period of Byzantine reconquest
541–52	Totila		
552–53	Teias	⎭	

Above Marcian (?)   *Below* Justinian

Trajan's Army

Apollodorus of Damascus, the designer of Trajan's column and of the monumental complex which provided its setting, was one of the great practical geniuses of antiquity. The column presents a narrative of the two Dacian wars of Trajan (101–02 and 105–06 AD) in the form of a continuous relief spiral over 200 meters in length. Though hard to see from ground level, the sculptures would originally have been viewed from galleries in the buildings of the Bibliotheca Ulpia surrounding it. Despite difficulties of detail, and in the almost complete absence of other evidence, the narrative of the Dacian campaign can be traced with considerable precision.

Apart from the interest of their narrative technique and artistic style, the reliefs are full of accurately perceived details of the Roman army at work. They illustrate not only the actual fighting but the marching, the building and engineering, the medical and transport facilities, and, not least, the religious observances, which framed the working life of the Roman army.

Throughout the series, the figure of Trajan recurs, usually accompanied by advisers: addressing and reviewing his troops, performing sacrifice, receiving embassies and prisoners, sometimes (as *right*) simply gazing forward with a studied calm foresight. He is presented as the "fellow soldier" of his men, and with this word, *commilitones*, he would address them in speeches.

The musicians (*below*) are from a procession associated with a sacrifice. Their instruments are valveless, but the leader of the band, who plays a pipe with a hollow mouthpiece, rather like a cornett, is using his right hand to produce a change of pitch or tone. The Legio III Augusta at Lambaesis in Africa had on its strength 39 trumpeters (*tubicines*) and 36 horn players (*cornicines*, as here).

Roman *ballistae*, resembling large crossbows, could attain considerable accuracy and range (up to 500 meters has been estimated). The two arms were operated by torsion springs of sinew cord, held in the drums at each side. Here two varieties are shown. *Below* a *ballista* is being brought up in a cart to be transferred to its prepared emplacement. The reconstruction (*right*), with its much sturdier carriage, is of a genuinely mobile version – a sort of Roman field gun, drawn by two mules.

In this scene (*below*), from the early stages of the first Dacian war, a camp is being built by legionaries, whose pikes, helmets and shields are propped up nearby. Some soldiers excavate a double ditch, carrying the earth away in baskets, while others construct the ramparts with squared pieces of turf, some of which are laid out in the foreground. The ramparts are stabilized with wooden cross-ties; the sculptor has shown the ends of these, apparently without understanding what they are. Trajan is shown looking out from his camp. To the left, more legionaries build a wooden bridge over a stream, beyond which (earlier in the narrative) is another, completed camp with its sentry. Below, a Dacian prisoner is brought to Trajan (off left) by two auxiliaries.

The detail (*below*), from the final assault on the Dacian capital of Sarmizegetusa, shows auxiliary troops leading the attack, both regular infantry, armed with short swords and rectangular shields, and archers clad in scale armor. The latter were recruited from the east, notably from the regions of Commagene, Emesa and Ituraea. Seen in their full context, they are covering the infantry from the rear, firing over their heads at the defending Dacians. Slingers and legionaries are also involved in the attack. As they appear on the column, legionaries wear rounded, while auxiliaries wear conical, helmets. Auxiliaries usually, though not in this instance, carry oval shields.

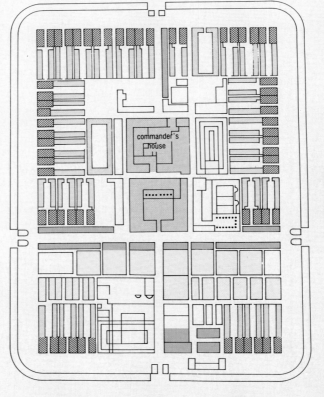

Left The standard bearer of a praetorian cohort. The shaft of his standard is decorated with the victory crowns won by his cohort, and with the image of the emperor, and is surmounted by the emblem of his unit.

Right Novaesium (Neuss), on the Rhine frontier in Lower Germany, was a typical permanent legionary fortress. Its neat barrack blocks accommodated upwards of 5000 legionaries divided into ten cohorts, and each of these into six centuries, nominally of 100 men but in practice rather smaller.

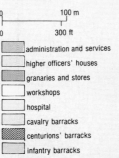

commander's house

	100 m
0	300 ft

- administration and services
- higher officers' houses
- granaries and stores
- workshops
- hospital
- cavalry barracks
- centurions' barracks
- infantry barracks

Above the most famous of all Roman military formations, the *testudo* or "tortoise," used for approaching the walls of an enemy in siege warfare. It is here being used in an attack on the citadel of a Dacian hill fort.

A POLITE AND POWERFUL EMPIRE

Imperial affairs

During the century and a half from 70 to 235 AD, the Roman Empire was by common consent at its height both of political and of cultural achievement. It was a period of slow development rather than of rapid change or spectacular events. Gibbon could write of the emperor Antoninus Pius (138–61) that he "diffused order and tranquillity over the greatest part of the earth," with the result that his reign provided few materials for history – "which is, indeed, little more than the register of the crimes, follies and misfortunes of mankind." Gibbon was thinking of regular narrative history with a military and political bias; yet, behind the obvious prosperity of the Antonine age, some of the changes which occurred in the military balance of the Empire in relation to its neighbors ultimately transformed the social basis of imperial power and led to the very different conditions of the 3rd century and late Empire. At the same time, in changes in the sensibilities of the 2nd century one detects the origins of some of the most distinctive cultural and religious features of late antiquity.

From a political point of view, this was a period of generally well-established imperial dynasties, the main moments of upheaval occurring in the civil wars of 69–70, which brought the Flavians to power, and of 193, from which emerged the dynasty of the Severi. The principle of succession under the Flavians was one of family inheritance, Vespasian being succeeded by his sons: the popular but short-lived Titus (79–81) and Domitian (81–96). The latter was a complex personality combining moral puritanism and religious archaism (he had an adulterous Vestal Virgin entombed alive) with a tyrannical intolerance which caused the last years of his reign to decline into a bloody persecution of those, especially philosophers, who expressed opposition to him. His denigration by the satirist Juvenal as a "bald Nero," lashing a half-dead world and enslaving Rome (*Satires* 4.38), was from this point of view at least not inappropriate.

The attractions of Nerva as imperial candidate upon the unexpected murder of Domitian in a palace plot (18 September 96) were in part his childlessness, which seemed to allow some room for political maneuver, as well as his personality and reputation as a mild, blameless senator. But Nerva's brief reign (96–98) was insecure and turbulent, and a major crisis and perhaps renewed civil war were only averted by his hasty adoption of Trajan, commander of the armies of Upper Germany. Trajan and his successor Hadrian, being without children, had recourse to adoption as a means of securing continuity of power; but both the accession of Hadrian in 117 and the preparations for his succession were marred by political unrest and the executions of potential rivals.

With the exceptions of Domitian and Commodus, the political conduct of the emperors of the Flavian and Antonine dynasties was relatively restrained,

and opposition, though intermittently expressed, was not widespread. Hostility to the memory of Hadrian can be ascribed to the confusion and acrimony surrounding his attempts to secure the succession; his first choice, Aelius Caesar, adopted in 136 from an Italian senatorial family, died prematurely and was replaced by the later emperor Antoninus Pius. There was little unrest among the provincial armies, such as had brought Vespasian to power in 69 after the proclamations of other candidates in Spain, Germany, Africa and at Rome. Domitian had to suppress the rebellion of Antonius Saturninus in Germany in 89–90, and Marcus Aurelius was threatened by the uprising in the east in 175 of Avidius Cassius, governor of Syria. This rebellion, perhaps set afoot in the knowledge of Marcus' advancing age and the apparent unsuitability of Commodus for the succession, seems to have won some support in court circles close to Marcus himself. His wife Faustina was believed to be implicated, but Marcus refrained after Cassius' suppression from investigations that might have proved embarrassing.

The government of the Flavians and Antonines was characterized, again with relatively few exceptions, by restraint and sobriety. This was especially true of Vespasian, who alleged in support of his notorious financial parsimony the immense cost to the Empire of the civil wars of 69–70. But even Vespasian spent heavily on rebuilding at Rome, and the short reign of Titus was marked by lavish expenditure, especially on the occasion of the inauguration of the Flavian Amphitheater (the Colosseum), and on further rebuilding after a fire at Rome. Titus was also much praised for relief measures after the destruction of Pompeii and Herculaneum by the eruption of Vesuvius in 79. It has been argued that Domitian was confronted by serious financial crisis, perhaps consequent on his raising of military pay by one-third. This would indeed provide a motive for his prosecutions of senators, but the extent of the financial crisis, if it existed, remains uncertain. The Flavians also exacted responsible conduct from provincial governors, Domitian especially being insistent on this. The biographer Suetonius, no lover of Domitian, remarked that governors were at no time more restrained and honest than under this emperor.

The military policy of the Flavians shows care and consistent planning, especially in their re-designing of the frontier in the upper Rhine and Danube regions. Domitian's Dacian wars, at first catastrophic, with major defeats in 85 and 86, were later successful at the battle of Tapae (88), and prepared the way for Trajan's wars and annexation of Dacia. Among the terms agreed by Domitian with the Dacian king Decebalus was the provision to the Dacians of Roman engineers, an early instance of the "foreign aid programs" which have so often introduced outside influences to less advanced though previously independent peoples.

This silver sestertius was issued by the emperor Titus to commemorate the inauguration in 79 AD of the Flavian amphitheater. Begun by Vespasian as part of his embellishment and reconstruction of Rome after the civil wars of 68–70, the amphitheater could seat upwards of 70000 spectators, and remained in use until the 6th century.

A silver tetradrachm issued by Shimeon bar-Kosiba, or Bar-Kochba, the leader of the third Jewish revolt of 132–35 AD. The legends are (*above*) "Shimeon," with an image of the Temple facade, and (*below*) "of the freedom of Jerusalem."

The relief (*top*), from the *lararium*, or household shrine, of L. Caecilius Jucundus of Pompeii, vividly expresses the effect of the earthquake which in 62 AD damaged large parts of the city before its destruction by the great eruption of Vesuvius in 79.

The two Dacian wars of Trajan resulted in the annexation of Dacia as a Roman province (107 AD). Here, in a relief from Trajan's column (*above*), is shown part of the final battle against Decebalus, after which the Dacian king committed suicide. A recently published inscription records the exploit of the Roman soldier, Tiberius Claudius Maximus, who took Decebalus' head to Trajan.

The annexation of Dacia can be seen as a defensive maneuver in the overall strategic context of the northern frontiers of the Empire, but Trajan's wars of 101–02 and 106 were presented to the Roman public in a spirit of open imperialism; the sculptures of the Column of Trajan depict his campaigns with a wealth of detailed illustration covering all aspects of army life. The building of the Column, and of the Forum of Trajan in which it was placed, was largely financed by the royal treasures of the defeated Dacian king. Trajan's other military venture, an invasion of Parthia, apparently with annexation in mind, cannot be explained except as aggressive imperialism influenced by the desire to emulate Alexander the Great. Begun in 115, the project foundered in 117 with the emperor's illness and death in Cilicia, leaving unsecured annexations and unrest in Judaea, Egypt and Cyrenaica to be suppressed by Hadrian. Hadrian abandoned the attempt to conquer Parthia – if indeed Trajan had not already done so. After the second Jewish revolt of Bar-Kochba (132–35), he destroyed Jerusalem, establishing in its place the legionary camp of Aelia Capitolina.

In temperament Hadrian was very different from his predecessor. Trajan was a plain soldier, Hadrian a restless, inquiring intellectual with a deep love of Greek culture. During his 21-year reign, he traveled ceaselessly, visiting his armies all over the Empire (an inscription preserves a speech delivered by him to the soldiers stationed at Lambaesis in Numidia after he had reviewed them and watched their maneuvers) and cultural centers like Athens and Alexandria. The versatility of his tastes is well represented by his two most famous monuments: the imperial residence at Tibur (Tivoli), reflecting in its design the influence of his worldwide travels, and Hadrian's Wall, massively defining the military frontier of Britain and of the entire Roman Empire at its most northerly and remotest point.

By contrast with both Trajan and Hadrian, Antoninus Pius never left Italy while he was emperor; he lived quietly at Rome, devoted to the government of the Empire and surrounded by a sober household and honest family virtues. In this latter respect too he was unlike Hadrian, whose wife Sabina was neglected and unhappy, and whose relationship with the boy Antinous was notorious; Hadrian indeed named a town in Egypt after him, following Antinous' accidental death by drowning in the Nile. For the later years of his reign, Pius ruled jointly with his nephew and adoptive son, M. Annius Verus (Marcus Aurelius), and died peacefully in 161. Marcus ruled as joint emperor with his adoptive brother L. Verus until 169, when Verus died while returning with him from Germany, having previously conducted a successful Parthian campaign. From 177 until 180 Marcus ruled with his son Commodus. His reign brings out acutely the tensions which were increasingly to affect the Roman Empire and change the structure of its government. A Stoic philosopher and, both in ancient and modern times, one of the most admired of all Roman emperors, Marcus set out in Greek in his *Meditations* his most personal thoughts, as they occurred to him and without literary elaboration (their original title was simply "To himself"). He had not aspired to the office of emperor and did not much enjoy wielding the power which it gave, but through his philosophy possessed an immensely strong sense of the obligations of the station in life to which he had been called, and to which he owed the full exercise of his moral and intellectual powers. Marcus wrote the *Meditations* while involved in the wars against the northern enemies of Rome, the Quadi and Marcomanni, which for several years of his reign required his presence in the theater of war. The campaigns, like those of Trajan, were narrated on a column at Rome, in a coarser, but in some ways more vigorous and no less aggressive style than that of Trajan's Column; they were not for aggrandizement, but for the defense of the Empire against mounting pressure on the Danube frontier. This was to be the abiding pattern of Roman military history in the next century.

Marcus died at Vindobona (Vienna) in 180, while conducting these wars. His son and successor, Commodus, was criticized for the haste with which he made a settlement with the barbarians and returned to Rome. Commodus clearly preferred living at Rome to conducting campaigns on the frontiers. The history of his reign largely concerns his activities in the capital, especially conspiracies mounted against him and violently suppressed, his excessively lavish generosity in providing public games, to which he was personally devoted, the food riots which led him to sacrifice his favorite, the freedman Cleander, and the religious ambition which led to his adoption of Hercules as his personal deity and in due course to his identification of himself with the god; Commodus appears on coins and in statue busts dressed in a lionskin and wielding a club, as worn and carried by Hercules.

Commodus fell to a conspiracy on New Year's Eve

Above Marble bust of the emperor Hadrian, c. 120 AD.

Right Hadrian's villa at Tivoli (Tibur), well characterized as a group of freely related pavilions or as a "contrived architectural landscape" (B. Cunliffe), was influenced in its various stages by monuments admired by the emperor during his travels. The effect is sophisticated, cultured and rather nostalgic. Here is seen the "Canopus", reproducing an architectural feature seen at this Egyptian city. Hadrian's memories of Egypt were mixed, for his young lover Antinous, seen *below* in one of many idealized representations, was drowned there.

The boar-hunt roundel (*below center*), reused in the 4th-century arch of Constantine, shows Hadrian in a typical pose of imperial leisure. The Sasanian image shown below (p. 168) forms an interesting comparison.

Right The new Pantheon or "shrine of all the gods" at Rome, shown here in Panini's painting of c. 1750, is a Hadrianic masterpiece, although the original dedicatory inscription of Agrippa was allowed to remain. The diameter of the huge cupola – at over 45 meters the largest ever built by preindustrial methods – corresponds exactly to its height from the floor, so that it forms in effect the upper half of a perfect sphere. It is an image of the vault of the heavens, and the opening at its summit symbolizes the sun.

192. His successor, P. Helvius Pertinax, was a military officer whose service in the wars of Marcus Aurelius had raised him swiftly from equestrian rank to the consulship in 175. Pertinax failed to satisfy his supporters and, partly by the rigor of his policies, acquired too many new enemies; after less than three months in power he was murdered by the Praetorian Guard. He was succeeded by Didius Julianus, a hitherto respectable senator and the grandson of a great jurist of the time of Hadrian, who was able to raise the money to secure his acceptance by the Praetorians to the tune of 25 000 sestertii per man. At once, however, the armies of Pannonia proclaimed their commander, Septimius Severus, as emperor. In a rapid march to Italy Severus suppressed Julianus and then, in a pattern of civil war reminiscent of 69–70, defeated in battle his rivals Pescennius Niger, the commander of the armies of Syria, in 194, and Clodius Albinus, proclaimed in Britain but defeated near Lugdunum (Lyon), in 196. After overcoming Niger, Severus had already embarked on a campaign against Parthia, intending partly at least to divert public attention from civil war to a successful foreign conquest; he returned to the east after his victory over Albinus, in order to consolidate his conquests. The result of Severus' wars against the Parthians was the annexation of northern Mesopotamia and the setting of the Roman frontier at the Tigris, but he failed to capture the caravan city of Hatra further to the south.

Septimius Severus bestowed on his sons Caracalla and Geta official nomenclature implying continuity with the Antonine dynasty, and in early coin issues appears himself with the designation "son of the deified Marcus Pius." His reign was notable for his generous building programs and public expenditure, particularly at his native city of Leptis Magna in Tripolitania. He conducted military campaigns in Britain, where he died after a painful illness in 211. His successor Caracalla (M. Aurelius Antoninus) campaigned on the Rhine and Danube frontiers and visited Alexandria before embarking in 216 on a Parthian campaign. In the following year Caracalla was assassinated near Carrhae (Harran) in Syria, in favor of his Praetorian Prefect Macrinus.

As far as their domestic policies are concerned Septimius Severus and his son are not well regarded by the ancient sources; both he and Caracalla are reported, with some but not total exaggeration, to have put to death large numbers of senators and men of equestrian rank. Severus' deathbed advice to Caracalla was reputed to have been to preserve concord with his brother, enrich the armies and ignore the rest. Caracalla disregarded the first part of this advice, killing the young Geta in 212. As for the second part, the army was increased in size under the Severan emperors and better paid, and it received certain privileges, such as the right of soldiers to contract legal marriages while still in service. Despite the benefits received by the army it is not clear that the Severi particularly deserve the reputation which they have gained for "militarizing" the Roman Empire. More relevant to this process is the steady pressure on the northern frontiers which by its nature made the army more important and required its commanders to demonstrate military expertise to a degree not expected in the 1st and earlier 2nd centuries.

After the brief intermission of Macrinus (217–18), an eastern conspiracy produced an imperial candidate from among the Syrian relatives of Septimius Severus' wife, Julia Domna. This was Varius Avitus Bassianus, better known as Elagabalus, a boy priest from the temple of Elagabal, the indigenous god of Emesa (Homs). In a brief but eccentric reign, the most notable event was the importation to Rome of the black conical stone representing the god of Emesa, an event which is suggested on some coin issues of Elagabalus. The emperor is reported to have preceded on foot the carriage bearing the stone, walking backwards in obeisance. The more lurid of the stories told by some ancient sources on the reign of Elagabalus must be treated with caution, as must the fictionally idealistic picture which they present of Alexander Severus, Elagabalus' successor upon his murder in 222. Alexander, another easterner from the same family, was a weak emperor, dominated by his mother Julia Mammaea. After a fair start, his reign soon brought political disorder with the murder after little more than a year of his praetorian prefect, the jurist Ulpian, and continued without distinction. In 231 he set out on a campaign against Parthia but was compelled to return to face a more immediate threat on the Rhine frontier. At Moguntiacum (Mainz) in 235 he and his mother were murdered by the soldiers and a new emperor, C. Julius Maximinus, proclaimed. The conspiracy was inspired by the sheer insufficiency of Alexander to meet the military crisis facing the Empire, and the accession of the military officer Maximinus inaugurates a new phase of Roman history.

Military and economic expansion

Tacitus, writing in the early 2nd century, ascribed to the admirers of Augustus in 14 AD the view that the Roman Empire had already at the time of his death achieved a state of strategic completeness; the Empire was "enclosed by the Ocean or by distant

The commemorative medallion (*above*), issued in the last month of Commodus' reign, shows the emperor wearing the lion-skin headdress of Hercules. The reverse of the medallion, not illustrated, has Hercules with the features of Commodus and the legend "HERCULI ROMANO" – "to the Roman Hercules!"

The detail from the column of Marcus Aurelius (*above right*) shows a barbarian captive on the point of his dispatch by a Roman soldier. His face is distorted in agony and his outstretched right hand expresses despairing supplication; the movement of his hair suggests the shock of the impact of the spear in his back.

rivers, with legions, provinces, fleets, all linked together and interconnected" (*Annals* 1.9). The validity of this judgment is debated, some critics thinking it more relevant to the situation in Tacitus' own day than to the time of Augustus. Apart from the conquest and annexation of Mauretania and Britain by Claudius – which might be taken to refine rather than to contradict the judgment reported by Tacitus – considerable improvements to the strategic defense of the Empire were made during the Flavian and Trajanic period. Under the Flavians, the agreement reached by Nero with Parthia in 66 AD, and the suppression of the Jewish revolt by Titus, were followed by an intensified occupation of Syria, the introduction of a garrison to Cappadocia for the defense of the upper Euphrates crossings and systematic road-building for purposes of military communication in the region between Palmyra, the cities of northern Syria and the Euphrates. In Germany an equally well-designed and carefully executed policy involved the annexation and fortification of the reentrant salient between the upper Rhine and Danube, the territory known as the *Agri Decumates*. This policy, begun by Vespasian, continued by Domitian and brought to completion in the first half of the 2nd century, permitted more economical and flexible deployments in the north, in that it became possible to release troops from the Rhine frontier to the Danube, where the military threat from barbarian peoples was more pressing and seemed likely to increase. Already under Nero a governor of Moesia had encountered kings "previously unknown and hostile" to the Romans, suppressed an "eastern movement" of Sarmatians and entered into diplomatic relations with Bastarnae, Roxolani and Dacians, and had settled 100 000 Transdanubians on the Roman side of the river, with their wives, children and princes. The Dacian wars of Domitian prepared the way for those of Trajan, the outcome of which was the annexation of the kingdom of Decebalus as a new province, bounded in the east by the Aluta river (Olt), in the west by the Marisia (Mures) and Tisia (Theiss), and in the north and northeast by the barrier of the Carpathian mountains. This annexation, like the unfulfilled intention ascribed to Marcus Aurelius to create new provinces of Marcomannia and Sarmatia, can be interpreted as defensive. The province of Dacia secured the Roman bank of the Danube by forming a powerful salient, defined by natural geographical features, projecting into barbarian territory beyond the river.

In the east, Septimius Severus, as we have seen, established a new province of Mesopotamia covering the area south of Armenia as far east as the Tigris and as far south as Singara on the Djebel Sinjar. This acquisition was potentially provocative, in that it deprived the Parthians of what they regarded, and continued to regard, as their ancestral dominions, but it offered protection in depth to the Roman cities of Syria, which now stood far behind the front line. At the same time cities in Mesopotamia such as Nisibis (modern Nisaybin), Resaina and Singara were colonized. Particularly interesting is the Severan expansion into southern Numidia, which took the Romans westwards along the edge of the Sahara desert, for a short period as far as Castellum Dimmidi (the oasis of Messad). Aerial photography

and field surveys on the southern and western fringes of the Aurès mountains, especially in the region of El Kantara and around the Chott el-Hodna, have revealed field-systems, irrigation works and settlement of the Roman period, on a scale and of a sophistication never achieved at any other time in history. Further north, in the plains between the Aurès mountains and the city of Sitifis (modern Sétif), can be traced large-scale settlement organized by imperial procurators through the medium of substantial townships, described on their inscriptions, of the later Severan period, as *castella*. The early 3rd century saw the greatest physical expansion of the Roman Empire and provides the most consistent evidence of the systematic exploitation of the agricultural resources of its border regions.

During the course of the first two centuries the provinces of the Roman Empire gained steadily in prosperity. A spectacular instance of this is the evidence for wine and oil imports, particularly from Spain, in the huge pile of broken pottery (50 meters in height) known as the Monte Testaccio or "Hill of Sherds" in the ancient warehouse quarter at Rome. In the 2nd and 3rd centuries, imports of olive oil from Numidian and proconsular Africa won a leading position in the popular market for this product. The great city of Thysdrus (El Djem) in proconsular Africa, with its immense amphitheater (the third largest in the Empire) of the early 3rd century and its rich mosaics, owed its prosperity to the expansion of the export trade in oil. In Numidia there developed on the same basis a thriving inland economy of substantial village communities and townships. For the Roman metropolitan market, supplies of African corn organized by imperial agents both in the province and in Rome, produced and shipped by specialized methods, vastly outweighed those brought from other sources or grown in Italy itself, though Africa did not gain proportionately from the transaction. Other parts of the Empire, like Britain and northern Gaul, Germany and the Danubian provinces, achieved a high standard of material culture, despite having begun as what would now be called underdeveloped countries.

As this survey implies, the wealth of the Roman Empire was based almost entirely on land. Commercial activity, though fundamental to the wealth of great trading cities like Alexandria, Palmyra and Dura-Europus, and an important part too of the prosperity of coastal cities like Leptis Magna in Tripolitania, did not rank with agriculture as a producer of wealth over the Empire as a whole. In any case the greater part of trade and commerce in the Empire was local in extent (the high costs of land transport would in themselves be enough to ensure this), and the commercial functions of the cities would often be performed by the landowners themselves and their agents. Industrial activity also, though more significant than sometimes assumed and obviously contributing to the material life-style of the Empire's cities, was not developed in such a way as to achieve large-scale production.

The visible urban prosperity of the Roman Empire was therefore based on the production of wealth by the labors of an agricultural population, of which relatively little is specifically known from the surviving evidence. The status of this agri-

The sun god of Emesa, shown on a coin of Elagabalus as a fire carried on a four-horsed chariot. Elagabalus had himself been boy-priest of the cult and, on becoming emperor, imported the god to Rome.

provincial capital, where known
Roman acquisitions to 201 BC
Roman acquisitions to 100 BC
Roman acquisitions to 44 BC
Roman acquisitions to 14 AD
Roman acquisitions to 96 AD
Roman acquisitions to 106 AD

ATLANTIC OCEAN

Cantabrian wars c 19 BC

LUSITANIA 27 BC province

EMERITA AUGUSTA

CORDUBA

BAETICA 27 BC province

TINGI

MAURETANIA TINGITANA

Provinces and frontiers of the Empire to 106 AD. On the completion of Trajan's Dacian wars, the Roman Empire had essentially reached its full extent. With the Flavian annexation of the "Agri Decumates," the northern land frontier was as short as it could be without the further advances into central Europe attempted, but abandoned, by Augustus. Dacia was less exposed than it looks, since its limits were based on geographical features and the Romans controlled the territory to the east and west of it; yet it was the only major province to be abandoned in the 3rd century (maps pp. 171 and 173). The only further acquisitions of any note after 106 AD were the annexation of Mesopotamia and some short-lived advances in Mauretania.

The formal distinction between "senatorial" and "imperial" provinces, though increasingly effaced in practice, remained valid, but the 2nd and 3rd centuries saw a considerable growth in their number, by division for ease of administration. Compare the provinces of the Severan and Tetrarchic periods (map p. 173).

cultural population varied widely, many being tenants of private landowners, whether local or absentee, or of the emperor, whose landed property throughout the Empire, acquired by gift, confiscation and intestacy, was very extensive. In the case of absentee landlords, the administration of estates would be performed by agents; in the case of imperial property by procurators. The oppressive behavior of imperial procurators in part of North Africa happens to be known from the inscriptions recording the successful attempts by the emperor's tenants, or *coloni*, to secure protection.

The degrees of wealth produced by agricultural exploitation varied very widely, providing at one extreme landowners of immense resources, like Herodes Atticus at Athens. At the same time many landowners, especially in smaller cities, barely reached the qualifying census for membership of the local council, or *curia*, the relatively modest figure of 100 000 sestertii. At a level below that of curial status and economically continuous with it, it is clear that there existed in most parts of the Empire a free peasantry of sometimes quite substantial farmers and smallholders, owning their land and

disposing of its produce in local markets.

An expression of the economic advance of the western provinces of the Empire during the first two centuries is to be found in the origins of the most significant Latin writers of the period. Following the two Senecas and Lucan from Corduba, the poet Martial and the writer on oratory Quintilian were also from Spain (respectively from the native towns of Bilbilis and Calagurris). Though an African origin has been suggested, the satirist Juvenal is more likely to have come from Aquinum in central Italy, and the younger Pliny was a Transpadane Italian from Comum. Tacitus, however, was a southern Gaul who married into a wealthy family from Forum Iulii (Fréjus). Africa provided a particularly rich contribution, with the biographer Suetonius coming from Hippo Regius in proconsular Africa, Fronto from Cirta, Apuleius from the Flavian colony of Madauros and the Christian polemicist Tertullian from Carthage. No known writer came from Pannonia until Victorinus, bishop of Poetovio (Ptuj, formerly Pettau) in the early 4th century, and Britain is absent from the register for almost another hundred years. Yet

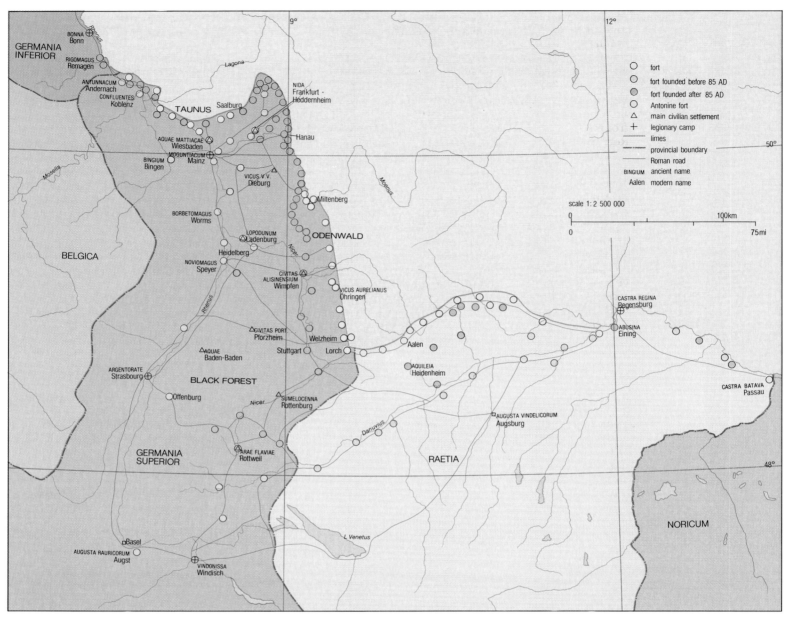

appearances can be deceptive. Central and western Gaul, after a long silence in the first three centuries, suddenly produced an efflorescence of distinguished writers in the 4th century, which is inexplicable unless the province had earlier possessed its share of literary culture. Britain produces the only known allusion on a Roman coin to Virgil as well as mosaic illustrations of episodes from the *Aeneid*, and its spoken Latin is argued to have been of a conspicuously high standard.

The steady extension of the Roman citizenship during the first two centuries of the Empire, by grants to individuals and to communities, meant that by the Severan period its possession had ceased to be a real asset or distinction. By a constitution of Caracalla, the *constitutio Antoniniana* of 212 AD, all free inhabitants of the Empire became Roman citizens. It is clear from the number of individuals who from this time appear in documents with the names M. Aurelius, after the official titulature of Caracalla, that many were enfranchised. The measure was nevertheless not of fundamental importance except, in the view of contemporaries (shared by modern critics), as a fiscal measure; Caracalla had thereby increased the numbers of the

inhabitants of the Empire liable to taxation. The privileges previously inherent in the citizenship — such as the privilege claimed by St Paul of freedom from arbitrary beating by order of Roman officials (Acts 22:24ff.) — were maintained as part of a now more precise social distinction, that between men of ''more honorable'' and ''more humble'' status (*honestiores* and *humiliores*): the former can be broadly identified as the members of the curial class of the cities of the Empire. *Honestiores* were exempt from certain punishments, such as consignment to the state mines, corporal punishment and torture (except in certain defined cases such as treason), and execution by burning alive or exposure to wild beasts. The distinction between the two classes first appears in legal texts in the time of Hadrian, but it is evident that it was applied in practice before this, and reflects well-established Roman assumptions as to the differing values to be attached to men of different social rank.

The widening origins of the ruling classes
The origins of the emperors of the Flavian, Antonine and Severan dynasties reflect in social terms the steadily expanding political franchise and economic

The German-Raetian *limes* from Vespasian to the Antonines. The map brings out the coherence of the advance of the *limes*, as the line of frontier forts is pushed forward from the Rhine and Danube to the advanced positions of the Antonine period. The greater east-west mobility provided by the new frontier, and the possibilities for greater freedom of military deployment, are also apparent. The advanced frontier was itself, however, based on no great physical barrier and was maintained largely by moral prestige. In the late Empire the annexed region was abandoned and frontier defense again based on the Rhine and Danube, heavily reinforced by fortification on and behind the rivers (see p. 192).

development of the Roman world. The Flavians came from municipal origins at Reate (Rieti), in old Sabine territory; Vespasian was said by Tacitus to have promoted an atmosphere of "domestic parsimony" typical of new men from Italy and the provinces after the excesses of the Julio-Claudian period. Trajan and Hadrian were from Spain, from the city of Italica in Baetica. Antoninus Pius was from Nemausus (Nîmes), an ancient tribal center and Roman colony in southern Gaul, and his dynasty, through the prematurely deceased Aelius Caesar and through Marcus Aurelius (whose grandfather was from Spain), presents an example of connections between wealthy provincial and Italian families such as often occurred in the first two centuries among the aristocracies of the west. Septimius Severus and his family widen the range still further. Severus himself was from Leptis Magna, an ancient Punic city which, through the generosity of its leading families, had very quickly asserted its prosperity and civic pride under the Roman Empire. It has been suggested that Septimius Severus was descended from a family of Italian émigrés to Africa in the time of the late Republic. This was indeed the background of several provincial senators at Rome, such as Seneca and the poet Lucan, perhaps also of the emperor Trajan; but it seems certain that Severus was in fact a member of a leading Punic family of Leptis, whose great-grandfather had come to Rome as a senator in the later 1st century. By his marriage to Julia Domna, whom he met while serving in Syria, Severus allied himself with a prominent Oriental family; we have already seen the political consequences of this marriage, in the rise to the imperial throne of the candidates of Syrian background, Elagabalus and Alexander Severus. The accession of the Danubian C. Julius Maximinus, popularly known as Maximin the Thracian, represents a new element in the widening of the social base of Roman political life which will be discussed later.

The imperial dynasties reflect the broadening provincial composition of the senatorial and equestrian governing classes of the Roman Empire. Statistical precision cannot be attempted on the basis of the surviving evidence, extensive though this is, but it is clear that those senators known in the Julio-Claudian period to come from central and northern Italy, southern Gaul and Spain, were followed under the Flavians by aspirants from Africa, where the city of Cirta (Constantine), with its huge and productive territory, plays a particularly prominent role. The Greek cities of Asia Minor, such as Ephesus and Pergamum, soon make their appearance; one family which has been studied in detail is that of the Plancii, from the less well-known city of Perge in Pamphylia. In the early 2nd century Trajan imposed a requirement, with what effect is not known, that all senators should possess a third of their landed property in Italy. He was evidently worried by the increasing numbers of provincial senators without connections in Italy, who were unlikely to commit themselves to the full obligations of a Roman senator.

Some parts of the Empire are conspicuously absent from the list of the provinces producing senators in this period. None came from northern or western Gaul, Germany or Britain, or from the Danubian provinces, though there is no reason to believe that these regions lacked the economic resources necessary to produce senators. Indeed, it had appeared to the critics of the policies of Claudius in the 1st century that many Gallic notables would, if admitted to the Roman senatorial order, eclipse their Italian counterparts in wealth (Tacitus, *Annals* 11.23). Sometimes, as in the case of Britain, sheer physical remoteness from the center of empire was obviously a factor, while elsewhere, as especially in Gaul, the existing social patterns were oriented towards local forms of expression, based on the countryside and on a developed villa economy rather than on the more urban life-style of the Mediterranean. In the case of Dalmatia, the coastal cities lacked the rich agricultural hinterland which might have generated the wealth necessary to the establishment of senatorial status. The economy of the inner Balkan area was and remained closely linked with the presence of the Roman army. The only known senator from Pannonia in the first two centuries was Valerius Maximianus, from Poetovio, who rose to senatorial rank, and to the consulship in 184 or 185, through his unbroken military service, especially in the wars of Marcus Aurelius. The case of Maximianus provides a good precedent for the transformation of the Roman governing class in the 3rd and 4th centuries. It is unlikely that he ever went to Rome to attend meetings of the senate or to assume his consulship, which he will have held in absence. Maximianus anticipates the growth of a provincial senatorial class in the late Empire, acquiring its rank from imperial service but not participating in the political and social life of the senate at Rome.

The widening social base of the governing class of the early Empire was thus an expression of two things: of the growth of provincial wealth as it developed under the *pax Romana* of the first two centuries, and of a tradition of service to the emperors and to the Empire which drew men into public careers and bestowed on them aristocratic status without involving them in the traditional duties of Roman senators. The importance of the senate in this development shifts from its political functions to its role as representing an order in Roman society.

Beside the regular senatorial career, broadly military or civil in its emphasis but with no clear or formal distinction between the two, developed similar opportunities for men of the equestrian order. These opportunities took them through posts known as procuratorships, of which something has already been seen; they were administrative positions connected with the emperors' possessions in the provinces but leading to a wide range of functions in which the procurator played an important role alongside the official governor of the province. It was the view of the jurist Ulpian that, in a fiscal matter involving the interests both of proconsul and of imperial procurator, the proconsul would "do better to abstain" (*Digest* 1.16.9). From such positions a procurator might advance to governorships of smaller provinces of equestrian status. The summit of the system of promotion was the high prefectures (see above, p. 74).

It is important not to exaggerate the degree of formalization implied by these careers. The crucial element in the promotion of an individual might, in this as in any other type of career, be his access to

Linguistic divisions of the Empire and physical conditions in relation to the distribution of cities. The distribution of urban settlement indicated is based on the physical development of cities rather than on their juridical status: the latter can disguise widely varying economic functions. In the most northerly provinces the importance of villa culture may yet again be emphasized (see p. 82). In the south and east, bordered by desert, the relationship between urbanization and the 250 mm isohyet, representing the limit of regular agricultural exploitation, is striking: cities lying outside this limit depend either on oases or on the delivery of water from distant mountains by major river systems. The correspondence of the olive-growing area with that of urbanization is also evident.

effective patronage, or the accident of the emperor's recognition of his merit at a fortunate moment, when others remained unnoticed. But a letter of appointment from Marcus Aurelius to a promoted procurator emphasizes his need to retain the emperor's favor by the vigor and integrity of his conduct. This clearly implies standards of conduct attaching to the office as such. The fact that the rank of procuratorships was defined by the salary attached to them – "centenariate" and "ducenariate" procurators, for instance, receiving respectively annual salaries of 100 000 and 200 000 sestertii – suggests that we have here at least the beginnings of a "bureaucratic" system. This is important in considering the origins of the late Roman state.

The financial qualifications required of candidates for political office ensured that members of this imperial "aristocracy of service" were still the products of the propertied upper classes. They were not specialized bureaucrats by background or training, but men educated in the traditional literary culture of the Roman Empire. It was assumed that a literary education provided the moral qualifications necessary for a good governor, and not until the late Empire were more specialized qualifications considered relevant.

Government and rhetoric

The actual processes of government of the Roman Empire remained much the same throughout the period from the Flavian to the Severan dynasties. The emperors did not customarily take major initiatives of their own, save in matters of military policy, nor were they equipped to do so. They neither possessed the means nor felt the need to consult public opinion; nor did they devise the instruments of active policy making which modern governments take for granted. Provincial governors administered their provinces at their own discretion, usually with only the most general guidelines from the emperors. The financial administration of the cities was one of the few areas where the

emperors did intervene, and did so more intensively as time went on, partly by the appointment of officials instructed to supervise the financial management of the cities and partly by requiring the consent of the emperor or provincial governor to municipal decrees on financial matters. In general, the emperors governed by responding to approaches made to them. If a community wished to address itself to an emperor, it would do so by passing a decree in proper form by council and assembly and sending it to the emperor, either by letter through the governor of the province, or by sending an embassy mandated to present its case in support of the decree. Inscriptions show that the participating in and financing of embassies was one of the forms of civic munificence most frequently undertaken by the leading men of local communities.

The normal procedure for an embassy, as illustrated by many anecdotes and by the advice given in handbooks of rhetorical practice, was simply for it to appear before the emperor, present the decree and make its supporting case as persuasively as it could. This procedure naturally involved the use of rhetoric (which was precisely the art of persuasion), and it is against this background of practical utility that it is at least partly possible to understand the immense prestige enjoyed by rhetoric in the Empire of the Antonine age. The literary movement known as the "Second Sophistic" is characterized by an amalgamation of literary and philosophical cultures to produce what has well been called a form of "concert oratory," often indulged in purely for display purposes. The framework of reference of this oratory (which survives mainly in Greek, with some examples in Latin) was set in past literature, especially in Homer and the Greek writers and orators of the 5th and 4th centuries BC. When, as in one episode, an Arabian sophist, addressing the emperor Caracalla in Germany, compares himself to Demosthenes appearing nervously before Philip of Macedon, the

Roman coinage, as here in an issue of Trajan, sometimes exemplifies what a modern observer might call social policy. Here is illustrated the "alimentary scheme," by which financial benefits were provided, by entailment on local estates, for young boys and girls of Italian cities. The coin beautifully catches a spirit of charitable paternalism, as the children reach out their hands to receive their benefits from the emperor.

comparison can appear forced and remote; but it was understood by all present as apt for the occasion, and provided the background of sympathy and common understanding against which more practical issues could be determined. It has been supposed that, in making constant appeal to a distant past, Greeks of the Roman Empire were compensating for their lack of any significant political power in their own day. There is some truth in this; on the other hand, this cultural framework did provide a mode of communication between individuals, and between communities and their emperor.

Civic munificence: the nature of the Antonine age

The period from the Flavians to the Severans is that in which the material prosperity of the Roman Empire can be seen at its most impressive. The surviving ruins, largely dating from this period, of the cities of the provinces were in themselves the proof, for Gibbon, that these provinces were "once the seat of a polite and powerful empire." The building inscriptions associated with the monu-

ments, as well as the commemorative inscriptions set up in honor of public benefactors, show that this civic grandeur was achieved through devotion to public duty and to the enhancement of their own prestige by the leading individuals of the cities. These worthies, who can be identified with the wealthier among the class of provincial councillors, took upon themselves in a spirit of willing generosity the provision not only of the material amenities of their cities, but of many of their social needs also, such as corn and wine distributions, the heating of public baths, the provision of games, the cleaning and lighting of the streets, the preservation of order in the countryside, as well as the supervision of many aspects of their financial and legal administration. It was men of this class who traveled abroad on embassies, offering this service too as an expression of civic pride and munificence.

During the later 2nd and early 3rd centuries, evidence begins to appear that the spirit of munificence which sustained the public life of the cities of the early Empire was beginning to be replaced by a reluctance to assume civic offices and their associated duties. The full extent and causes of

northern limit of vine growing
northern limit of olive growing
northern limit of date-palm growing
250mm annual isohyet
open desert
land over 1000 meters
distribution of cities
— — — division between Latin and Greek languages
CELTIC major local language surviving Roman period
Punic local language survival

this tendency to avoid public office, which if it grew would threaten the essential nature of the civic prosperity of the Empire, are not fully understood. One factor appears to have been the growing influence within the class of decurions of a minority of particularly wealthy members of the order, known as *principales viri*, whose rivalries with each other and with their neighbors in other cities tended to raise the cost of munificence to a level which only they could reach; at the same time, through their political influence, they were more successful than their colleagues in gaining exemptions from the less attractive civic burdens.

Anotner possible factor was growing imperial influence on municipal affairs. From the later 1st century the emperors had begun to intervene more directly in the financial management of the cities, for example by sending out officials, or *curatores*, to supervise individual cities, and by imposing more specific terms of reference upon provincial governors. The correspondence of the younger Pliny, who was appointed governor of the province of Bithynia and Pontus under Trajan, illustrates the activities of a senatorial governor sent out with instructions to inquire closely into the finances of the cities of his province, "since many things," wrote Trajan, "appear in need of correction." This concern of the government with civic finances appears to have arisen from uncontrolled expenditure rather than financial stringency: the letters addressed to Trajan by Pliny show such problems as the mismanagement of civic funds, over-ambitious building projects begun and then abandoned and the embezzlement of public funds by individuals, rather than any shortage of money. If this was true of Bithynia-Pontus, it must have applied still more strongly to the adjacent, more spectacularly wealthy province of Asia Minor. Both Bithynia-Pontus and Asia Minor show another feature which inevitably attracted the emperors' attention; civic unrest generated within communities by the competition for influence among members of the upper classes, and by rivalry between cities, as, in Asia, between Ephesus and Smyrna, and in Bithynia, between Nicaea and Nicomedia. This led to faction fighting and to riots, which the emperors were obviously unable to ignore.

The civic prosperity of the Antonine age derived from a successful combination of two potentially contradictory features – public-spiritedness and individualism. The combination was based on the classical recognition of virtue as essentially public, or civic, in nature. At the same time, the 2nd century was marked by the development of a more personal conception of individualism (see below, pp. 176–77). It involved the increasing popularity, for instance, of religions of personal salvation, like the cult of Isis, commemorated in the tenth book of Apuleius' *Metamorphoses*, and, of course, Christianity. Another source, the *Dream Book* of Aelius Aristides, is a document of the relationship of an individual with a tutelary deity, the healing god Aesculapius, who in Aristides' account expresses himself personally, through dreams and visions, to his devotee. Aristides was a neurotic hypochondriac, but hypochondria is nothing if not a personal preoccupation; it has been well described as one of the more disquieting features of the

Antonine age, embodied perhaps in the tremendous prestige of the doctor Galen. The individual fame, based on their personal talents, of the sophists and teachers of the Second Sophistic is well shown by the biographer of the sophists, Philostratus, who also wrote an account of the life and travels of a famous sage and wonder-worker, Apollonius of Tyana. Apollonius, to whom a cult was devoted and whose working of miracles later gained him comparison with Jesus Christ, can be set beside the philosophers and wise men of religious inspiration such as Peregrinus and Alexander of Abounoteichos, presented with satirical intent in the writings of Lucian.

The essential character of the Antonine age may then be summed up as residing in the balance which it achieved between private individualism and public munificence, the one seen as reinforcing the other. It is possible that the "slow and secret poison" that Gibbon detected in the age was not so much the disappearance of the spirit of liberty from a people over-indulged in peace, but the exuberant growth of a personal individualism, and the progressive weakening of the ideal of collective civic responsibility among many of those best placed to sustain it. In this period the lives of the cities and of their great individuals could flourish freely, and the Empire suffered no really damaging military threat, though the wars of Marcus Aurelius were a portent of what was to happen. It was in the 3rd century, after 235, and in the radically changed military, economic and political conditions which then came about, that the exuberance of the Antonine age was dissipated and a new social order evolved.

In an episode of the time of Nero, illustrated in the wall painting from Pompeii shown here, riots erupted between the Pompeians and visitors from neighboring Nuceria, in town for the gladiatorial games. The riots, in which the Pompeians' greater numbers gave them the advantage, so that "many Nucerians mourned the deaths of children or parents" and others were carried home injured (Tacitus), began with the exchange of insults at the games, but in the violence with which they developed they expressed a more deep-seated rivalry between the cities. This is suggested also by graffiti at Pompeii, such as "Nucerinis infelicia!" – "Bad luck to the men of Nuceria!" The episode resulted in the compulsory closure of the amphitheater for ten years. It illustrates the circumstances in which legitimate competition within and between cities could explode into destructive violence, and the restriction of local autonomy that could ensue.

PART THREE
PROVINCES OF THE EMPIRE

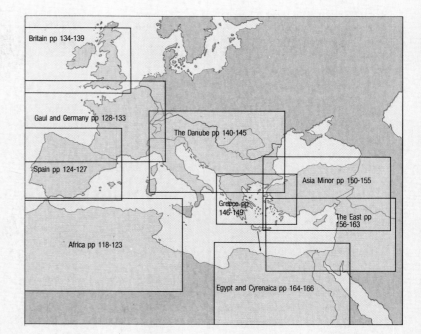

Britain pp 134-139

Gaul and Germany pp 128-133

The Danube pp 140-145

Spain pp 124-127

Asia Minor pp 150-155

Greece pp 146-149

The East pp 156-163

Africa pp 118-123

Egypt and Cyrenaica pp 164-166

Communications in the Roman World

The direct, meticulously surveyed and engineered roads of the Roman Empire are among its most durable monuments: their distinctive traces exist everywhere from Scotland to the Syrian desert. They were often first constructed for military purposes. They also carried the *cursus publicus*, or imperial courier service for the use of authorized officials. For the general traveler they possessed staging posts, or *mansiones*, where towns were more than a day's traveling distance apart.

The roads quickly acquired economic uses and sustained a heavy volume of commercial traffic. Import taxes were levied at provincial frontiers, and in the late Empire officials were detailed to inspect vehicles to prevent overloading. The costs of maintaining the roads fell partly on the communities through which they passed, and which shared their benefits.

The economic importance of the roads was limited by the slowness and high costs of land transport, especially of bulk goods: it was cheaper to ship corn to Rome from Egypt and Africa than to bring it by land from southern Italy. Most of the commercial traffic on the roads of the Empire was of a local nature. The efficiency of the administration, too, was restricted by the physical speed with which messages could travel. Yet in the effectiveness of its communication the Roman Empire outclassed its predecessors, and long-distance contacts were better maintained then than at any subsequent time until the modern period.

Left The paved main street, or *decumanus*, of the Roman colony of Timgad (see p. 123). It led to the legionary camp of Lambaesis, and to the plains of southern Numidia, currently being developed by imperial initiative.

The milestone near the arch of Severus at Leptis Magna (*above*) marks the length of the road inland as 44 miles.

The horse-drawn carriage (*far left bottom*), on a Gallo-Roman relief, is reminiscent of a stage coach, with passengers seated on the roof as well as inside. Its simple solidity well evokes the laborious nature of travel by land even on the fine roads of the Roman Empire.

Trajan's bridge over the Danube at Drobeta (shown *far left top*, from the simplified representation on Trajan's column) was designed by the famous architect, Apollodorus of Damascus. The historian Cassius Dio thought it the greatest of Trajan's achievements: "it has 20 piers of squared stone, 150 feet high excluding the foundations, and 60 feet wide. These are placed 120 feet from each other and connected by arches." Its building was an engineering miracle, in water "so deep and full of eddies, and on a bed so muddy." When after Trajan's death the superstructure was demolished to reduce access from the Dacian side, the piers remained in place, "as if erected solely in order to demonstrate that there is nothing which human ingenuity cannot accomplish."

The roads of the Roman Empire, the "Devil's causeways" of the medieval period, frequently underlie the modern road systems of former provinces. Here (*center left*) the Fosse Way, the highway from Exeter to Lincoln, passes through Somerset, its direct course contrasting with the winding nature of the local roads seen in the photograph, and with the varied patchwork of the field system.

The Peutinger Map

The Peutinger map, a 13th-century copy of a late Roman original, owes its name to a town clerk of Augsburg, who inherited it in 1508 from the humanist scholar, Konrad Celtes. In the form of a continuous, elongated chart, 6·80 × 0·34 meters, the map shows the known world from Britain to

India, though the most westerly portions are missing. The distorted projection is well illustrated by the section (VI) shown here. The land masses appear as horizontal strips, separated by the Mediterranean and Adriatic seas. Mountains and rivers are indicated, and towns represented by little groups of buildings, as in the illustrations to the *Notitia Dignitatum* (see pp. 118, 124, and for the more elaborate images of Rome and Ostia, p. 92). The map should, however, not be seen as an attempt to attain geographical accuracy, though in detail it does sometimes achieve this. It is rather a schematic diagram for the traveler, indicating towns, the distances between them and their location in the road system. It relates to the geography of the Roman Empire in much the same way that a diagram of a metropolitan railway system may relate to the actual configuration of the districts which it serves.

AFRICA

Map labels:
ICOSIUM Algiers, IOL CAESAREA Cherchell, TIPASA, CARTENNA Ténès, AQUAE CALIDAE, ARSENARIA, Cheliff, TIGAVA ZUCCABAR, CASTELLUM TINGITANUM El Asnam, QUIZA, Mostaganem, PORTUS MAGNUS, Oran, TASACCURA, MINA, COLUMNATA, MAURETANIA CAESARIENSIS, Tiaret, COHORS BREUCORUM, CASTELLUM DIMMI Messa, CASTELLU DIMM, RUSADDIR Melilla, SIGA, NUMERUS SYRORUM, POMARIA Tlemcen, ALTAVA, TINGI Tangiers, LIXUS, OPPIDUM NOVUM, RIF, MAURETANIA TINGITANA, BANASA, Beht, THAMUSIDA, VOLUBILIS, Subur, Fès, SALA Rabat, Casablanca, MOYEN ATLAS, ATLAS MOUNTAINS, Moulouya, HAUTS PLATEAUX, ATLAS SAHARIEN, Marrakech, HAUT ATLAS

8° 4° 0°
36° 34° 32° 30°

Urbanization in Africa was rapid and relatively uniform, though rather diversely based — in the east on Punic settlements and further west on the romanization of native centers. Penetration of the province followed the lie of the mountains, which run from west to east, allowing few easy communications from the interior to the sea. The Aurès mountains, encircled and penetrated during the 2nd century, were watched by the single legionary fortress of Lambaesis, with support from the colony at Timgad. The natives of the interior retained their identity: a confederation assembled during a 4th-century rebellion consisted, according to the historian Ammianus (29.5.28), of peoples "diverse in culture and in the variety of their languages," presumably dialects of "Libyan."

Romanized Africa was one of the most articulate of provinces. Renowned as the home of lawyers, it also produced many senators and *equites* and distinguished literary figures. Possessing links with the east, it received Christianity early, and in the 4th century, under the impulse of competition between Catholics and Donatists, developed an advanced episcopal structure.

The economy of Africa was closely linked with the outside world, not always to the advantage of the province. As well as its famed olive oil, profitably exported, Africa supplied Rome with corn under far less favorable terms. The evident wealth of the province would have been still greater, but for the profits that went overseas.

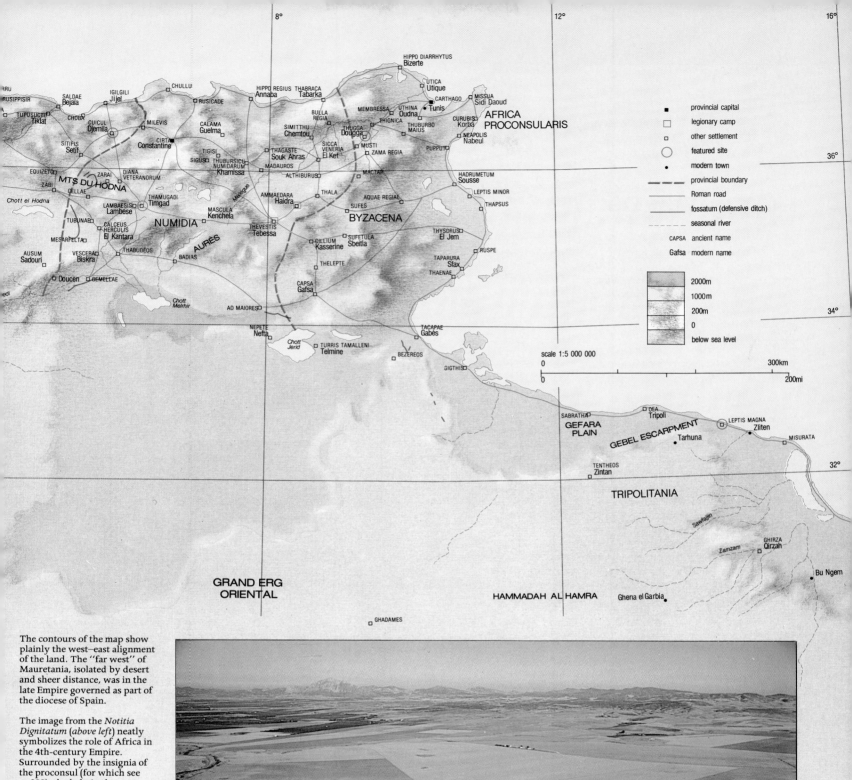

The map shows the following labels:

HIPPO DIARRHYTUS
Bizerte

RRU
RUSIPPISIR
SALDAE
Bejaïa
TUPUSUCTU
Tiklat
IGILGILI
Jijel
CHULLU
RUSICADE
HIPPO REGIUS
Annaba
THABRACA
Tabarka
UTICA
Utique
CARTHAGO
MISSUA
Sidi Daoud

CHOBA
CUICUL
Djemila
MILEVIS
CALAMA
Guelma
SIMITTHU
Chemtou
BULLA
REGIA
MEMBRESSA
THIGNICA
UTHINA
Oudna
Tunis
CURUBIS
Korba
AFRICA
PROCONSULARIS

SITIFIS
Setif
CIRTA
Constantine
TIGISI
SIGUS
THUBURSICU
NUMIDARUM
Khamissa
THAGASTE
Souk Ahras
THUGGA
Dougga
THUBURBO
MAIUS
NEAPOLIS
Nabeul

ZARAI
DIANA
VETERANORUM
THAMUGADI
Timgad
MADAUROS
SICCA
VENERIA
El Kef
MUSTI
ZAMA REGIA
PUPPUT

MTS DU HODNA
EQUIZETO
ZABI
QELLAE
MASCULA
Kenchela
ALTHIBURUS
MACTAR
HADRUMETUM
Sousse

Chott el Hodna
LAMBAESIS
Lambese
THAMUGADI
Timgad
AMMAEDARA
Haidra
THALA
AQUAE REGIAE
LEPTIS MINOR

NUMIDIA
AURES
CALCEUS
HERCULIS
El Kantara
THEVESTIS
Tebessa
SUFES
THAPSUS

MESARFELTA
VESCERA
Biskra
BADIAS
CILLIUM
Kasserine
SUFETULA
Sbeitla
THYSDRUS
El Jem

AUSUM
Sadouri
THABUDEOS
THELEPTE
RUSPE

Doucen
GEMELLAE
CAPSA
Gafsa
TAPARURA
Sfax
THAENAE

edi
Chott
Melrhir
AD MAIORES
TACAPAE
Gabès
GIGTHIS

NEPETE
Nefta
Chott Jerid
TURRIS TAMALLENI
Telmine
BEZEREOS

BYZACENA

GRAND ERG
ORIENTAL

SABRATHA
OEA
Tripoli
LEPTIS MAGNA
Zliten
MISURATA

GEFARA
PLAIN
GEBEL ESCARPMENT
Tarhuna

TENTHEOS
Zintan

TRIPOLITANIA

HAMMADAH AL HAMRA
Ghena el Garbia
GHIRZA
Qirzah
Zamzam
Bu Ngem

GHADAMES

■	provincial capital
□	legionary camp
□	other settlement
○	featured site
•	modern town
– – –	provincial boundary
——	Roman road
——	fossatum (defensive ditch)
– – –	seasonal river
CAPSA	ancient name
Gafsa	modern name

2000m
1000m
200m
0
below sea level

scale 1:5 000 000

0   300km
0   200mi

The contours of the map show plainly the west–east alignment of the land. The "far west" of Mauretania, isolated by desert and sheer distance, was in the late Empire governed as part of the diocese of Spain.

The image from the *Notitia Dignitatum* (*above left*) neatly symbolizes the role of Africa in the 4th-century Empire. Surrounded by the insignia of the proconsul (for which see p. 202), the lady in the upper register brandishes ears of corn; below are the ships laden with bags of wheat, under sail for Rome.

The countryman pouring wine (*left*), seen on a mosaic in the Bardo Museum, Tunis, illustrates the changeless face of rural life. He sits before one of the thatched huts built in the traditional native style, called by their Punic name, *mapalia*.

Carthage drew water supplies from a source near Zaghouan, over 50 kilometers distant. The water was conveyed to the city by the magnificent aqueduct, seen here (*right*) as it crosses a shallow valley near Uthina, and stored there in huge covered cisterns.

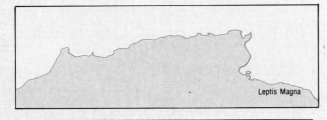

Leptis Magna

Leptis Magna, one of the group of three cities which gave its name to the district of Tripolitania (and to modern Tripoli), was a Punic foundation, perhaps of the 5th century BC. Little is known of its early history, but the wealth of Punic Leptis is shown by its payment of 1 talent a day to its overlord Carthage, and by the annual fine of 3 million pounds of oil later imposed by Julius Caesar on the city for its part in African resistance to him. The development of Leptis was continuous over the first two centuries of the Empire, with two particularly notable phases. In the first, under Augustus, monuments were provided by members of the Punic aristocracy which still dominated the city. The second was in the time of Leptis' most famous native, the emperor Septimius Severus, who visited the city, furnished a new forum and basilica, modernized the harbor and built the imposing colonnade leading from there to a monumental piazza by the Hadrianic baths.

In the late Empire Leptis remained prosperous, though with some retrenchment. It was the seat of the governor of Tripolitania and provides many inscriptions, but little new building, from this period. In the mid-4th century Leptis and its neighbors were troubled by tribal incursions from the desert. The fortunes of the city declined sharply under the Vandals, and by the time of the Byzantine reconquest the site was largely deserted.

The wealth of Leptis derived in part from trade and commerce. The main source of wealth, however, was agricultural development of the hinterland, based on the olive and on wheat.

The great Severan forum and basilica are seen (*above*) from the west, beyond (in the foreground) the market and Chalcidicum of the Augustan period. They, like the theater (*opposite*), were provided by members of the Punic aristocracy of the city. In the distance is a glimpse of the fertile coastal territory on which the wealth of Leptis depended. Shown *right* is a detail from one of a pair of pilasters of the Severan basilica, later reused to flank an apse of the church built in its ruins by Justinian. It shows scenes relating to Dionysus (Liber Pater), one of the patron gods of Leptis. A corresponding pair of pilasters shows scenes of the life of Hercules. The style of the sculpture has its closest affinities in the imperial art of Asia Minor.

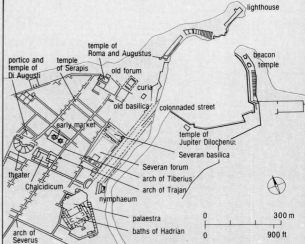

The Punic settlement was on the headland west of the harbor; the roads leading westward along the coast and to the country south of Leptis, and their influence on the later development of the city, are clearly visible on the plan of the site (*left*). The enlargement of the early settlement is suggested by the distance between the harbor and old forum and the theater, the latter built on the site of a Punic cemetery. The extent of the fully developed Roman city can only be appreciated with reference to the area still unexcavated. The circus stood at a distance of 1000 meters from the eastern habor mole, but the area between them remains unexplored.

The theater (*above*) was built in 1/2 AD by the Punic noble Annobal Rufus, son of Himilcho Tapapius, whose dedicatory inscription, beautifully engraved in Latin and Punic, is pictured (*left*). Immediately behind the stage facade, added under the Antonines, is a courtyard and portico built in the time of Claudius to enclose a small temple of the Di Augusti, or deified emperors. The title ''ornator patriae'' in the inscription represents a traditional Punic expression commemorating civic munificence. The title ''sufes,'' a civic magistracy equivalent to the Roman duumvirate, disappeared in 110 AD, when Leptis became a Roman colony. Its last bearer was the grandfather of Leptis' greatest benefactor, Septimius Severus.

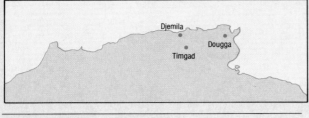

Dougga

Dougga (ancient Thugga) stands in a strong defensive position about 90 kilometers southwest of Carthage. A prosperous city long before the arrival of the Romans, its original population was a mixture of Punic and native Libyan: among its monuments is a mausoleum of the late 3rd or early 2nd century BC commemorating a Numidian prince, with an inscription in Punic and Libyan. After its annexation as part of the new province of Africa, the native inhabitants of Dougga continued to be governed by their own institutions, living side by side with a community of Roman citizens initially dependent on Carthage. Dougga became a formal municipality only in the early 3rd century. The irregular street plan (*below right*) and the buildings rising in terraces up the hillside reveal the native origins of the community. Nevertheless, Dougga acquired the standard amenities of a provincial Roman city – temple of the Capitoline gods, forum and senate house, and so on. The wealth of the city, derived from exploitation of the plains below, is expressed by the magnificence of some of its public buildings, notably the splendid theater, built in 168/9 AD, and the temple of Caelestis.

The street plan of Djemila clearly illustrates the city's course of development, the regular layout of the original foundation contrasting with the more casual pattern of the streets in the area of 2nd-century development. The architectural function of the Severan forum and basilica in unifying the now rather elongated city can also be clearly seen. The usual description of the southeast sector of the site as the "Christian quarter" is strictly misleading. The Christian monuments were built in the area of residential development of the 2nd century, but there is no reason to suppose that there was ever a time when this quarter of Djemila was Christian but the rest still pagan.

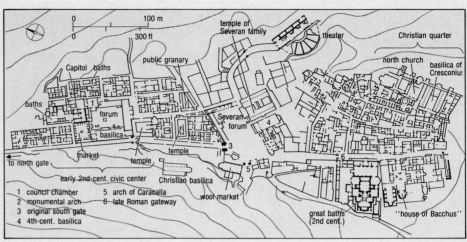

The Capitoline temple of Dougga (*left, above*) was dedicated in 166/7 through the generosity of members of the same family which donated the theater. No doubt because of the hillside terrain of the city, the main forum and associated public buildings face its flank rather than front steps and pediment. The wall around the base of the temple dates from the time of the Byzantine reconquest of Africa. The mosaic (*left, below*), showing a man fishing from a rock with line and landing net, is from a room in the "House of Dionysus and Ulysses". It is a conventional design, intended to reinforce the maritime character of the scenes shown in other mosaics in the room, Ulysses passing the rock of the Sirens, and Dionysus' encounter with the Tyrrhenian pirates.

The Severan arch at Timgad (*below*) marked the entrance to the original colonial foundation on the road from Lambaesis. It occupies the site of the west gate which, with the west wall, had been overrun by the 2nd-century development of Timgad.

Djemila

Djemila (ancient Cuicul) was founded under Nerva or Trajan as one of a series of veteran colonies along the road leading from Sicca Veneria (El Kef) to Cirta (Constantine). Cuicul soon received additional settlers from other parts of Africa and rapidly outgrew its original site. It spread to the south and up the slope of the hill behind the colonial settlement; the 2nd-century theater and bath complex in this district drew the focus of the town away from its original center, balance being restored by the creation of a new forum, basilica and other monumental buildings in the Severan period. Cuicul retained its importance in the late Roman and Byzantine periods. Fourth-century churches and an episcopal residence were constructed in the southeast quarter of the city, and the houses both in this district and in the region of the old forum have produced late mosaics of high quality. The prosperity of Cuicul was presumably based on the exploitation of its agricultural resources.

Timgad

The strictly regular layout of Timgad (ancient Thamugadi), shown as clearly in the aerial photograph (*left*) as in any site plan, demonstrates the circumstances of its foundation in 100 AD as a veteran colony by the Third Legion stationed at Lambaesis. By the mid-2nd century the settlement had already outgrown the limits of its original enclosure. As is especially clear on the western and southwestern sides, the new suburbs developed with a cheerful unconcern for the design of the military planners. The foundation was immensely successful and possessed every civilized amenity (including no fewer than 14 identified sets of bath buildings). It had a library, and in the 4th century among its many churches a great Donatist basilica.

SPAIN

Roman settlement of the Iberian peninsula was first directed to the eastern seaboard and to the valley of the river Baetis (Guadalquivir). The cities of these regions produced early senatorial families: an orator from Corduba founded one of the principal literary dynasties of early imperial Rome, while an imperial legate from Italica was father of the first provincial emperor.

The mountains to the north and northwest required subjugation, which was provided by Augustus' Cantabrian wars. Though also urbanized, these areas retained much of their indigenous character – Basque is a pre-Roman language – and a legion was maintained (at León) to ensure their contentment.

Partly in consequence of its small garrison, the contribution of Spain to the main political events of the Roman Empire did not match its social and economic importance. Rebellion there inaugurated the "year of the four emperors," and Spain played an important role in the political disintegration of the Empire in the early 5th century.

The peninsula yielded precious metals and copper, especially from mines in the Rio Tinto valley northeast of Huelva, and at Vipasca near Beja (Pax Iulia) in Portugal. Among other products, exports of wine to Rome reached massive proportions in the first two centuries.

Christianity came early. The records of the council of Elvira (Illiberris) in 306 provide evidence for the distribution (see p. 179), organization and moral concerns of the immediately pre-Constantinian church. In the Gallaecian emperor Theodosius Spain contributed Catholic intolerance, supported by legislation, to the christianization of the Empire, and in the ascetic teacher Priscillian the first "heretic" martyr.

The Spanish peninsula suffered considerably in the 5th-century invasion, but its centuries of Roman, followed by Gothic and Arab, occupation lend to its early cultural landscape an almost unique complexity.

Above Spain in the *Notitia Dignitatum*. The provinces of the diocese are shown as ladies wearing mural crowns, carrying baskets – the fruits of the provinces in taxation. The *vicarius*, like the proconsul of Africa (p. 118), has the inkstand symbolizing judicial competence (see p. 203).

The splendid chariot team (*below*) is from a circus mosaic from a villa near Barcelona. Two of the horses' names are shown, Pa[n]tinicus ("Winner") and Calimorfus ("Beauty"): the substitution of *f* for *ph* is common in later Latin. Spain was in the 4th century a leading producer and exporter of racehorses.

BAY OF BISCAY

CANTABRIAN MOUNTAINS

PYRENEES

MEDITERRANEAN SEA

SIERRA DE LA DEMANDA

SIERRA DE GUADARRAMA

SERRANIA DE CUENCA

SIERRA DE GREDOS

MONTES DE TOLEDO

TARRACONENSIS

SIERRA MORENA

SIERRA NEVADA

GIGIA
Gijon
PORTUS VICTORIAE   FLAVIOBRIGA
IULIOBRIGA
Retortillo
LANCIA
UXAMA BARCA
Osma
ARACELI
Araquil
POMPAELO
Pamplona
IACA
Jaca
IUNCARIA
Figueras
VIROVESCA
SEGISAMO
Sasamon
LIBIA
Leiva
VAREIA
CALAGURRIS
Calahorra
GRACCURIS
Alfaro
CASCANTUM
Cascante
OSCA
Huesca
AESO
Avella
EMPORIAE
Ampurias
PALLANTIA
Palencia
TURIASSO
Tarazona
AUGUSTOBRIGA
ILERDA
Lerida
IESSO
Guisona
AUSA
Vich
GERUNDA
Gerona
RAUDA
Roa
CLUNIA
NUMANTIA
Soria
CAESARAUGUSTA
Zaragoza
BAETULO
Badalona
SEPTIMANCA
Simancas
UXAMA ARGELA
Osma
BARCINO
Barcelona
TERMES
BILBILIS
CELSA
CAUCA
Coca
ARCOBRIGA
Arixa
TARRACO
Tarragona
MANTICA
Salamanca
SEGOVIA
SEGONTIA
Siguenza
DERTOSA
Tortosa
AVELA
Avila
COMPLUTUM
CARACA
ERCAVICA
POLLENTIA
Pollensa
Minor
MAGO
TITULCIA
Tagus
SEGOBRIGA
Cabeza de Griego
LEIRIA
(EDETA)
Liria
SAGUNTUM
PALMA
BALEARES
CAESAROBRIGA
Talavera de la Reina
VALERIA
Valera Vieja
Turia
Maior
TOLETUM
Toledo
VALENTIA
Valencia
AUGUSTOBRIGA
Talavera la Vieja
CONSABURA
Consuegra
Cabriel
Jucar
MIROBRIGA
Capilla
SISAPO
Almaden
LAMINIUM
LIBISOSA
Lezuza
SALTIGIS
SAETABIS
Jativa
ORETUM
AD ARAS
DIANIUM
Denia
MELLARIA
Fuente Obejuna
Segura
ILICI
Elche
TUCENTUM
Alicante
CASTULO
Cazlona
BEGASTRUM
Cehegin
EPORA
Montoro
CORDUBA
Cordoba
OBULCO
Porcuna
CARTHAGO NOVA
Cartagena
ASTIGI
Ecija
UCUBIS
TUCCI
Martos
URSO
Osuna
BASTI
Baza
ANTICARIA
Antequera
ILLIBERIS
ACCI
Guadix
MALACA
Malaga
ABDERA
Adra
MURGI
URCI
Huercal
ARUNDA
Ronda
CALPE
Gibraltar

Noguera
Ebro
Duero
Pisuerga
Oca
Genil
Guadiana

scale 1:3 400 000

■	provincial capital
☐	legionary camp
▫	other settlement
○	featured site
---	provincial boundary
—	Roman road
BASTI	ancient name
(EDETA)	later name
Baza	modern name

2000m
1000m
200m
0

3°   0°   42°   40°   38°   36°

0   200km
0   150mi

Italica

Italica, the native city of Trajan and Hadrian, was the oldest community of Roman citizens in Spain, but came late to municipal status. Long overshadowed by the romanized native city of Hispalis (Seville), Italica underwent a transformation in the time of Hadrian. The city was redesigned in Hellenistic fashion. It acquired a huge amphitheater with a capacity of 25 000, hardly justified by the population of Italica itself, and fine town houses with elegant mosaics. The development of the city was always to some extent artificial; in the 3rd and later centuries Italica again yielded local primacy to Seville.

Below Fine mosaic floors of a house that has been excavated in the northern sector of Italica. They date from the time of Hadrian's embellishment of the city. Surviving sculptures are Greek in inspiration and it is possible that Greek craftsmen were employed.

Right The famous aqueduct at Segovia. Its 128 arches stride across the center of the city for 800 meters.

Below right The bridge at Alcantara over the Tagus river. Nearly 200 meters in length, it carried the Roman road between Norba and Conimbriga in Lusitania.

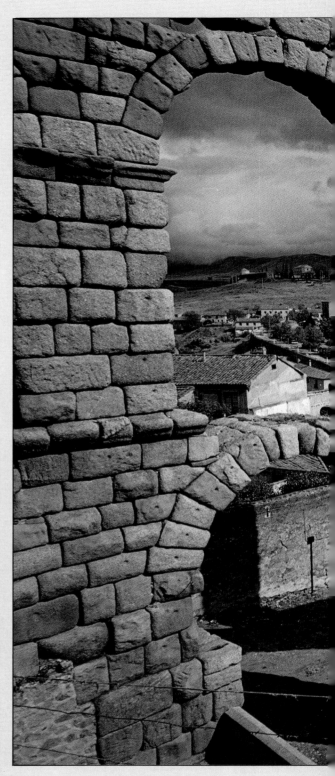

Segovia

Segovia, a relatively unimportant Roman town, formerly a Celtic stronghold, is famous mainly for its fine aqueduct, which brought water from a source about 16 kilometers distant to a distribution point, or *castellum*, from where it was fed to the township. Like the bridge of Alcantara it is a fine example of the transformation of civic amenities made possible by the combination of Roman engineering skills and local initiative. The pride of the people of Segovia in their aqueduct is evident: sculptured images of it are sometimes shown on their epitaphs.

Alcantara

The bridge of Alcantara is a particularly notable instance of public initiative and cooperation under the Roman Empire, being built by 11 Lusitanian communities whose names were listed on inscriptions on the bridge. The height of the roadway above the water may seem excessive and wasteful, but in winter spate the river can rise almost to the level of the arches. The expertise and pride of the architect, C. Julius Lacer, are eminently justified: in an inscription at the site, he declared that his achievement would "last for ever through the ages."

GAUL AND GERMANY

Below left The command of the Dux Tractus Armoricani in the *Notitia Dignitatum*. Armorica (roughly Brittany and Normandy) was not a province but a coastal command. Among the posts shown is the *litus Saxonicum* or "Saxon shore" (see p. 171).

The social history of the Gallic provinces was dominated by the geographical contrast between the urbanized south, already hellenized through cities like Massilia (Marseille) and Antipolis (Antibes), and the regions north and west of the Massif Central, known expressively as Gallia Comata – "long-haired Gaul." Here, with heavier open soils permitting large-scale agricultural exploitation, the countryside comes into its own. Cities are more widely separated and great villas like that of Estrées-sur-Noye (overleaf) and rural shrines like Sanxay are typical. A third area, the military zone adjoining the Rhine, fostered a population of soldiers and their dependants. These lived, married and often retired locally, requiring civilized comforts in their cities and country houses.

Despite the social conservatism of non-Mediterranean Gaul, a substantial commercial and trading class emerged, as suggested by many grave reliefs illustrating its activities. There was also technical innovation, in the use of waterpower and in agriculture (pp. 182–85).

In the late Empire the balance changed in favor of the north, as an imperial court based at Trier attracted increased financial and material resources, and was the center of a vastly increased bureaucratic establishment.

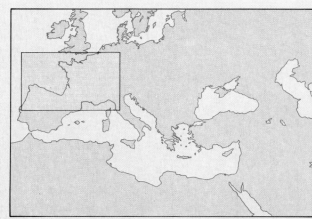

The bronze statuette from Trier (*below*), originally part of a larger group, shows a countryman, who is evidently working outdoors – possibly, as suggested by his forward movement and by his hands, which once held circular poles or handles, guiding a plow.

The city of Autun (Augustodunum) quickly emerged under the Empire as a center of liberal studies, with an early theater and amphitheater and a large wall circuit with well-proportioned monumental gates. One of these, the "Porte d'Arroux" leading north across the river, is shown *above*.

Rhineland glassware was often both very handsome and of extremely delicate workmanship. The jug shown (*above right*), with snake thread decoration, comes from Urdingen.

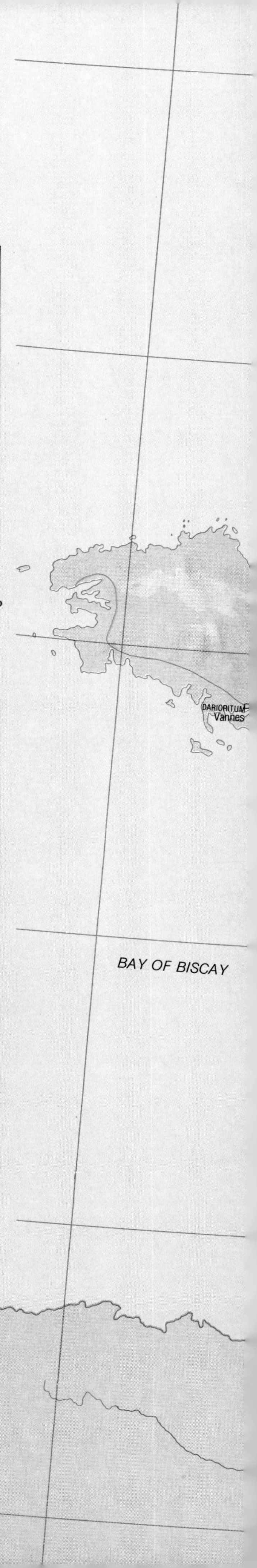

DARIORITUM Vannes

BAY OF BISCAY

ENGLISH CHANNEL

MEDITERRANEAN SEA

provincial capital
legionary camp
other settlement
featured site
provincial boundary
Roman road
LUTETIA *ancient name*
(BONONIA) *later name*
Dijon *modern name*
= *Alpine pass*

2000m
1500m
400m
200m
0
below sea level

GERMANIA INFERIOR

BELGICA

LUGDUNENSIS

GERMANIA SUPERIOR

AQUITANIA

NARBONENSIS

ALPES GRAIAE ET POENINAE

ALPES COTTIAE

ALPES MARITIMAE

TAUNUS

VOSGES

BLACK FOREST

JURA

ALPS

MASSIF CENTRAL

PYRENEES

scale 1:4 000 000

0   150km
0   100mi

LUGDUNUM BATAVORUM
Valkenburg
TRAIECTUM
Utrecht
fossa Corbulonis
FORUM HADRIANI
(MUNICIPIUM CANANEFATUM)
Voorburg-Arentsburg
NOVIOMAGUS
Nijmegen
VETERA
Xanten
ATUATUCA
Tongeren
TEUDURUM
Tüdden
NOVAESIUM
Neuss
DIVITIA
Deutz
COLONIA AGRIPPINA
Köln
IULIACUM
Jülich
BONNA
Bonn
RIGOMAGUS
Remagen
ANTUNNACUM
Andernach
CONFLUENTES
Koblenz
AQUAE MATTIACAE
Wiesbaden
MOGUNTIACUM
Mainz
BINGIUM
Bingen
NOVIOMAGUS
Neumagen
OROLAUNUM
Arlon
BUZENOL
Buzenol
AUGUSTA TREVERORUM
Trier
BORBETOMAGUS
Worms
NOVIOMAGUS
Speyer
LOPODUNUM
Ladenburg
TABERNAE
Rheinzabern
CASTELLUM NENAPIORUM
Cassel
GESORIACUM
(BONONIA)
Boulogne
TARVENNA
Thérouanne
TURNACUM
Tournai
BAGACUM
Bavai
NEMETACUM
Arras
CAMARACUM
Cambrai
AUGUSTA VIROMANDUORUM
Vermand
SAMAROBRIVA
Amiens
CORIALLUM
Cherbourg
IULIOBONA
Lillebonne
AUGUSTODURUM
Bayeux
BRIVODURUM
Briare
ROTOMAGUS
Rouen
CAESAROMAGUS
Beauvais
MINATIACUM
Nizy
Estrées-sur-Noye
NOVIODUNUM
Soissons
DUROCORTORUM
Reims
DUROCATALAUNI
Châlons-sur-Marne
DIVODURUM
Metz
NASIUM
Naix
TULLUM
Toul
ARGENTORATE
Strasbourg
AQUAE
Baden-Baden
SUMELOCENNA
Rottenburg
ARAE FLAVIAE
Rottweil
NOVIOMAGUS
Lisieux
MEDIOLANUM
Evreux
AUGUSTOMAGUS
Senlis
LUTETIA
Paris
DUROCASSES
Dreux
COROBILIUM
Corbeil
AUTRICUM
Chartres
LEGEDIA
Avranches
SEII
Sées
NOVIODUNUM
Jublains
SUINDINUM
Le Mans
AGEDINCUM
Sens
AUGUSTOBONA
Troyes
ANDEMATUNNUM
Langres
NOVIOMAGUS
Dijon
AQUAE MATTIACAE
CENABUM
Orléans
AUTESSIODURUM
Auxerre
ALESIA
Alise
DIBIO
Dijon
BESONTIO
Besançon
AUGUSTA RAURICORUM
Augst
VINDONISSA
Windisch
IULIOMAGUS
Angers
CAESARODUNUM
Tours
TASCIACA
Thésée
AVARICUM
Bourges
ABALLO
Avallon
BIBRACTE
Beuvray
AUGUSTODUNUM
Autun
AVENTICUM
Avenches
EBURODUNUM
Yverdon
PORTUS NAMNETUM
Nantes
SEGORA
Bressuire
LIMONUM
Poitiers
ARGENTOMAGUS
Argenton
DECETIA
Decize
CAVILLONUM
Chalon-sur-Saône
TINURTIUM
Tournus
VIVISCUS
Vevey
Sanxay
RAURANUM
Rom
AQUAE NERI
Néris-les-Bains
VOROGIUM
Vouroux
NOVIOBUNUM
Nyons
GENAVA
Geneva
OCTODORUM
Martigny
Great St Bernard Pass
MEDIOLANUM
Saintes
NOVIORIGUM
Royan
AUGUSTORITUM
Limoges
ICULISMA
Angoulême
AUGUSTONEMETUM
Clermont-Ferrand
FORUM SEGUSIAVORUM
Feurs
GERGOVIA
Gergovie
LUGDUNUM
Lyon
VIENNA
Vienne
AXIMA
Aime
DARANTASIA
Moutiers
AUGUSTA PRAETORIA
Aosta
Little St Bernard Pass
MEDIOLANUM
Milan
VERCELLAE
Vercelli
BLAVIA
Blaye
VESUNNA
Périgueux
UXELLODUNUM
Puy d'Issolu
SEGUSIO
Susa
Mt Genèvre Pass
AUGUSTA TAURINORUM
Turin
BURDIGALA
Bordeaux
VALENTIA
Valence
BRIGANTIO
Briançon
EBURODUNUM
Embrun
VASATES
Bazas
AGINNUM
Agen
DIVONA
Cahors
ANDERITUM
Javols
VASIO
Vaison
SEGUSTERO
Sisteron
DINIA
Digne
ELUSA
Eauze
CACTORA
Lectoure
SEGODUNUM
Rodez
ALBA
Aps
ARAUSIO
Orange
CARPENTORATE
Carpentras
SANTIUM
Senez
VINTIUM
Vence
AQUAE TARBELLICAE
Dax
VIRODUNUM
Verdun
TOLOSA
Toulouse
ELIMBERRIS
Auch
LUTEVA
Lodève
NEMAUSUS
Nîmes
GLANUM
St Rémy
UCETIA
Uzès
TARASCO
Tarascon
VENNIO
Avignon
CABELLIO
Cavaillon
AQUAE SEXTIAE
Aix-en-Provence
CEMENELUM
Cimiez
NICAEA
Nice
ANTIPOLIS
Antibes
ALBITIMILIUM
Ventimiglia
FORUM IULII
Fréjus
AQUAE CONVENARUM
Bagnères-de-Bigorre
LUGDUNUM CONVENARUM
St Bertrand-de-Comminges
BAETERRAE
Béziers
AGATHE
Agde
CARCASO
Carcassonne
NARBO
Narbonne
MASSILIA
Marseille
ARELATE
Arles
RUSCINO
Castel Roussillon
VALENTIA
Valence
CULARO
(GRATIANOPOLIS)
Grenoble

Estrées-sur-Noye

Despite its being a relatively unknown site of which nothing stands above ground, the great rural villa at Estrées-sur-Noye (Somme) is no less typical of the economic development of provincial life in the west than great cities like Nîmes and Trier. The villa is one of many in northern France surveyed in recent years by systematic aerial photography. *Below* appears an artist's reconstruction of the villa based on its actual site plan. It consists of a main residence, at the far end of the photograph, and before it a courtyard lined with cottages and storehouses. Near the front gateway is an isolated building, presumably a shrine. The whole complex is a self-sufficient farming establishment typical of the northern provinces of the Empire. The main difficulty in the interpretation of these sites, which can only be resolved by excavation, is to know how many were occupied simultaneously and how many were abandoned to be succeeded by others nearby. On any account, the density of rural occupation of northern Gaul was remarkably high.

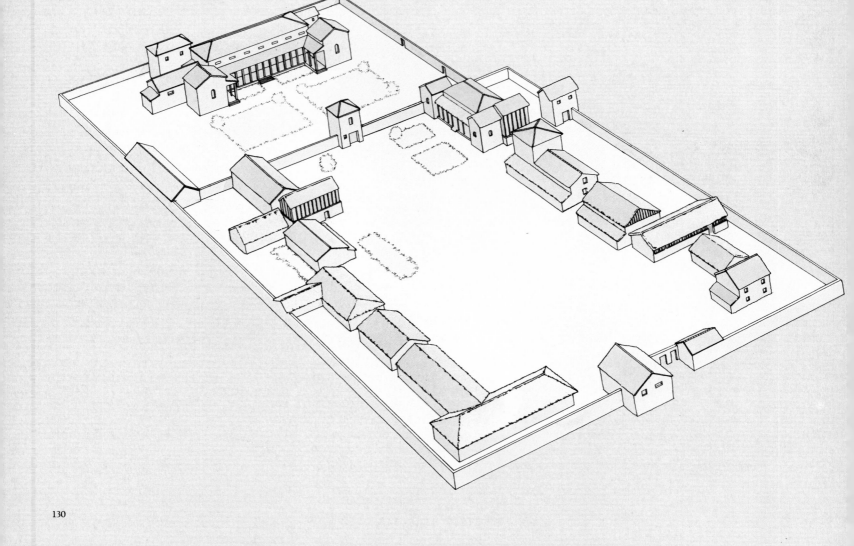

The famous aqueduct constructed in the time of Augustus over the river Gard (or Gardon) was part of a system which delivered water to Nîmes from a source near Uzès (see also p. 185). The accuracy of the surveying and engineering involved is most impressive; the water dropped only 17 meters over the distance of 50 kilometers for which it was conveyed. The local quarries from which the stone was brought for the construction of the aqueduct can still be seen.

After the capture of Alexandria by Octavian in 30 BC, Egyptian Greeks were settled at Nîmes; this is reflected by the coin issues showing the heads of Augustus and Agrippa with reverses (shown *left*) of a crocodile with the legend COL[onia] NEM[ausus]. The beautifully preserved temple in the forum of ancient Nîmes, known as the "Maison Carrée" (*left*), was dedicated to the princes Gaius and Lucius Caesar. It is a perfect example of classical style, conforming exactly to the proportions laid down by Vitruvius. The famous amphitheater of Nîmes (*top*), still used for bullfights, dates from the late 1st or early 2nd century.

Nîmes

Nîmes, ancient Nemausus, fell under Roman control in the late 1st century BC and became a colony of Roman citizens in the time of Augustus. Standing on the main road from Italy to Spain and with access to the Mediterranean, it was one of the most populous and important cities in southern Gaul. Its wealth nevertheless derived chiefly not from trade, in which it was surpassed by Narbonne, but from the exploitation of the agricultural potential of its territory; the early senators whom it produced can be shown, on the basis of their nomenclature, to have been romanized Gauls, the ancestral owners of the land, rather than Italian immigrants. The city was in the 2nd century the native city of the emperor Antoninus Pius. Apart from the other monuments illustrated on this page, Nîmes possessed an elaborate complex of baths and pools fed by the sacred spring of the god Nemausus. This, elaborately remodeled in the 18th century, can still be seen, but other public monuments, for example the circus which the city once possessed, are now lost.

Augst

Augst (Augusta Rauricorum, in the later period simply Rauraci) was founded as a military colony in 44 BC by a lieutenant of Julius Caesar, partly as a safeguard for Caesar's recent conquests in Gaul. It was also important in the German wars conducted by Augustus and by the Flavians. The defensive advantages of the site are apparent from its contours: it is a plateau with steeply falling land on three sides, set back a little from the banks of the Rhine. Excavation is revealing a varied and well-equipped town with porticoed streets, theater and senate house, fountains, temples, two sets of baths and trading establishments including a sausage maker's. Like other sites in the northern provinces, Augst acquired substantial stone buildings only in the late 1st century AD. After the invasions of the mid-3rd century the apparently declining population concentrated in the smaller fortified settlement of Kaiseraugst; Ammianus Marcellinus described Rauraci in the 4th century as situated "on the very edge of the Rhine." Kaiseraugst should however not be regarded as an entirely separate settlement but rather as a contraction of the earlier one, involving a displacement from its monumental area.

Trier

Trier was an ancient capital of the mixed Celtic, and possibly also Germanic, peoples of the Treveri; near the city stand important religious sanctuaries, including a native precinct, the Altbachtal, and a temple of Lenus Mars, a romanized native god. The name Augusta Treverorum derived from the presence of Augustus during his Gallic visit of 15–13 BC. In the early Empire the city flourished, owing its success to its position, on a waterway with easy access to the military establishments on the

The theater at Augst underwent various adaptations, visible in the aerial photograph and more fully on the site plan. It was first a small theater of orthodox design, with some of its seating in wood, then an amphitheater (or combined theater and amphitheater), and in its final transformation, c. 150 AD, a slightly larger classical theater with a capacity of 8000. To coincide with this phase a second amphitheater was built to the south. All this is a sign of a flourishing and expanding community. The city walls exist in two stretches but were never finished.

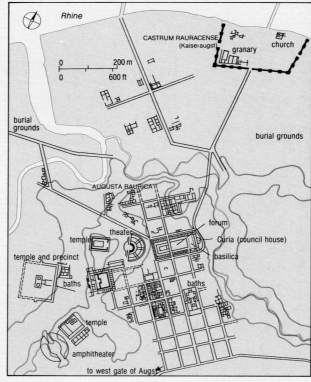

Rhine. To the early period belong the baths known as the Barbarathermen, the amphitheater and the remains of many elaborate private houses. Trier was in the first two centuries an important administrative center as the seat of the procurator of Belgica and the two Germanies, and several of its natives make appearances in written history. From the late 3rd century the city acquired a vastly enlarged role as the main imperial residence in the west. The emperors Constantius and especially Constantine the Great were particularly influential in this development, the most notable monuments from the time of Constantine being the great imperial basilica (Aula Palatina), the imperial baths, all of which formed part of a new "palace precinct," and several churches. An orator speaking at Trier in 310 evokes the atmosphere: "I see a great circus to rival the one at Rome, I see basilicas, forum, a seat of justice, rising to such heights as to be worthy neighbors of the stars. All of which are the fruits of your presence." As the imperial capital Trier attracted literary men, both as teachers and as civil servants. It drew embassies from the provinces, and churchmen like Martin of Tours and Ambrose of Milan went there on various errands. Until its transfer to Arles in the late 4th or early 5th century, the praetorian prefecture of Gaul, Britain and Spain, with its associated offices such as a mint and state workshops, had its seat at Trier. The position of the city, which had given it such great advantages in the earlier period, exposed it to the barbarian raids of the 5th century, and its decline as a Roman city was hastened by repeated barbarian sack.

Above In this painted fresco from Trier rural workers are seen outside a country house. One wears the hooded cloak seen in grave reliefs from the region and also from Britain. It was presumably as appropriate for the northern climate in those days as it would be now.

The great north gate of Trier (*far right*), known as the Porta Nigra or "Black Gate," and the city walls of which it formed part, are probably to be dated to the late 2nd or early 3rd century, but the gate is on any account an appropriate symbol of the later role of the city as imperial capital. In the Middle Ages it became a church, an apse being added to the east tower. The painted fresco (*right*), possibly representing the wife of Constantine, is from the Constantinian palace, on the site of the later cathedral.

BRITAIN

The conquest of Britain was in part provoked by its relations with Belgic Gaul, and its social history under the Roman Empire is an extension of that of its continental neighbor. The cities of Britain, though large in expanse, would undoubtedly have seemed more diffuse and less monumental than their Mediterranean counterparts. As in Gallia Comata, villas played a proportionately more important role, as the vehicles of commercial life and agents of romanization.

The continuing insecurity presented by the peoples of Wales and north of Hadrian's Wall meant that Britain always required a substantial military presence. The development of the province, indeed,

falls into two halves. South of the Fosse Way, the road from Exeter to Lincoln, was civilian settlement; north and west of this line, occupation was generally under strong military influence.

As in the case of Gallia Comata but without the advantage of a late imperial presence, natives of Britain made little direct contribution to the political life of the Roman Empire except, in the 4th century, through repeated usurpation. Though Britain exported materials such as tin and lead, a little gold, and sometimes provided corn to the Rhine armies, it can hardly have covered the costs of its occupation. Yet we must not underestimate the intrinsic quality of romanization achieved there. The Roman cities and roads, built, it was supposed, by giants or the Devil, haunted the imagination of later writers. So an Anglo-Saxon poet (translated by R. Hamer) evokes the ruins of Roman Bath – "where long since/a host of heroes, glorious, gold-adorned .../shone in their armour, gazed on gems and treasure .../on this bright city with its wide domains ..."

In the symbols presented by the *Notitia Dignitatum* for the civil and military governors of Britain, the province is shown notionally as an island, with no attempt to achieve exact, or even relative, geographical accuracy in the location of the cities and forts. Shown here are the insignia of the Vicarius Britanniarum.

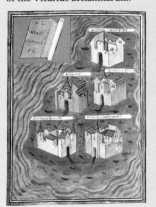

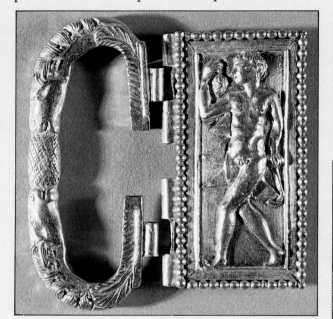

The Thetford treasure, discovered in 1979 beside the Icknield Way in Norfolk, is one of the largest hoards of Roman gold and silver to come to light in Britain. The quality of the working suggests that it was done on the Continent in the late 4th century. This gold buckle (*top*) has a hinged bow in the form of two confronted horses' heads and a rectangular plate with a relief of a dancing satyr.

The building inscription (*above*), from the fort of High Rochester north of Hadrian's Wall, records work done by a detachment of the Twentieth Legion from Chester. The crudely carved figures flanking the inscription are Mars and Hercules, appropriate military patrons. The date is probably early 3rd century, when there was much rebuilding after the British campaign of Septimius Severus.

The 4th-century mosaic (*above*) from the bath buildings of a villa in Somerset is part of a series illustrating the story of Dido and Aeneas. Apart from its mildly erotic appeal, the mosaic attests a knowledge of Virgil's *Aeneid* – or at least of its most romantic book. Augustine, too, as a student in 4th-century Africa, "wept on the death of Dido" (*Confessions* 1.13).

The strategic concept of Hadrian's Wall (inset map), of a patrolled linear frontier supported by an occupied military zone, has analogies with other 2nd-century frontiers, such as the Raetian palisade (p. 108). The wall, with its associated works, seems to be almost as concerned with what lay behind as beyond it. Possibly it was intended to separate and so control restless peoples on both southern and northern sides.

Hadrian's wall is seen (*overleaf*) looking east near Housesteads on a day of striking scenic contrasts. In conditions like these one can find some sympathy for the Palmyrenes and other Middle Easterners stationed there.

GRAMPIAN MOUNTAINS

Inchtuthil

Tay

Carpow

Antonine Wall

Inveresk

TRIMONTIUM
Newstead

SOUTHERN UPLANDS

BREMENIUM
High Rochester

CILURNUM
Chesters

SEGEDUNUM
Wallsend

CASTRA
EXPLORATORUM

Hadrian's Wall

PONS AELIUS
Newcastle

NORTH SEA

MAIA
Bowness

LUGUVALIUM
Carlisle

CORSTOPITUM
Corbridge

CONCANGIUM
Chester le Street

CHEVIOT HILLS

ALAUNA
Maryport

VOREDA
Old Penrith

DERVENTIO
Papcastle

LAVATRAE
Bowes

VERTERAE
Brough

CUMBRIAN MTS

CATARACTONIUM
Catterick

YORKSHIRE
MOORS

PENNINE CHAIN

Tees

ISURIUM
Aldborough

Ouse

IRISH SEA

BREMETENNACUM
Ribchester

CALCARIA
Tadcaster

EBURACUM
York

LAGENTIUM
Castleford

PETUARIA
Brough

MAMUCIUM
Manchester

NAVIO
Brough

AQUAE ARNEMETIAE
Buxton

LINDUM
Lincoln

VARAE?
St Asaph

DEVA
Chester

SEGONTIUM
Caernarvon

DERVENTIO
Littlechester

Trent

CAUSENNAE
Ancaster

BRANODUNUM
Brancaster

VERNEMETUM
Willoughby

THE FENS

VIROCONIUM
Wroxeter

LETOCETUM
Wall

RATAE
Leicester

DUROBRIVAE
Water Newton

VENTA
Caister

Caersws

Severn

SALINAE
Droitwich

VENONAE
High Cross

DUROVIGUTUM
Godmanchester

DUROLIPONS
Cambridge

Alcester

Nene

Gt Ouse

Great Chesterford

MAGNIS
Kenchester

LACTODORUM
Towcester

CAMBRIAN MTS

Llandovery

Wye

COTSWOLD
HILLS

Avon

CAMULODUNUM
Colchester

MORIDUNUM
Carmarthen

GOBANNIUM
Abergavenny

BLESTIUM
Monmouth

GLEVUM
Gloucester

Alchester

CAESAROMAGUS
Chelmsford

CHILTERN HILLS

VERULAMIUM
St Albans

NIDUM
Neath

VENTA
Caerwent

CORINIUM
Cirencester

Dorchester

LONDINIUM
London

DUROBRIVAE
Rochester

ISCA
Caerleon

Thames

DUROVERNUM
Canterbury

RUTUPIAE
Richborough

AQUAE SULIS
Bath

CUNETIO
Mildenhall

CALLEVA
Silchester

DUBRIS
Dover

EXMOOR

SALISBURY PLAIN

SORVIODUNUM
Old Sarum

VENTA
Winchester

LEMANIS
Lympne

LINDINIS
Ilchester

CLAUSENTUM
Bitterne

PORTUS ADURNI
Portchester

SOUTH DOWNS

ANDERITA
Pevensey

NOVIOMAGUS
Chichester

Fishbourne

DARTMOOR

ISCA
Exeter

Maiden Castle

DURNOVARIA
Dorchester

ENGLISH CHANNEL

scale 1:2 700 000

0 .... 150km

0 .... 100mi

■ provincial capital

□ legionary camp

● colonia

○ civitas capital

△ other important civil settlement

□ other settlement

○ featured site

Roman road

Roman road, course uncertain

Roman canal

Roman waterway

Roman wall

VENTA ancient name

Caerwent modern name

500m

200m

0

marsh

6°   4°   2°   0°

56°

54°

52°

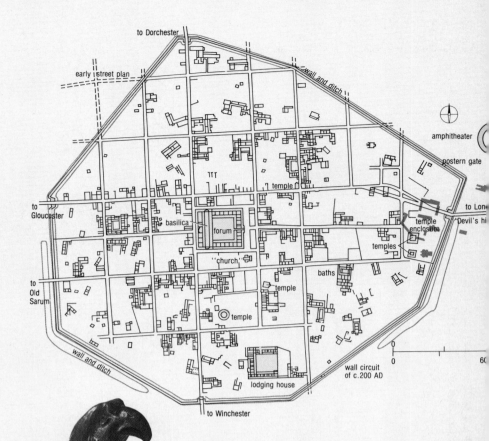

Silchester

Silchester (Calleva of the Atrebates) was the capital of one of the native states, or *civitates*, given as a client kingdom to the British chieftain Cogidubnus at the time of the Claudian conquest. The site, abandoned as an urban center after the Roman period, now consists of open fields, surrounded by the remains of the city walls, added to the existing earthen ramparts in the late 2nd or early 3rd century. Of modern buildings there is only a church and a farm near the east gate of the Roman town. The remains of the small amphitheater are visible nearby as a circular embankment. Its capacity has been calculated at about 2700, which might roughly represent the adult population. A recent estimate of the population of Silchester as 1000 seems far too low, and takes no account of the seasonal variations which must have been considerable in a rural center with such a large agricultural territory.

Right The bronze Silchester eagle, found in the Roman basilica, is evidently not, as was originally supposed, a legionary standard, but part of a larger statue once in the basilica complex.

Below The aerial photograph shows clearly the course of the Roman defenses of the 2nd/3rd century, the inner earthwork rendered superfluous by the early development of the town, and the regular street plan. The amphitheater is in the clump of trees at the far left corner of the site. The driveway crossing the site transversely is modern.

Above The town plan has some interesting features. The early forum and baths are roughly aligned with each other but not with the street grid, suggesting that they were already built when the grid was laid out. The grid extends beyond the walls, its outer area being presumably still undeveloped when the walls were planned. The density of occupation is in any event more sparse towards the ramparts; evidently Silchester took on a semirural appearance immediately beyond the area of its public and administrative buildings.

Below The Great Bath at Bath. Still fed by Roman conduits, it measures 24 by 12 m and is 1·8 m deep.

Below right The temple of the Celtic goddess Sulis, romanized as Minerva, was first discovered during the construction of the Pump Room at Bath in the late 18th century. The bearded male "Medusa" head here shown, with entwined serpents for hair, formed the striking central feature of the sculptured pediment of the temple. The decorative flair of Celtic art is applied with splendid effect to a somewhat adapted classical subject. The stylized vigor of the work is emphasized by the contrast with the calm poise of the classical head of Minerva also from Bath (*bottom*), a gilt-bronze piece, probably from a cult statue of the goddess, found in the Great Bath in the 18th century.

Bath

Roman Bath (Aquae Sulis), founded under the Flavians, was one of many settlements in the Roman Empire which owed their often long-lived prosperity to their medicinal springs. Parallels in the continental Empire, like Vichy and Néris-les-Bains in France, and in Germany Baden-Baden and Wiesbaden, can easily be found. Like them, Bath retained its popularity as a health and holiday resort into modern times, though the waters have recently been found contaminated by bacteria and unfit for use. Because of the continuous development of the city, little is known of Aquae Sulis apart from its well-preserved bath complex. The 2nd- or 3rd-century walls of the town survived, however, until the early 18th century.

Fishbourne

The Roman palace at Fishbourne in Sussex, by the main road leading west from Chichester (Noviomagus), has been spectacularly revealed by recent excavation. It stood at the head of a creek which at that time reached further inland than it does now, and was also the site of wooden granaries and a naval station associated on archaeological grounds with the Claudian conquest. The fully developed palace of the Flavian period was an enlargement of an earlier residence. It has been connected with the king Cogidubnus mentioned above – Roman citizen and friend of the emperor Claudius. The identification cannot be positively attested, but the magnificence of the palace – unsurpassed for its date in the west Roman provinces – makes Cogidubnus' candidacy for its ownership a strong one.

Its remains still suggest something of the sophistication of the palace at Fishbourne. The mosaic (*left*), showing sea monsters and a trident-bearing winged Cupid riding a dolphin, is in a room in the north wing reconstructed in the 2nd century. It is likely that more than one craftsman worked on the mosaic; this is suggested in particular by the different standards of workmanship visible in the sea horses in the north and south panels, the south panel being far better.

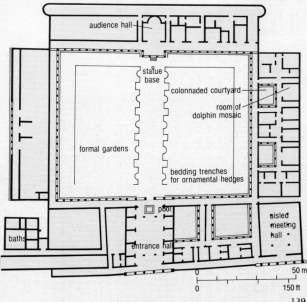

audience hall

statue base

colonnaded courtyard

room of dolphin mosaic

formal gardens

bedding trenches for ornamental hedges

pool

baths

entrance hall

aisled meeting hall

0   50 m

0   150 ft

THE DANUBE

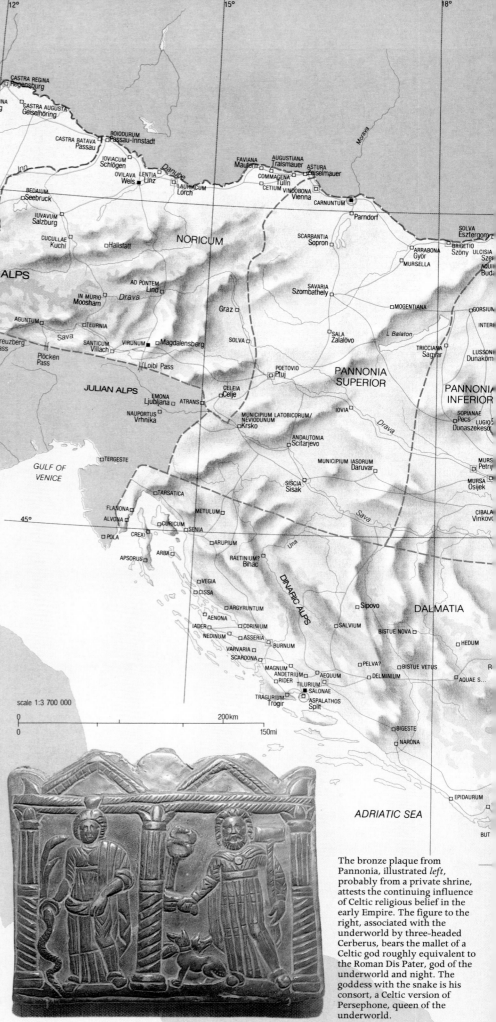

Cassius Dio, a Bithynian Greek who governed Pannonia under Alexander Severus, thought of it as a backward region and its people as uncultivated and bloodthirsty. His opinion, which fails to acknowledge the standard of material culture achieved there by his day, expresses a Mediterranean educated man's prejudice towards a profoundly non-Mediterranean, but still prosperous and crucially important region of the Empire.

The Danubian provinces, taken together, span the whole range of Roman civilization, from the settled Celtic tribes of the west and the urbanized seaboard of Dalmatia to the ancient Greek cities of the Black Sea coast. The Thracian regions east of the pass of Succi were Greek-speaking and their cities have Greek names. The "latinization" of Dacia, after an occupation of little more than 150 years, is actively attested by modern Romanian.

That the area was in any sense a unity derives from its importance as the military backbone of the Empire. Roman fortresses such as Carnuntum (see overleaf) provided the stimulus for urbanization, and for the development of agriculture and villa settlement. The Danubian provinces were a prime source of army recruits, men often of country or small-town origins who in the 3rd and 4th centuries provided the officer elite, and in due course (p. 109) filled the imperial office. In the 4th century particularly, the regions entered a new prosperity through the presence of the emperors: "Pannonia," wrote a 4th-century source, "is a land rich in all resources, in fruits, beasts, commerce and also slaves. It is the constant residence of the emperors and possesses great cities, like Sirmium ..."

Linking east and west, and also confronting barbarian invasion, the Danubian provinces are a constant test of the well-being of the Empire. It was on their stability that the survival of the Roman Empire, as Dio knew it, depended.

The bronze plaque from Pannonia, illustrated *left*, probably from a private shrine, attests the continuing influence of Celtic religious belief in the early Empire. The figure to the right, associated with the underworld by three-headed Cerberus, bears the mallet of a Celtic god roughly equivalent to the Roman Dis Pater, god of the underworld and night. The goddess with the snake is his consort, a Celtic version of Persephone, queen of the underworld.

scale 1:3 700 000

ADRIATIC SEA

Left Scythia is shown in the *Notitia Dignitatum* as a group of cities with the river Danube running symbolically (and inaccurately) through their midst.

Carnuntum

Carnuntum and Aquincum illustrate a process of urban development characteristic of the northern military provinces of the Empire. Founded in the time of Tiberius as a legionary base on the Danube bank, the military camp of Carnuntum soon attracted settlers – traders, artisans, soldiers' concubines and others who saw their prospects of fortune in the vicinity of an establishment of 5000 men and more who received regular salaries from the Roman government. These immigrants congregated in informal settlements known as *canabae*, communities with no independent legal status but falling under the jurisdiction of the legionary legate. The civilian municipality, founded later, is to the west of the camp and *canabae*, its central area lying under the modern village of Petronell. It possessed its own amphitheater, provided in the 2nd century by an immigrant from Syrian Antioch named C. Domitius Zmaragdus, a decurion, or town councillor, of the municipality: 2nd-century Carnu-

The aerial view of the *canabae* of the legionary fortress of Carnuntum (*below right*), with buildings and streets clearly seen as differences in the growth of standing crops, well indicates the spontaneous but substantial nature of the settlement. The main street forks as it enters the *canabae* from the southern gate of the fortress, which lies a little distance off the bottom of the picture, beyond a cleared area adjoining the rampart.

ntum was in its composite form a very substantial urban community.

It remained important until the time of the later Empire, although its military function was never lost. It was here that Marcus Aurelius undersigned the second book of his *Meditations* while engaged in war against the Quadi, and at Carnuntum Septimius Severus was proclaimed emperor in 193 AD. In the 4th century Ammianus Marcellinus described it as a "deserted and unkempt town" but militarily convenient. The emperor Valentinian spent three months there before moving on to Aquincum. Carnuntum was apparently abandoned with the Hunnish occupation of the plains to the north and Roman evacuation of the right bank of the Danube. Indeed, the presence of such well-appointed cities on the extreme fringes of the Roman Empire has often been seen as a standing temptation to the barbarian tribes who adjoined it.

The plan of Carnuntum (*below*) shows the relative positions of legionary camp and *canabae* and civilian *municipium* and suggests the overall size of the conurbation.

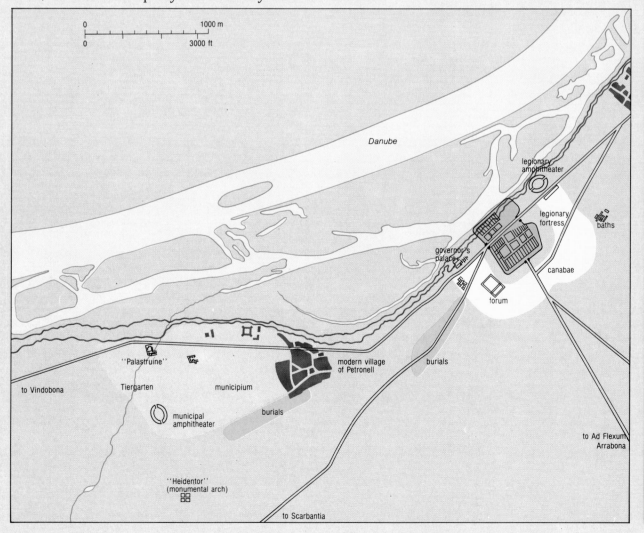

The civilian amphitheater of Carnuntum stood by the main road leading towards Vienna (Vindobona). In the aerial photograph (*bottom right*) the traces of extensive surrounding buildings are clearly visible.

Below This portable organ was found in the basement of the Collegium Centonariorum, or guild of firemen, and casts an intriguing light on the nature of its meetings. By coincidence, Aquincum also produced the touching epitaph set up by the legionary organist to his wife, a lady of musical accomplishments, in which "she alone excelled her husband."

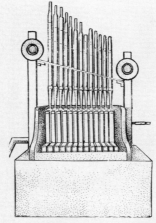

Aquincum

An identical process of development, from legionary camp and *canabae* to later *municipium*, took place at Aquincum as at Carnuntum. Here, too, as at Carnuntum, are two amphitheaters, military and civilian, the latter built after the foundation of the *municipium* in the 2nd century. Despite its annihilation by modern Budapest, Aquincum has furnished numerous artifacts, and richly decorated wall paintings which attest the standard of life achieved by the more opulent members of its society. Inscriptions also reveal the contribution to the civilian life of Aquincum which was made by veterans of the legion stationed there.

143

Split

Split, or Spalato, was originally a suburb of the city of Salona, an ancient tribal capital and in the Roman Empire a great city of Dalmatia. In the 4th to 6th centuries Salona was a notable center of late Roman Christianity, with monumental basilicas and many engraved sarcophagi, and in the 5th century was for a time the capital of an independent Dalmatian principality. Since medieval times the position of the two communities has been reversed, for with the development of Split as the nucleus of an urban settlement, Salona progressively became little more than a quarry for building materials. In modern times Split is a flourishing city while Salona is a deserted site.

The medieval town of Split (its ancient name, Aspalathos, the Greek name for the thorn plant which grew there, reflects the early Greek influence on this part of Dalmatia) grew in and around the seaside palace built by Diocletian for his retirement after his abdication from the imperial throne in 305. His octagonal mausoleum adjoining the peristyle (*below*) later became a Christian church – an ironic fate for the emperor whose last years had been spent in Christian persecution. The palace was laid out in strict Roman fashion like a military camp, with main streets crossing at right angles. It seems evident that, despite his reputation for simple tastes such as gardening, Diocletian was not deprived in retirement of the ceremonial grandeur that had attended him as emperor.

Above Diocletian, the builder of Split, as seen in a portrait bust from Nicomedia.

Right The architect Robert Adam was one of many European artists and designers to be attracted by the ruins of Diocletian's palace, and spent five eventful weeks in 1757 surveying and measuring the site. This is his reconstruction of the south facade of the palace, overlooking the sea. The artist has exercised some licence in clarifying the authentic parts of the ancient structure but his drawings give a good impression of the buildings at a time when they were better preserved than now. The architectural focus of the palace was formed by the colonnaded peristyle (*below*) which functioned as a ceremonial courtyard and, in due course, monumental approach to the mausoleum of Diocletian.

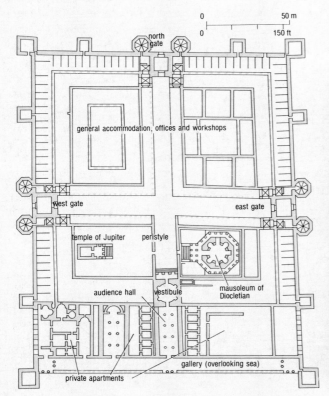

Below The "pastor bonus" (Good Shepherd) sarcophagus, found at Salona and now in the Archaeological Museum at Split. The quality of the carving (early 4th century) is superb, and it has been claimed that the same craftsman later worked on the arch of Constantine in Rome.

Adamclisi

The Roman city of Tropaeum Traiani, near Adamclisi in the Dobrudja, is known to have existed from the 2nd century until late antiquity. Destroyed by Gothic raids in the 3rd century, the city was rebuilt by Constantine and Licinius and in the later period possessed a number of fine churches. It took its name from the "Trophy of Trajan," of which a modern reconstruction is shown *below*. Erected by Trajan as a local reminder of his victories in the Dacian wars, it was also intended to mark retribution for the defeats suffered by Domitian. Nearby were built a mausoleum and commemorative altar, the latter containing the names of nearly 4000 soldiers killed in Domitian's Dacian wars.

Left The metopes of the Adamclisi trophy show scenes of warfare in a style which is a striking contrast with that of Trajan's column at Rome. Here are shown an auxiliary horseman dressed in chain mail, and sheep representing spoils of war. Some have argued that the metopes are Constantinian in date, connected with the late rebuilding of the city of Tropaeum Traiani; on any account they are a remarkable example of provincial style.

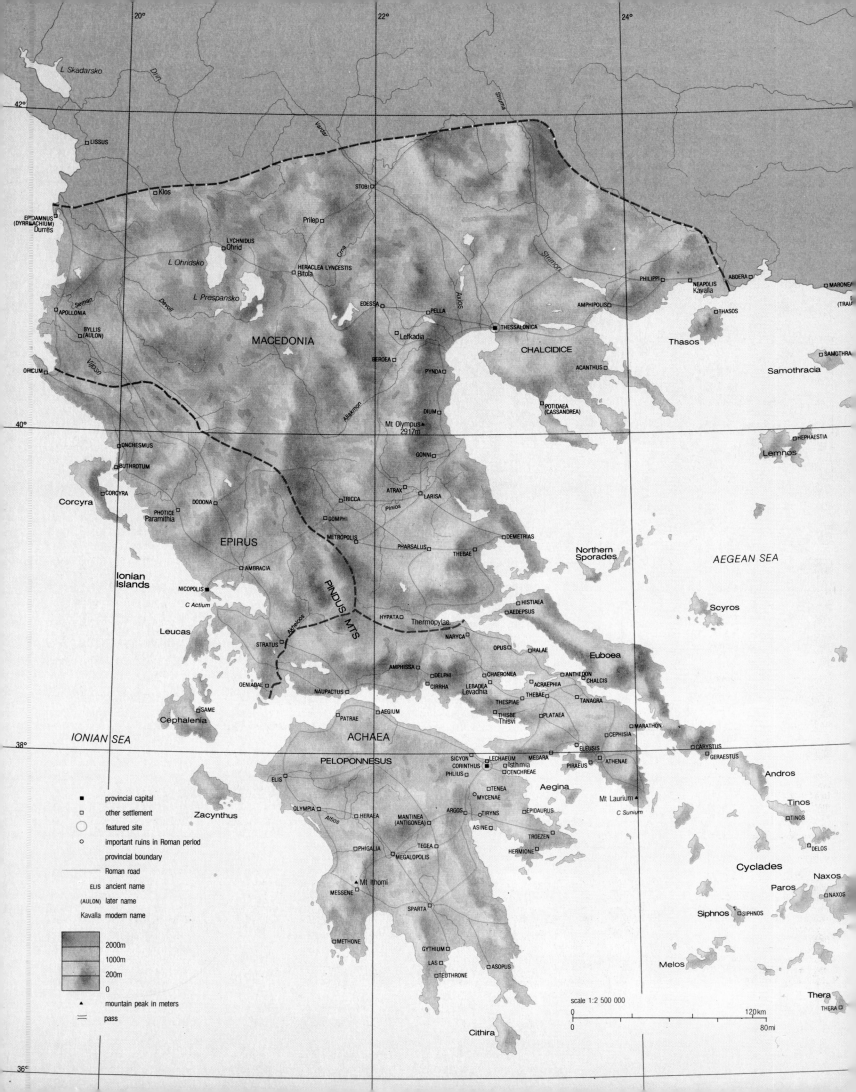

Map legend:

- ■ provincial capital
- □ other settlement
- ◯ featured site
- ○ important ruins in Roman period
- ——— provincial boundary
- ——— Roman road
- ELIS ancient name
- (AULON) later name
- Kavalla modern name

2000m
1000m
200m
0

- ▲ mountain peak in meters
- = pass

scale 1:2 500 000

0 ———————— 120km

0 ———————— 80mi

Labels on map:

L Skadarsko, Drin, Vardar, Struma, Strimón, Crna, Axós

LISSUS, Klos, EPIDAMNUS (DYRRACHIUM) Durrës, LYCHNIDUS Ohrid, STOBI, Prilep, HERACLEA LYNCESTIS Bitola, APOLLONIA, Seman, Devoll, L Ohridsko, L Prespansko, BYLLIS (AULON), EDESSA, PELLA, AMPHIPOLIS, PHILIPPI, NEAPOLIS Kavalla, ABDERA, MARONEA, (TRAIA, THASOS, Thasos, SAMOTHRA, Samothracia

ORICUM, Vijosë, MACEDONIA, Lefkadia, THESSALONICA, CHALCIDICE, BEROEA, PYNDA, ACANTHUS, POTIDAEA (CASSANDREA), Aliakmon, DIUM, Mt Olympus 2917m, HEPHAESTIA, Lemnos

ONCHESMUS, BUTHROTUM, GONNI, CORCYRA, Corcyra, PHOTICE Paramithia, DODONA, TRICCA, ATRAX, LARISA, Pinios, GOMPHI, EPIRUS, METROPOLIS, PHARSALUS, THEBAE, DEMETRIAS, Northern Sporades, AEGEAN SEA

Ionian Islands, AMBRACIA, NICOPOLIS, C Actium, Leucas, PINDUS MTS, HYPATA, Thermopylae, HISTIAEA, AEDEPSUS, Scyros

STRATUS, Achelóos, NARYCA, OPUS, HALAE, Euboea, ANTHEDON, CHALCIS, AMPHISSA, DELPHI, CHAERONEA, ACRAEPHIA, CIRRHA, LEBADEA Levadhia, THEBAE, TANAGRA, OENIADAE, NAUPACTUS, THESPIAE, PLATAEA, THISBE Thisvi, MARATHON, CEPHISIA

SAME, Cephalenia, AEGIUM, PATRAE, ACHAEA, EEUSIS, CARYSTUS, GERAESTUS, PELOPONNESUS, SICYON, LECHAEUM, MEGARA, CORINTHUS, Isthmia, PIRAEUS, ATHENAE, Andros, PHLIUS, CENCHREAE, Aegina, TENEA, Mt Laurium, Tinos, ELIS, MYCENAE, C Sunium, TINOS, Zacynthus, OLYMPIA, Alfios, HERAEA, MANTINEA (ANTIGONEA), ARGOS, TIRYNS, EPIDAURUS, ASINE, TROEZEN, HERMIONE, DELOS, Cyclades, PHIGALIA, TEGEA, Naxos, MEGALOPOLIS, Paros, NAXOS, Mt Ithomi, MESSENE, Siphnos, SIPHNOS, SPARTA, IONIAN SEA, Melos, METHONE, GYTHIUM, LAS, ASOPUS, TEUTHRONE, Cithira, Thera, THERA

GREECE

The Roman conquest of Greece, starkly symbolized by Mummius' sack of Corinth in 146 BC and Sulla's capture of Athens 60 years later, was the culmination of a complex military, diplomatic and commercial involvement in the affairs of Greek cities and their leagues dating back to the 3rd century (see pp. 50–51). The resulting provinces, Achaea (initially including Epirus) and Macedonia, though both governed by proconsuls, differed in character. Achaea retained throughout the Roman period a special prestige based on the historic distinction of classical Greece. Macedonia, by contrast, was except for its western seaboard a remote and rural land, its society based on villages rather than cities; the latter, when they occurred in the interior, often developed in succession to native fortresses.

In some respects the Roman presence made possible the development of a greater material prosperity than before, or perhaps only of greater extremes of wealth. Certain families, like the Euryclid dynasty of Sparta and that of Herodes Atticus at Athens (see overleaf), acquired wealth on a scale far beyond anything achieved in classical times: in this respect Achaea follows the pattern yet more spectacularly achieved in the cities of Asia Minor. The writer Plutarch, from Chaeronea in Boeotia, is the counterpart of those literary figures from Asia Minor who flourished under the Empire: his works, especially the *Parallel Lives* in which a selected Greek is compared with a Roman, reflect the attitudes of a not unsympathetic Greek under Roman rule.

Some cities, like Corinth, Patrae and Thessalonica, acquired a progressively increasing prosperity, but others declined into insignificance, and in general the economic potential of Greece did not match that of Asia Minor, or of some newer provinces "opened up" by Roman exploitation.

In the 3rd century, and again in the late 4th, the peninsula suffered from barbarian invasion, that of Alaric in 395–97 being particularly destructive. By the mid-5th century Macedonia, passing firmly into the eastern sphere of influence and possessing in Thessalonica the new capital of Illyricum, had become a frontier against the barbarian north.

Above The symbols of the proconsul of Achaea, as shown by the *Notitia Dignitatum*. Achaea was one of only three provinces still governed in the late Empire by titular proconsuls (the others were Africa and Asia), a reflection of their prestige as senior senatorial provinces.

Above The old and the new in later Greco-Roman culture, seen in a fascinating 4th-century marble at Athens. Christ appears as Apollo with his lyre, in an unusually explicit piece of syncretism, but one in particular accord with the tradition of the cultural center of Greece.

Right The Roman road, the famous Via Egnatia, seen as it runs across Macedonia between Philippi and Neapolis. The road was strategically crucial in the civil wars of the late Republic (see p. 70), but under the Empire, with the consolidation of the frontier at the Danube, a more northerly route replaced it in military importance.

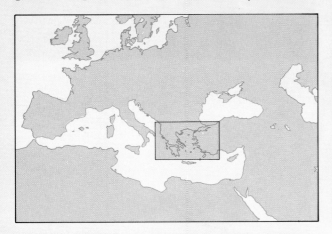

Athens

Tertullian's expression of the incompatibility of Christianity and classical culture, "What has Athens to do with Jerusalem?," epitomizes the moral and intellectual distinction of Athens which, surviving the destruction of the city's political power, remained the basis of its prestige in the Roman Empire. Many of the more important intellectual figures of all periods of the Empire studied, taught, or, as in the case of St Paul (Acts 17:16ff.), sought an audience there. The Eleusinian Mysteries retained their appeal; the emperors Hadrian and Julian the Apostate, and the late pagan senator Praetextatus (p. 193), were among the most famous of their many initiates.

Despite the benefactions of Hellenistic kings like Attalus of Pergamum, Roman Athens was very much a showpiece of imperial patronage, with its market of Caesar and Augustus, odeion of Agrippa and, provided by the philhellene Hadrian, gymnasium, Panhellenion or shrine of all the Greeks, magnificent library and, after a lapse of more than six centuries since it was started, temple of Olympian Zeus. A few years later Athens's own Herodes Atticus provided the odeion named for him, and a new stadium.

The philosophical tradition of Athens evolved in the late Empire into a mystic Neoplatonism influences by magical elements (see p. 177). Despite the damaging occupation of the city by Alaric, it remained in sufficiently good order to accommodate the 5th-century Neoplatonic school of Syrianus and Proclus, but this late efflorescence of its intellectual development, and the historic role of Athens as a shrine of classical learning, were ended in 529 by Justinian's closure of the schools.

Right Old and new in Roman Athens. Below the Acropolis, on which little new building was done among the masterpieces of Periclean Athens (a significant exception being a temple of Rome and Augustus), is seen the odeion of Herodes Atticus, given by the millionaire to his compatriots in about 160 AD.

Below left The "Tower of the Winds," or Horologion of Andronicus of Cyrrhus, built in the 1st century BC. It stood in an open space near the later market of Caesar and Augustus. It is decorated with reliefs of the eight winds, and was originally surmounted by a weathervane. Inside was a 24-hour clock driven by waterpower.

Below The cuirass of this torso of Hadrian, with the Acropolis in the background, stands for the Roman rather than the Greek in Hadrian's tastes. It shows figures of Victory, and the she-wolf with the twins, Romulus and Remus.

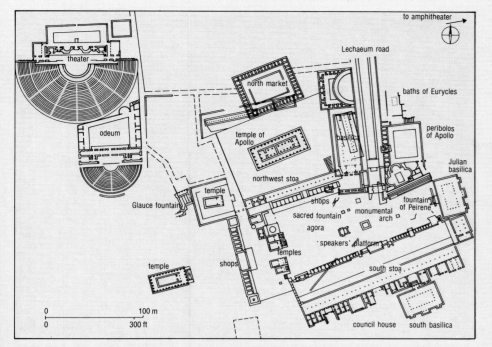

Corinth

Corinth (see plan, *left*) was refounded in 44 BC after its destruction by Mummius in 146, and became the capital of the province of Achaea, a distinction which reflects its earlier status as chief city of the Achaean League. It was here that St Paul appeared before the proconsul Gallio (Acts 18:12ff.). Its history under the Roman Empire is the rather generalized one of a great commercial city with wide connections. Nero visited it during his tour of Greece in 66 AD and initiated one of many unsuccessful attempts at different times to dig a canal through the Isthmus. Corinth was destroyed by an earthquake in 521 AD.

Thessalonica

Thessalonica, at the eastern end of the Via Egnatia, displaced Pella as both capital and main port of Macedonia. Though enjoying rapid civic development in the 2nd century and promoted as a Roman colony in the mid-3rd, its greatest magnificence came with the later shift of the resources of the Roman Empire towards the regions of the Bosphorus. As a Tetrarchic capital, Thessalonica acquired a palace complex including a hippodrome and the so-called octagon, possibly a throne room. This phase of its history illustrates the passion for building ascribed by Lactantius to Diocletian and more familiarly associated with Nicomedia in Asia Minor.

The city remained important as an occasional imperial residence. Riots, provoked by the imprisonment of a popular charioteer, resulted in the massacre in the hippodrome for which Theodosius was forced by Ambrose to do penance (p. 198). The third main phase of the physical enlargement of Thessalonica occurred in the mid-5th century, with its adoption in place of Sirmium as seat of the Illyrian prefecture. To this period belong the church of St Demetrius, a new palace for the use of the prefect, and the massive wall circuit.

Above The elegant arch of Hadrian, erected by the Athenians in his honor in about 130 AD, carries two inscriptions: on one side, facing the old city, "This is Athens, the ancient city of Theseus," and on the other, "This is the city of Hadrian and not of Theseus." It stands on a road by the precinct of the temple of Olympian Zeus. Hadrian clearly saw himself as the refounder of the city.

Right Monuments from the later phases of the growth of Roman Thessalonica. The triumphal arch of Galerius celebrates his victory over the Persians (see p. 171) with typical scenes of military and religious life. The Byzantine walls of Thessalonica (*far right*), long believed to be of 4th-century date, have now been associated with the promotion of the city as the seat of the prefecture of Illyricum after the abandonment of Sirmium.

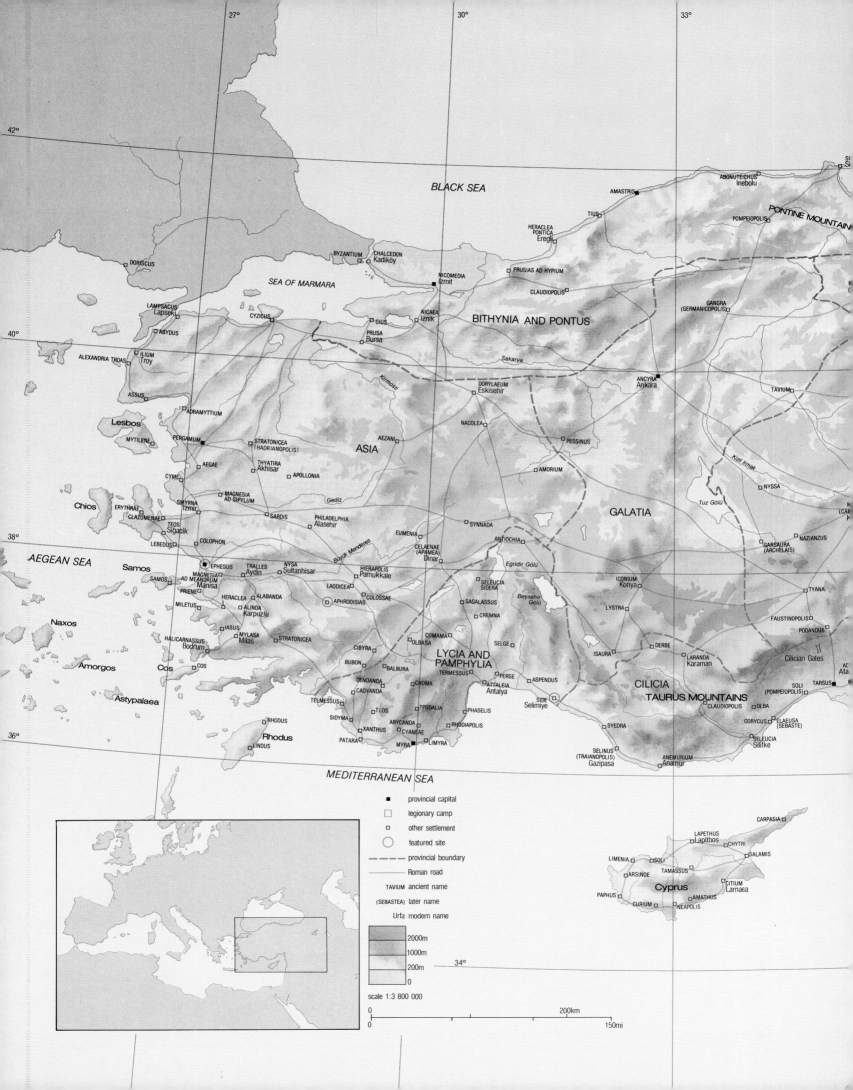

BLACK SEA

SEA OF MARMARA

BITHYNIA AND PONTUS

PONTINE MOUNTAIN

DORISCUS

BYZANTIUM
CHALCEDON
Kadiköy

NICOMEDIA
İzmit

PRUSIAS AD HYPIUM

CLAUDIOPOLIS

HERACLEA
PONTICA
Ereğli

TIUS

POMPEIOPOLIS

AMASTRIS

ABONUTEICHUS
İnebolu

SI
Si

LAMPSACUS
Lapseki

ABYDUS

CYZICUS

CIUS

PRUSA
Bursa

NICAEA
İznik

Sakarya

DORYLAEUM
Eskişehir

ANCYRA
Ankara

GANGRA
(GERMANICOPOLIS)

TAVIUM

ILIUM
Troy

ALEXANDRIA TROAS

Kırmıstı

ASSUS

ADRAMYTTIUM

NACOLEA

PESSINUS

Kızıl Irmak

Lesbos

MYTILENE

PERGAMUM

STRATONICEA
(HADRIANOPOLIS)

AEZANI

ASIA

GALATIA

AEGAE

CYME

THYATIRA
Akhisar

APOLLONIA

AMORIUM

NYSSA

Chios

ERYTHRAE

CLAZOMENAE

SMYRNA
İzmir

MAGNESIA
AD SIPYLUM

Gediz

SYNNADA

Tuz Gölü

GARSAURA
(ARCHELAIS)

NAZIANZUS

TEOS
Sığacık

SARDIS

PHILADELPHIA
Alaşehir

EUMENIA

ANTIOCHIA

ICONIUM
Konya

TYANA

LEBEDUS

COLOPHON

Büyük Menderes

CELAENAE
(APAMEA)
Dinar

Eğridir Gölü

AEGEAN SEA

Samos

EPHESUS

TRALLES
Aydın

NYSA
Sultanhisar

HIERAPOLIS
Pamukkale

SELEUCIA
SIDERA

LYSTRA

FAUSTINOPOLIS

PODANDUS

SAMOS

MAGNESIA
AD MEANDRUM
Manisa

PRIENE

LAODICEA

COLOSSAE

SAGALASSUS

Beyşehir
Gölü

AD
Ata

MILETUS

HERACLEA

ALABANDA

ALINDA
Karpuzlu

APHRODISIAS

CREMNA

ISAURA

DERBE

LARANDA
Karaman

Cilician Gates

Naxos

IASUS

MYLASA
Milas

STRATONICEA

COMAMA

OLBASA

SELGE

TARSUS

HALICARNASSUS
Bodrum

CIBYRA

LYCIA AND
PAMPHYLIA

SOLI
(POMPEIOPOLIS)

Amorgos

Cos

COS

BUBON

BALBURA

TERMESSUS

PERGE

ASPENDUS

CILICIA
TAURUS MOUNTAINS

CLAUDIOPOLIS

OLBA

OENOANDA

CADYANDA

CHOMA

ATTALEIA
Antalya

SIDE
Selimiye

CORYCUS

ELAEUSA
(SEBASTE)

TELMESSUS

?PODALIA

PHASELIS

SELEUCIA
Silifke

SIDYMA

TLOS

ARYCANDA

RHODIAPOLIS

SYEDRA

RHODUS

XANTHUS

CYANEAE

PATARA

MYRA

LIMYRA

SELINUS
(TRAIANOPOLIS)
Gazipaşa

ANEMURIUM
Anamur

LINDUS

Rhodus

Astypalaea

MEDITERRANEAN SEA

■ provincial capital

□ legionary camp

▫ other settlement

◯ featured site

— — — provincial boundary

——— Roman road

TAVIUM ancient name

(SEBASTEA) later name

Urfa modern name

2000m
1000m
200m
0

34°

scale 1:3 800 000

CARPASIA

LAPETHUS
Lapithos

CHYTRI

LIMENIA

SOLI

SALAMIS

ARSINOE

TAMASSUS

Cyprus

CITIUM
Larnaca

PAPHUS

AMATHUS

CURIUM

NEAPOLIS

0   200km
0   150mi

ASIA MINOR

The expansion of Roman influence in Asia Minor, initiated by the acceptance of the legacy of Attalus of Pergamum (p. 57), proceeded steadily by annexation and the incorporation of client kingdoms, being defined in the east by the presence of Arsacid Parthia. With the wealth produced by agricultural exploitation, the cities of Roman Asia Minor expressed themselves with a vivid exuberance. Their leading citizens acquired immense and sometimes overbearing prestige. They served as effective spokesmen for their cities before the imperial authorities, and drew their communities into levels of expenditure which might, as in Bithynia, overstretch their means and invite Roman interference.

Further east, the picture changes. The Anatolian plateau was a land of villages and of a peasantry often sought as recruits for Roman armies. The mountains of Lycia and Pamphylia, Cilicia, and especially Isauria, harbored pastoralists who turned in hard times to brigandage, local raiding, and, in extreme cases, to revolt. Here were Roman colonies, outposts of Latin culture gradually absorbed by their Greek environment. To the east, Commagene and Lesser Armenia, attached to Cappadocia, were oriental principalities more closely aligned with the Syrian and Iranian east than with Greek Asia Minor.

Left The Isauria of the *Notitia Dignitatum* splendidly evokes the threat of the mountains to the security of the plains and coast of southern Asia Minor.

Below left The beautifully preserved theater of Aspendus in Pamphylia well illustrates the scale of expenditure and standards of construction achieved in 2nd-century Asia Minor.

Below Equally expressive of private opulence are the 4th-century mosaics in the "house of Eustolion" overlooking fields and the sea at Curium in Cyprus.

Ephesus

Ephesus, the first church of the Apocalypse, was also the home of the great temple of Artemis, one of the Seven Wonders of the World and a masterpiece of Hellenistic architecture in a predominantly Roman city, and of the legendary Seven Sleepers, who were supposed to have woken after centuries of slumber to find themselves living under a Christian government. The life of Roman Ephesus is revealed, not only by the extensive archaeological remains, but by inscriptions which show the munificence of the leading families and its rivalries with Smyrna for the title "first city" of Asia. The riot provoked by St Paul, in which the silversmiths roused the people in favor of their goddess, is an episode which reveals much of the life of this great eastern city (Acts 19:22ff.). The great theater (see *opposite*), in which the demonstration occurred, could seat 24 000 spectators. Among the many other facilities of the metropolis was the famous library of Celsus, dedicated in the early 2nd century in honor of Tiberius Julius Celsus Polemaeanus by his brother, also a Roman senator.

The city was attacked by Goths in the 3rd century, but recovered and passed undiminished into the Christian period. In the church of the Virgin Mary, built in the 4th century, met the council of Ephesus of 431 (see p. 000). The main street known as the Arkadiane, leading from the great theater to the harbor, dates from the early 5th century, and the church of St John, over the supposed tomb of the evangelist, was lavishly rebuilt by Justinian.

Ephesus suffered at various times from earthquakes, and in the end yielded to the double process of slow subsidence combined with accumulation of alluvial deposits. By these processes, the sea has retreated from the site, leaving the harbor silted up and many other remains, including the platform of the Artemision, in a waterlogged condition.

Below The road leading down to the Magnesian gate, on the line of the Hellenistic city wall (see plan). The procession of the festival of Artemis led by this gate from the Artemision to the great theater.

Bottom left The splendors of the more opulent residences of Ephesus are well illustrated by these mural paintings in a villa in the central area near the Agora.

Bottom right The entrance to the temple of Hadrian, built in the early 2nd century and restored, with additions, in the late 4th. The four bases before the temple carried statues of the Tetrarchs.

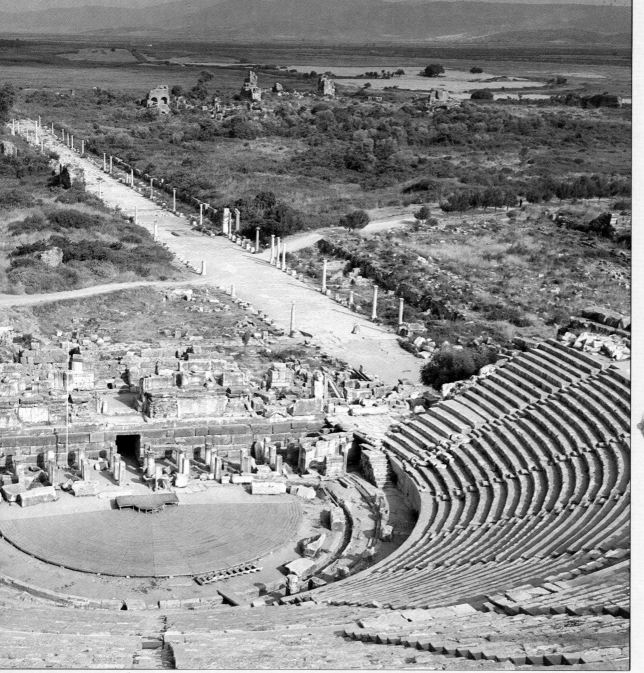

Left The view from the great theater along the Arkadiane to the harbor, which appears as a green swamp in the distance.

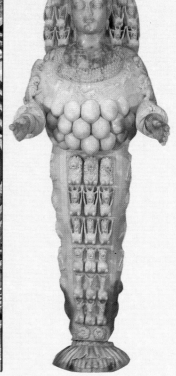

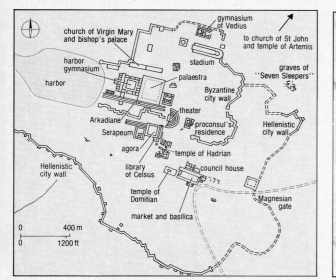

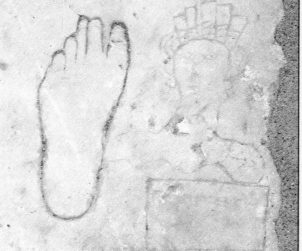

Above "Artemis of the Ephesians," seen in a Roman copy of the cult statue of the goddess, combines a classicizing archaism with a glimpse of a deeper past. The many breasts of this divine figure have little to do with the "Queen and Huntress, chaste and fair" of more orthodox classical conception.

Left A detail of a more secular side of Ephesian life, the self-explanatory sign on the sidewalk advertising a brothel.

153

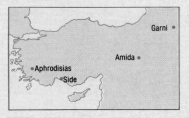

The theater of Aphrodisias (*below*) is built into the early acropolis, later a Byzantine fortress. It was adapted in the 2nd century AD to accommodate wild-beast and gladiatorial shows.

Aphrodisias was an important marble supplier and artistic center in the Roman Empire: its stylistic influence has been traced at Leptis Magna (p.120). Shown here is (*opposite top left*) the head of an imperial youth, possibly Britannicus, from the newly discovered temple of the Augusti.

Aphrodisias

The Carian metropolis of Aphrodisias (the name of the modern hamlet at the site, Geyre, preserves the name of ancient Caria) was particularly favored not only by Roman emperors such as Augustus and Hadrian but by Sulla and Julius Caesar in the 1st century BC. Both these republican magnates, regarding themselves as protected by the goddess Venus, were drawn to favor a city whose name represents the "hellenization" of an ancient local deity. In this respect Aphrodisias may be compared with sites further east such as Heliopolis (p.161). The temple of Aphrodite, built in the 1st century BC, was embellished by a new precinct, provided by Hadrian; in the 6th century it was transformed into a church. The wall of the theater, also built in the 1st century BC, has produced later copies of many *senatus consulta* and imperial letters confirming the city's special privileges, and on a more mundane level parts of Diocletian's Edict on Maximum Prices (p.172).

The defensive wall enclosing the fine stadium but excluding other parts of the city was built in the 260s against Gothic invasion, but the city continued to flourish in the late Empire and only declined in the Byzantine period. The plan of Aphrodisias (*below*), consisting largely of open spaces, reflects the current state of excavation of this constantly productive site. In so far as a road system has been identified, the plan was apparently that of a normal late Hellenistic or early imperial city.

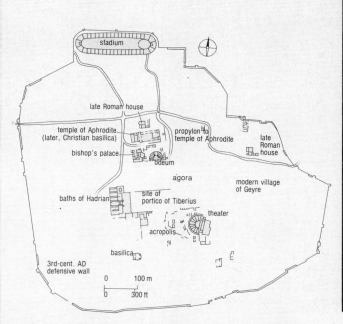

Side

Side in Pamphylia stands on a narrow peninsula and possesses a mainly artificial harbor used, until their suppression by Pompey, by Cilician pirates. Unfortunately it was liable to silting and required constant dredging to keep it clear; an ancient saying, "a harbor of Side," signified a job continually in need of repeating. It also possessed a rather narrow entrance, and it is unlikely that the main part of the prosperity of the city came from maritime trade. Like its neighbors Aspendus (see p. 151) and Perge, Side was essentially a city of the Roman Empire; its theater, like that of Aphrodisias, was converted by the addition of a wall in the orchestra for wild-beast hunts and similar dangerous displays. In the late Empire a defensive wall was built across the narrowest part of the peninsula, passing just behind the agora, but the city continued to flourish beyond these limits and only declined with the Arab invasions.

Amida

The previously unimportant city of Amida on the Tigris (*below*) was developed in the later years of Constantine as a nodal point in the defense of northern Mesopotamia and the Roman-controlled satrapies as far as Corduene (Kurdistan). It was besieged and captured in the Persian invasion of 359, but remained in Roman hands and after Jovian's surrender of Nisibis in 363 received some of its population. The wall circuit, much repaired in later times, is in essence that given it by Justinian. It is of dark basalt, hence a saying: "black the walls, and black the hearts of the men of Amida"!

Garni

Castellum Gorneae, Garni in Soviet Armenia, is the site of the classical building illustrated below (*left*), perhaps the 2nd-century tomb of a romanized client king. The place is mentioned by Tacitus as a fortification occupied by the Romans during the eastern campaign of Nero. It is the most easterly point reached by the Romans, unless we count the Flavian centurion from Melitene who, in unknown but intriguing circumstances, carved his name on a rock face near Baku.

Right A general view of the ruins of Side and the sea, suggesting mainly in its confusion the immense amount of work still to be done in Roman Asia Minor.

THE EAST

Roman control of the east was built on the ruins of the Seleucid kingdom, incorporated by Pompey as the province of Syria, extended by the progressive absorption of "client kingdoms" friendly to Rome, such as Commagene and Judaea, and completed by the annexations of Arabia and Mesopotamia.

These provinces, taken together, comprised the western arc of the "Fertile Crescent," a region of ancient civilization running up the east Mediterranean seaboard, across Syria and northern Mesopotamia, and descending into Babylonia. Along this band of territory fell enough rain to permit systematic crop cultivation and the growth of cities. The open desert to the east and south of the Roman provinces, inhabited by transhumant and nomadic Bedouin, was otherwise penetrated only by caravans from trading cities, often, like Palmyra (see overleaf) and Hatra, based on oases.

Roman occupation made little real difference to the cultural life of the area. Greek remained the language of its upper classes, Syriac of the ordinary people in the towns and more particularly the countryside. Latin made little headway, though it was used at Berytus (Beirut), the home of Roman law in the east, and in the late Empire in the administrative capital of Antioch. Easterners, on the other hand, like Paul of Tarsus, Lucian of Samosata and the jurist Ulpian, found their way all over the Empire; while, writing of a less elevated level of society, the conservative Italian, Juvenal, complained that "the Orontes has flowed into the Tiber" (*Satires* 3.62)! Along the same route came some of the most innovative and important philosophical and religious ideas of the later Greco-Roman world.

The insignia given by the *Notitia Dignitatum* for the Dux Arabiae. Garrison towns are indicated in the usual manner; note the snakes and a pair of ostriches.

The frieze of a 5th-century mosaic from a villa at Daphne near Antioch (*bottom*) shows an itinerary from Antioch to this fashionable resort. Here are seen "the workshops of the martyr's shrine" (of St Babylos at Daphne), before which a reclining man, Markellos, is being served by an attendant named Chalkomas. Then comes "the Olympic stadium," "the private [baths] of Ardabourios," and "Kastalia" and "Pallas," the famous springs of Daphne. Below Kastalia is a semicircular basin with portico, possibly the nymphaeum built by Hadrian. The attractive "Still Life with Boiled Eggs" (*below*) is a detail from another mosaic from Daphne.

The upper-class family group (*right*), from a cave tomb at Edessa in Osrhoene, well expresses the cultural diversity of the Roman world. Its members, whose names are written in Syriac, wear the colorful robes, slippers, trousers and headgear evocative of an Iranian rather than Roman provincial background.

The view from the upper citadel (*opposite*) shows the commanding position of Edessa. Until the 3rd century it was ruled by an ancestral royal dynasty: a statue of Queen Shalmath, possibly wife of Abgar IX, "the Great" (179–216), surmounted one of the two free-standing columns on the citadel.

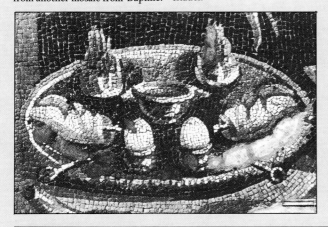

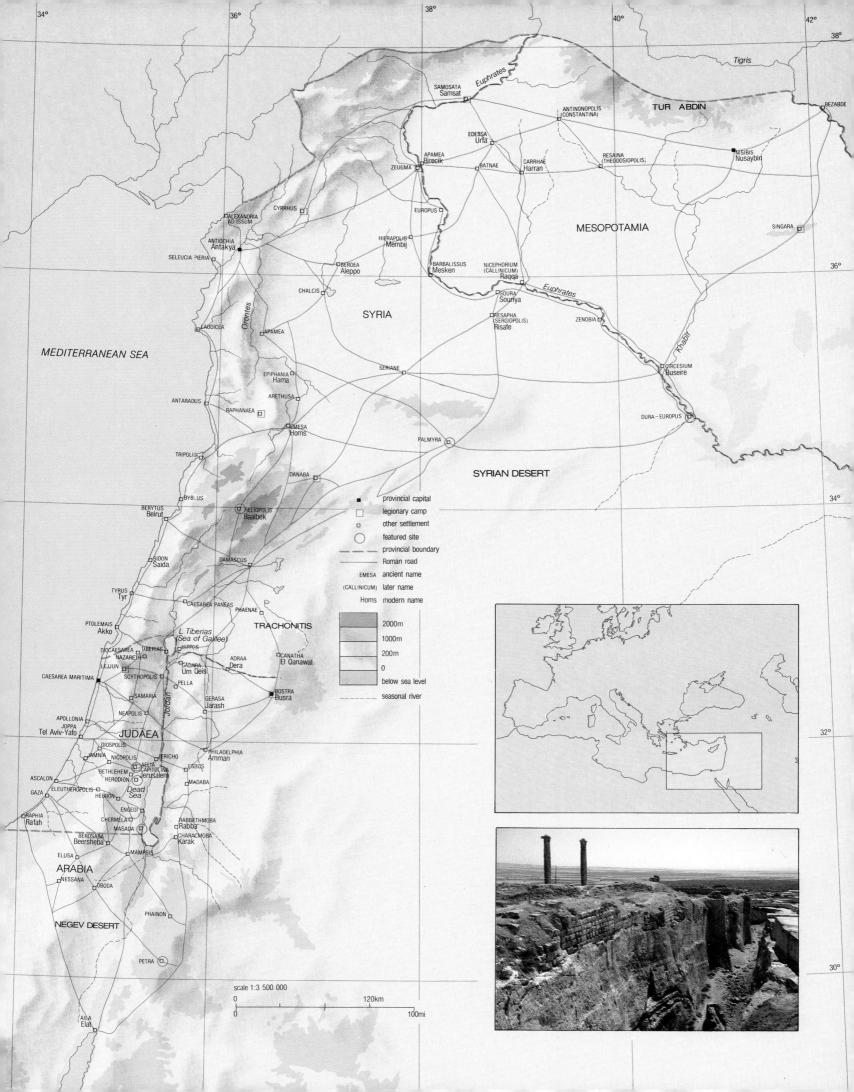

34° 36° 38° 40° 42°

38°

Tigris

SAMOSATA
Samsat

Euphrates

ANTINONOPOLIS
(CONSTANTINA)

TUR ABDIN

BEZABDE

EDESSA
Urfa

NISIBIS
Nusaybin

APAMEA
Birecik

ZEUGMA

BATNAE

CARRHAE
Harran

RESAINA
(THEODOSIOPOLIS)

36°

ALEXANDRIA
AD ISSUM

CYRRHUS

EUROPUS

MESOPOTAMIA

SINGARA

ANTIOCHIA
Antakya

HIERAPOLIS
Membij

SELEUCIA PIERIA

BEROEA
Aleppo

BARBALISSUS
Mesken

NICEPHORIUM
(CALLINICUM)
Raqqa

CHALCIS

Euphrates

LAODICEA

APAMEA

SYRIA

SOURA
Souriya

RESAPHA
(SERGIOPOLIS)
Risafe

ZENOBIA

Orontes

MEDITERRANEAN SEA

EPIPHANIA
Hama

SERIANE

Khabir

CIRCESIUM
Buseire

ANTARADUS

ARETHUSA

RAPHANAEA

EMESA
Homs

TRIPOLIS

SYRIAN DESERT

DANABA

PALMYRA

DURA–EUROPUS

34°

BERYTUS
Beirut

BYBLUS

HELIOPOLIS
Baalbek

■ provincial capital

SIDON
Saida

DAMASCUS

□ legionary camp

▫ other settlement

TYRUS
Tyr

○ featured site

PTOLEMAIS
Akko

CAESAREA PANEAS

PHAENAE

─ ─ ─ provincial boundary

──── Roman road

*L Tiberias
(Sea of Galilee)*

TRACHONITIS

EMESA ancient name

DIOCAESAREA

TIBERIAS

HIPPOS

(CALLINICUM) later name

NAZARETH

ADRAA
Dera

CANATHA
El Qanawat

Homs modern name

LEJJUN

SADARA
Um Qeis

CAESAREA MARITIMA

SCYTHOPOLIS

PELLA

2000m

32°

SAMARIA

1000m

NEAPOLIS

GERASA
Jarash

BOSTRA
Busra

200m

APOLLONIA

0

JOPPA
Tel Aviv-Yafo

Jordan

below sea level

JUDAEA

DIOSPOLIS

─ ─ ─ seasonal river

JAMNIA

NICOROLIS

JERICHO

PHILADELPHIA
Amman

NICOROLIS

AELIA
CAPITOLINA
Jerusalem

ESBUS

ASCALON

BETHLEHEM

HERODION

MADABA

GAZA

ELEUTHEROPOLIS

HEBRON

*Dead
Sea*

ENGEDI

RAPHIA
Rafah

CHERMELA

MASADA

RABBATHMOBA
Rabba

CHARACMOBA
Karak

BEROSABA
Beersheba

MAMPSIS

ELUSA

ARABIA

NESSANA

OBODA

PHAINON

NEGEV DESERT

PETRA

scale 1:3 500 000

0   120km

0   100mi

AILA
Elat

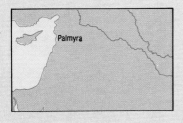

Palmyra

Palmyra or Tadmor, the "city of palms," produced under the Roman Empire a spectacular explosion of urban prosperity. Roman interest in Palmyra had begun as early as Mark Antony, who attacked it but failed to capture its legendary wealth, which was carried beyond the Euphrates by its mobile owners. In the earliest years of the Empire it could be regarded as an independent state between the empires of Rome and Parthia, but Germanicus visited it as Tiberius' envoy during his tour of the east in 18 AD and Palmyra was incorporated in the province of Syria. Its trading links with the east always gave it a degree of independence unusual for a Roman city. Its chief families organized the luxury caravan trade over the desert to the Euphrates and Mesene (Maisan) in the Persian Gulf, connecting there with the sea route to India. An inscription, written in both Palmyrene and Greek, tells how one merchant "on many occasions nobly and generously assisted the merchants, caravans and fellow citizens established at Vologesias," and had "defended from great danger the caravan recently arrived from Vologesias." The "danger" probably came from Bedouin tribesmen along the route.

In the 260s and 270s the Palmyrene dynasts Odaenathus, Vaballath and Zenobia established their city as the capital of an independent empire which performed important military services against the Sasanians. Palmyra was however destroyed by Aurelian and never regained prosperity.

The view from the northwest (*right*) well evokes the geographical setting and monumental splendor of the city. The great temple of Bel stands in the distance, built in 19AD on the tell, or ruin mound, which shows the antiquity of the settlement, with the colonnaded avenue leading from it through the city. On the near side of the temple is a group of buildings including the theater and, surrounded by columns, the agora (or caravanserai). Beyond the temple are the trees of the oasis, and the desert across which the caravans made their way to the Euphrates and the Persian Gulf.

Left A 2nd-century tombstone of a young man. The tower tombs of Palmyra to the west of the city are among its best-known landmarks and attest the wealth of its great families.

Below Architectural fragment from Palmyra. The vine leaves and tendrils reflect oriental influence in their studied decorative symmetry.

The most striking feature of the plan of Palmyra is its irregularity. The temple of Bel, the houses behind it, and the theater are out of alignment, and the arrangement of the theater and adjoining agora is asymmetrical. The great colonnade assumes three different directions and the transverse colonnade is not perpendicular to it. The explanation of the irregularity lies in the pattern of pre-Roman occupation of the site, itself dependent on the position of the oasis and location of the water sources. It has been suggested that the inhabitants had retained something of their Bedouin lifestyle, encamped in different areas of the site, which developed as different quarters of the Roman city.

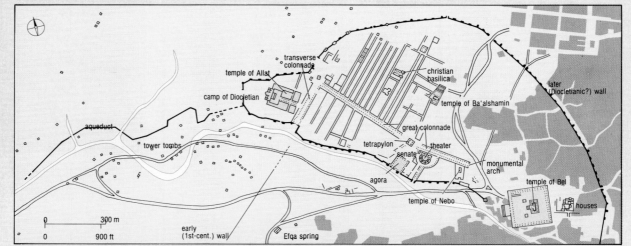

Dura-Europus

Dura on the Euphrates, named Europus by its Hellenistic settlers, was a city with, on one level, a clearly articulated history. Built as a fortress by the Seleucids in 300 BC, it fell in the 2nd century BC under Parthian, and from 165 AD, under Roman domination. In 256 it was destroyed by the Persians under Shapur I, and never resettled.

The sudden abandonment of Dura brings to an end the Roman phase of its existence, and the city has produced much evidence of Roman military organization. More significant, however, is the persistence of its indigenous Semitic character through all periods of foreign control. The rectangular agora was rapidly filled by the informal structures of a Levantine bazaar. The inscriptions are mostly in Greek, but Aramaic and Arabic dialects and Pahlavi are also represented. The same mixture occurs in the religious life of Dura. Apart from the Roman state cults, there was a synagogue, Mithraeum, and Christian house church.

The aerial view of Dura (*above*), supported by the plan, shows its strategic position on a scarp overlooking the Euphrates. Both show clearly the main design of a Hellenistic city: oriental influence is more apparent in the details of domestic architecture. The church and synagogue adjoin the inner face of the rampart to the right of the photograph.

The wall paintings from the synagogue at Dura shown here portray (*top*) the discovery of the baby Moses in his reed boat on the river Nile and (*above*) the Ark of the Covenant under Philistine attack; the Philistine soldiers wear contemporary Sasanian military dress. The Jewish community had links with the Aramaic-speaking Jews of lower Mesopotamia, the presence of wall paintings in the synagogue suggesting in any case a less than strictly rigorous attitude to the teaching of the Law.

Right The view southeast from the platform of the temple of Jupiter-Baʿal. In the foreground is another temple, known as the temple of Bacchus, but most probably of Venus-Atargatis, one of the triad of Semitic deities worshiped at Heliopolis. The plan of the sacred precinct (*below*) illustrates the combination of open enclosures and *cellae* which, better than any individual architectural features, shows the "oriental" nature of the site. The Christian basilica was constructed in the late 4th century: Heliopolis was one of those cities where paganism maintained a long-lasting tenacity (see p. 194).

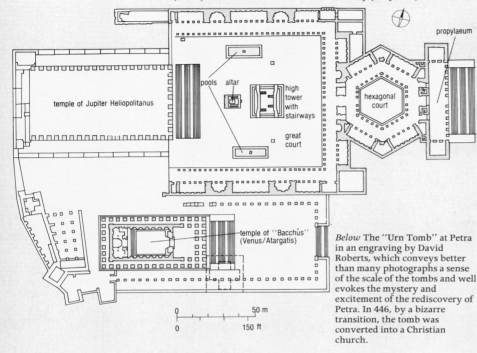

temple of Jupiter Heliopolitanus · pools · altar · high tower with stairways · great court · hexagonal court · propylaeum · temple of "Bacchús" (Venus/Atargatis)

0 — 50 m
0 — 150 ft

Below The "Urn Tomb" at Petra in an engraving by David Roberts, which conveys better than many photographs a sense of the scale of the tombs and well evokes the mystery and excitement of the rediscovery of Petra. In 446, by a bizarre transition, the tomb was converted into a Christian church.

Baalbek

Like Dura-Europus and Petra, Heliopolis (the ancient Baalbek) rose to prominence in the later Hellenistic and Roman periods, its main phase of civic development coming, as so often, in the 2nd and early 3rd centuries. Standing in the valley between the mountain massifs of Lebanon and anti-Lebanon, Heliopolis possessed the usual facilities of a large Greco-Roman council hall, theater and hippodrome, together with houses which have produced, especially from the late Roman period, fine mosaics, both classical and "orientalizing" in style.

The real claim of Heliopolis, however, is in its marvelous temple precinct, and especially in the temple of Jupiter-Baʿal, built like its counterpart at Palmyra (p. 158) during the 1st century AD on a tell, or ruin mound, which shows the antiquity of the site. Jupiter-Baʿal was one of a triad of divinities worshiped at the site: the others were Venus-Aphrodite, the classical equivalent of the Semitic Atargatis, and Mercury-Hermes, whose Semitic equivalent is not known.

Petra

Petra, the capital of the Nabataean kingdom visited by Germanicus Caesar in 18 AD, owed its development to the local kings of the later Hellenistic era whose achievement in urban settlement in Jordan and the Negev is currently becoming better appreciated. The great prosperity of Petra had derived from its role as a caravan city on the route from India to Rhinocorura (El Arish) and Gaza on the Mediterranean, but it seems that already by the 1st century AD such trade was taking the more northerly route by Palmyra or going by the Red Sea to Alexandria, and that the prosperity of Petra had reached its limit. The Roman remains are nevertheless impressive, with a theater and a colonnaded street leading by way of a triple-arched gateway to a sacred precinct. But Petra is most famous for its rock tombs, their facades evoking in massive relief the style of Hellenistic palaces.

Jerusalem

Jerusalem, the ancient capital of King David, was described by the elder Pliny in the first century of the Roman Empire as "by far the most famous city, not only of Judaea, but of the east" (*Natural History* 5.70). This it owed largely to Herod the Great, who gave Jerusalem a quite spectacular magnificence, with extensions to its fortified area, a theater and amphitheater (presumably outside the walls), palaces and monumental buildings including the Temple, dominating the city from its massive platform. As these works suggest, Herod achieved a balance between Jewish and Greco-Roman culture hardly attempted by his Hasmonean predecessors. The independence of Judaea did not long survive Herod's death in 4 BC, before it was made into a Roman province with its capital at Caesarea, another of the cities rebuilt by Herod.

Jerusalem and its Temple were taken and destroyed by Titus during the Jewish revolt of 66–70 AD (see pp. 80–81), and the city occupied by the Tenth Legion. Under Hadrian it was refounded as a Roman colony with the name Aelia Capitolina. With the christianization of the Roman Empire it entered a new period of fame and prosperity through its association with the last teachings, death and resurrection of Christ. By the late 4th century Jerusalem was the object of frequent pilgrimage and site of monastic settlements, a phase of its history which continued into the Byzantine period. Notable benefactions were made by the exiled empress Eudocia (p. 217), and under Justinian. Jerusalem fell to the Arabs in 638 and was equally famous as a holy city of Islam.

Bottom Jerusalem, as it appears on a 6th-century mosaic map from Madaba in Jordan. Conspicuous among the monuments are the colonnaded main street of the Hadrianic city and the Church of the Holy Sepulcher midway along it, clearly recognizable by its rotunda (seen upside down as the picture is printed). The Wailing Wall (*below*) is actually the platform of the Temple, as extended by Herod the Great.

Herodion

The citadel of Herodion, built by Herod the Great 12 kilometers from Jerusalem and clearly visible from there, was the focal point of a large settlement "not inferior to a city," according to the historian Josephus. It was equipped with "diversions" or pleasure grounds, and water had to be taken there from some distance by aqueduct. The citadel itself contained an elaborate palace, with baths, synagogue and gardens, and was a clever feat of architectural deception. It was built upon and masked by an artificial mound added to the natural hilltop. The palace would reveal itself to a visitor only as he mounted the 200 steps of polished stone and entered through the deep-cut entrance by the main tower. It was among the residences in which Herod entertained M. Agrippa in 14 BC.

After his death, Herod was buried at Herodion — as some scholars believe, in the still unexcavated north tower. The site was one of the last strongholds in the Jewish revolt of 66–70 AD and was also occupied in the rebellion of Bar-Kochba.

Masada

Masada, a spur of the barren mountains to the west of the Dead Sea, was used as a fortress by the Hasmoneans, but massively developed by Herod as a palace-cum-stronghold, to secure himself from challenges from both inside and outside his kingdom. The ruins contain extensive storehouses as well as heated baths, synagogue and two main palaces, the western with descending terraces perched dizzily on the edge of the precipice.

After Herod's death the palace was disused, but was taken by Zealots from the Roman garrison which occupied it at the beginning of the revolt of 66–70. The reduction of Masada was completed by Vespasian's legate Flavius Silva, only after a lengthy siege which ended (in 73) with the suicide of the defenders. A pottery fragment inscribed with the name of their leader, Ben Ya'ir, may possibly be one of the pieces by which the defenders drew lots to determine which ten of them would kill the others (390 in all, men, women and children), the last survivor of these ten taking his own life.

The aerial photograph of Herodion (*left*) clearly shows the four towers, and the artificial mound raised to their level. The north tower, in which Herod may lie buried, is to the right of the picture, with the approach and entrance to the palace visible beside it (the sloping ramp is modern).

The aerial view of Masada (*far left*) shows some of the Roman siege fortresses, part of the wall of circumvallation and the huge ramp up which were moved the siege engines that finally ended the Zealot resistance. Josephus explains that the flat top of Masada was fertile and left clear for cultivation, so that the place should enjoy some self-sufficiency: the general truth of this is also clear from the plan (*left*). The summit is approached from the Dead Sea by the "Snake Path," the hair-raising nature of which is described by Josephus in vivid but possibly exaggerated terms (*Jewish War* 7.283). The western approach was easier, but blocked by Herod with a defensive tower.

EGYPT AND CYRENAICA

Map labels:
MISURATA
MEDITERRANEAN SEA
APOLLONIA
Marsa Susah
PTOLEMAIS
Tulmaythah Qasr el-Lebia
TAUCHIRA
(ARSINOE)
Tukrah
HADRIANOPOLIS
Driana
BARCA
CYRENE
Shahhat
OLBIA
DARNIS
Derna
EUHESPERIDES
(BERENICE)
Benghazi
CYRENAICA
CHARAX
to Sabe

The geographical proximity of Egypt and Cyrenaica is deceptive, for the two provinces were very different in their economic structure and manner of government. Egypt, acquired by Octavian after the capture of Alexandria in 30 BC, was treated by him and his successors as an imperial domain, a special position which they inherited from a centuries-old tradition of monarchical government by the pharaohs and Ptolemies. Evidence for the manner of government, and for all aspects of Roman life in Egypt, is abundantly provided by the many thousands of papyri found at Oxyrhynchus and at other sites, but the extent to which this evidence can properly be applied to other provinces of the Empire remains doubtful. The peculiar geographical nature of Egypt is unique in the Roman Empire, being most similar to that of Mesopotamian Babylonia. Linked by the Nile, its cities were more easily subjected to central control than those elsewhere; conversely, only under central control can the country achieve its full agricultural potential. The annual flooding of the Nile provided the essential rhythm of Egyptian life; it was officially measured at Elephantine by a gauge known as the Nilometer.

In Alexandria, Egypt had a great Hellenistic city. Elsewhere in the delta and in the Nile valley community life was founded on settlements, often described in the sources as "cities" but in reality resembling large villages. Greek culture penetrated Egypt through Alexandria to the cities of the Nile, but there is an essential distinction between the hellenized city populations of Egypt and the country folk, who retained their Egyptian language and in the late Empire produced the vernacular Coptic church.

Cyrenaica, the group of five cities known as the Pentapolis, was under the Empire governed together with Crete by a senatorial proconsul. The economic life of the Pentapolis was made possible by the well-watered coastal ridge known as the Gebel el Akdar. Though Cyrenaica seems in local terms rather remote, this was less true in the broader context of the eastern Mediterranean. Its cities flourished under the Roman Empire as they had under the Ptolemies, and the port of Apollonia in particular grew in importance as a link in the communications between the cities of proconsular Africa, Tripolitania and Alexandria.

The insignia of the "Count of the Egyptian Frontier" from the *Notitia Dignitatum* (*below right*) show the symbolic features of the land – river Nile and pyramids. Emerging from the cities are the devices of the administrative divisions of Egypt. The funerary portrait painted on wood (*below*) is one of many from the later Roman period which often, as here, combine Hellenistic with local influences. Scenes inspired by the Nile landscape, much like the "chinoiserie" of more modern times, were a popular decorative feature, as in this mosaic from Pompeii (*bottom right*).

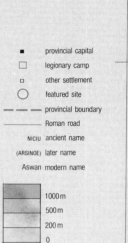

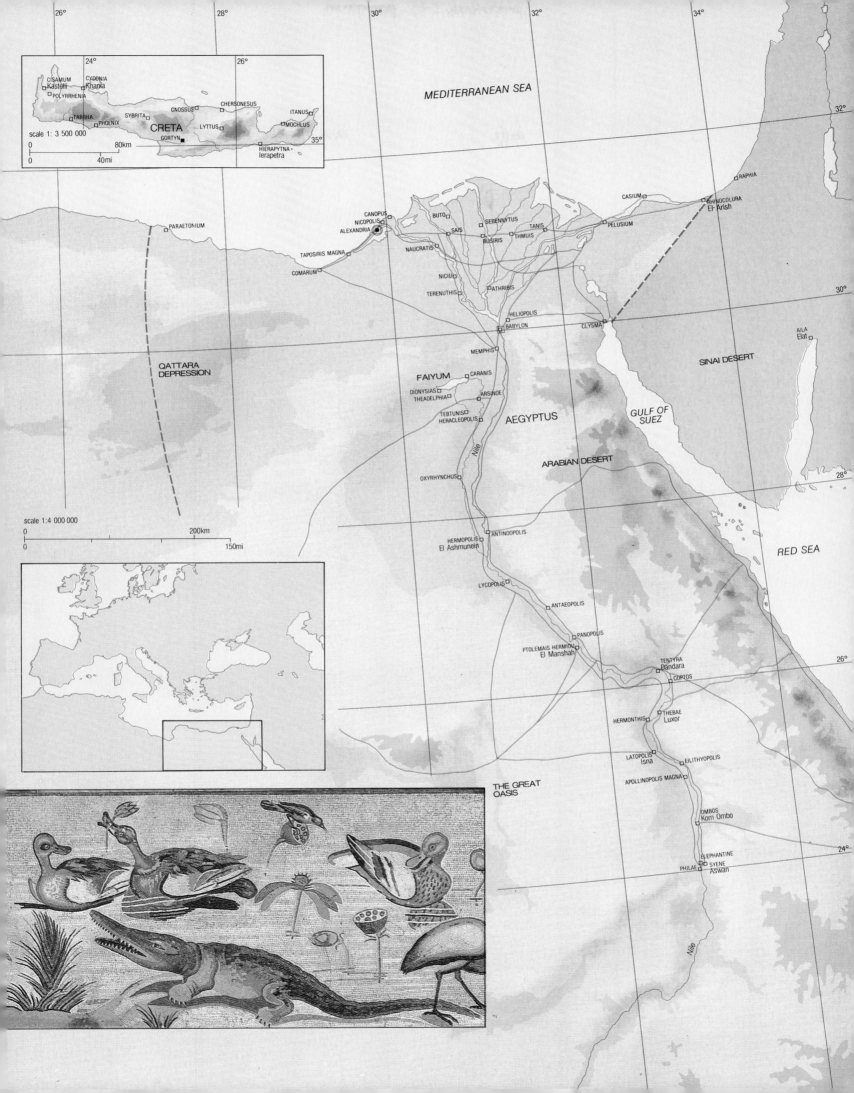

MEDITERRANEAN SEA

CRETA

scale 1: 3 500 000

CISAMUM
Kastelli
POLYRRHENIA
CYDONIA
Khania
TARRHA
PHOENIX
SYBRITA
CNOSSUS
CHERSONESUS
ITANUS
MOCHLUS
GORTYN
LYTTUS
HIERAPYTNA
Ierapetra

0   80km
0   40mi

PARAETONIUM

CANOPUS
NICOPOLIS
ALEXANDRIA
TAPOSIRIS MAGNA
COMARUM
NAUCRATIS
NICIU
TERENUTHIS
BUTO
SAIS
BUSIRIS
SEBENNYTUS
TANIS
THMUIS
ATHRIBIS
HELIOPOLIS
BABYLON
CASIUM
PELUSIUM
RHINOCOLURA
El-Arish
RAPHIA
CLYSMA

QATTARA
DEPRESSION

MEMPHIS

FAIYUM
CARANIS
DIONYSIAS
THEADELPHIA
ARSINOE
TEBTUNIS
HERACLEOPOLIS

AEGYPTUS

SINAI DESERT

GULF OF
SUEZ

AILA
Elat

ARABIAN DESERT

OXYRHYNCHUS

Nile

scale 1:4 000 000

0   200km
0   150mi

HERMOPOLIS
El Ashmunein
ANTINOOPOLIS

RED SEA

LYCOPOLIS

ANTAEOPOLIS

PANOPOLIS

PTOLEMAIS HERMIOU
El Manshah

TENTYRA
Dandara
COPTOS

HERMONTHIS
THEBAE
Luxor

LATOPOLIS
Isna
EILITHYOPOLIS

THE GREAT
OASIS

APOLLINOPOLIS MAGNA

OMBOS
Kom Ombo

ELEPHANTINE
SYENE
PHILAE
Aswan

Nile

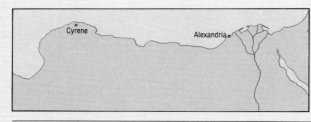

As with most Greek cities of the east Mediterranean, the visible remains of Cyrene are of the Roman period; yet the layout of the city is Hellenistic. In the photograph the "street of Battus" is seen as it passes the magnificent Caesareum, or temple of the imperial cult. Adjoining the Caesareum to the north is a basilica of Roman imperial date, to the west a small odeion, or recital hall, and across the "street of Battus" the Roman theater. It was obviously a most imposing civic center.

Alexandria

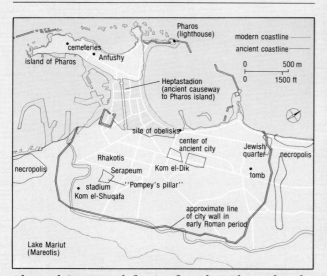

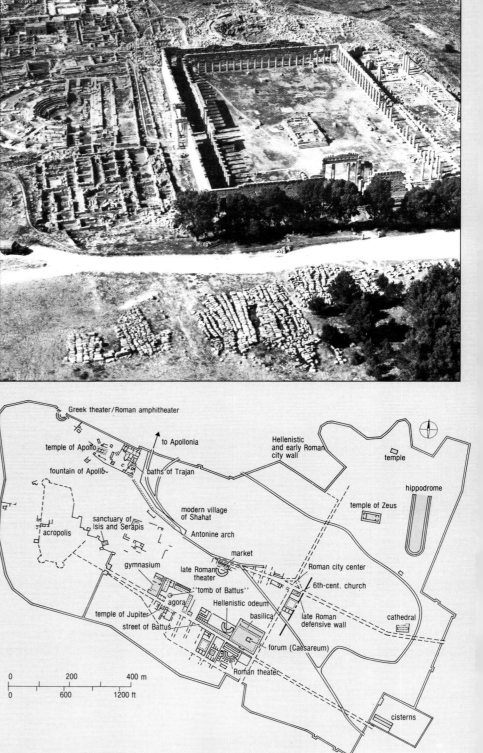

Alexandria, named for its founder Alexander the Great and vigorously developed by the Ptolemies, has been so successful a city that little archaeological trace of the ancient site remains. The ground plan, however, laid out by Dinocrates of Rhodes, was a famous example of Hellenistic urban design. Alexandria was in the Roman Empire an immense and exuberant metropolis, surpassed in size only by Rome, to which it was in intellectual distinction far superior. Its fortune came from trade; it was a clearing house for eastern imports, and in the Roman Empire dispatched the corn ships to Rome and, after 330 AD, to Constantinople. Prominent among its cosmopolitan population, the Jews possessed their own political organization and in 39 AD sent the philosopher Philo as ambassador to Caligula to protest about their treatment by the Greeks of Alexandria. Yet, as Philo shows, the Jews also were profoundly influenced by the persistent Hellenistic atmosphere of the city.

Cyrene

The prosperity of Cyrene was maintained for over a millennium after its foundation by Battus from Thera as one of the most famous and best-documented early Greek colonies. From the late 4th century it fell under a local dynasty of the Ptolemies, the last of whom bequeathed it to Rome in 96 BC. Its development under the Romans differed little from that of other Hellenistic cities. In the Jewish revolt of 115 AD it was occupied and badly damaged by a rebel leader; its recovery was assisted by the munificence of Hadrian. Damaged by earthquakes in the mid-3rd and mid-4th centuries, Cyrene, like its Tripolitanian neighbors, was afflicted in the late 4th and early 5th centuries by desert incursions. Yet the city remained active until the Byzantine period. It contained two Christian churches in the central area and a splendid cathedral with baptistery, which fell outside the Byzantine walls and served as a fortified outpost.

PART FOUR
THE EMPIRE IN DECLINE

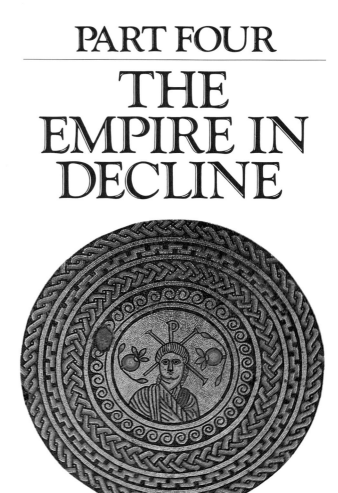

DISORDER AND RECOVERY

Maximinus to Carinus, 235–284

The half-century from the accession of Maximinus in 235 to the death of Carinus in 284 was a period of political disturbance made no easier for the modern historian by the fragmentary condition of its sources. Cassius Dio, particularly interesting on the personalities and events of his own time, comes to an end in the late 220s; the much less impressive history of the Syrian Herodian ends with the death of Maximinus in 238. The Greek historical works of an Athenian, Dexippus, were clearly of great interest, but survive only in the tantalizing fragments preserved by Byzantine epitomators. In the Latin tradition, the imperial biographies known as the *Augustan History*, often very informative on the 2nd century, are in the 3rd reduced to fiction and fantasy, the interest of which, great though it is, is not primarily of a historical order. Also writing in the later 4th century, a group of epitomators — Aurelius Victor, Eutropius and an anonymous successor of Victor — offer brief accounts of the 3rd century deriving from a lost Latin historian of the age of Constantine (died 337). The study of the interrelationship of these sources is however a technical and often controversial matter.

Any treatment of the 3rd century must necessarily be thematic, and cannot offer narrative and chronological precision. This is not necessarily a handicap. It is more serious that the historian is more or less forced to see the age in terms of that ill-used historical concept, an "Age of Transition," in that its meaning has to be inferred largely from what precedes and follows it. But contemporaries could not wait for the 4th century to tell them what their lives had been about; the historian must make some attempt to see the period in its own right and to read its character.

On a narrower view, that of the development of the imperial office, the 3rd century has been characterized as an age of anarchy. Between 235 and 284 there were 18 or more "legitimate" Roman emperors, holding office for an average of less than three years each; but this count is only a fraction of the story, for it leaves aside sons appointed to hold office with their fathers, and other colleagues, and it ignores usurpers and pretenders whose full number may never be known. Nearly all met violent deaths in civil or foreign war, or by conspiracy.

The circumstances and motives surrounding these monotonously repetitive events are often extremely obscure. Personal ambition alone can hardly account for the claims made by so many for an office which offered so few prospects of survival. Usurpations usually took place in areas of military occupation and barbarian invasion, especially among the armies of the Rhine and Danube. The phenomenon of usurpation should be regarded, not as an accumulation of acts of individual ambition, but as a facet of the structure of the Empire in this period.

The most obvious, and surely correct, inter-

pretation is that usurpations were a response to the military pressures that increasingly beset the Empire. The incursions of the Goths into Asia Minor, of Alamanni and Franks into Gaul and Spain, of Heruli into Attica — whence they were repelled by local resistance led by the historian Dexippus — led to a need for effective power which a distant emperor could not supply, for locally provided finance and for imperial authority if negotiations with the invaders were to be successfully concluded. The independent Gallic empire of the 260s and 270s, established by the usurper Postumus, provided a better-organized response to the Germanic invasions than the legitimate emperor Gallienus, with his preoccupations in the east and with the Danube frontier, could hope to offer. It is a tribute to Gallienus' sense of reality as well as a comment on the limitations of his power, that he left his Gallic rival to get on with the job undisturbed.

In the east, there was a significant shift in the balance of power in the rise of a vigorous and ambitious new royal dynasty, that of the Sasanians under Shapur I, which succeeded in unifying and invigorating the Persian empire and in presenting an effective challenge after a long period in which the ascendancy had rested with the Romans. In 260 the emperor Valerian was taken prisoner by the Persians under Shapur I in a battle near Edessa; the figure of the humiliated Roman emperor, together with the supposed submission to Shapur of his predecessor Philip in 244, was portrayed on the monumental rock carvings at Bishapur and Naqsh-i-Rustam. From the mid-260s Gallienus, sole emperor after his father's capture, committed the defense of the eastern frontier to the Palmyrene dynast Odaenathus who, succeeded by Zenobia and Vaballath, governed a quasi-independent empire extending at its greatest from Egypt to southeastern Asia Minor.

The reign of Gallienus both illustrates the predicament of the Empire in the 3rd century and

Shapur I (240–72 AD), "king of kings" and inspirer of the resurgence against Rome of her ancestral enemy in the east, brings down a galloping stag on this beautiful silver and gilt presentation dish, perhaps the earliest of many showing Sasanian kings at their characteristic pleasure. The animals for hunting were kept in great walled parks, which often attract the attention of classical sources. The historian Ammianus Marcellinus, who visited Persia with the campaign of Julian in 363, commented on them and remarked also that the Persians "show nothing in their painting and sculpture than war and various forms of slaughter."

suggests the structural reforms by which it might be overcome. The reign was regarded by later sources as the time in which the frequency of rebellion had reached its climax, large tracts of Roman territory, in Spain, Gaul and Britain, and in the Orient, being governed as separate "empires." But this division of the Empire, with Gallienus holding Illyricum as the link between east and west, resembles the collegiate structure of the Tetrarchy and the 4th-century system of regional prefectures. The frequent usurpations were the painful early stages of the development of a collegiate imperial office, lacking only the adaptation of the ideal of imperial unity which made collegiality acceptable. One of the strangest aspects of the 3rd century was the determination and expenditure in manpower with which, despite their other preoccupations, legitimate emperors suppressed the claims to power of rivals who were in fact performing an effective local function.

The second development for which Gallienus was later criticized, was his alleged exclusion of the traditional Roman governing class, the senate, from the tenure of military power. One ancient source ascribes this to a "decree" of Gallienus forbidding senators from holding military commands, supposedly in order to keep the "best men" away from the armies. But this is much too simple a view: the elimination of senators from army commands in favor of men of equestrian rank and military background was part of a general process of change which can be traced back into the 2nd century, to the wars of Marcus Aurelius.

Economic aspects of the 3rd-century crisis

The condition of the Roman Empire in the later 3rd century can, on any account of its political history, only be described as critical. Within the tendency of provincial regions to split away into self-governing blocks, further levels of disaffection can also be perceived. In central Gaul, local rebels known as Bacaudae staged some sort of insurrection against imperial authority. In other parts of the Empire there is evidence for the flight of peasants from the land to take up more promising occupations such as banditry, and for an increase in the amount of deserted agricultural land. It is impossible to

quantify the extent of these developments, as it is to assess the likelihood, based on the effects of plague and the incidence of war and disorder in the later 2nd and 3rd centuries, of a general decline in population, and therefore in the manpower available to the government and in the agricultural productivity of the Empire. Statistical evidence is lacking, and such tendencies are in any case unlikely to have affected the Empire uniformly in its different areas.

The most readily measurable expressions of the 3rd-century crisis are in economic developments. The later 3rd century saw a momentous weakening of the monetary system. The causes of this were complex, one of them being the Roman authorities' own lack of comprehension of any theory of monetary circulation, and so of the economic consequences of their own actions. The functioning of ancient coinage was based on the assumption that the value of a coin was that of its metal content: in this sense, one might regard the official legends stamped on the coins – as in the cases of the Lydian and early Greek coinages – as the state's guarantee of their purity and weight. But this assumption, if it was ever explicitly made, was not rigorously observed, for it was considered permissible, in times of a shortage of precious metals, to debase the coin by the admixture of base metal, without any idea of reducing its face value. This had been done, without disastrous consequences, by Nero, who issued silver denarii at a purity of 90 per cent, and increasingly by later emperors. Marcus Aurelius issued silver coin at a purity of 75 per cent, Septimius Severus at 50 per cent. But such things were noticed; Cassius Dio accused Caracalla of paying good gold coin in subsidies to barbarians and allowing debased silver to circulate in the Empire.

In the later 3rd century, an apparently severe shortfall in the supply of precious metals, combined with extremely heavy government expenditure, forced the emperors to issue an increasingly debased silver coinage in order to meet their financial needs. It is obvious that, with the recognition by the public that the coins were grossly overvalued in relation to their metal content, their value as currency would fall and prices rise. The result was an inflationary spiral in which an ever more heavily debased coinage pursued and then created still higher prices. In addition, coin of higher intrinsic value was hoarded and never returned as taxation, forcing still greater debasement as the government's access to sources of precious metal declined yet further.

Already by the time of Gallienus, the standard of purity of the silver denarius stood as low as 5 per cent. Before many years had passed, the government was reduced to issuing silver-plated copper coin. The inflation rate between the 2nd century and Diocletian's Prices Edict of 301 (see below, pp. 172–73) can be judged from a single, fairly reliable figure, deriving from the recorded price of wheat: a measure (*modius*) of wheat, normally valued in the 2nd century at about half a denarius, is listed in the Prices Edict – which gives a low estimate – at 100 denarii. The denarius was thus worth, at most, 0·5 per cent of its earlier value.

It is as difficult to comprehend how the government could persist with its self-destructive

A Persian view of Roman history. In this monumental rock carving from Naqsh-i-Rustam near the tomb of Darius the Great, Shapur publicizes his recent triumphs. He receives the obeisance of the emperor Philip (244), and holds by the right wrist Valerian, defeated and captured near Edessa in 260.

monetary "policy" as it is to see how, with the combination of inflation, high government spending and a shortage of precious metals, it could escape from it. The chief victim of the inflation was the government itself, as its tax receipts declined in real value and it was required to make large cash payments in salaries to its officials and soldiers. The government's solution was to secure its needs by exacting them directly in the form of requisitions of food and material supplies, transportation facilities and so on. Over the course of time these exactions became more regular and remained as a standard feature of the late Roman tax system.

An area of public life directly affected by the monetary collapse was the civic munificence which was the characteristic mark of the Empire in the Antonine age. Public building, the provision of shows and amenities and other such acts of public generosity, can be seen from an economic point of view as a means of disposing of large cash surpluses derived from agricultural production. Ancient society, as we have seen, lacked the variety of resources and instruments which in the modern industrial world absorb surpluses; there was little to do with surplus money except spend it, often ostentatiously. It is therefore not surprising that the collapse of the monetary system entailed a sudden and very noticeable decline in civic munificence during the later 3rd century. This does not merely imply a stabilization at an existing level of provision: the period is marked by a positive loss of public amenities and entertainments, as theaters and amphitheaters fall out of use, are filled with rubbish and their arcades inhabited by squatters. In some cases, as at Tours and Périgueux, the amphitheaters formed part of city defenses constructed in the later 3rd century, in response to invasions.

The transformation in the appearance of cities of the later Roman period, especially in the west, is sometimes taken to reflect a contraction of urban life also implied in the decline of civic munificence — especially when the process is accompanied by the continued prosperity and in some cases enlargement of great, self-sufficient rural villas. It is inferred that the civic dignitaries who had sustained the urban vigor of the Antonine age now neglected their cities in favor of a self-contained life with their dependants on their estates. Such inferences must be treated with extreme caution. It is true that, in Gaul at least, the cities underwent a transformation; instead of the expansive cities of the early Empire, with ostentatiously large wall circuits and imposing gateways intended more for show than for defense, there now appeared confined wall circuits enclosing the monumental area of the city, that is, only a small proportion of the actual urbanized area. The building materials include reused blocks and column drums from earlier public buildings now clearly out of commission, as well as funerary monuments, inscriptions and so on.

The provincial economies of northern Gaul, Germany and Britain were at all times dependent on a villa culture; archaeology and aerial surveys reveal the existence, especially in northern Gaul, of many self-contained country houses, equipped with storehouses and habitations for estate workers. This was the situation throughout Roman imperial history, and not merely the later period. Nor does

the appearance of fortified citadels within the urban areas of late Roman towns imply that the economic functioning of the cities as such was permanently impaired. It is clear from many examples in Gaul that there was continued habitation of the urban areas outside the later wall circuits. Despite the apparent transformation of the cities of the western Roman Empire and elsewhere (for example at Athens, where the wall built after the Herulian invasion blocked the ancient Panathenaic Way), and despite the loss, for the economic reasons already described, of civic amenities, it should not be assumed that the 3rd-century crisis caused a permanent decline in urban life, leading to an enhancement of what are sometimes called the prefeudal or "seigneurial" aspects of the position of rural landowners.

It was argued in rather different terms by the great social and economic historian, Michael Rostovtzeff, that in the 3rd century an alliance was formed between the peasantry and a Roman army mainly recruited from the peasantry, directed against the cities and their propertied classes as the source of social and economic oppression. The interpretation owes much, as Rostovtzeff acknowledged, to the model provided by the activities of the Red Army in revolutionary Russia, which Rostovtzeff left in 1918. Applied to the Roman Empire of the 3rd century, it fails to convince, against the weight of evidence for the hostility felt by the peasantry towards an army which was invariably a more acute and more immediate oppressor than ever the cities had been. The army may have been recruited from the peasantry, but it behaved as an army, taking what it wanted from the land without too much reflection on its own social origins.

An extremely significant economic change, for which the military crisis of the Empire was responsible, was a shift of resources from the Mediterranean area to the frontier regions in which the wars were fought, and in which the emperors had of necessity to spend most of their time. Cities such as Trier on the Moselle, and Sirmium, Naissus and Serdica in the Danubian regions, emerge during the 3rd century in the role of regular imperial capital cities, a role which they retained in the 4th century. There was also a shift to the east. It was said that, before deciding on Byzantium, Constantine the Great had once favored Serdica as the site of a new capital city. Constantinople itself was the successor of Diocletian's Nicomedia; both sites held a strategic position between east and west, closely linked both with the Mediterranean and with the military land routes into Illyricum and eastwards to the Persian frontier.

In this shift of resources and of imperial interest, the ancient capital of Rome became increasingly isolated and, as an interesting consequence, under the dominance of its senatorial class it enjoyed an enhanced independence which made of it, in the absence of the emperors, still one of the most flourishing and lively of late Roman cities. But there can be no doubt that the 3rd century brought about a substantial shift of resources away from the Mediterranean towards the landbound northern frontier, which had for long been, but in the 3rd and 4th centuries was openly revealed as, the real military backbone of the Empire. The significant

The porphyry group of the "Tetrarchs," Venetian loot from Constantinople now set into the wall of the cathedral of San Marco, Venice. Though the identification of the group as Diocletian and his colleagues involves some difficulties, it beautifully captures the spirit of unity and "togetherness" required of late Roman emperors.

Right: Invasions and frontiers of the Empire in the 3rd century AD. The areas actually abandoned as a result of the mid-3rd-century crisis, of which the map gives a necessarily simplified impression, were surprisingly limited: the "Agri Decumates" in Germany, Dacia, and part of Mesopotamia (recovered by Galerius). The main effects were on the internal structure of the Empire. The immense length of the land frontier under simultaneous threat would necessitate devolution of power among "colleges" of emperors, and government would be carried on from military capitals in the frontier zones. In the 3rd century, usurpation secured a *de facto* devolution which "legitimate" emperors were reluctant to concede in principle. The Gallic and Palmyrene "empires" of the 260s and 270s formed, with the Balkan lands between, the self-financing and self-governing blocks represented in all essentials by the 4th-century prefectures (see map p. 173). Other rebellions, like those of the Quinquegentiani in Africa and the Bacaudae of central Gaul, arose from general uncertainty and required expenditure and effort in their suppression without affecting the structure of the Empire.

division in the Empire was as much that between the Mediterranean and the north as that between east and west, which ultimately provided the formal basis of its partition.

Diocletian and the Tetrarchy

The circumstances of the rise of Diocletian were, even for the 3rd century, melodramatic; he is said to have denounced and with his own hand struck down Numerian's praetorian prefect, Aper, before the eyes of the assembled army. This was in 284. Diocletian was proclaimed emperor at Nicomedia in the late summer of the year. The next spring he defeated the surviving emperor, Carinus, in Pannonia, and for the moment held unrivaled power. Nothing in this sequence of events gives any hint of the character of the reign of Diocletian as it was to emerge over the 20 years of vigorous government and reform on which the political structure of the late Roman state was based.

Diocletian's success was based on his recognition of the need to devolve power to colleagues. In 286 he promoted as Caesar another Illyrian officer, Maximian, and in the next year made him Augustus. Maximian devoted himself as co-emperor to the western part of the Empire, where he won victories over the Alamanni, while Diocletian confronted the Persians on the eastern frontier.

On 1 March 293 the arrangement which historians know as the "Tetrarchy" or "Rule of Four" came into being, when two more officers of Illyrian origin, Galerius and Constantius, were appointed Caesars. They held this rank below Diocletian and Maximian, by whom they were respectively adopted. Constantius put away his wife (or concubine) Helena, who took her young son Constantine to be educated in the east, and married

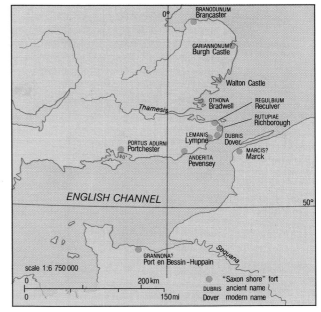

Diocletianic defense system: the "Saxon shore." The defense system of the "Saxon shore" (*litus Saxonicum*), anticipated in some respects by the British usurpers of the late 3rd century but developed and systematized by the Tetrarchs, was a means of coastal defense and surveillance designed to prevent the penetration of Saxon raids through the Straits of Dover to the coasts of southern Britain and northern Gaul. This map is derived from the commands of the "Counts" (*comites*) of the Saxon shore as given by the *Notitia Dignitatum*, but the number of actual forts listed here, especially in northern Gaul, is clearly incomplete. The former view that *litus Saxonicum* designates districts occupied and garrisoned by Saxons on behalf of the Romans is certainly mistaken.

a stepdaughter of the retired emperor Maximian, who was supporting his son Maxentius.

The devolution of power yielded most satisfactory results. Galerius fought the Goths on the lower Danube and in 297–98 won a spectacular victory over the Persians. His lucky capture of the harem of King Narses enabled him to negotiate a Roman frontier along the upper Tigris as far east as Kurdistan and Singara. Meanwhile Diocletian settled a revolt in Egypt, and in the west Constantius recovered Britain from the usurpation of Allectus and won victories on the Rhine frontier, and Maximian suppressed a native insurrection in Mauretania.

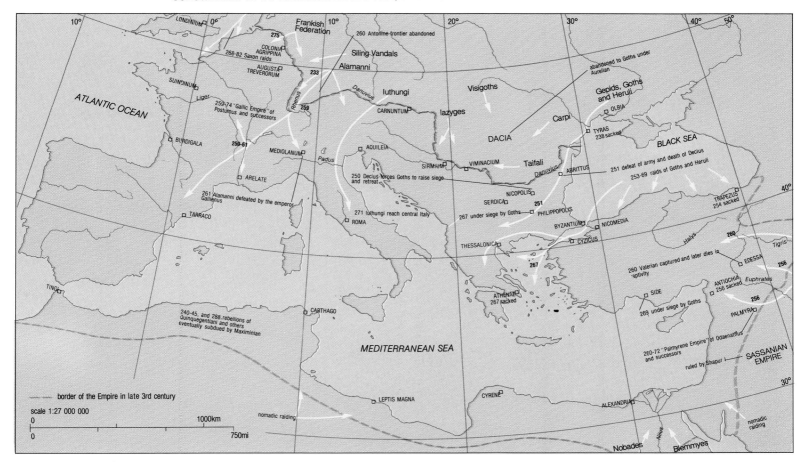

Top The rather crudely modeled but high-quality silver denarius of the British usurper Carausius is remarkable for the Virgilian echo, unique in Roman coinage, with which the province welcomes Carausius as its deliverer. "EXPECTATE VENI" is an allusion to the appearance of the ghost of Hector to Aeneas in a dream before the sack of Troy.

The medallion of Constantius, by contrast (*above*), shows the emperor in his turn being welcomed by LON [dinium], as the "Restorer of Eternal Light" – the "light" of legitimate government in place of the "tyranny" of Carausius and Allectus. The crossing of the Channel by Constantius is symbolized by a warship.

The section of Diocletian's massive Prices Edict shown *below* lists maximum prices for a variety of plant and mineral products including sponge (used to make eye lotion), lime and fish glue, followed by the tariffs for sea transportation from Alexandria to Rome, Nicomedia and Byzantium.

The formation of the Tetrarchy was a progressive achievement, in which the "centrifugal" tendencies in the structure of imperial power, so obvious in the 3rd century, were contained by being legitimized. In an act of self-denial perhaps more astonishing than any other of their achievements, Diocletian and Maximian resigned as Augusti in 305. Galerius and Constantius took their places and two new Caesars were appointed in an attempt to renew the Tetrarchy. The prompt collapse of these arrangements, described below, makes still more remarkable the mutual loyalty achieved by Diocletian and his colleagues. It seems evident that this was not the expression of any sudden change in the attitudes or structure of Roman society but that it was based on the personal and professional loyalty of Illyrian officers known to each other and prepared to accept the dominance of Diocletian.

The survival for 20 years of the government of Diocletian was the precondition for the extraordinary series of reforms which changed the entire tempo of Roman history and were the basis of late Roman government and social organization. Many of the reforms, taken in themselves, had precedents. In their reorganization of the army, for example, Diocletian and his colleagues pursued the development of a mobile field army to complement the role of static frontier garrisons. The promotion of a field army can be seen in the times of Gallienus and Aurelian, and was already implicit in the use made by the early emperors of legionary detachments (*vexillationes*) in active campaigning, while the main legion remained in its camp.

The distinction between a fully mobile field army and static frontier defense is fundamental to late Roman strategy. It has been thought that the frontier garrisons, sometimes referred to as *limitanei*, formed a sort of local militia, occupying land in return for their performance of military duties when required. It is now generally accepted that the word *limitanei* means simply "frontier troops," without these further and far-reaching implications. In certain regions, however, such as Tripolitania and Mauretania, where the defense system was manned by local federate tribesmen, the description of the frontier garrison as a "local militia" seems more apt.

Under the Tetrarchy the numerical strength of the army was greatly increased. A hostile contemporary witness, Lactantius, alleges that the army was quadrupled, and although this is an obvious exaggeration, modern writers are prepared to accept an increase of up to double. The implications of this increase for the problems of finance and supply are very evident, and lead naturally to the question of the monetary and tax reforms of the Tetrarchy.

The Tetrarchs did not at once succeed in stopping inflation, but by a combination of methods they checked it and left a partially stable monetary system to their successors. This was achieved by a series of monetary reforms, the most important of which was the creation of a new gold coin, struck at a high standard of purity at a rate of 60 coins to the pound of gold bullion. With a devaluation of one-fifth by Constantine, this system formed the basis of the stable gold currency of Byzantium. There was also a standard of silver coinage, which held its value relatively well in relation to gold, and of

copper, which did not. The result was continuing inflation in prices as expressed in copper coin, the everyday currency of the Empire's populations. The complaints of the army provoked from Diocletian his Edict on Maximum Prices of 301. Inflation is naively ascribed in the Edict's preamble to "furious avarice . . . which with no thought for mankind hastens to its own gain and increase, not by years or months or days, but by hours and even minutes," and an attempt is made to impose maximum legal prices upon an immense range of products and services. Lactantius claimed that the Edict was an immediate and total failure as goods

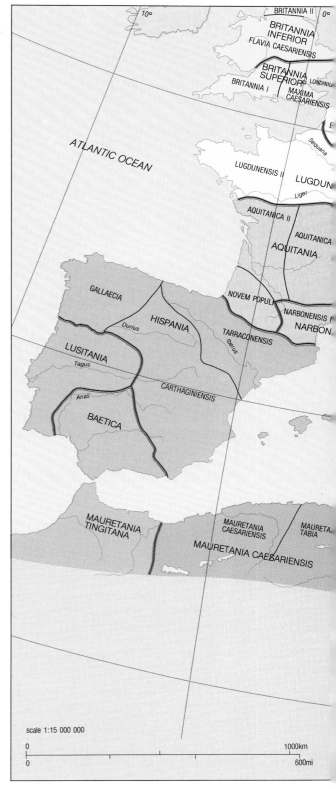

The later Empire in the time of Diocletian. The Diocletianic hierarchy of prefectures, dioceses and provinces is shown in relation to the provinces of the Severan period. The main changes are in the treatment of an enlarged Italy as a diocese with provinces, and in the abandonment to barbarian occupation of the "Agri Decumates" and Dacia, the name of the latter (and part of its population) being transferred to the Roman side of the Danube. The campaigns of Galerius, on the other hand, have added territory along the upper Tigris.

were driven off the market, and his opinion has generally been accepted. Yet the seriousness with which the government took its attempt to control inflation is demonstrated by the many sites which have produced fragments of this massive inscription. Its most effective contribution may have been psychological rather than economic, showing the willingness of a Roman government, after the trauma of the 3rd century, even to contemplate exerting its authority on such a scale and in such meticulous detail.

The implementation of such a complex piece of legislation clearly implies the possession by the government of considerable administrative manpower. This is equally clear in relation to the tax reforms of Diocletian and his colleagues. Again introduced progressively, and with allowance for regional variations and local custom, these reforms involved, in essence, the introduction of a standard unit of taxation, based on the labor (including women and slaves) and animal stock employed on agricultural land, and on the area of land exploited. The latter part of the assessment was variable, depending on the type of use to which the land was put – whether for cereal crops, vines, olives, grazing and so on. The figures were then combined to yield

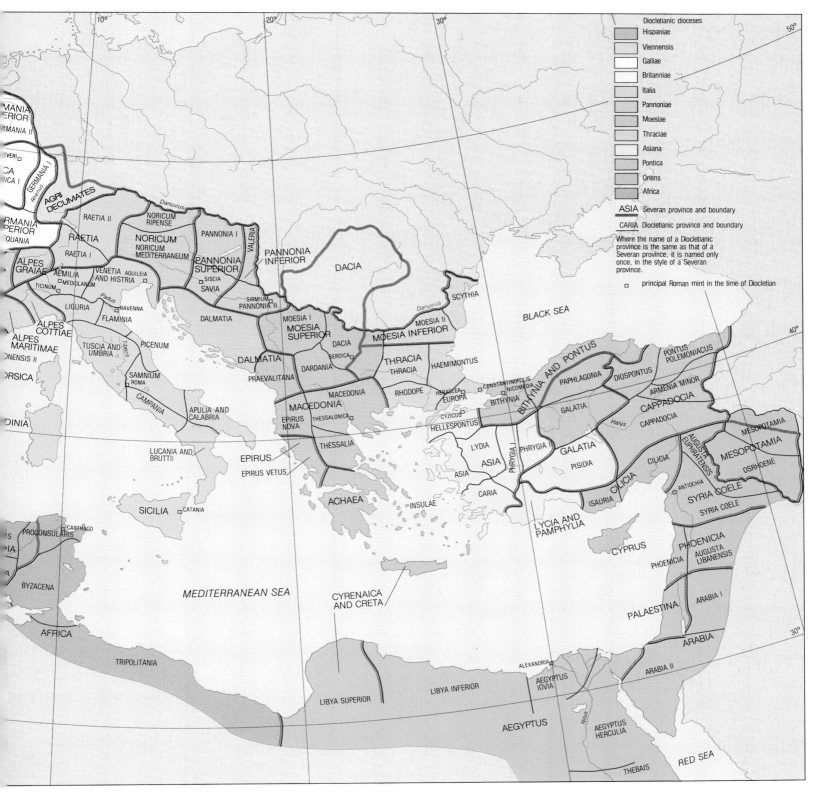

Diocletianic dioceses
- Hispaniae
- Viennensis
- Galliae
- Britanniae
- Italia
- Pannoniae
- Moesiae
- Thraciae
- Asiana
- Pontica
- Oriens
- Africa

ASIA Severan province and boundary
CARIA Diocletianic province and boundary

Where the name of a Diocletianic province is the same as that of a Severan province, it is named only once, in the style of a Severan province.

□ principal Roman mint in the time of Diocletian

173

a unit of tax liability which made allowance for different modes of cultivation and degrees of fertility, and the actual rate of taxation was imposed uniformly at so much per unit. In the early 4th century, the city of Autun successfully petitioned Constantine for a reduction of its assessment from 32000 to 25000 units, its main argument being the amount of uncultivated land in its territory which had been included in the assessment.

In principle, this was an equitable method of taxation, based on the variable productivity of different types of land and of different modes of cultivation; it allowed, for the first time in Roman history, for rational budgeting. If the government could estimate in advance its financial obligations, then, by simply dividing this figure by the total number of tax units in the Empire (or any part of it), it could calculate each year the rate of taxation required to meet its predicted outlay. To what extent this ideal was achieved is another question. It is clear that there was often a shortfall in the taxes received, which the emperors remedied by making "supplementary assessments."

Various other forms of exaction existed alongside the new tax units. Additional taxes, not in themselves onerous, were levied on senatorial estates, and the emperors continued to receive cash and bullion on their various anniversaries; this was tantamount to additional taxation and clearly made a substantial contribution to imperial finance. As in the 3rd century, the government exacted by requisition services such as transportation facilities and the billeting of troops, and supplied most of the material needs of the armies and the bureaucracy by exacting produce directly from the land. Frontier garrisons were regularly supplied in kind from the estates of provincial landowners. Municipal services were devolved as an obligation onto local councils, which were also made responsible, against the personal fortunes of their members, for the collection and payment of taxation to the imperial authorities. The limitations of the system can be seen, not only from the need for the "special assessments" just mentioned, but from the frequency with which the emperors "wrote off" uncollected taxes by making remissions.

Lactantius alleged that as a result of Diocletian's tax reforms the Empire contained more tax-collectors than tax-payers. Despite Lactantius' obvious exaggeration, the enlargement of the imperial bureaucracy was one of the most characteristic features of the later Roman period (see below, pp. 199–200), and reflects the increased "incidence" of government on Roman society initiated under the Tetrarchy. The same development took place in the provincial administration. The division of the provinces already undertaken by the Severan emperors into smaller and more manageable units, was further pursued to produce a total of over 100 provinces, about twice their number in the 3rd century. Italy, for the first time in Roman history, was divided into provinces and subjected to regular taxation. The provinces were arranged in regional groups known as "dioceses," each under the authority of an official known as a *vicarius*, or "deputy" (of the praetorian prefect). The function of *vicarii* was apparently connected with taxation, since each diocese as a general rule housed an imperial mint, to which its product in monetary

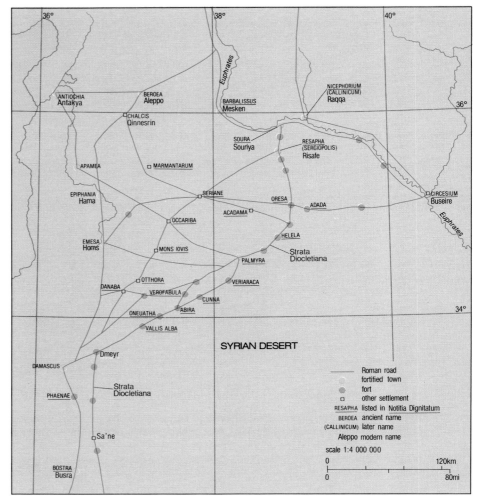

taxation was returned for restriking as new coin. One of the main functions of the praetorian prefecture of the 4th century was precisely the assessment and administration of regional taxation.

Many of the characteristics of the developed bureaucracy of the 4th century emerged progressively, under Constantine and his successors. But there is no doubt that its decisive enlargement is attributable to Diocletian, and reflects the intense governmental and legislative activity of his reign.

Late Roman ceremonial and art

Diocletian is credited by 4th-century sources with the introduction of a ceremony known as "adoration of the purple." In this an individual granted audience with the emperor was offered the edge of the imperial purple robe to kiss as an act of homage. The ceremony is taken by these sources to symbolize a change in the position of the Roman emperor from civil magistrate (a pretense maintained since the days of Augustus, but obviously with weakening force, especially during the military crisis of the 3rd century) to Oriental despot. *Adoratio purpurae* was only one aspect of a process whereby the late Roman emperors surrounded themselves by a much more elaborate ceremonial protocol than their predecessors. Although many of the individual elements in this development can be found in Roman practice of earlier periods, their combination marked a real change in the nature of the imperial office. The emperors' persons were attended by a religious aura; petitioners and panegyrists addressed their words to the "sacred ears" of the emperor, and replies, falling from his

The eastern frontier of Diocletian (strata Diocletiana). The map shows the essentials of the Diocletianic eastern frontier, as reconstructed from the evidence of the *Notitia Dignitatum*, field archaeology and aerial surveys. There is nothing original in a garrisoned frontier based on a military road (the *strata Diocletiana*) lying in advance of and communicating with the cities which it defended. This line is in effect that of the Flavio-Trajanic period, and analogies with Diocletian's system can be found in late Roman Africa, where inscriptions show it evolving already in the 3rd century. Nevertheless, the eastern frontier required much new construction, as at Palmyra and Circesium, the latter in particular being seen as a crucial defensive point against Persian attack. It is uncertain to what extent the system was designed for security against local Bedouin, but this was evidently a factor in its operation, especially since the Bedouin ("Saracens" in our literary sources) might ally themselves with Persia.

The frontier was manned by regular frontier troops known as *limitanei*. Though these, like their African counterparts, certainly engaged in farming activities around their forts, there is no justification for describing them as a "peasant militia" engaging in military duties in return for assignments of land.

This detail from the mosaics of the palace of Piazza Armerina in Sicily (see also p. 186) well conveys the color and brilliance of late Roman dress. A group of attendants awaits the embarkation of a captured animal; on their decorated tunics appear the embroidered emblems typical of the costume of their period. The mosaics are dated to the 4th century; it is widely argued that the villa was owned by the retired emperor Maximian, but this remains extremely uncertain.

"sacred mouth," were put into official rhetorical language by his "sacred secretariat." The official council of state was known as the *consistorium* because its members stood in the imperial presence. Diocletian, adopting the name "Jovius," presented himself as the vice-regent of Jupiter on earth; Maximian, his colleague, was "Herculius," representing the god who had by his untiring labors relieved mankind from terror and affliction. These titles were inherited by the respective junior members of the Tetrarchy. The language of administration becomes filled with abstractions, such as "Our Serenity," "Our Majesty," "Our Eternity," the emperors thereby being presented not as individual personalities but as the vehicles of the abstract virtues by which the Empire was protected. The emperors' victories in war become attached to them as a permanent attribute; they are "always victorious" (*semper victores*), even "extremely invincible," (*invictissimi*). The collegiality of the imperial office is strenuously asserted. Laws issued in one part of the Empire, though they may be of no interest at all to the other, bear the names of all the legitimate emperors of the time.

As part of the elaboration of the imperial office, the palaces became filled with officials and attendants of all kinds, who controlled and made difficult access to the emperor. This again contrasts with the earlier period, when a pretense at least was kept up that an emperor should be accessible to his subjects, and should find time to listen to their individual grievances. The enlarged administrative bureaucracy of the late Empire had as its counterpart a swelling palace staff, headed by "chamberlains" (*cubicularii*), who are often eunuchs (another sign of the "orientalization" of the imperial office); these individuals at times gained an immense and, in conservative opinion, scandalous influence.

The ceremonial elaboration of the late Roman imperial office did not come about in isolation. Late Roman public life in general was characterized by an increasing sense of "theatrical" effect; the emperors with their ceremonial audiences and great processions provide only the most spectacular examples. Many artistic expressions of this tendency, as in the mosaics from the palace at Piazza Armerina in Sicily or the marble intarsia from the audience hall at Rome of the consul Junius Bassus, illustrate how late Roman public life adopted a color and style, a theatrical panache more reminiscent of Renaissance Florence than of a classical city. Literary sources, like Ammianus Marcellinus' description of the fancy clothes worn by Roman aristocrats of the later 4th century, made of brightly colored, airy silk, with fringes and vividly embroidered figures, bear out this impression.

Ceremony is a mode of communication, and it is possible that in the late Roman period it functioned in a more positive and open way than is often assumed. It was not merely a reflection of the new despotism but it provided also a sense of identity to a new governing class, the imperial bureaucracy, which was still in the process of consolidation, and presented the imperial office to the late Roman public in a way which was found intelligible and reassuring. During the 3rd century the emperors must often have seemed very remote from the ordinary civilian populations of the Empire, and the prestige of their office can hardly have been unimpaired by the political disorders of the 3rd century. It may be that their emergence amid such splendor under the Tetrarchy and later was effective in persuading the late Roman public that imperial permanency was once again firmly established and confident.

Changes in the public presentation of the emperors appear to find expression in the art and iconography of the late Empire. During the 3rd and especially the 4th century, Roman public art is characterized by an increasing formalism both of feature and of design. The new style, of which the most obvious aspects are in the stiff, frontal presentation of human figures and the schematic arrangements of groups, together with a weakened sense of perspective, is already seen in the sculptures of the Arch of Septimius Severus at Leptis Magna (early 3rd century), and, more conspicuously, of the Arch of Constantine at Rome (c. 315). Here, the formality and simplicity of the sculptures are emphasized by their juxtaposition with works of the Antonine period, ransacked to embellish the new monument.

Affinities with the new style can be found in the provincial sculpture of the early Empire, but its prevalence in late Roman art is plausibly ascribed to the need to convey the enhanced ceremonial presentation of the emperors of that period, and in general the element of the theatrical. It is in this context that we can most readily understand the frontal poses, the calculated gestures, the neatly articulated rows of figures and carefully designed spaces of so much late Roman representational art. The increasingly stylized "expressionism" of individual portraiture seems also, at least in the case of imperial portraits, to reflect the development mentioned above, in which the emperors are seen less as individuals than as the embodiments of

This relief from the arch of Constantine at Rome illustrates the stiff "frontality" characteristic of much late Roman ceremonial art. The intention is deliberate: to define the roles of the various participants by separating the visual registers in which they respectively appear, and to represent the relationship between emperor and audience as a sort of theatrical set piece. The contrast with the more informal spontaneity of the 2nd-century sculptures incorporated in the arch is very marked (see p. 104).

certain virtues, the symbols of stereotyped abstractions.

Against this shift to a greater formalism, art historians have often seen the reign of Gallienus as marking a "renaissance" of classical style, not only in the fields of philosophy and literature, but also in the visual arts. The main stylistic feature in question is a renewed naturalism reminiscent of the art of the Antonine age, but with the addition of a greater emotional intensity, "an essentially romantic rendering of life in transience" (Gervase Mathew). Yet, apart from the difficulty of dating with sufficient accuracy the works under discussion, they may simply reflect an autonomous classical tradition, continuously developing in its own terms alongside the more "modernistic" developments in the visual arts. The evidence is far too insecure to support any such notion as that of a "renaissance," if by this is meant a movement with more or less consciously conceived aims and fostered by the deliberate support of the emperor and other patrons. It is better to see the various styles of 3rd-century art as expressions of diverse contemporaneous traditions pursued in their own right, not always as closely linked as the critic might suppose with the social and political situation which surrounded them, and ultimately far less easy to explain.

Religious developments

Writing in the early 2nd century, Plutarch had complained of the neglect of the ancient oracles of Greece, a situation which no doubt reflects the loss of the political independence of the Greek states. At Rome, the rise of Stoicism during the 1st century has been seen in terms of a shift of interest away from the state cults to a code of moral conduct deriving from concepts of individual duty, again as part of a response of a once great governing class, the senate, to its loss of political influence under the emperors.

These examples take us to the heart of religious changes of immense importance in the Roman Empire of the 2nd and 3rd centuries. New forms of devotion were drawn from the Greco-Oriental cultures of Egypt, Judaea and Syria, and from Mesopotamia – the cult of Isis and Osiris, Christianity and various forms of Gnosticism, later Mithraism and Manichaeism. Together with some of the more personal mystic cults from Asia Minor, like those of Dionysus and the Phrygian Great Mother, these seem to have become increasingly popular. They offered the individual a variety of attractions: hope of the salvation of his soul, in some cases exotic rituals of initiation to membership of a purified elite, allegorical myths explaining the cosmic order, a definition of the individual's place in the universe; sometimes, in their conception of the human soul as descended from a divine realm and trapped in a hostile world of matter or on a battleground between good and evil, they offered explanations of suffering and wickedness. The ancient public cults of the Greeks and Romans were interested in none of these matters.

The prevalence of the mystery cults has often been linked, more precisely, with the 3rd-century crisis. It has seemed natural to suppose that increasing disorder and insecurity in the outside world would have provoked a corresponding withdrawal by individuals into an inner life.

Possibly, in addition, the failure of traditional belief to protect the Empire encouraged men to turn their attention to the mystery religions, to astrology, and, for their personal protection against misfortune, to magic arts, which are seen as increasing in popularity, both absolutely and relatively, in the later Roman period.

Such conclusions must be examined very critically. The evidence, being circumstantial and fragmentary, does not permit any proper analysis of the incidence of such beliefs in one period as opposed to another. The late Roman period, being in general more plentifully and more diversely documented than earlier periods, naturally reveals more cases, for example, of the use of magical practices. Further, such views as those just described are often linked to a more general conception of late Roman society as in an advanced stage of decline from the clear rationalism of the classical age, to an age of less "rational," more superstitious attitudes and beliefs. Such impressions may involve both the imposition of inappropriate concepts of rationalism, and a failure to appreciate the religious complexity of earlier Greco-Roman society.

The practice of magic and astrology was immemorial in ancient society. Government action against the magic arts, together with the expulsion of astrologers and "philosophers" from Rome, was already frequent in the 1st century, by which period a temple of Isis was standing in the central area of the city. Second-century sources are full of references to magical practices, action taken in response to dreams and many other "irrational" but, in the view of their practitioners, effective courses of action. The so-called "Chaldaean Oracles," a collection of utterances on the nature of the universe and of God, and on the techniques for raising the soul to God by the use of magical arts, were collected and circulated in the time of Marcus Aurelius. Indeed, if mysticism is linked too closely with the increasing misery of the 3rd century, it becomes difficult to account for Marcus himself, anxiously addressing his soul in the *Meditations*, in the prosperous days of the Antonine golden age.

The view that the popularity of the mystery religions was connected with the crisis of the 3rd century thus encounters the objection that, in many essential respects, they preceded it. It would be better to associate the development with the ever-increasing mobility of men and ideas in the Mediterranean world under the peaceful conditions provided by the Roman emperors as part of their unification of the Latin, Greek and Middle Eastern worlds. If there was a response on a religious level to the political and social crisis of the age, this is as likely to have taken the form of a reassertion of traditional values as a search for new ones. Such was the basis of the persecution of the Christians in the times of Decius and Diocletian (see below, p. 178), and of the Manichees by Diocletian. In his edict against the Manichees he denounced the wicked arrogance of these men who had set themselves against the common wisdom, opposing their new sect to the old-established religions and preferring their own beliefs to those long ago entrusted by the gods to mankind.

The emperors were not totally conservative. They had already reflected a widely held religious conviction of the age, in associating themselves with

The portrait bust from the theater of Dionysus at Athens has at different times been identified as a portrait of Christ, of an "unknown barbarian" (i.e. the representative of a "Semitic race"!), as a masterpiece of the Antonine age and of the "Gallienic renaissance" of the mid-3rd century. A more recent view is that it shows the emperor Gallienus himself in the guise of the god Serapis. The piece clearly looks back to the Hellenistic age through (or from) the age of the Antonines, with a "dreamy melancholy" of introspection which sets it firmly apart both from the severe modernism of the portrait bust shown *opposite* and from the uncomplicated clarity of the portrait of Aurelian (*below right*).

The coin of Aurelian (*right*) shows the emperor in military dress, wearing the radiate crown characteristic of the sun (see p. 188 for an example associated with Constantine). The reverse bears the legend "ORIENS AUG [ustus]," "rising emperor," with a rather spidery figure of the sun, again wearing radiate crown and carrying orb. The celestial imagery is confirmed by the appearance of a star in the field of the image.

"Expressionism" in late Roman portraiture, as seen in a porphyry bust from Cairo of an unidentified emperor of the late 3rd or early 4th century. The modeling is notable for the abstract symmetry in which the personal character of the subject has been immersed. Though exaggerated and lively, the features are imposed statically on the surface of the material and their physiological structure has been simplified. There is no sense of the introspective complexity of mood so beautifully caught by the bust of "Gallienus" shown *opposite*.

certain particular gods under whose protection they lived. Commodus went so far as to identify himself with the god Hercules, but this was something of an eccentricity, as was the association of Elagabalus with the sacred stone of Emesa (see above, p. 105). From the mid-3rd century, particularly from the time of Gallienus, the emperors linked themselves with the "Unconquered Sun," whom they regarded as their familiar "companion" (*comes Augusti*). Aurelian established a public cult of the Sun at Rome, creating a new college of priests to administer it, which survived until the end of official state paganism. Diocletian and Maximian too associated themselves with the Unconquered Sun as well as with Jupiter and Hercules.

This tendency reflected both the popularity of Sun-worship, in the figure of Mithras, in the Roman army, and contemporary religious beliefs in which the sun was seen as identical with or the symbol of the ultimate deity, the source of physical life and intellectual illumination, of whose all-pervasive power the gods of the classical pantheon were the divine agents.

Contemporary philosophical developments, on a narrower definition, expressed the same tendencies as religious thought in general, in their pre-occupation with an array of doctrines set in an all-encompassing theology derived from Plato. Emphasis is given to the religious aspects of Platonic thought, especially to Plato's myths of the descent of the soul from the realm of divine Ideas to the world of matter and its longing to return to God. This "return of the soul" was to be achieved by rational contemplation or by the use of magical, or "theurgical," techniques designed to exploit the "symbols" of divine presence in the universe in physical objects, in numbers, magical spells and incantations. The former, purely intellectual, approach was that adopted by Plotinus, the founder of what is now known as Neoplatonism, a systematization of Platonic thought in terms of a hierarchy of different levels of being and of reality through which the soul must by contemplation make its way in its return to the "One," the supreme principle from which it was derived. Plotinus' most important follower in this approach was Porphyry, a Syrian from Tyre. The alternative and in every sense more popular method, that of the elevation of the soul by theurgy, was supported by the school of another Syrian, Iamblichus. The theurgical tradition of Iamblichus passed down to the 5th-century Athenian Neoplatonic school of Syrianus and Proclus.

For all these philosophers, Plato was not merely the dominant intellectual influence, but the "divine teacher," and they themselves were regarded as divinely inspired men. Their aims went beyond those of the traditional classical philosopher, in that they wanted to teach and to attain not merely virtue and goodness, but perfection. As divinely inspired men, they were believed to have special powers, enabling them to levitate, perform wonders, evoke the gods and receive divine oracles. Again, it must be emphasized, the origins of such a development must be sought at least as early as the Antonine age, in figures such as Apuleius and the miracle-working "philosophers" satirized by Lucian. It is best seen as an organic development in its own right, owing little or nothing to the insecurity of surrounding events; on the contrary, the origins of such rampant individualism as one sees in these movements are more satisfactorily ascribed to the leisure and security of an age of peace and prosperity like that of the Antonines.

The growth and persecution of Christianity

The 2nd and 3rd centuries were, for the Christian church also, a time of expansion. This was much more marked in the eastern provinces of the Empire, in Africa, and in those parts of the west most exposed to the Mediterranean, which as always bore the main current of intellectual and cultural influences from the east. The churches of the west were generally Greek-speaking until the end of the 2nd century. Bishop Hippolytus of Rome wrote in Greek; the early bishops of Lugdunum (Lyon) were Greek-speaking. Yet in Tertullian (?c. 170–220) the African church produced a major Latin writer, and it seems that, both there and in Italy, the Greek element in Christian congregations was by this time beginning to be overtaken by Latin-speaking local converts.

The growth of the church can be measured, from another point of view, by the 87 bishops who attended the council of Carthage organized by Bishop Cyprian in 256. At Rome the number of widows and orphans receiving charitable aid is put at 1500, which would suggest the existence of a substantial Christian community. At Antioch Bishop Paul, convicted of heresy and deposed in 268, is described by an opponent as lording it in his city as if he were an imperial procurator.

Some parts of the Empire, notably the European provinces of Pannonia, northern Gaul, Germany and Britain, were less immediately affected by Christianity, but it is clear that by 300 AD there were many districts in which its adherents formed at least a prominent minority.

The church historian Eusebius of Caesarea, writing soon after 300, remarked that the period since the reign of Decius had been one of peace and prosperity for the church, which the Devil had exploited by sowing dissension in its ranks. The persecution initiated by Decius was itself the first general attack against Christianity ever undertaken by the Roman government as a matter of deliberate policy. Earlier, persecution had been conducted on a local basis, often by governors under pressure from local populations and civic leaders. The existence of such action may be known to us only because the governor in question, like Pliny in the time of Trajan, consulted the emperor on points of procedure – what to do with Roman citizens who were admitted Christians, whether or not to countenance anonymously posted denunciations (on which point Trajan's reply was firmly in the negative). It is important not to underestimate the frequency of such local persecution. At the same time, it is essential to recognize that no emperor before Decius, in the mid-3rd century, mounted a centrally organized campaign against Christianity, and that until that time the issue was never particularly important in the mind of any Roman emperor.

The general causes of persecution are fairly clear, though it is not always easy to say why it occurred at a particular time. Tertullian complained that the Christians were blamed for any misfortune afflict-

177

ing a community: "If the Tiber floods or the Nile fails to, the cry goes up: the Christians to the lion!" Outbreaks of plague, earthquakes or violent storms were other disasters which could be attributed in popular opinion to the withdrawal of the favor of the gods. For Romans believed that the universe was kept in balance only by the goodwill of the gods to men, which must be maintained by the collective piety of the community, that is, by the performance of duly established rituals and sacrifices. The Christians, a dissenting group who refused to participate in such rituals, were believed to be undermining the relations between the community and its gods, and by disturbing the "peace of the gods" (*pax deorum*) to be provoking the withdrawal of their protection.

In addition, the social and religious habits of Christians themselves caused suspicion. Their rituals were secret and involved the consuming of symbolic flesh and blood in the Eucharist: anti-Christian propagandists offer lurid allegations of cannibalism – "Thyestean banquets" (in Greek mythology Thyestes was served the bodies of his sons in a stew) – and of incest, since Christians were exhorted to love their brothers and sisters. Christians took mysterious oaths of loyalty to each other: it surprised Pliny to discover that the oath was "to commit neither theft, robbery, nor adultery, nor to betray a trust, nor to refuse to return a deposit on demand." They absented themselves from much of the social intercourse of a community, since this was linked up with the performance of religious rituals (Tacitus had already accused the Christians of a "hatred of the human race"); some Christian writers, like Tertullian, went so far as to maintain that a Christian should as a matter of fundamental principle have no part in the social life or culture of secular society. "What has Athens," he wrote, "to do with Jerusalem?" This was by no means the whole picture. Other Christian spokesmen argued that Christians too were loyal citizens, who paid their taxes and prayed to their own God for the emperor's safety. It is clear that not all Christians took Tertullian's rigorous view of classical culture and education; in this issue is anticipated one of the most important debates of the time of Christian empire (see below, pp. 194 ff.).

Decius' initiation of a persecution of the Christians, like the other evidence sketched above, suggests that Christianity was a relatively prominent religion, at least worth picking out as the cause of the Empire's ills. The reign of Decius coincided with the onset of serious military crisis, especially in the Gothic invasions, and it may be that it was felt necessary to reassert the loyalty of the Empire to its traditional gods. This feeling was possibly sharpened by a sense that the recent celebration of the millennium of Rome by the emperor Philip had not provided the confirmation of Rome's fortunes that might have been expected.

The actual process of persecution involved, first, the arrest and punishment of members of the clergy; later, all citizens were required to sacrifice to the gods of Rome and the emperor's genius, or guiding spirit. On the completion of sacrifice, a certificate (*libellus*) was issued to this effect; examples of these documents survive on papyrus. It was suspected, and must sometimes have happened, that *libelli* were obtained through bribery by Christians who did not wish to sacrifice but were terrified of the penal consequences. The clergy were also required to surrender the holy scriptures, but it does not appear that, in the Decian persecution, damage was done to church buildings. Many communities no doubt still met in the private houses of their wealthier members.

The persecution initiated by Decius was revived for a time by Valerian, but lapsed after Valerian's capture by the Persians (260). Among its victims was Cyprian of Carthage, who in the time of the Decian persecution had withdrawn from Carthage and escaped, but who under Valerian faced exile and, in 258, martyrdom by beheading. It nevertheless appears that it was relatively easy for a Christian to escape persecution by quietly disappearing for a time; the authorities were not equipped to track down everyone who might do this, especially if he were harbored by other members of his community. Presumably in this, as in the Great Persecution, some victims were Christians who actually wished to undergo martyrdom and thereby secure instant promotion to sainthood. This appears from the exasperated comments of Roman governors unwilling to impose execution and from the perplexity of Christian writers faced with the issue of voluntary martyrdom.

The Great Persecution of Diocletian is unlike that of Decius in that, although much more is known of the circumstances of its outbreak, the period of Diocletian's reign in which it began was not, from a political or military point of view, particularly critical or uncertain. There must be some truth in the allegation of contemporary Christian sources that the motivating force was Diocletian's junior colleague Galerius, stirred by a personal hatred of Christianity and imposing this attitude on the aging, weakening Diocletian. Diocletian's own wife and daughter were among those compelled to sacrifice as Christians or Christian sympathizers.

General persecution was occasioned by the failure of a sacrifice at Nicomedia, when an imperial official present was seen to cross himself to avert pollution by the rites. It is interesting to find the presence of Christianity in court circles so close to the emperor, and it may be that this was what disturbed and enraged Galerius. The first edict of persecution, dated 23 February 303, ordered the closure of churches and the surrender of the scriptures, and this was followed by an order to the clergy to perform sacrifice. So far only the ecclesiastical authorities were involved, but a third edict extended the obligation to sacrifice to all members of the Christian community. The edicts, posted at Nicomedia (where one was torn down by an angry Christian who was immediately executed by burning), were sent out to the praetorian prefects, passed on by them to provincial governors and by them to municipal officials for local enforcement. A papyrus from Oxyrhynchus records the experience of a Christian who came to Alexandria for litigation and found that all those appearing before the court were being made to sacrifice. He overcame this problem by empowering his brother, who was evidently not a Christian, to act on his behalf.

It is difficult to estimate the incidence of persecution and the numbers of those who suffered

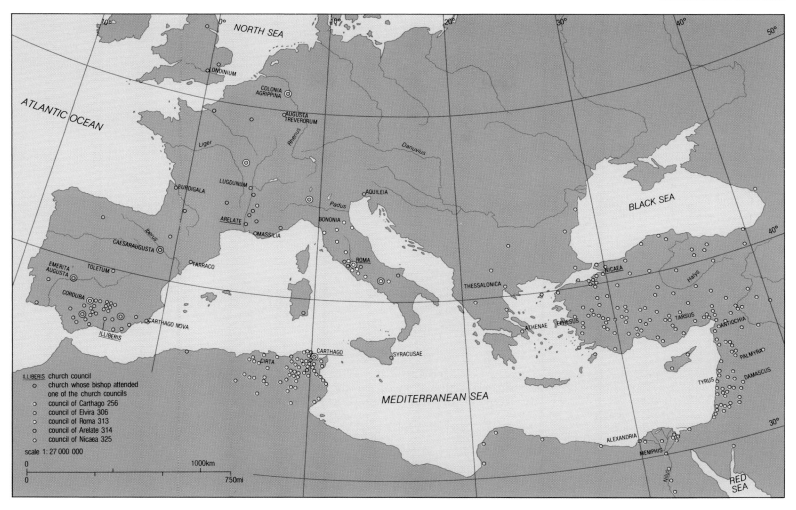

The purpose of
the map is to indicate only those
churches known to have
attended the councils indicated.
It omits churches recorded,
sometimes reliably but often on
late and untrustworthy
evidence, as existing elsewhere,
and gives no indication of the
actual size of Christian
communities. It suggests the
"potential" rather than actual
distribution of Christian
churches, based on the evidence
provided by the councils for
certain regions. This evidence is
obviously incomplete; one
wonders, for example, what
would have been revealed by a
council held in southern
Dalmatia. Nevertheless, the
council of Nicaea gives a fair
indication of the distribution of
churches in the east at the outset
of Constantine's reign there, and
in other areas the distribution
coincides sufficiently closely
with the density of urbanization
in the Empire (see p. 111) to
suggest that the general
impression is not a misleading
one.

ILLIBERIS church council
o church whose bishop attended
   one of the church councils
o council of Carthago 256
o council of Elvira 306
o council of Roma 313
o council of Arelate 314
o council of Nicaea 325

scale 1: 27 000 000

1000km

750mi

The distribution of Christian churches, 3rd and early 4th centuries AD.

the penalties of exile, condemnation to the mines, mutilation or death. The picture given by Eusebius for the heavily Christianized provinces of Palestine and Egypt is that there were indeed many individual victims; in the case of Egypt, he mentions for instance two convoys, respectively of 97 and 130 Christians, men, women and children, being led off to hard labor in the state mines. Yet it seems unlikely that more than a small proportion of the Christian population in the Empire at large suffered penalties. What is clear is that the persecution was a central issue in public policy for several years and that its aftermath provided the Christian church with its main ideological preoccupation in the period after the granting of the peace of the church by Constantine and Licinius. The proper attitude to take to clergy who had compromised their faith by surrendering the scriptures, and to ordinary Christians who had sacrificed, and the rancorous disputes arising from allegations of such behavior, created the Donatist schism in North Africa and temporarily soured the life of many other churches.

The persecution was maintained by Galerius in the years after Diocletian's abdication, but was allowed to lapse in the regions controlled by Constantius (Gaul and Britain, where there were in any case few Christians) and the usurper Maxentius (Italy and Africa). In 311 Galerius fell ill of a terminal disease and, apparently in fear of death, suspended the persecution in terms which reveal clearly its original motivation. He had hoped by coercion to restore the Christians to a sound mind, but had discovered that, while they had been deprived of opportunities to worship their own God, they were not praying to the traditional gods either. He therefore restored freedom of worship, inviting Christians to pray to their God for his safety, their own and that of the Empire. Shortly afterwards Galerius died, the victim, according to gleeful Christians like Lactantius, of divine vengeance.

After Galerius' death the persecution was revived, with a somewhat different emphasis, by his successor Maximinus Daia. Maximinus received delegations from the cities petitioning for the persecution of Christians. The propaganda activities of pagans such as Theotecnus of Antioch, who circulated forged memoirs of Pontius Pilate full of blasphemies against Christ, give us a glimpse of the local feeling which may well have sustained the persecution for so many years. Maximinus also attempted, in anticipation of the policy of Julian the Apostate (see below, p. 191), to found a provincial priesthood charged with the administration of a restored paganism. Before any of the effects of these policies could be seen, Maximinus fell to the new emperor Licinius. In 313 Constantine and Licinius had issued a declaration of freedom of worship, and restored to the Christian church its confiscated property. This was the beginning of the peace of the church and the conversion of the Roman Empire to Christianity, welcomed with alacrity by Eusebius as the fulfillment of divine prophecy. But this is to anticipate the question of the conversion of Constantine which is to be discussed in the next chapter.

Roman Portraiture

The development of individual portraiture is generally considered one of the principal achievements of Roman art. This view is perhaps somewhat paradoxical, since the artists who produced the majority of the surviving portraits were in fact Greeks. But they were working under the patronage of wealthy Romans, and their work is a response to Roman needs and a reflection of Roman tastes. The distinguishing characteristic of this style of portraiture is an extreme realism, with a particular emphasis on the ugly and unattractive features of the subject. The origins of this "veristic" style are difficult to determine, but there is no doubt that it appealed strongly to the Romans, who liked to see themselves as a tough, honest, no-nonsense people.

During the late Republic and early Empire the realistic portrait style was adopted by all classes of society, including artisans, traders and freedmen, as can be seen from the numerous funerary portrait reliefs which are among the most characteristic expressions of plebeian art. In public portraiture there was a distinct change under Augustus and the Julio-Claudians, who favored a classicizing style of idealized portrait (see above, p. 76). But verism reappeared under the Flavians, and again in the 3rd century under Caracalla, who rejected the revived classicism that had prevailed since Hadrian and introduced a new harsh realism. Imperial portraits in the period of the 3rd-century crisis convey with remarkable frankness the energy, strength and vitality of the unsophisticated soldiers who ruled the Empire. But under Diocletian and his successors imperial portraits took on a fixed and abstract quality expressing the majesty of emperors separated from their subjects by an elaborate court ritual; in later imperial portraiture there is no longer any attempt to represent the real features of living men.

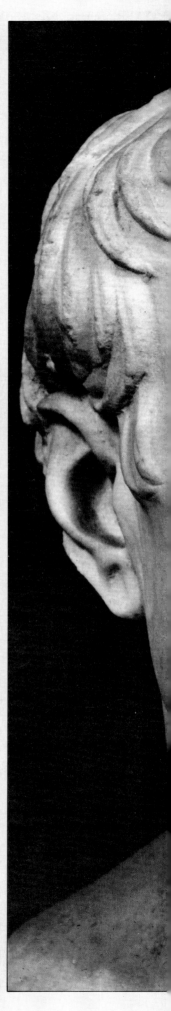

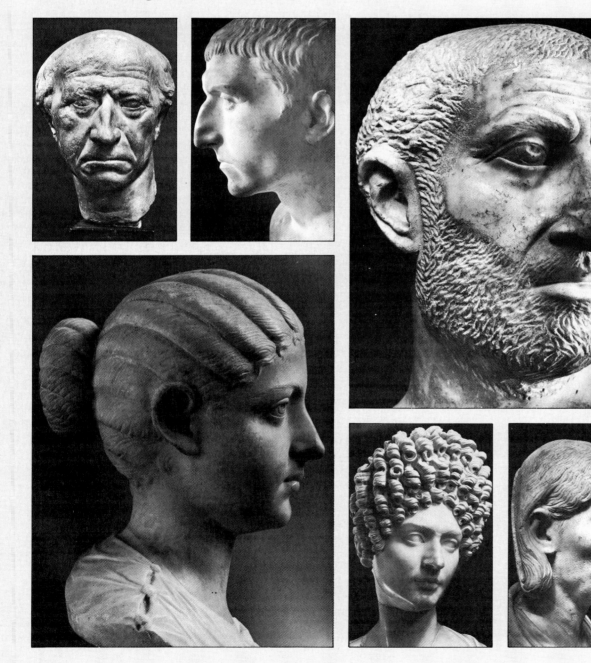

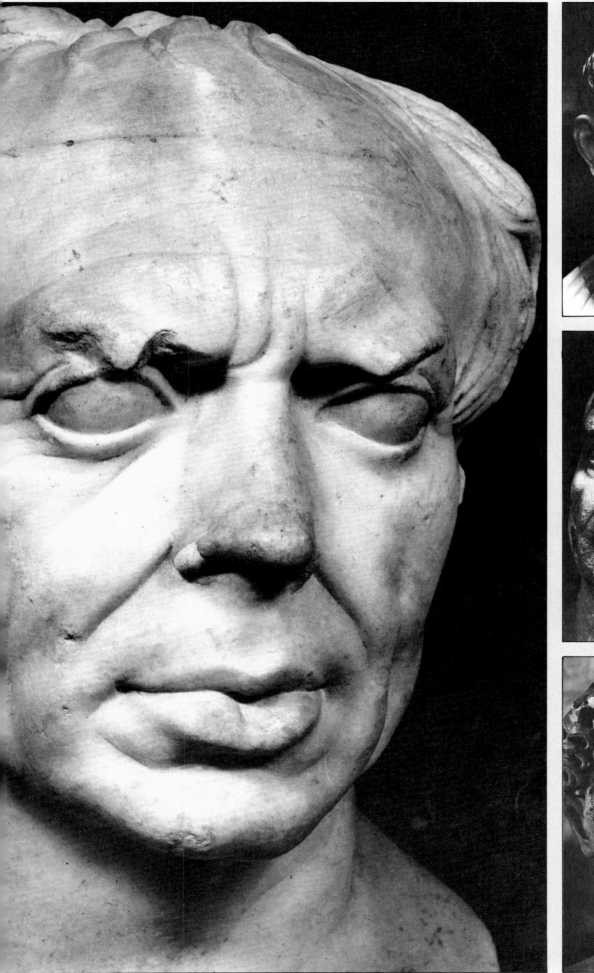

Everyday Life

The greengrocer.

The shopkeeper.

The blacksmith.

The ironmonger.

The apothecary.

There was no sharp distinction between the means of production and of distribution in the ancient world. Manufactured articles for sale, such as those displayed in the ironmonger's shop (*far left*), would be produced in workshops on the premises, like the smithy shown *above*. The relief *below* seems to show the payment or changing of money, perhaps in the form of rents paid to an agent; it distinguishes the figures who have come in from outside (shown in hooded cloaks) from those working indoors. In the butcher's shop (*below left*) the owner's wife (or is it a customer?) seems to be keeping records with a writing implement. Many examples of the yardarm, shown on the right of the relief, have been preserved.

The butcher.

The rent collector.

young apprentices; it was an economy of craftsmen rather than of industrial organization. The great state industries, such as the arms factories of the late Empire, were exceptional, and here too it is likely that the manufacturing process was not large-scale but a multiplication of small operations.

A carpenter's plane.

The bargeman.

In the smithy (*above*) an assistant is heating the forge with a pair of bellows, while shielded by a screen from the heat. The smith's tools are displayed separately, together with what appears to be one of his products, a spearhead. The carpenter's plane from Silchester (*top*) shows how little this implement has changed in design. Many reliefs survive of wine barrels being transported on boats; here (*left*) the barge is being pulled from a towpath by three men with ropes attached to a pivot, and steered by a helmsman. The large wine barrel (*right*), also from Silchester, is made of silver fir from the Pyrenees. It has survived through being reused as part of the lining of a well.

The sole of a boot.

The cobbler and the cord maker.

A wine barrel.

Mills and Technology

Roman society never developed an industrial economy, nor did it evolve any general theory of economic progress. It lacked the financial instruments necessary for industrial investment and was without such notions as productivity and consumer demand. It was not that the Romans were deficient in technical inventiveness or failed to apply it when a specific need was perceived and understood. In military technology, for example, ballistic and siege warfare reached a high level of sophistication and effectiveness. The Romans could produce stunning theatrical effects and their achievement in building and in water management speaks for itself. Yet manufacture continued to be pursued on a small scale, on the level of craft rather than industry.

This failure to develop an industrial technology is sometimes ascribed to the presence of slavery, which is argued to have removed the incentive to reduce labor costs by mechanization. Clearly, more is at issue than this. Many societies have lacked slavery but failed to industrialize, and in the Roman Empire there was often a surplus of free-born labor, especially in the large cities. When the need was felt, as in areas of lower population, the motive to economize on labor was present. It was partly for this reason that an agricultural writer recommended the reaping machine illustrated below.

There were practical limitations. Ancient society lacked an advanced metallurgical technology. Its mechanical devices were made of wood and not equipped to sustain the stresses undergone by power-driven machinery. The gears in the Barbegal water mills shown opposite were wooden, and held to their axles by lead plugs. They must have required constant repair and maintenance.

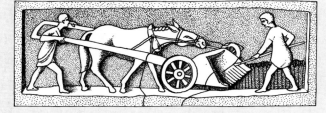

The *vallus* or reaping machine (*above*) was used in the flat, open plains of northeastern Gaul, from where all its known representations come. It operated by being pushed from behind, the tapered teeth cutting or tearing off the ears of corn and letting them fall in a container. The remainder of the plant was left to stand as tall stubble.

The ox-powered boat (*below*), with vertical capstans geared to paddle wheels, was one of a set of military inventions submitted to the emperors c. 370. The idea was ingeniously adapted in 537 by Belisarius who suspended paddle wheels from pairs of boats and used the waterpower to turn millstones on the boats.

The lifting device illustrated (*above*) is described by the architect Vitruvius. The beam or arm of the device is secured by guy ropes and the load borne by ropes on an arrangement of triple pulleys. In the case of heavier loads a geared windlass was used, operated in extreme cases by a man or men in a treadmill, as shown here in a reconstruction derived from a funerary relief from Syracuse.

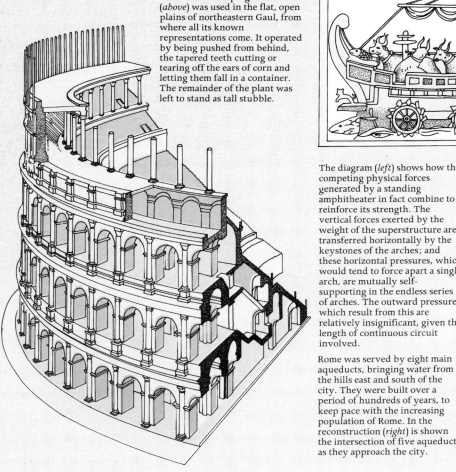

The diagram (*left*) shows how the competing physical forces generated by a standing amphitheater in fact combine to reinforce its strength. The vertical forces exerted by the weight of the superstructure are transferred horizontally by the keystones of the arches; and these horizontal pressures, which would tend to force apart a single arch, are mutually self-supporting in the endless series of arches. The outward pressures which result from this are relatively insignificant, given the length of continuous circuit involved.

Rome was served by eight main aqueducts, bringing water from the hills east and south of the city. They were built over a period of hundreds of years, to keep pace with the increasing population of Rome. In the reconstruction (*right*) is shown the intersection of five aqueducts as they approach the city.

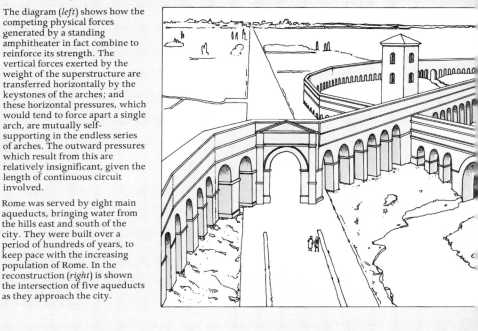

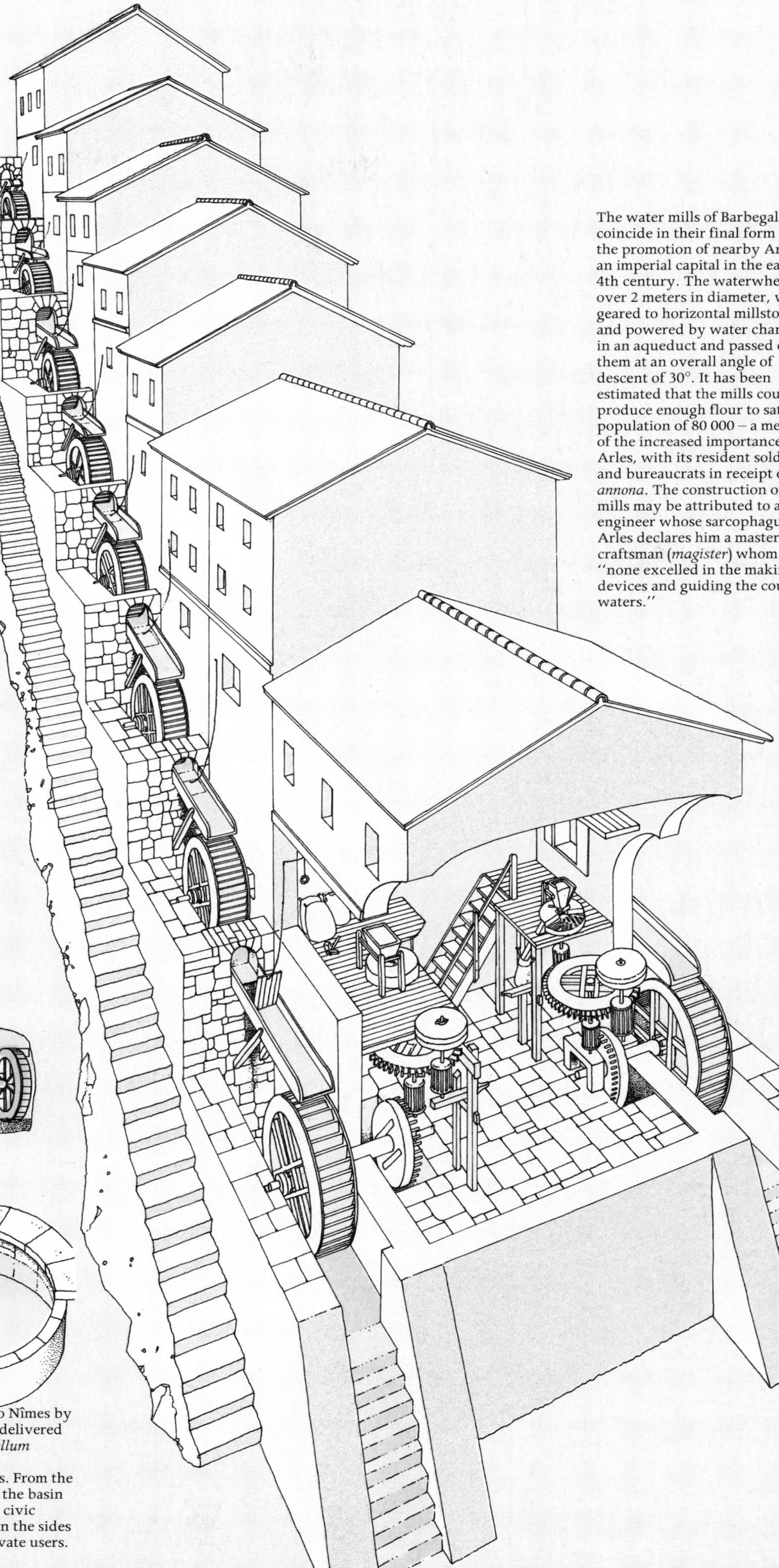

The Romans greatly advanced mining techiques in their ability to raise water from the lower levels, as in the copper mines of Rio Tinto in Lusitania, illustrated here (*below*). The pumping is done by a series of waterwheels which lift the water through successive reservoirs to the surface. The wheels themselves were probably powered by treadmills.

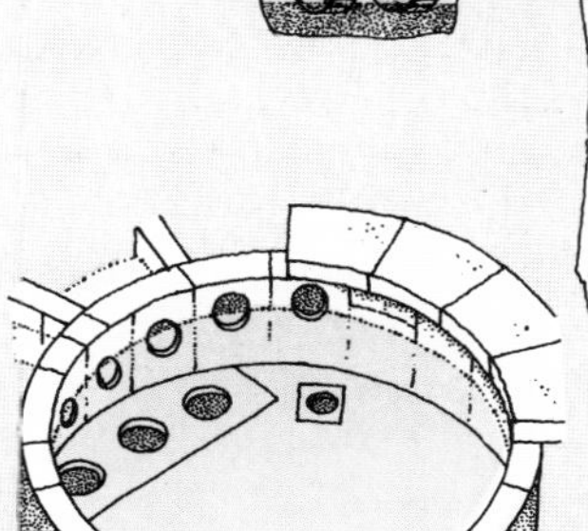

The water mills of Barbegal (*left*) coincide in their final form with the promotion of nearby Arles as an imperial capital in the early 4th century. The waterwheels, over 2 meters in diameter, were geared to horizontal millstones, and powered by water channeled in an aqueduct and passed over them at an overall angle of descent of 30°. It has been estimated that the mills could produce enough flour to satisfy a population of 80 000 – a measure of the increased importance of Arles, with its resident soldiers and bureaucrats in receipt of the *annona*. The construction of the mills may be attributed to an engineer whose sarcophagus at Arles declares him a master craftsman (*magister*) whom ''none excelled in the making of devices and guiding the course of waters.''

The water conveyed to Nîmes by the Pont du Gard was delivered to the city in this *castellum divisorium*, a basin for distributing the waters. From the ducts in the bottom of the basin ran water for essential civic purposes; the outlets in the sides delivered water to private users.

185

Public Shows

The satirist Juvenal's contempt for the taste of the Roman people for "bread and circuses" (*Satires* 10.81) is often cited by critics who cannot easily imagine the deprivation of urban poverty or the boredom of unemployment. In fact, public shows were not only a consolation for the underprivileged, but an extremely important aspect of the social life, and social relations, of a Roman city. They were provided by the local dignitaries, who thereby asserted their wealth and social prestige in rivalry with their peers, and established their patronage over the common people, whose gratitude was expressed by acclamations in theater, amphitheater or circus. In 1st-century Rome, the emperors could "undercut" the position of the senatorial aristocracy by their overwhelming generosity in providing shows – a position reversed in the late Empire, when the emperors rarely visited the city.

It is difficult to say whether the games relieved, or intensified, social tensions. They could explode into destructive violence, as in the riots between Pompeii and Nuceria under Nero (see p. 112), and civic disorders were often aggravated by the rivalries of local aristocrats. This provided one motive for the intervention of the emperors in the lives of provincial cities.

The games involved frantic danger and excitement, as in chariot races, and, in gladiatorial combats and wild-beast fights, systematic bloodletting. Exposure to beasts in the arena was a punishment reserved for slaves and the low-born, and for outsiders like the wretched desert tribesmen shown below. In other cases, combats between animals and men appear rather as feats of acrobatics, and one suspects that, as in modern professional wrestling, genuine combat was often presented with a certain histrionic contrivance. It is unlikely that those senators who presented themselves as gladiators under Nero took much risk with their lives, though in general it seems evident that a career as a gladiator was actually sought only by the desperate.

Scenes of gladiatorial combat, circus races and hunting shows are common in Roman decorative art. They give the artist the opportunity to show human and animal forms in vigorous action, and allow the patron to commemorate his munificence in providing the games. The mansion at Rome of the senator Junius Bassus produced the vivid marble intarsia shown *above*. Bassus as consul (in 331 AD) leads the parade. Behind him are the charioteers arrayed in the colors of their teams, or factions, whose fortunes were followed avidly by their partisans. The combat scene (*above left*) is from a mosaic at Bad Kreuznach in Germany, picturing various types of gladiatorial combat. Here in mid-action are a pair of gladiators armed in the "Samnite" fashion with sword, oblong shield and crested helmet. The extensive mosaics from the late Roman palace at Piazza Armerina in Sicily display hunting scenes: not only the ostriches shown here (*center left*), but tigers, antelopes and a rhinoceros are shown being loaded for export from Africa. The mosaic from Zliten in Tripolitania (*left*) is remarkable for its pitiless realism: captured desert tribesmen defenselessly exposed to beasts, and various forms of fighting with animals.

The wide-eyed circus audience shown *above* is captured from a mosaic of the Byzantine period from Gafsa (Capsa) in Tunisia. It does not attest the continuance of chariot racing in this 6th-century provincial town but derives from an earlier design, or conventional theme, associated with Roman Carthage.

Shown *above* on a papyrus from Oxyrhynchus is a 6th-century circus program. The attractions include six chariot races, interspersed by a parade, singing rope dancers (two appearances), gazelle and hounds, mime dancers and a troupe of athletes.

The amphitheater at El-Djem, ancient Thysdrus (*left*), was among the largest in the Empire. Built in the early 3rd century, it superseded an earlier structure already possessed by the city.

The ivory diptych of the Lampadii (*above*) is typical of the gifts which senatorial families would distribute to friends invited to their games, usually held to celebrate the public office of one of their members.

CONSTANTINE THE GREAT AND THE 4th CENTURY

The rise and conversion of Constantine

The retirement in 305 of the Augusti, Diocletian and Maximian, entailed the promotion in their place of the existing Caesars, Galerius in the east and Constantius in the west. At the same time, by a second tier of promotion, the relatively unknown Maximinus Daia and Severus became Caesars. This choice put at risk the loyalty and coherence of policy so laboriously achieved by Diocletian, for it involved the exclusion from the prospects of imperial power of Maxentius, son of the retiring Augustus Maximian, and Constantine, son of the promoted Constantius. The collapse of Diocletian's arrangements can be attributed in part to the personal ambitions of the disappointed candidates, but ambition must have its opportunity and it is perhaps as significant that the arrangements went against the general expectation, especially in the army, for the restoration of a directly hereditary succession.

In 305 Constantine, who was still residing in the east, was allowed by Galerius to join his father in Britain. In the following year Constantius died at York, and Constantine was proclaimed Augustus by the army, though he initially claimed from Galerius only the title of Caesar. Constantine at once embarked on the energetic civil wars which by 324 made him sole ruler of the Roman Empire. Crossing to Gaul, he won the support of the restless old Augustus, Maximian, and married his daughter, Fausta. Maximian had already supported his own son Maxentius in a proclamation at Rome before quarreling with him and joining Constantine, and it was not long before he turned against Constantine also and was forced to suicide (310). Constantine now marched against Maxentius and defeated him at the battle of the Milvian Bridge (28 October 312). Since Maxentius had himself earlier eliminated Severus, Constantine was now master of the entire west.

In the east, meanwhile, Galerius had died, and his successor Licinius shared the eastern empire with Maximinus Daia. Constantine and Licinius met for mutual recognition at Milan and agreed, among other things, to restore freedom of religious worship and allow the Christians to recover their property, confiscated in the Great Persecution. The two emperors lived in peace until 316 (Licinius in the meantime defeating Maximinus), when Constantine gained territory in the Balkans from Licinius, and from 317 until 324. In 324, however, Constantine moved against Licinius, defeating him at Hadrianople and in a sea battle at Chrysopolis, and from then until his death in 337 was sole ruler of the Empire, appointing as Caesars his sons Constantine, Constantius and Constans.

The rise·of Constantine cannot be understood, even so far, without reference to his conversion to Christianity. The outward signs of this can be traced fairly closely. In the earliest stages of his quest for power, Constantine relied on a variety of claims of connections with the Tetrarchy. Then, after the suicide of Maximian in 310, a Gallic panegyrist announced that Constantine had experienced a vision of Apollo in a shrine somewhere in Gaul. Occurring in the same speech as a fabricated family connection with the emperor Claudius II (Gothicus), the vision would most naturally be taken as part of a double claim, for divine support, and for the legitimation of his quest for power at a time when, with the death of Maximian, Constantine most needed it. Our knowledge of the second phase depends ultimately on Constantine himself, in an account given late in his life to his Christian panegyrist, Eusebius of Caesarea. Constantine recalled how he had witnessed a vision of a cross standing over the sun, accompanied by the words, "Conquer with this," and the following night had been visited by a dream in which Christ explained to him the meaning of the vision. The third stage was another dream, experienced by Constantine on the evening before the battle of the Milvian Bridge. In this dream, he was told to paint on his troops' shields the Christian monogram (☧) and go to battle "armed with this sign." Doing so, he was victorious over Maxentius. To this point, Constantine's religious affiliations combined two tendencies. They were associated with the sun, the symbol of the all-powerful and all-embracing God of contemporary religious thought, and within this conception had come to focus on Christ as the particular representative of that power who had revealed himself and offered his support to Constantine.

The fourth, and most public, stage of the conversion involves a variety of pronouncements, by Constantine himself in his letters, by panegyrists and on monumental inscriptions, to the effect that his victories had been achieved by his piety to the One True God, to whom the emperor had now devoted himself. Two such statements among many are worth particular emphasis. The Arch of Constantine at Rome bears an inscription stating that the emperor had defeated the tyrant Maxentius "by the inspiration of the Divinity and the greatness of his [i.e. Constantine's] mind," and Constantine himself, writing in 314 to African bishops, measured by his own experience the extent of God's mercy. Referring directly to his conversion, the emperor wrote that there had originally been many things in himself which seemed to "lack justice," and which should have been rewarded with the fate that befalls all wickedness; but God had rescued Constantine from the darkness of ignorance and bestowed on him the salvation which he least deserved. Such statements in the emperor's own letters, in his legislation and in the comments of observers preclude any doubt that Constantine's "conversion," whatever its explanation in terms of his personal psychology, was an event publicized by the emperor, and recognized by contemporaries, as a genuinely religious experience with definite consequences.

Top Constantine and Trier, his early capital, in a gold medallion of 310/15. The emperor, with scepter, stands over the gate of the walled city, below which runs the river Moselle. On either side are defeated barbarians. The medallion of 313 (*above*) shows Constantine "the Unconquered" with his companion the sun, in an explicit recognition of the importance of the sun in Constantine's early religious development. On the shield is the four-horsed chariot of the sun.

Coin issues from later in Constantine's reign, as in this example of about 327 (*opposite top*), show him wearing a diadem, with an upward gaze symbolizing his intimacy with heaven. A medallion of 315, shown *opposite above* in the best of very few surviving examples, is generally taken to show the monogram (☧) on the crest of Constantine's helmet, but it is more likely that the apparent device is merely one of the rosette designs forming the crest. On Constantine's shield are Romulus and Remus with the she-wolf.

In his pronouncements, Constantine frequently emphasizes the personal nature of his relationship with the Christian God, as with the Apollo whom he had seen in his vision at the shrine in Gaul; the orator of 310, addressing Constantine, refers to this as a vision of *"your* Apollo" (*Apollinem tuum*). Further, dreams and visions were part of the regular "technology" of ancient religious experience – one of the standard means whereby the gods were accustomed to communicate with men. Many examples can be found of actions, of the widest possible variety, undertaken in response to dreams and visions. The conversion of St Paul on the road to Damascus is an obvious parallel to the experience of Constantine, but not all such divine messages were as sensational as these. However they are to be explained in terms of individual or collective psychology, it is clear that Constantine's experiences, in which he received revelations and instructions from his God, were part of the regular mode in which men of the ancient world believed these things to happen.

Constantine's religious attitudes were involved also in one of the most significant of all social and political events of antiquity, the foundation of Constantinople. The emperor had visited Rome in 315, for the celebrations of the 10-year anniversary of his rule. Repeating the visit in 326 after his victory over Licinius, Constantine offended the senate and people of Rome by refusing to attend a procession and sacrifice on the Capitol. His rupture with the old capital was followed by the deliberate promotion of Constantinople, the foundation of which, on the site of ancient Byzantium, he had already decided on before his visit to the west. The "New Rome" was built on seven hills, was divided into 14 city districts and possessed its own senate, which was further enhanced in dignity by Constantine's successor, Constantius. The city was dedicated in 330. Despite the report that secret pagan rites were involved in the consecration ceremonies (in 324), Constantinople was from the beginning a city without active pagan cults, except possibly for that of the "Tyche," or Fortune, of the city. Though it contained classical statuary collected from the cities of the east (including what was left of the tripod of Apollo from Delphi), this was "secularized" by being detached from its former religious associations, and the existing pagan temples of old Byzantium were put out of use. The new capital was a city of Christian worship and of great churches, among which those of Holy Peace (Hagia Eirene) and of the Apostles are the best-attested Constantinian foundations. The most famous of all, the church of Holy Wisdom (Hagia Sophia) was probably begun by Constantius.

Constantine's momentous visit to Rome was also connected in some way with a mysterious political crisis affecting his close family. In 326 his son Crispus was executed at Pola in Dalmatia. Then, a little later, Constantine's wife Fausta (Crispus' stepmother) also died, allegedly by being scalded to death in her bath. Not long afterwards, Constantine's mother Helena embarked on a visit, or pilgrimage, to the Holy Land. It has naturally been suspected that part of her intention was to expiate the guilt which had fallen on her family; indeed, the Greek pagan tradition, hostile to Constantine, could inaccurately but with evident plausibility assert that Constantine had been converted to Christianity in order to gain "instant forgiveness" for the murder of his relatives. Helena's visit was associated with a lavish program of church building at Jerusalem and at other places in the Holy Land, in which Constantine took an intense personal interest. He wrote to the bishop of Jerusalem on matters of design and furnishing, and promising financial and administrative help, transportation facilities and other assistance in the works. A pilgrim who went to Jerusalem from Bordeaux in 333 remarked on several occasions on the fine new churches, built by order of Constantine. The most celebrated was the church of the Holy Sepulcher, purporting to mark the very spot of Christ's burial; the church is shown by the 6th-century Madaba map as the dominating feature of Jerusalem. Within a few years of Constantine's death, fragments of the "True Cross" were also displayed at Jerusalem; on one occasion a pilgrim bent over as if to kiss the relic,

The arch of Constantine at Rome (*right*) was erected to mark the victory over the "usurper" Maxentius in 312. Some of the reliefs of the arch were reused 2nd-century pieces (cf. p. 104), but new sculptures were added which give a summary narrative of the campaign against Maxentius. Here are shown (*below right*) the siege of Verona and (*below*) a detail from a scene at Rome in which Constantine demonstrates his liberality by largesse. The officials take coin from a chest and hand it down for distribution, while one of them keeps a record of expenditure. The furrowed brows are presumably meant to suggest concentration rather than anxiety.

then ran off with a piece between his teeth! The connection of Helena with the Invention of the Cross is, however, first found only in the last years of the 4th century; it is not part of the contemporary tradition.

Constantine was the founder of other famous churches: the Lateran basilica and St Peter's at Rome, and churches at Cirta (Constantine) in Numidia and at Trier, where he had spent some years in the early part of his reign. It was to Trier that Constantine had summoned the old teacher of rhetoric Lactantius, the author of works of Christian exegesis, and of a ferociously hostile pamphlet denouncing the persecutors of the Christians, to be the tutor of his son Crispus. Lactantius, an African, had taught rhetoric at Nicomedia, the capital city of Diocletian, before coming to Trier in 317 or earlier.

Both in the time of Constantine and throughout the 4th century, a decisive impulse in the process of the Christianization of the Empire was provided by the imperial court. Many of the supporters of Constantine at the highest levels, such as his praetorian prefect Ablabius and the Spaniard Acilius Severus, who was known to Lactantius and is the first known Christian prefect of Rome (326), were Christians whose example and influence undoubtedly had a great effect on the imperial court and through it on society at large. In addition, the bureaucracy drew its recruits from precisely those areas of society, the urban middle classes, in which Christianity had earlier made its deepest impact. In this sense, the conversion of Constantine, though in its own right a personal and unpredictable event, did not exercise its influence in a vacuum, but through the medium of what became one of the major social institutions of the late Empire (see below, p. 201).

The successors of Constantine

The policies of Constantine were not confined to matters of religion, though contemporary critics ascribed the many changes which he introduced in the administrative, financial and military organization of the Empire to the same restlessness of mind which led to his religious innovations. Constantine brought in new taxes, especially the

chrysargyron, a monetary tax, which was bitterly criticized, on all forms of trade and commerce, and established the basic unit of gold currency, the *solidus*, at the new rate of 72 to the pound which it retained for centuries. In his military policy, Constantine further developed the role of a mobile field army, some believed at the cost of effective frontier defense. He conducted successful foreign wars against German tribes, and later against Goths and Sarmatians on the Danube frontier; his death in 337 took place in the midst of preparations for a major Persian campaign. Constantine was baptized on his deathbed, and his body was taken to Constantinople and buried there in his church of the Apostles. The memorials of the 12 were arranged, six on each side of the emperor, who thereby presented himself as a sort of thirteenth Apostle.

Through his father's second marriage to a stepdaughter of Maximian, Constantine possessed numerous half-brothers and nephews whom he sometimes used to further his political and diplomatic projects. Immediately after the emperor's death these relatives and most of their children were murdered, obviously by a concerted plan, leaving Constantine's own sons, Constantine II, Constantius and Constans as emperors respectively of Gaul with Spain and Britain, of the east, and of Illyricum with Italy. The most obvious direct beneficiary of the assassinations was Constantius, but he was under 20 years old at the time, and it seems more likely that those responsible were powerful politicians and generals who wished to preserve an orderly dynastic succession, free from disputes between different branches of the family.

Constantine II survived only three years before he was suppressed by Constans, who then ruled the west for a further 10 years. In 350 Constans himself fell to a military usurper, Magnentius. Constantius defeated Magnentius at Mursa (351) and Mons Seleucus (353), and became sole ruler of the entire Roman Empire, but it quickly became clear that, in the face of renewed German hostility, the western provinces required separate government by an emperor with local authority. In 355 Constantius overcame his personal dislike and appointed his nephew Julian, the son of one of those massacred in

The city of Jerusalem, seen here (*above left*) in a mosaic from the triumphal arch of the 5th-century church of St Maria Maggiore at Rome, and its companion Bethlehem, stand for the churches of the circumcised and of the gentiles. Within the city appear its most distinctive Christian monuments, the Constantinian foundations also shown (*above*) in the relief from a Roman sarcophagus of St Peter being warned by Christ that he will thrice deny him before cockcrow. The three buildings to the left are identified as the church of the Holy Sepulcher and its baptistery, with domed rotunda (known as the Anastasis) over the supposed site of the burial of Christ. The prominence of the baptistery underlines the theme of repentance implied by Peter's denial of Christ.

Right: Mesopotamia and the campaigns of Julian, 363 AD. Julian's strategy in the Persian campaign of 363 was to divert the main army of Shapur by a feigned invasion of northern Assyria, then to attack Ctesiphon rapidly before the king could redeploy his forces. The plan foundered on the resistance of fortified cities like Pirisabora and the garrison near Besouchis, and on the Persians' willingness to obstruct Julian's passage by breaching river and canal banks and flooding the terrain. Julian reached Ctesiphon, but, threatened by the approach of the king's army, abandoned any attempt to take the city, burned the huge fleet which had carried his supplies down the Euphrates but was now an encumbrance, and turned north under constant Persian attack, to be killed in a skirmish. The map suggests the nature of the terrain, with ancient ruined cities left waterless by changing river courses, and complex canal systems. It also acknowledges a fact only fleetingly mentioned by classical sources on the campaign, the presence of a large Jewish population with its famous Rabbinical academies.

337, as Caesar in Gaul, summoning him from his studies at Athens.

Constantius intended that Julian should be in nominal control of the German wars, leaving their active management to the generals and other officials whom he appointed on his Caesar's behalf. Julian initially acquiesced, and under this arrangement achieved a great victory over the Alamanni near Strasbourg in 357, but as he became progressively more competent at and interested in warfare he asserted his personality more forcibly. Constantius, after visiting Rome in 357, returned to the east to meet a major invasion of Mesopotamia. Needing to strengthen the eastern armies, in 360 he requested reinforcements from Julian, whose response was his proclamation as Augustus, allegedly spontaneous and reluctantly accepted on his own part. In 361 Julian marched east against Constantius, and a potentially destructive civil war which Julian would probably have lost was averted by Constantius' death. He was still under 44 years of age.

Julian's short reign was one of frantic and in some ways ill-balanced activity. Disliking the elaborate ceremony of the imperial office, Julian severely reduced the size of the palace and bureaucratic staffs (the sources select barbers, cooks and eunuchs as the particular victims of these economies), and was strenuous in personally hearing judicial and other matters which were brought to his attention. His chief ambition as emperor was the restoration of the worship of the ancient gods, allied with a program of civic, moral and cultural renewal. His attempt to restore the Temple at Jerusalem was abortive, but restorations in other cities were successfully undertaken. Julian took the first steps towards the creation of a reformed pagan priesthood under which the temples would be administered; social and charitable institutions like those offered by the Christian churches were to be founded for the support of widows and the sick. Believing that a love of classical literature was incompatible with belief in Christianity, he issued an edict, which was widely criticized, forbidding Christians to act as

teachers of literature and rhetoric. One of the greatest classical scholars of the day, Marius Victorinus, was forced to resign his chair of rhetoric at Rome, and became equally famous for his Christian doctrinal works; another, Prohaeresius of Athens, was also prevented from teaching but is said to have consulted the hierophant of Eleusis and to have learned that the emperor would not reign long.

Julian's personal religious sympathies were with the school of theurgical Neoplatonism propounded by Iamblichus (see above, p. 177). He was a devotee of Mithras and of Magna Mater, and wrote obscure allegorical tracts on their behalf as well as harsh polemical works against the Christians; the most famous of the latter, *Against the Galilaeans*, is only known from its refutation by a 5th-century writer, Cyril of Alexandria. He sacrificed with unrestrained enthusiasm to the pagan gods, and for this too he was criticized even by his supporters. It is far from certain what degree of sympathy he would have retained from pagans with different religious tastes from his own and more tolerant than he was of their opponents. His policies naturally incurred the bitter hostility of Christian writers, but before they could be fully implemented or their prospects of success demonstrated, the emperor was killed on his ambitious Persian campaign mounted from Antioch in 363.

Julian's successor, Jovian, was proclaimed by the army in Mesopotamia, in the crisis caused by Julian's death in battle. To secure the escape of the army from Persian territory, Jovian was obliged to cede territories in northern Mesopotamia, including five satrapies along the upper Tigris and all the land east of Nisibis and Singara; for these necessary concessions Jovian took the blame deserved by his predecessor. In contrast to Julian, Jovian was a Christian of apparently moderate temper, but before any real policies or attitudes could emerge he too was dead, overcome by the fumes in a recently plastered room in the house in Galatia where he was staying on his journey to Constantinople.

Jovian was succeeded by another military officer, Valentinian, who was nominated by a caucus of high military and civil officials and accepted without demur by the army. Valentinian appreciated the need to share the imperial power and selected as colleague his brother Valens, an apparently unpromising choice with the advantage that it seemed best suited to secure the loyalty between eastern and western parts of the Empire which recent experience had so clearly shown to be essential. In conferences held at Sirmium in the winter of 364/5, the emperors divided the provinces, army and administration between them. Valentinian then went to the Rhine frontier to confront the renewed barbarian threat which had followed the departure of Julian from Gaul in 361. Intent on the need to secure this frontier, Valentinian left his brother to meet and overcome from his own resources the usurpation of Procopius in 365.

The reign of Valentinian was devoted to the military defense of the Rhine frontier, and in its later years of the Danubian frontier of the Empire; his general Theodosius also suppressed a major barbarian incursion into Britain. Valentinian's policy is well attested by archaeology; it involved a

Julian the Apostate, seen here (*below*) as consul, appears on his coinage as the bearded philosopher-emperor, an image also taken up by the leader of another pagan "revival," the rhetorician Eugenius (*bottom*). Proclaimed in 392 by the Frankish general Arbogast and supported by members of the Roman aristocracy, Eugenius was defeated by Theodosius at the battle of the Frigidus river (394).

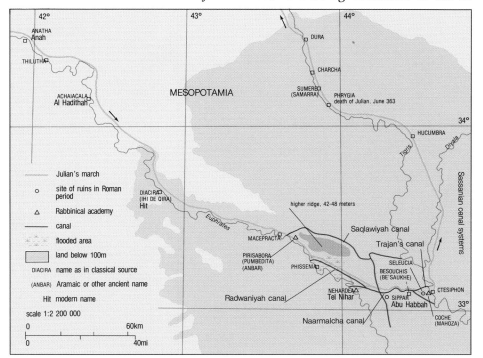

Julian's march
o   site of ruins in Roman period
△   Rabbinical academy
─   canal
     flooded area
     land below 100m
DIACIRA name as in classical source
(ANBAR) Aramaic or other ancient name
Hit modern name
scale 1:2 200 000
0   60km
0   40mi

systematic program of fort construction, both along the rivers themselves and at sites lying behind them on routes of penetration into the Roman provinces, supported by punitive raids and reprisals in barbarian territory. His administration was generally characterized by rigor and thoroughness, not to mention the brutality now typical of late Roman government. Nonetheless, the attempts of Tripolitanian cities to confront tribal incursions from the desert were undermined by maladministration and corruption in both provincial and central government, Illyricum suffered from the oppressive administration of its praetorian prefect and Mauretanian Africa was threatened by a serious tribal rebellion, suppressed by Theodosius in 373–75. At Rome, Valentinian's organization of the corn supplies and his building projects won him a lasting reputation, but he provoked the hostility of the Roman nobility by instigating prosecutions there for magic and adultery from 369 onwards. Valentinian died in 375 of a stroke, brought on by his anger at the conduct of envoys of the Quadi whom he was receiving in his camp at Brigetio on the Danube.

The reign of Valens was concerned mainly with foreign wars, against the Goths, whom he attacked successfully in 367–69, and Persia, an indecisive conflict involving the status of Armenia. Valens,

like his brother, conducted trials for magic, in which members of the eastern upper classes were involved. These trials involved genuine political dissent among members of the eastern intelligentsia rather than merely, as in the case of those conducted by Valentinian, the immoral behavior of the nobility. The crisis of the reign of Valens came in 376, when the emperor was persuaded to agree to the admission to the Empire of the Visigoths, pushed against the Roman frontier by the expansion of the Huns from their homelands east of the Dnieper river. The attractions of this policy to the emperor lay in the opportunity to acquire large numbers of recruits, which would allow the peasantry to remain on the land rather than be enrolled in the Roman army, and would thereby increase cash revenue from taxation. But the crossing of the Danube was inadequately supervised, the Goths flooded into Thrace in an uncontrolled mass and forced Roman armies to meet them in battle. In August 378 Valens himself encountered the Goths at Hadrianople (Edirne, in European Turkey). The battle was lost; Valens himself was killed and two-thirds of the Roman army destroyed.

In the crisis Theodosius, son of Valentinian's former general, was recalled from private life in Spain and made emperor (January 379). Theodosius

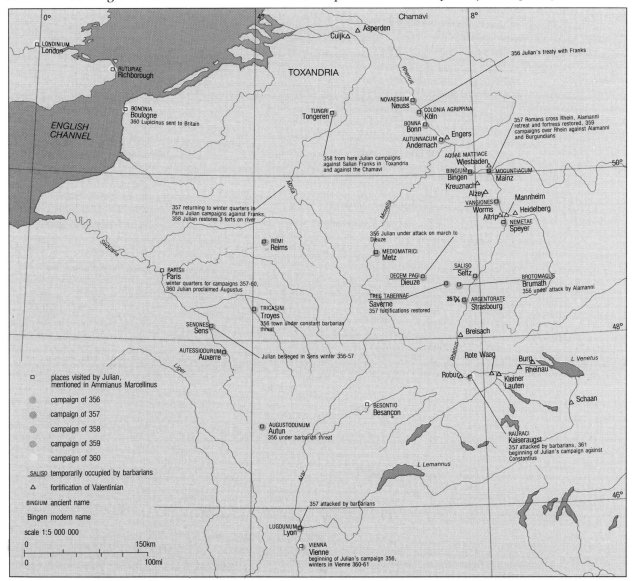

The German campaigns of Julian and Valentinian. On the appointment of Julian as Caesar in Gaul, after several years of political disturbance there, the area under barbarian occupation or threat reached as far west as Lyon, Autun, Sens and Troyes. Julian's campaigns reestablished the frontier as the Rhine, an achievement for which he claimed personal credit and deserved much of it, though there are several signs of his inexperience and the role of the advisers given him by Constantius was probably greater than Julian's admirers would admit. Julian's declaration of war against Constantius deprived Gaul of many troops, and the Persian campaign of 363, undertaken against the explicit advice of the praetorian prefect of Gaul, undermined much of his achievement. The situation was restored by the good sense and patience of Valentinian. It is likely however that the ancient sources, attracted by the personal glamor of Julian's achievements, underrepresent the less spectacular work which he put in hand, in engineering and the construction of frontier defenses.

The beautiful diptych leaf headed "SYMMACHORUM," with its companion "NICOMACHORUM" (in the Cluny Museum at Paris), commemorates some event, possibly a marriage, jointly involving these two leading late 4th-century families. The imagery is both pagan and classical. A priestess makes an offering at an altar, behind which is the oak tree symbolic of Jupiter, while the companion leaf presents images of Ceres and Cybele in a similar composition. Q. Aurelius Symmachus and Nicomachus Flavianus were champions of the traditional cults of Rome in this last generation of their existence. Flavianus fell in the pagan revival of Eugenius (392–94). Symmachus did not actively participate in the civil war and was able to retain his political influence during the last few years of his life and to use it in favour of some who had opposed Theodosius.

devoted the first years of his reign to the Gothic problem, and a treaty of alliance was concluded in 382, whereby the Goths were settled in Lower Moesia and allowed to serve in the Roman army as federates under their own tribal leaders. Theodosius also made a treaty with the Persians in 386. Both alliances are commemorated on the base of the obelisk of Theodosius at Constantinople, erected in 390.

In the west, Valentinian had been succeeded by his sons, Gratian and Valentinian II, then respectively aged 16 and four years old. Both were evidently controlled by their advisers, and Valentinian also by his mother, the forceful Justina, but neither regime made much impact on the government of the Empire, and in 383 that of Gratian fell to the usurper Maximus. Proclaimed in Britain, Maximus had Gratian murdered at Lyon, set up his court at Trier and hoped for recognition by Theodosius. In 387, however, he invaded Italy and unseated Valentinian, who fled to Theodosius. In response, Theodosius marched against Maximus in 388, defeated him and restored Valentinian, whom he sent to Gaul while he himself resided at Milan. Theodosius visited Rome in the summer of 389.

Returning to Constantinople in 391, Theodosius left Valentinian at Trier under the supervision of a Frankish general, Arbogast. In the next year the young emperor was found hanged, probably by suicide, and Arbogast elevated as Emperor Eugenius, a former teacher of rhetoric. Eugenius was used by a group of Roman senatorial supporters as the "front" for a pagan revival at Rome, but in September 394 their forces, under the command of Arbogast and the senator Nicomachus Flavianus, were defeated by Theodosius at the battle of the Frigidus (Wippach) river east of Aquileia. Theodosius came again to Milan and set up his court there, but in January 395 he died, apparently of heart disease, and left the Empire jointly in the hands of his young sons, Honorius in the west, and Arcadius, who ruled the east with equally nominal authority from Constantinople. From this time, if not already from 364, the Roman Empire can be considered effectively divided into eastern and western parts.

The Christianization of the Roman Empire

Writing in the late 4th century, Augustine remarked that the conversion of the Roman world to Christianity had happened "extremely fast." He was quite right in this, especially considering the extent to which the old pagan religion was embedded in the culture, moral values and social organization of classical antiquity. In the splendid chapter 15 of his *Decline and Fall*, Gibbon vividly described the difficulties faced by the early Christians, if they wished to keep their faith pure and yet take part in the regular life of society; in any social event in which they wished or were obliged to participate – weddings, funerals, litigation, "all the offices and amusements of society" – they would be drawn against their will into religious rituals and gestures, "infernal snares" from which they could not stand back without setting themselves apart from everyday life. From the same sources, the ancestral religion gained a tremendous tenacity when forced onto the defensive by an aggressive Christianity supported by the emperors. It proved almost impossible, for the purpose of government

action, to isolate the religious elements from the social and cultural contexts with which they were so intimately linked. Constantine himself permitted the establishment of a temple of the second Flavian dynasty at Cirta in Numidia, and at Hispellum in central Italy, with the recorded proviso in the second case that the temple was to be kept free of any suspicion of the "contagion" of sacrifice. Imperial legislation throughout the 4th century, culminating in the laws of Theodosius in the 380s and early 390s, restricted and finally abolished pagan sacrifice; the ancient temples were closed and their estates confiscated, but it proved necessary to reiterate that the games and festivals traditionally associated with the temples were to continue, having been established "for the common enjoyment of all men." By a law of 382, the great temple at Edessa in Osrhoene was closed to religious observance, but maintained as a work of art and museum of antiquity. It was a situation with which the Christian emperors of the 4th century found themselves increasingly familiar.

The most conspicuous element of continuity with the pagan past in the emperors' own position was their retention of the title of *pontifex maximus*. The title was only abandoned by Gratian, probably as late as 382 under the influence of Bishop Ambrose, when an embassy came to Milan from Rome to offer him the pontifical robes. Gratian accompanied his refusal of the robes and rejection of the title *pontifex maximus* by more positive measures. He withdrew from the priestly colleges and Vestal Virgins the financial subsidies and other privileges which they had received for centuries, and removed from the senate-house the altar of Victory, where ever since the days of Augustus senatorial sessions had been inaugurated by a sacrifice. Gratian's action drew from the prefect of Rome, the pagan orator Symmachus, a petition of protest addressed on behalf of the senate to his successor, Valentinian II. Symmachus pressed the claims of the ancestral religion on grounds of custom and utility. The old gods, he argued, had defended Rome through the ages, and their support should not be casually set aside. Symmachus' arguments were unsuccessful against the assertion by Ambrose of the claims of an expanding religion under the patronage of an emperor whose Christian duty it was to support it. The pagan revival of Eugenius and Nicomachus Flavianus in 393–94 was no more than a last gesture of the pagan cause, which went down with its leaders at the battle of the Frigidus.

While the public battle was fought over the preservation of the ancient cults of the Roman state, the attitudes of the late pagans themselves were no less vitally involved with the so-called "Oriental" cults which they had adopted, sometimes in great profusion. The senator Praetextatus (died 384), as we know from his epitaph, combined priesthoods and initiations in no fewer than six Greek and Oriental mystery religions as well as four public priesthoods in the old state cults. These mystery cults, among which those of Magna Mater (Cybele), Mithras and Serapis were prominent, offered purification of the soul and a hope of eternal life to their initiates, and required of them a genuine religious devotion and, at their highest level, philosophical learning. For Praetextatus, as for Julian the Apostate, the gods of the pagan pantheon were united in a Neoplatonic interpretation as the diverse functions of the all-powerful Sun. Initiation into the cult of Magna Mater was by the rite known as the *taurobolium*, in which the initiate stood in a pit under a grille while a bull was slaughtered above him, spraying him with its blood. This rite especially drew the fire of Christian polemic, partly because of its intrinsically distasteful nature, but also because, like other such rites, it functioned as a sort of pagan "baptism" and showed that paganism, as expressed in these cults, had the capacity to appeal to the religious imagination of individuals as well as to the sense of public duty of Roman senators and priests.

Though judgments differ, it seems likely that at the time of Symmachus' appeal to Valentinian, the Roman senate was already, as Ambrose claimed, composed of a majority of Christians. There is at least no doubt as to the *direction* of the change, from paganism to Christianity, as a result of political and social pressure, genuine conversion (though recorded cases of this are rare) and, perhaps most pervasively effective, mixed marriages between Christians and pagans in which the Christian upbringing of the children secured the faith of the next generation.

Whatever point in the transition had been reached by the nobility of the city, the common people of Rome were surely Christianized by the second half of the 4th century, and took a lively interest in the life of its church (on one occasion riots over the election of a bishop of Rome left 137 corpses on the floor of one of the churches). This was also true of the populations of other great cities of the Empire. The case of Antioch is relatively well documented from the writings of the pagan rhetorician Libanius and the Christian priest John Chrysostom. Antioch contained a core of supporters of the old gods, among whom Libanius was prominent. Yet, as Julian the Apostate was shocked to find on arriving there in 362, the general population of the city, a large proportion of its aristocracy and no doubt the majority of the imperial officials there were already firmly Christianized by his day.

As to other Syrian cities, Carrhae was pagan and remained so until much later, while such cities as Heliopolis (Baalbek), Emesa, Arethusa and Berytus retained strong (if not always unanimous) traditions based on ancient cults, as, further south, did Gaza in Phoenicia. Edessa, on the other hand, with its traditions of St Thomas, its martyrs' memorials and its possession of the alleged letters written by Christ to King Abgar, was already strongly Christianized by the time of Julian; he refused even to visit it when invited to do so by an embassy in 363.

Elsewhere in the Empire, Athens retained pagan intellectual traditions into the 5th and 6th centuries; moreover, the rarity of Christian symbols on the many 4th-century clay lamps excavated in the Agora, and the absence of any definitely identified church building or of any well-known bishop in the same period, suggest that the general population also was resistant to Christianity. Alexandria, a center of study for Neoplatonic philosophy and the sciences, was at the same time a hotbed of Christian fanaticism, led by forceful bishops such as Athanasius, whose dominating influence in the city led on several occasions to his exile by the emperors. Apart

from its intellectual traditions, Alexandria was notorious for its civic disorders, for which religious divisions no doubt provided yet further opportunities. In 391 a mob, led by monks and incited by the bishop, tore down the great statue and temple of Serapis in the city, one of the great marvels of the ancient world.

The evidence is less full for the western than for the eastern provinces. In the predominantly rural provinces of Gaul, bishops were by the later 4th century turning their attention to the evangelization of their communities, and such sources as the *Life of St Martin of Tours* by Sulpicius Severus show these efforts being directed against traditionally conservative rural areas, with the destruction of local shrines and the beginnings of the organization of parish churches based on townships and villages. The cities, as one would expect, were ahead of the countryside. To take one example, while waiting at Vienne in 360 to embark on his campaign against Constantius, Julian the Apostate, who had already secretly committed himself to paganism, maintained an open profession of Christianity and attended the services for Epiphany. He maintained this pretense in order not to alienate his support, an action which implies clearly that Vienne was a predominantly Christian city.

In Africa, where Christianity had gained an early hold (see above, p. 177), disputes between Catholics and Donatist schismatics seem to presuppose strongly Christianized communities, often with rival bishops, one belonging to each sect. But there were still in the late 4th century spokesmen for paganism, like Augustine's correspondent Maximus of Madauros, and as late as 408 anti-Christian riots occurred at Calama in Numidia when the bishop tried to break up a pagan procession. In general it seems clear that, although most parts of the Empire were predominantly Christian by the late 4th century, local pockets of pagan belief still persisted, often based on traditional associations with certain gods, and that at its more articulate levels paganism, though by now a minority interest, still presented a serious intellectual case requiring reasoned criticism.

Julian, like other Greek intellectuals, used the word *Hellen* ("Greek," that is, educated Greek), to mean a believer in the old gods. Julian's opinion was shared, from the opposite point of view, by Jerome, who argued that the acceptance of Christianity implied the rejection of classical culture and all its links with the pagan past. A third view, represented by the Christian bishop Gregory of Nazianzus, asserted that classical culture was the common possession of all men. Christians, he argued, were capable of appreciating classical literature and benefiting from it without succumbing to its dangers. They too were "Greeks" (Gregory challenged Julian's restrictive use of this word) and it was intolerable that they should be deprived of their heritage as educated human beings. Other writers, like Augustine, wrote tracts defining the use which could properly be made by Christians of classical culture, comparing it sometimes with the "gold of the Egyptians" seized by the children of Israel (Exodus 12:35), but it is clear that it was in effect the position of Gregory that was adopted by the majority. The importance of a classical education for recruitment into the Roman government, and of

Right Late Roman sarcophagi and mosaics, with their iconography of images often taken from the Old Testament and interpreted as a prefiguration of the *tempora Christiana*, provide vivid expressions of the Christian culture of late Roman society. Here are shown the three brothers of the Book of Daniel in the "burning fiery furnace" (*top left*), and Daniel in the lion's den on a 4th-century sarcophagus (*top right*) and on a 6th-century African mosaic (*center right*) – images of triumph over persecution frequently found on the monuments. On the sarcophagus of the Roman senator Petronius Probus, who died after baptism in about 390 and was buried in a family mausoleum at St Peter's (*center left*), Christ hands to the Apostles copies of the "New Law" of Christianity, an allusion interpreted by reference to the Tables of the Law broken and the new Tables received by Moses in Exodus. The detail of Pilate washing his hands, on a sarcophagus from the catacombs of Domitilla, is self-explanatory (*bottom left*), while Jonah and the whale, from an early 4th-century mosaic from the basilica at Aquileia (*bottom right*), symbolizes death and resurrection, or more specifically the salvation of the soul after baptism, an image of obvious appropriateness for a church.

Above Christian and pagan motifs on lamps from the Athenian Agora: Athena, an early 4th-century type revived in the 5th (*top*) and St Peter (*bottom*; 5th century).

Left The Corbridge *lanx*, a rectangular presentation dish, is remarkable for the erudition of its mythological imagery. Its subject is the birth of Apollo and Artemis to Leto on the island of Delos; the "omphalos," or "navel" of the earth, is shown as a column behind the seated figure of Leto. It has been persuasively argued that the version of the legend shown, including the local Delian nymph Asteria (between Leto and Athena), involves a recondite knowledge implying active pagan belief rather than a merely formal classicism of taste. The gesture with which Athena addresses Artemis is very characteristic of the late Roman period.

rhetoric in its conduct, is no less conspicuous in the 4th and later centuries than it had been in the 2nd and 3rd. The examples of men such as Themistius the philosopher (a pagan) and the poet Ausonius (a Christian), who held office under the Christian emperors of the 4th century, could be multiplied many times over without difficulty.

At the same time, the 4th century saw the emergence of a specifically Christian culture, based on the Bible, expounded by bishops and developed in works of exegesis by Christian writers. Jerome's new Latin version of the Bible, the Vulgate, was a conscious attempt to provide a new Christian public with a scholarly and accurate translation; it was supported by a vast program of biblical commentaries, dedicated to Jerome's friends among the Christian aristocracy of Rome but clearly intended for a wider audience.

The Christianization of the Empire involved the acquisition of a new culture, based on the Bible, by a public which did not, in general, expect to lose its old one. This situation implies a certain difficulty in the interpretation of much of the surviving intellectual culture and artistic creation of the late Roman period. In cases where we do not know the religion of a poet, of the recipient of a literary dedication or of the owner of a villa containing mosaics with classical themes, it is tempting to infer this from the nature of the work of art of which he is the author or with which he is associated. On this basis, however, the poet Ausonius, whose work is full of classical themes, might be inferred to have been a pagan, though the evidence for his Christianity is explicit. The coexistence of a genuinely devout Christianity with a continuing love of classical culture was not only a possible but a frequent occurrence.

The church and the emperors

From the moment of the conversion of Constantine, the position of the Christian church in Roman society was transformed. By the so-called Edict of Milan (313) the church received back its property confiscated in the Great Persecution, and, beginning in Africa in the early years of Constantine's reign, acquired additional financial and other benefits from the emperor. The church gained for its clergy exemption from civic obligations (though a cleric was supposed on ordination to guarantee their performance by a substitute), bishops received rights of civil jurisdiction, with or without the consent of both parties. There is no doubting the practical benefits to litigants, who were released from what Constantine called the "interminable meshes of litigation" by this more speedy and honest method of jurisdiction. But there could be obvious abuses, as when Libanius complained of the activities of the bishop of Antioch, who by the exercise of episcopal jurisdiction settled land disputes in favor of the monks who had brought them to him. By their acquisition of such power, bishops quickly became prominent figures in their communities; their churches became important and, by their receipt of donations and legacies, often very wealthy institutions.

Jerome once made a tantalizing unfulfilled promise to write a history in which he would show how the church during the 4th century "grew richer in wealth and possessions but poorer in virtue." Jerome would have enjoyed the historian Ammianus Marcellinus' description of magnificently attired prelates parading around the city of Rome surrounded by crowds of admirers, and eating dinners fit for kings. In this, wrote Ammianus, they contrasted with the humbler and

Right Ambrose, bishop of Milan in the late 4th century, as he is presented, shortly after his lifetime, in a mosaic from the chapel of St Victor at Milan. Although it cannot be proved that it is a realistic portrait, the questioning but confident alertness of the features is a convincing expression of certain aspects at least of the character of this formidably gifted and determined man.

commendable manners of provincial clergy. Yet Jerome's own patron, Damasus (367–83), was not among those bishops of Rome least known for their sense of the high dignity of the office.

Jerome was also thinking of the religious divisions which beset the church in the 4th century. Constantine was dismayed at the outset of his reign by the division in the African church between Catholic and Donatist parties, the latter opposing the ordination as bishop of Carthage of a candidate who was believed to have surrendered the scriptures in the Great Persecution. This schism, which in the 4th century dominated the life of the African church, was only suppressed, amid much rancor, by the efforts of Augustine and his colleagues in the early 5th century, with the help of carefully managed councils supported by imperial legislation.

On his arrival in the east in 324, Constantine was at once confronted by the problem of Arianism. Arius, a priest of Alexandria, had developed theories concerning the nature of God, which owed much of their conceptual framework to Neoplatonic philosophy. He thought of the Trinity as a hierarchy of divine beings, with God the Father at its summit, and argued that the Son, or Logos, though existing before time, was created by the Father and subject to him. In this and related theological systems, the Son is seen as the Demiurge, or creating agency, and as the intermediary between the Father and the world of creation. Orthodox opinion refused to accept any such distinction between the members of the Trinity. At the Council of Nicaea, summoned in 325 to resolve the issue, Constantine himself offered the compromise formula that Father and Son were "consubstantial" (in Greek, *homoousios*) and succeeded in forcing its acceptance on all but two or three recalcitrant clergy, who were exiled. In the event, neither the Council of Nicaea, nor the Creed which it issued incorporating Constantine's formula, could reconcile the differences between the Arian and orthodox positions. The Arian movement remained the dominant opinion of the eastern Empire until Theodosius enforced a strictly "Nicene" definition of orthodoxy and eliminated Arianism as a serious issue in the east.

The emperors were obliged to participate closely in these theological controversies, and sometimes seem to have enjoyed doing so. They were constantly approached by ecclesiastical embassies, they summoned church councils, influenced their proceedings and used secular authority to impose their decisions, and deposed and exiled recalcitrant bishops like Liberius of Rome and Athanasius of Alexandria. Ammianus Marcellinus wrote, albeit with deliberate exaggeration, that in the time of Constantius the imperial transportation service, the *cursus publicus*, was near collapse because of the numbers of bishops traveling to and from synods with imperial permission.

Despite their involvement in the conduct of church councils and their use of the secular arm to enforce their outcome, and despite the great and threatening authority which they sometimes brought to bear on the church, the 4th-century emperors were never in the position of themselves defining official doctrine, nor were they in any way conceived of as heads of the church. Indeed, the position aspired to by Julian, who wrote letters to the priests of his reformed paganism showing them how they should dress and behave in public, what they should read and what doctrines they should accept, was far more theocratic and "Caesaropapist" than that of any of the Christian emperors.

In the west, Bishop Ambrose of Milan exerted great influence over the emperors who were at various times resident in the city. In 389, by publicly challenging Theodosius in his crowded cathedral at Milan, he forced the emperor to rescind an order to the bishop and congregation of Callinicum on the Euphrates to restore a synagogue which they had destroyed; the following year by similarly direct methods he made Theodosius perform penance for a massacre carried out by his soldiers at Thessalonica. Ambrose had a very clear conception of the duties of a Christian emperor, yet no contemporary source interprets any of these occasions as an issue of principle between "church" and "state." Despite the advantages won by the church and the immense influence exercised by certain bishops, the church acquired no recognized formal position in the constitutional structure of the late Roman state. Its relationship with the imperial government was and remained that of a privileged and well-organized pressure-group.

The ascetic movement

The end of persecution produced for the Christian community a dilemma as to the nature of spiritual virtue. A "martyr" in earlier times was precisely what the Greek word means, a "witness," one who publicly "confessed" his faith under the extreme threat of death. After persecution ended, a new form of expression was required by those Christians who still felt the need to confess their faith as vigorously as seemed to be implied by the New Testament. The Donatist movement in 4th-century Africa maintained the authentic attitudes of early Christianity, in a society in which the position of Christianity had been transformed, a position which evoked the more measured and realistic approach of their opponent Augustine. "Like frogs," he wrote, "they sit in their marsh, croaking 'We are the only Christians!'"

The need felt by some 4th-century Christians to belong to an elite of sanctity was partly answered by the growth of the ascetic movement. A sense of self-perfection by physical and intellectual discipline, as we have seen (p. 177), was a central aspect also of late classical philosophical practice; the emperor Julian, according to Ammianus Marcellinus, lived a life of quite conspicuous austerity, "as if he would soon return to the philosopher's cloak" (25.4.4). Yet the view maintained by late classical philosophy, of the physical body as an encumbrance to be mastered by discipline in order to free the mind for a higher contemplation of God, takes on in the Christian ascetic movement a more disquieting aspect. The body comes to be seen as actively hostile to the spirit, not merely to be trained by discipline but to be punished by extreme forms of ascetic behavior. The resulting body-spirit dualism led to suspicion of heresy. It was associated with the Gnostics and Manichees, according to whom the individual human being was the battleground of the opposing forces of good and evil, with the body, the vehicle of the evil forces, being the creation of the devil. The problem of the source of evil was central

to Augustine's intellectual development; the difficulties inherent in the need to reach a proper balance in ascetic behavior are the subject of many treatises on virginity, and of letters of instruction written to prominent Christian laymen by spiritual advisers such as Jerome.

The main traditions in the development of the ascetic movement are represented by two men, both Egyptians: Pachomius and Antony. In the late 3rd century Pachomius had established a mode of living for societies of monks; they were organized in communities, owned essential possessions in common, satisfied their basic economic needs by their own labor, sold surpluses for charity and followed certain rules of religious and social conduct. This was the origin of the monastic movement, as further formulated in the *Rule* of Basil of Caesarea and in due course in the west by Cassian and Benedict, the founders of medieval monasticism. Antony, whose biography by Athanasius of Alexandria was immensely influential, represented the eremitic tradition in asceticism, living in increasing isolation from communal life and pursuing his spiritual perfection in solitary contemplation and self-imposed privation. The temptations of St Antony by the devil in the wilderness were a potent theme in the religious art of later ages.

The ascetic movement influenced the life of the 4th-century church in a variety of ways. Earlier in his religious career, Jerome had passed an unhappy period as a hermit in the Syrian desert. For Jerome, the monastic setting was the base for intellectual and academic work, for the writing of the translations and commentaries mentioned earlier and for the bitter theological controversies for which he was equally famous. For Jerome's contemporary Augustine, bishop of Hippo Regius in North Africa, a monastic community attached to the episcopal church was an environment for reading, meditation, discipline and communal living, from which new priests might emerge to become the bishops of the next generation. The community on the island of Lérins off the south coast of France performed a similar function in relation to the bishoprics of southern Gaul in the 5th century.

The establishment by Martin of Tours of the monastery of Marmoutiers (*maius monasterium*, the "greater monastery") in central Gaul introduces a further contribution of some importance made by the ascetic movement to late Roman society. From his association with the monastic life, Martin gained a reputation for spiritual authority going far beyond his office as bishop. He was believed to possess direct contact with divine power, by virtue of which he was able to perform miracles, and with which he charged his campaigns of aggressive evangelization. The activities of Martin bring out one of the most disturbing implications for traditional Roman society of the growth of the ascetic movement. Believing themselves to be directly inspired by the divine will, local monks banded together in some parts of the Empire to attack local shrines and pagan institutions. In doing so they were sometimes encouraged by the local bishop and apparently not restrained by the imperial authorities; on certain occasions, indeed, the local authorities gave their active support to these blatantly illegal activities. The Donatist controversy in North Africa produced the so-called "circum-

The distribution and influence of monasticism, 300–500 AD. The early diffusion of monasticism followed definite routes, often linked with geographical mobility arising out of ecclesiastical disputes. Contending bishops such as Athanasius of Alexandria from the beginning harnessed in their interests the prestige of the ascetic movement, while Hilary of Poitiers and Eusebius of Vercelli brought back the monastic example from their exiles in the east by the Arian Constantius II. The influence of other westerners such as Jerome, and of John Cassian in 5th-century Gaul, was linked with their respective roles in eastern theological controversies. The prestige of the ascetic was often seen as a challenge to episcopal authority, but bishops such as Martin of Tours and Augustine were able to harness the two and monasteries, like that of Lérins, became training grounds for episcopal office. The monastic traditions in 5th- and 6th-century Britain and Ireland reflect two phases: contacts between the Celtic peoples of Britain and those of western Gaul (represented also in the later diffusion of manuscripts from the Mediterranean via the western sea routes), and the conversion of Saxon Britain begun by Augustine of Canterbury.

cellions," bands of crudely armed fanatics who went around shouting "Praise to God" and intimidating, injuring and sometimes killing Christians of the opposing party. For pagan observers, such "tyrants" were violating all standards of civilized behavior, moral and legal; it is in this that the reproach sometimes leveled against the monastic movement, that it promoted an attitude which undermined the morale of Roman society, can be appreciated most keenly.

This reproach forms part of a general criticism of the 4th-century church, that it attacked the moral purpose and the physical resources of the Roman Empire. It did this, so it is argued, by encouraging an ideology which was at its highest other-worldly and at its lowest antisocial in its violence against secular institutions and property, and by absorbing resources of finance and manpower which the imperial government could not afford to lose. As for the first part of this criticism, the notion that the church was other-worldly in the 4th century was, as we have seen, doubted by Jerome. The leaders of the church in this period seem to have lacked neither ambition nor a genuine sense of charity and public responsibility, while the bishops acquired certain rights, such as episcopal jurisdiction, which gave them a definite and useful role in secular society. The violence of Christians against their opponents, pagan or heretic, is as likely to have reinforced existing attitudes as to have undermined them; the more likely danger here is that of polarization rather than of indifference. As for the criticism that the church diverted resources and manpower from the state, this had best form part of a general discussion of the nature of the 4th-century Roman state and its relationship with Roman society.

The late Roman state and society

That the late Roman Empire was above all a bureaucratic state is universally admitted; by the term "bureaucratic" is meant that it was a government organized by departments (*officia*) with defined spheres of activity, served by salaried officials among whom promotion was by rules of seniority and precedence, that serving officials felt a sense of loyalty to their departments and that at the regular administrative levels there existed a high degree of continuity of service, whatever political upheavals might take place at higher levels. It was also, by a more everyday definition of bureaucracy, a government characterized by masses of paperwork. One particularly important source gives the impression that the organization of the government might even be appreciated as a work of art in itself; this tribute to bureaucratic self-awareness is the

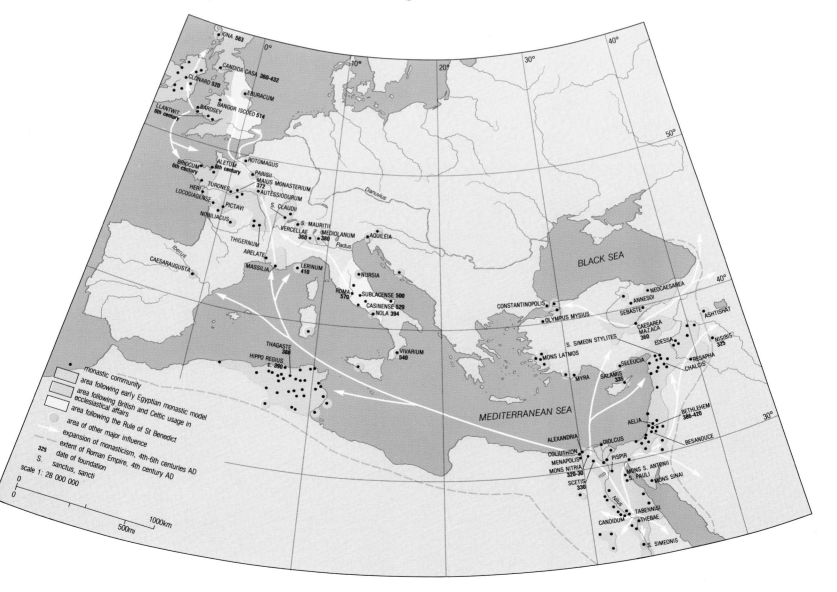

Notitia Dignitatum, a compilation, with illustrations of their insignia, of the administrative departments and military postings as they were at the end of the 4th and beginning of the 5th century.

The *Notitia Dignitatum* gives only a partial impression of the sheer scale of the operations of the late Roman government, whose agents must be numbered not only in those who held office at the imperial court, but throughout the provinces also: superintendents of provincial treasuries, accountants in charge of the supplying of regional armies, supervisors of mints and arms factories, officials sent out to draw up tax assessments, managers of imperial property and so on. Some, but not all, of these officials would be listed in another document, the *Laterculum minus* ("Register of Lesser Dignitaries"), which is mentioned once or twice by the *Notitia Dignitatum* but does not survive.

To the modern, as no doubt to the late Roman observer, the most obvious fact about the methods of this government, so elegantly illustrated in the *Notitia*, was the violence with which it tried to impose its will. The Theodosian Code, a compilation of 4th- and early 5th-century legislation made between the years 429 and 437 and covering all conceivable areas of legislative and administrative practice, provides a fearsome display of punishments. In two laws of Constantine, the hands of civil servants who accept bribes are to be cut off, and the mouths and throats of accessories to the abduction of unmarried girls are to be stopped with molten lead – outbursts of rhetorical aptness far from unparalleled in the Code and in other sources. Torture was regularly applied, not in its "proper" function of extracting truthful information in a court of law, but as a refinement before execution and as a punishment in itself. The use of such penalties and others is confirmed by many literary references, and especially by Ammianus Marcellinus, who takes us as close as any source to the atmosphere of terror with which the late Roman emperors defended their rights, especially when they feared that their position was being challenged by treason and its associated arts, magic and the reading of the future from horoscopes.

The moral tone of late Roman legislation was very little affected by the Christianization of the Empire. The influence of Christianity in individual cases can be seen very clearly. Constantine is said to have abolished the penalty of crucifixion and the breaking of legs, and one of his laws forbids branding on the face, "lest the image of divine beauty be disfigured." Laws were issued at various times in the 4th century on Sunday observance, and Easter amnesties were sometimes offered to criminals, certain categories always being excluded. It is possible, though far from certain, that increasingly harsh legislation on adultery, greater severity in divorce law and greater moral outrage on such matters as male prostitution and the immorality of actresses, were inspired by Christianity. In general, it is impossible to assert that late Roman legislation was more humane than earlier, and it is certain that in its treatment of religious dissent it became progressively more intolerant.

The political and social aims of late Roman legislation were in the emperors' own minds very clear: the maintenance of their own position and of public order, and the organization of society as best

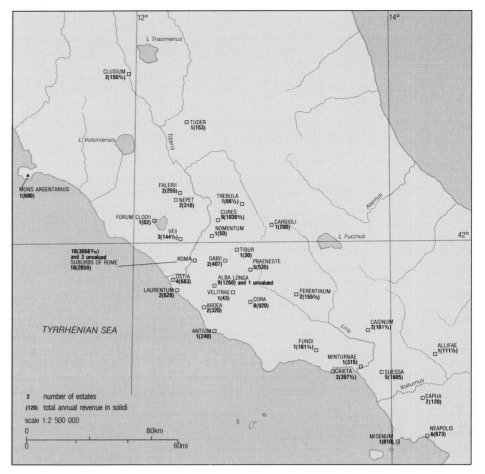

suited the needs of government. To this end, late Roman society was set out, as it were, as an array of economic instruments and agencies, each with its defined function in relation to the needs of the government.

The impression given by imperial legislation of the 4th century is that Roman society was more rigid and more firmly tied by hereditary obligation than ever before. It is possible however that the new image of late Roman society preserved in the laws is a reflection, less of actual changes in society itself, than in the needs of the government. There is no doubt that the *incidence* of late Roman government, as measured by its legislation and by the number of its officials, was far greater than at earlier times, and its impact more direct. Perhaps this should be seen as a consequence of the recognition by the imperial authorities of the late Roman period that they had more requirements to satisfy and more ends to meet, and they tried to achieve this by simply doing more governing.

Recent opinion is rightly inclined to emphasize two factors: the degree of social mobility still inherent in late Roman society, and, on the other hand, the conservatism of ancient society in general. As in many other times and places, sons tended to follow their fathers' occupations; bakers, soldiers, merchants and shipowners enjoyed certain advantages in life, a definite profession and a recognized role in society. It might not always be apparent that these attractions could be improved on. Still more evidently, peasant communities in any society are indifferent or resistant to change; they hang on to old ways of life and old modes of belief (it is no accident that the word *paganus*, used

The early 6th-century compilers of the *Liber Pontificalis* were able to include in their biographies of the Roman bishops from 314 to 440 AD lists of the estates with which 16 churches at Rome and one each in Ostia, Albano, Capua and Naples were endowed by their founders. Apart from 36 properties elsewhere in the Empire, there are 122 in mainland Italy; in addition to the name and location of each estate the lists give in all but four cases the cash revenue that each was expected to produce.

The donor of 84 of these Italian properties is stated to have been Constantine. The other estates come from a senator Gallicanus, the will of a woman of high social standing named Vestina, and several of the popes themselves.

While there were doubtless many other unrecorded church endowments in this period, the surviving details show an ownership pattern of large numbers of small and scattered estates that is likely to be typical not merely of the imperial or private donors and the recipient churches but also of other wealthy families and corporations such as temples. Land was wealth, and could be accumulated by "casual" acquisitions over many generations. Constantine's estates include former properties of the emperors Augustus and Tiberius, Maecenas, senators of the early Empire, and a Christian whose land had been confiscated in time of persecution – and even the abandoned barracks of a legion since stationed elsewhere.

in Christian polemic to denote a believer in the old gods, actually means "villager" or "countryman").

However, it is possible to assemble many individual cases of social mobility of types debarred or discouraged by legislation, "success stories" of escapes from hereditary obligations: a baker becomes a provincial governor, the son of a town councillor a teacher of rhetoric (and later a bishop), a soldier becomes a monk and so on. The problem, as always, is one of quantification. The examples give a certain impression, which it is impossible to measure by anything approaching a scientific method. But the impression is worth something, especially since it is confirmed by examination of a topic that yields to more analytic discussion: the role of the imperial court itself, ironically in view of its aims for society, as a source of social mobility and of opportunities for evasion.

The *comitatus* appears in late Roman sources in a wide variety of guises: as the center of government, the scene of earnest discussions at moments of crisis, of litigation, the petitions of embassies, of political dispute and sudden death, but also as a sort of intellectuals' "club," attracting the gifted, ambitious and educated, fostering literary pursuits, providing the setting for elegant dinner parties as well as for the serious discussions of religious and philosophical matters such as those recorded for the court society of Milan in Augustine's *Confessions*. All of these are facets of its activity which can be readily attested from the ancient sources.

The court also functioned as an economic stimulus in those regions where it settled. The presence of an imperial court at Trier opened opportunities for a flock of aspirants from the cities of central and southwestern Gaul, which had in the early Empire taken little part in Roman political life. The same is true, in relation to the court of Constantinople, of the inland districts of Anatolia, where the Cappadocian bishops, Gregory of Nazianzus, Basil of Caesarea and Gregory of Nyssa, are expressions of the cultural and political "arrival" of a previously unassertive part of the eastern Roman Empire.

The role of the court is more fully illuminated by the letter-collections of some prominent figures in public life who had dealings with it: in the west, the orator Symmachus, and in the east, the rhetorician Libanius of Antioch and the Cappadocian bishops. From such sources it becomes clear that in addition to their role as imperial officials, many of the correspondents at court of these influential patrons were also the sources of benefits, privileges and exemptions for them and their friends. What can appear from the Theodosian Code as a caste-ridden society, rigidly defined by imperial legislation, often dissolves in the other evidence into a series of inconclusive running battles between the emperors and the intended objects of their legislation, the latter only too often using the emperors' own agents to defend themselves and maintain their privileges.

It would be misleading to describe this simply as "corruption," though the emperors were fully aware of the collusion of imperial officials with private vested interests, and tried to prevent it (by yet more legislation); it was simply the manner in which the government functioned in its social context. The late Roman Empire should be seen as a pluralist society with a multiplicity of vested interests, impinging on the government as effectively as their influence allowed. Two of the better-organized vested interests are worth mention.

The role of the Christian church, and the privileges won by it under the Christian emperors of the 4th century, have already been described. The church, with the bureaucracy itself, has been seen by some modern critics as one of the main sources of weakness in the late Empire, in that it attracted to its service men who would otherwise have been of use to the state. But bishops, like rhetoricians and charioteers, were among the great individualists of the late Empire. It is far from certain that they would have shone in the imperial service as brilliantly as they shone in the church, or that the imperial service would have gained perceptibly from their support as bureaucrats and officials. If Ambrose had become a praetorian prefect like his father, could he have expressed himself in that office with the panache allowed him by his bishop's *cathedra*?

The second main vested interest was the Roman senate, representing through an institution of no great political power but of immense historical prestige the interests of the landed nobility of Italy and the western provinces. (The senate of Constantinople, recruited from the landed families of the east, was always entwined with the eastern imperial court and never possessed the same corporate independence as did its counterpart at Rome.) Under the guidance of the prefect of Rome and of the *princeps senatus*, the leading senator in seniority and prestige, the senate governed Rome and a large part of central and southern Italy as its own domain. Senators possessed great landed wealth in Italy, Sicily and North Africa, and fortified their influence in these areas by governorships and by inherited ties of patronage. Through their economic influence, prestige, and their political organization based on the senate, the Roman aristocracy was able to exert great and continuing pressure on the emperors.

The immense wealth of the senatorial nobility of Rome cannot be over-emphasized; it was spent conspicuously on luxurious building, traveling in style, dressing ostentatiously and maintaining great household establishments with whole "armies" of slave attendants, and in largesse to colleagues and to the people of Rome, especially in financing public games. The cash incomes of some senatorial families from rentals on their estates ranged, according to one contemporary source, from 4000 pounds of gold to 1500 in the case of senators of "moderate" wealth, with another third which could be realized by the sale of surplus produce. Senatorial expenditure on public games was also lavish. The orator Symmachus, a senator of "moderate" wealth, laid out 2000 pounds of gold on his son's praetorian games in 401. At a time when the imperial government was increasingly handicapped by financial difficulty, the Roman senatorial class has justly received blame for its part in the political collapse of the western Empire. Yet it must be admitted that the role of the aristocracy of Italy during the period after the Visigothic invasion and sack of Rome in 410 was fundamental in achieving a degree of Roman continuity in that period. It was a role which came to an end only with the reconquest of Justinian.

The Bureaucracy

"A splendid theatre, filled with players of every character and degree": so Gibbon described the late Roman bureaucracy, referring especially to the illustrations of the *Notitia Dignitatum*, of which a selection is shown on these pages. The *Notitia*, or "Register of Civil and Military Dignities," was compiled in the mid-390s and its western sections used in the imperial administration until about 425. It then passed out of official use, but survived as part of a dossier of late Roman official and quasi-official documents copied in the 9th century. The examples shown here are from a manuscript in the Bodleian Library, Oxford, copied in 1436 from the 9th-century Carolingian manuscript. The successive illustrators of the manuscript clearly tried to show accurately the late Roman insignia, though they exercised some freedom in presenting certain decorative features such as clothing.

The administrative structure of the late Roman state, as presented in the *Notitia*, was headed by the emperor (here Constantius II, on a gold multiple struck at Nicomedia); usually there was a college of two or more emperors, ruling independently but maintaining a front of unity. The administration was from the time of Diocletian strictly divided between military and civil functions. The mobile field armies, east and west, were commanded by Magistri, or "Masters" of cavalry and infantry. Shown here are the insignia of the western Master of the Infantry and some of his troops' shield devices. Below the Magistri were the commanders, entitled Comites and Duces ("Counts" and "Dukes") of the regional armies, listed by the *Notitia* for all provinces. The Comes Domesticorum commanded the elite palace guard, again divided, as shown below, into horse and foot. The duties of the Castrensis were to maintain the palace establishment, a more complicated task than one might suppose, given the constant mobility of late Roman emperors.

Heading the civil administration were the praetorian prefects of Italy with Africa and Illyricum, Gaul with Spain and Britain, and of the east, from Thrace to Arabia. Their responsibilities extended both to court and to provincial administration, in the latter being much concerned with taxation. The Master of the Offices controlled the administrative staffs, regulated audiences with the emperor and coordinated the general running of the court administration. The Count of the Sacred Largesses controlled mints and mines, received monetary taxation and supervised the payment of donatives and cash salaries; another official, the Count of the Imperial Portfolio, administered state property. The Quaestor of the Sacred Palace was responsible for framing imperial communications in a suitable literary form and was himself often a well-known literary figure. The Primicerius Notariorum headed the corps of imperial secretaries, or "notaries."

The insignia of officials are shown as a set of codicils — letters of appointment set in gold and ivory frames and bearing the imperial portrait — or as a book with formulae of goodwill emblazoned on its cover, and scrolls. The codicils, and sometimes the books, are set on a table with patterned coverlet. In some cases an engraved ivory column appears standing on a tripod base. This was a ceremonial inkstand, symbolizing judicial competence.

The insignia of the Comes Domesticorum, shields resplendent in purple and gold, express his position in the palace establishment. The winged Victories bearing the imperial portrait are, from a Christian perspective, readily transformed into angels. The first two units shown under the western Magister Peditum, "Joviani" and "Herculiani," preserve the Tetrarchic titles Jovius and Herculius.

Provincial armies are represented by a symbolic city or group of cities. The duties of the Count of Italy, a late innovation, are represented by the Alps with their barricades (actual or symbolic), the Claustra Alpium. Belgica Secunda was the coastal region of northern France; the Litus Saxonicum or Saxon Shore was part of a system of coastal defense (see map p. 171).

For the Castrensis, pictures of palace furniture including an embossed silver casket containing perfume flasks.

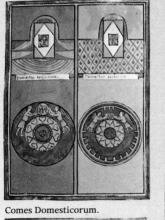

Comes Domesticorum.

Comes Italiae.

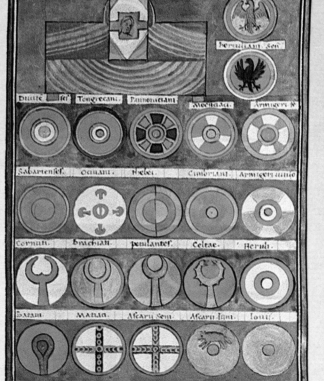

Magister Peditum.

Dux Belgicae Secundae.

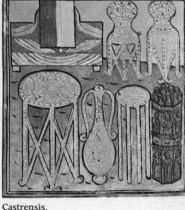

Castrensis.

The three ladies, Italia, Africa and Illyricum, represent the dioceses under the praetorian prefect of Italy. Their baskets contain the tribute in taxation of the provinces. Their "modernized" dress is self-evident; equally so is the accuracy of detail preserved in other cases by the Carolingian and Renaissance copyists, who did not always understand what they reproduced. The consular province of Campania is shown, rather unusually, as a lady with shield and placard, sitting on a platform in a curtained alcove. The table with book is cunningly worked into the composition as part of the furniture of the alcove. Apulia and Calabria are the example given by the *Notitia* of a province governed at the rank of Corrector. The abbreviated legend on the book, slightly corrupted, reads "I [?] feliciter; Vale corrector iussu dominorum" ("Go [?] in prosperity; farewell, Corrector by order of our lords").

Italia, Illyricum, Africa.

Campania.

Apulia, Calabria.

Praetorian prefect.

Magister Officiorum.

Comes Sacrarum Largitionum.

Quaestor.

Primicerius Notariorum.

The insignia of the praetorian prefect, apart from the ceremonial inkstand and codicil mentioned above and a set of candlesticks, were a four-horsed carriage, as also boasted by the prefect of Rome. Such details as the decorative heads on the carriage have been faithfully, and in the case of the inkstand uncomprehendingly, represented. The arms factories (*fabricae*), shown as the preserve of the Master of the Officers, were in fact only acquired by him in 390; this is one argument for the dating of the *Notitia Dignitatum*. The various items of equipment – shields, arrowheads, breastplates – were manufactured in specialized workshops. The functions of the Quaestor are shown by scrolls and a column, perhaps optimistically inscribed "beneficial laws," and those of the Count of the Sacred Largesses by items of wealth in a form suitable for distribution – gold and silver coins, buckles, laurel leaves, presentation dishes. Also seen are bags of money with symbols of value and a money chest. The *Notitia* itself, or Laterculum Maius ("Greater Register"), is illustrated (*bottom right*) as a bound book with straps and tags to fasten it. Its maintenance was among the duties of the Primicerius Notariorum.

203

The City of Constantine

From the first days of its construction, Constantinople grew with amazing speed, commanding unlimited financial resources and attracting craftsmen and materials from the entire east. The Megarian colonists who had settled Chalcedon in the 7th century BC had been called "blind" for ignoring the richer site of Byzantium. In the context of the late Empire, however, the new city came into its own, standing between east and west, more particularly between Asia Minor and the northern land mass of the Balkans.

Its expansion saw a building "boom," evidently with much profiteering. Within a couple of generations, claimed critics, mansions built for its new nobility were already collapsing. Constantinople also acquired monumental squares and public buildings (see plan) with a notable absence of pagan temples but many Christian churches. A 5th-century source, the *Notitia* of Constantinople, lists 14 of these, together with 11 palaces of emperors and empresses, five markets, eight public and 153 private baths, 20 public and 120 private bakeries, 52 porticoes, 322 streets and 4388 houses.

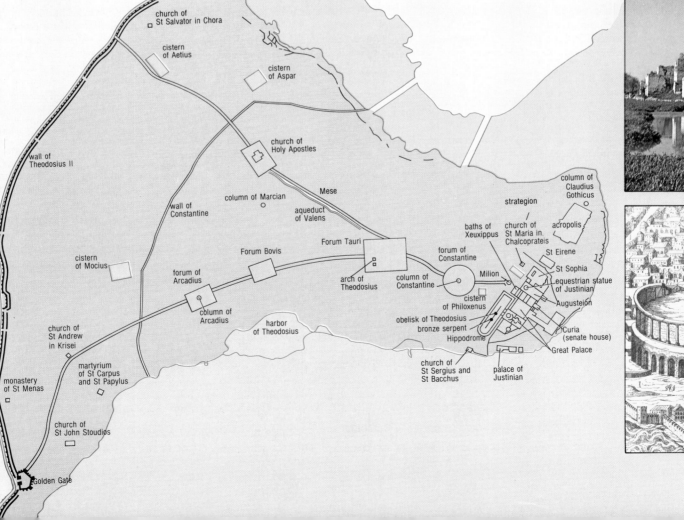

Below The frontispiece to the *Notitia* of Constantinople, as preserved in a manuscript of 1436. The vignette contains anachronisms, but well displays the configuration of the city, in which St Sophia and the Hippodrome are conspicuous. The equestrian statue is of Justinian.

The land walls of Constantinople (*below*) represent a doubling of the enclosed area of the city since its foundation by Constantine. Built in 413 by the Praetorian Prefect Anthemius, they were in 447 badly damaged by an earthquake and rebuilt within two months. The now vanished Hippodrome (*bottom*) is here seen in an engraving by Panvinio (c. 1580), showing the column of Justinian (here without its famous equestrian statue), the obelisk of Theodosius, which alone still survives *in situ*, and in the foreground the sea walls of Constantinople.

Justinian's new church of St Sophia (Holy Wisdom), the masterpiece of the architects Anthemius of Tralles and Isidore of Miletus, was consecrated in 537, five years after the destruction of its predecessor in the Nika riots (see p. 223). It is here seen (*below* and *opposite*) in two views published in 1852 by the architect Fossati, who had been commissioned by the sultan to supervise its restoration. Despite its massively imposing exterior (for contemporary historical accuracy the building must of course be imagined without the surrounding minarets), St Sophia is designed above all to be experienced from the inside; and here Fossati, choosing an ideal perspective, has beautifully conveyed its essential character – the rich splendor of the light, and the huge but harmonious space which it defines. These, and the dome, "floating as if suspended from heaven," were precisely the features which most appealed to a contemporary, the writer Procopius. The dome was, and remains, an architectural marvel; but it is worth recalling that the first attempt collapsed 20 years after its erection, to be replaced by the still more ambitious structure which stands today.

Late Imperial Rome

After the conversion of Constantine, Rome rapidly emerged as a great center of Christian culture. The vigor of the late imperial city was in part a consequence of the emperors' departure for their new capitals on the frontiers. In their absence from Rome – to its admirers still the "Eternal City" – its senatorial class and people asserted themselves with a lack of inhibition (not to mention periodic violence) lost since the late Republic. Simultaneously with its emergence as a Christian city, Rome also produced an efflorescence of classical culture, both literary and visual, and even a late revival of the ancestral pagan religion under a small group of pagan senators (see p. 193); but as the city was progressively christianized, old habits of patronage, intellectual and material, were transferred to the advantage of the Christian church, and great basilicas and martyr shrines were built everywhere.

The "Calendar of the Year 354," whose dedicatory frontispiece is shown *below*, includes both traditional and Christian material. Its designer Furius Dionysius Filocalus, was a calligrapher also employed by Pope Damasus; his name appears on the fragmentary inscription also shown (*opposite*). Like his

Roman churches and their modern equivalents

t = titulus (parish church by c.500)

t Aequitii (Silvestri) = St Martino ai Monti
t Apostolorum = St Pietro in Vincoli
t Byzantis (Pammachii) = St Giovanni e St Paolo
t Fasciolae = St Nereo e St Achilleo
t Gaii = St Susanna
t Iulii iuxta forum Traiani = St Apostoli
t Iulii trans Tiberim = St Maria in Trastevere
Basilica Lateranensis = St Giovanni in Laterano
in Lucinis = St Lorenzo in Lucina
t Praxedis = St Prassede
S Stephani = St Stefano Rotondo sul Celio
t Vestinae = St Vitale

The wooden door panels of the basilica of St Sabina, built in the 420s through the munificence of Peter, a wealthy priest from Illyricum, are among the most remarkable monuments of early Christian Rome. Seen below are (*left*) the ascent of Elijah in a "fiery chariot" (2 Kings 2:11), an Old Testament prefiguration of the ascension of Christ, and (*right*) an unexplained scene in which an angel presents an unidentified, but apparently lay, figure, who stands in the doorway of a sanctuary, to a waiting crowd, their hands raised in acclamation.

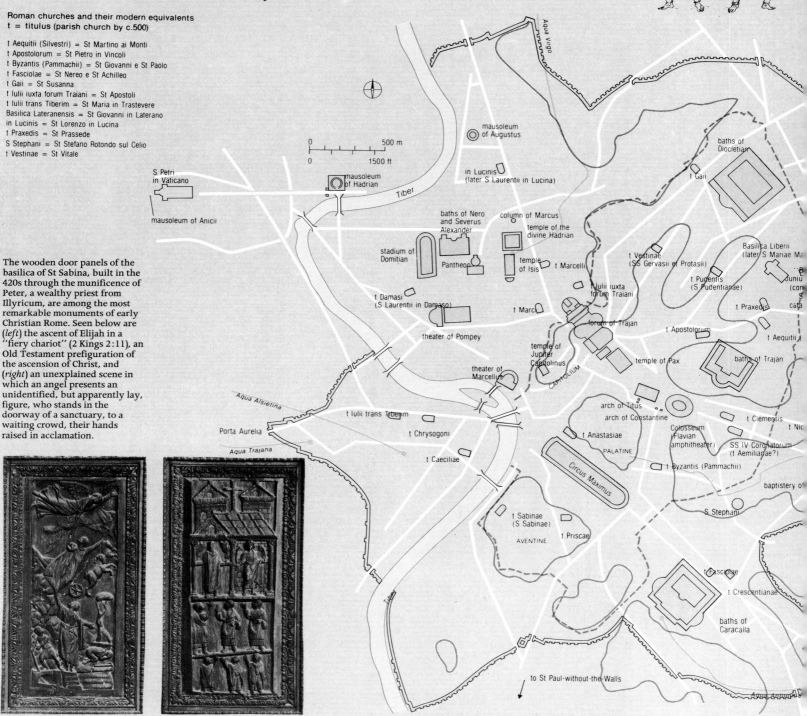

calendar, Filocalus illustrates the
continuity of classical themes in
the christianized culture of 4th-
century Rome.

Artists' impressions sometimes
offer the best available views of
early churches subjected to
subsequent rebuilding. Shown
here are (*left*) old St Peter's, in a
drawing of c. 1470, and (*below
left*) the interior of St John
Lateran, in a fresco by Dughet
(c. 1660). Both churches were
founded by Constantine.

Peter and Paul, the founders of
Christian Rome, are sometimes
described as the Christian
counterparts of Romulus and
Remus, and often appear
together in iconography. Shown
below is St Paul, in a mosaic from
old St Peter's. He appears in his
already conventional image as
teacher rather than martyr.

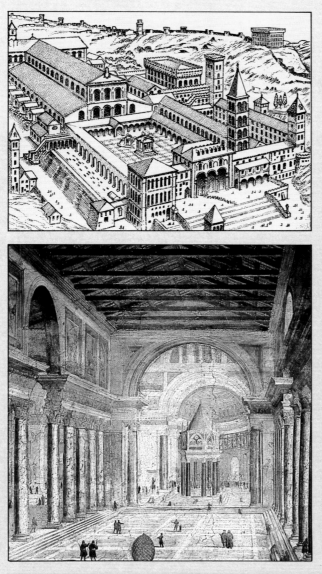

The great basilica of St Paul-
outside-the-Walls, dedicated
under Theodosius I but
completed by his successor
Honorius, is here seen in an
engraving by Piranesi (c. 1750),
particularly valuable since in
1823 the church was damaged by
fire and its original form largely
lost in the rebuilding. It was one
of the finest new churches of late
4th-century Rome: Prudentius
(c. 400 AD) well evokes the "royal
splendor" of the place, its gilded
beams, marble columns and
brilliant mosaic frescoes, and the
beauty of the light inside the
church, "glowing like the rising
sun."

THE FALL OF THE WESTERN ROMAN EMPIRE

Imperial disunity and barbarian threats

Theodosius I, who died at Milan in January 395, was the last emperor for over half a century who by military ability and force of character exerted any sustained personal control over the Roman Empire. It was in some ways ironic that his death should have left the Empire in the possession of two such nonentities as his sons: Arcadius, who nominally held power at Constantinople, and Honorius, emperor at Milan. The dynastic grip of Theodosius on the Empire had been further strengthened by his marriage, after the death of his first wife, to Galla, a daughter of Valentinian I. Their daughter, Galla Placidia, was born in 388.

At the time of his accession as senior Augustus, Arcadius was no more than 18, older by some years than Honorius. The later 4th century had accustomed the Empire to *Kinderkaiser* – emperors who assumed power in youth, even in infancy, and exercised it nominally, the actual government being conducted by great ministers of state and anyone who succeeded in establishing personal ascendancy. None of the successors of Theodosius possessed much individual personality, but yielded without resistance to the ceremonial constraints of their office and the influence of their advisers. Arcadius, who died in 408, was succeeded by his son Theodosius, who had been made co-Augustus in January 402, when he was less than one year old. Honorius, after a secluded reign of intense inactivity, died of disease in 423. It was maliciously said of him that he only recognized "Roma" as the name of his pet chicken. After the intermission of the usurpation of Johannes (423–25), the eastern court installed in the west the four-year-old Valentinian III, son of Galla Placidia by the gifted general Flavius Constantius.

The dynastic stability of the imperial office in this period, in itself impressive, was therefore secured at the cost of presenting to the Empire nominal emperors who lived in pampered seclusion and served merely to legitimize the powers of those ministers who succeeded in asserting their ascendancy. Several of these powerful ministers can be identified: in the east, among others, Theodosius I's former supporter Rufinus, the eunuch Eutropius, the praetorian prefect Anthemius, the urban and praetorian prefect Cyrus of Panopolis and Cyrus' enemy Chrysaphius, not to mention the influential women of the household of Theodosius II, his sister Pulcheria and wife Aelia Eudocia; in the west, a sequence of powerful military commanders, notably the half-Vandal Stilicho, Constantius, who became Augustus in 421, Flavius Aetius and the barbarian Ricimer.

The dynastic continuity achieved by the legacy of Theodosius did not prevent the usual political rivalries and violence among the supporters of the emperors, but its importance, in extremely difficult times, should not be underestimated. There were other conditions attached to the legacy, which

between them provided the setting for the political and military history of the early 5th century: the division of the Empire between the courts of Constantinople and Milan (soon transferred to Ravenna), and the presence within the Empire of the Visigoths under their own national leaders, as a powerful military force owing service to the empire but also in a position to extract concessions from it.

In the years immediately after 395 Stilicho, in accordance with Theodosius' alleged dying wishes, claimed a "protectorate" over both western and eastern emperors. The hostility he thus incurred from the east was intensified by his attempts to secure for the west the recruiting grounds of eastern Illyricum, then administered from Constantinople. To pursue this project, Stilicho required the help of Alaric the Visigoth, who had invaded Greece in 395–97 and Italy in 401–02, escaped successive encounters with Roman armies and was still at large, seeking a secure homeland for his people. In 407 Stilicho was about to use Alaric to secure control of Illyricum, but the enterprise was prevented by major barbarian invasions in Gaul and by a usurpation in Britain. Alaric's demands for payment for his unused services, at first refused by the senate, led to his second invasion of Italy in 408. Stilicho was executed by the emperor's order in August 408 and his reputation assailed for his

Portrayed on contemporary ivory diptychs are (*above*) the half-Vandal general Stilicho with his wife and son, and (*overleaf*) his imperial master Honorius. Stilicho was dismissed and executed in 408 for alleged complicity with Alaric.

In winter 409/10 Alaric sponsored an imperial regime under a Roman senator, Priscus Attalus, against the intransigent government of Honorius at Ravenna. The medallion of Attalus (*below*), with its legend "INVICTA ROMA AETERNA," is an ironic commentary on the sack of Rome by Alaric only a few months later.

Barbarian incursions and settlements in the west. The character of the barbarian invasions was not uniform. Some, like that of the Vandals and Suebi, were aimed at the forcible seizure of land and property, while that of the Visigoths was an extended quest for settlement and recognition by the Romans.

complaisant treatment of Alaric, but his successors in power proved incapable of meeting the barbarian threat. Stilicho's death was followed by three successive sieges of Rome, the last of these culminating in its capture and sack by Alaric in August 410.

It is worth trying to consider the situation from the viewpoint of the Goths themselves. Fourth-century sources show the Goths in the period before their entry into the Roman Empire as a quiet agricultural people, living in village communities, trading with and sometimes traveling as individuals to the Roman Empire. The migration of the Goths was caused by the pressure of the Huns from the east, and was not in any sense an aggressive move against the Roman Empire; this only emerged when the Goths were maltreated and oppressed by the Roman officials in charge of the crossing of the Danube.

The Goths may have seen the agreement of 382 as being with Theodosius himself rather than with the Roman government. The death of Theodosius placed Alaric in a precarious position, for he could not be sure that Theodosius' successors, whether in east or west, would honor the treaty. Throughout his relations with the regime of Honorius and

Stilicho, Alaric pressed the same claims: land for his people to settle on, financial subsidies and the provision of food supplies. After the sack of Rome in 410, he pressed south, trying to secure a crossing to Africa, but died in southern Italy, and his successor Athaulf led the Goths from Italy into Gaul. Here, in 414, a Gothic regime was set up, with a puppet Roman emperor. It was based at Narbonne, where Athaulf married Theodosius' daughter Galla Placidia, a hostage from the sack of Rome, and proclaimed his policy of sustaining the Roman name by the force of Gothic arms. The following year the Goths were forced by naval blockade to abandon Narbonne for Spain. After Athaulf's assassination, his successor, Vallia, tried unsuccessfully to organize a crossing to Africa and finally, in 418, by agreement with the Roman government secured a settlement in southwestern Gaul, between the Garonne and the Loire. From the Gothic point of view it was not a very successful sequence of events, but they had in the end achieved what they wanted.

Though the sack of Rome had an immense emotional impact, it was from a strategic point of view very far from the worst disaster to afflict the Empire in these years. At the end of 406 a huge

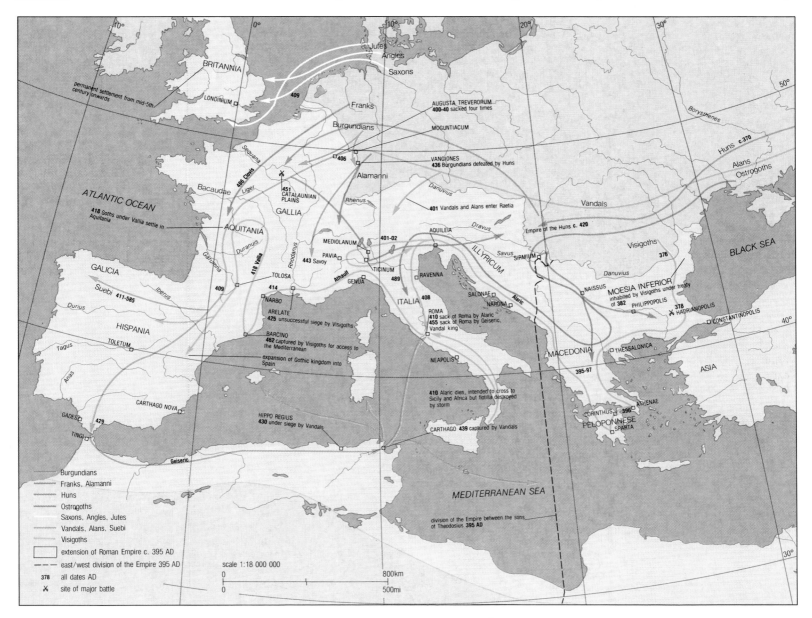

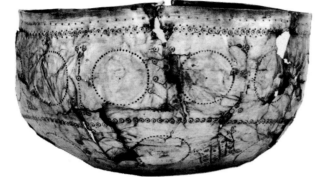

commands in the frontier regions and for the calling-in and upgrading of provincial troops to meet the invasions of Italy. Roman generals conducted campaigns in Spain against the Vandals and Suebi. In this they were assisted by Visigothic federates, and it seems certain that the settlement of the Goths in southwestern Gaul was intended to provide a bulwark in the Roman interest against the unrest in Spain and against the Bacaudae in central and northwestern Gaul. In Africa, some resistance

The silver bowl (*left*), reconstructed from the fragments into which it was broken, is from the "Coleraine hoard," a large deposit of silver coin, ingots and broken plate discovered in 1854. The coin series implies a 5th-century date (after 420), and the hoard may represent a cache taken as loot or paid in ransom after an Irish raid on western Britain or Gaul.

invasion of Germanic peoples, mainly Vandals, Suebi and Burgundians, crossed the Rhine, overwhelming Roman defensive positions, capturing cities in northern Gaul and the Rhineland and fanning out across Gaul to the southwest. By 409 the cities of Aquitania were threatened and the Suebi and Vandals forced their way over the Pyrenees into the rich, heavily urbanized provinces of Spain, the homeland of the dynasty of Theodosius. The whole of Gaul, as one contemporary put it, "burned in one vast funeral pyre," and letters of St Jerome to oppressed western provincials at this time reveal the disruption of material and family life caused by the invasions. Within a few years, the barbarian invaders of Spain were setting up kingdoms, competing for possession of the best lands, uprooting and scattering Roman landowners.

At the same time, local unrest in Britain and Saxon incursions around the coastline produced a series of imperial proclamations, as a result of which the usurper Constantine III crossed to Gaul in 407 and established his court at Arles, soon extending his power to Spain. Concerned at the time with the invasion of Alaric, the Italian government could do very little about the usurpation in Gaul.

After the proclamation of Constantine and his crossing to Gaul, Britain was never recovered as a Roman province. It was governed by men whom Roman sources describe as "tyrants," that is, local dynasts with a greater or lesser claim to continuity with Roman power, and from the mid-5th century it was progressively occupied from the east by the Saxons. The name of the shadowy Ambrosius Aurelianus survives to denote one of these post-Roman "tyrants" who resisted the Saxon encroachments in southwestern England. He may serve as a model for the "five princes" described by Gildas as wielding power in western Britain in the early 6th century, and for whatever truth lies behind the legendary figure of King Arthur.

In Gaul, Armorica (comprising Brittany and adjacent parts of the northwest) and a large part of the central region of the province were controlled after 410 by the insurgents known as the Bacaudae or by locally established barbarian enclaves. In 429 the Vandals crossed from Spain to Africa, and over the next few years worked their way eastwards towards Carthage. The bishop of Hippo, the now aged Augustine, died in 430 while his city was under Vandal siege.

The imperial government did what it could to counter these problems, but this was not very much. There is evidence for extensive recruitment by Stilicho among the barbarian peoples of the north, for the creation of emergency military

After his deposition as western Roman emperor in 475, Julius Nepos, like his uncle before him, maintained himself for some years as head of an independent principality based on Salona in Dalmatia. Here (*top*) is shown a coin of Nepos issued at Milan on his behalf by Odoacer between 476 and 480, and also (*above*) a similar coin of the last officially recognized Roman emperor, Romulus Augustulus.

to the advance of the Vandals was offered by an expedition sent from the east, but eastern Mauretania and Numidia were ceded to them in 435 and four years later, against the terms of the treaty, Geiseric seized Carthage and made himself master of proconsular Africa.

The establishment of the Huns from about 420 in the Hungarian plains north of the Danube, and the extension of their influence in succeeding years, threatened the land route between east and west which in the 4th century had been the military backbone of the Roman Empire, as well as access to traditional recruiting grounds. Treaties, involving the payment of subsidies, were conducted by the eastern government in about 430 with the Hunnish king Rua (or Rugila) and a few years later with his successors Bleda and Attila. Open war broke out in 441, in which Sirmium, Margus, Naissus and Philippopolis fell to the Huns, and again in 447. These wars were settled by the payment of increased subsidies, and by the Roman evacuation of territory on the Roman side of the Danube. The seat of the Illyrian prefecture was transferred from Sirmium to the coastal city of Thessalonica in Macedonia.

Because of their loose political organization and their lack of interest in settling within the Roman provinces, the Huns never achieved the devastating effect on the Roman Empire which they had once seemed to threaten. Their relations with the western court in the earlier 5th century were generally cooperative; they provided help to the troubled regime of Honorius in 409, supported the usurpation of Johannes and fought with the Romans against the Visigoths in the late 430s. Several figures prominent in western politics in this period had served some time as visitors or hostages among the Huns. In 451, after his agreement with the court of Constantinople, Attila advanced on the west but was defeated at the Catalaunian Plains (near Châlons-sur-Marne) by the combined forces of Romans, Visigoths and Burgundians. He retreated from Gaul, took and plundered Aquileia, Milan and Ticinum, but was persuaded by diplomacy and the threat of retaliation to withdraw from Italy. In 453 Attila died and the Hunnish empire fell apart.

The interest of the court of Constantinople in western affairs in this period was persistently, if not always effectively, expressed. In the time of Stilicho, Africa's adherence to the senior emperor of Constantinople had caused corn shortages at Rome until the "rebellion" was crushed by Stilicho. During the occupation of Italy by Alaric, Constantinople sent military aid to Honorius. The eastern government, under the influence of Galla Placidia, was responsible for suppressing the usurpation of Johannes and installing Valentinian III in 425. Valentinian was betrothed to the daughter of Theodosius, Licinia Eudoxia, and the marriage was performed at Constantinople in 437. On that occasion, western envoys went to Constantinople and returned in 438 with copies of the Theodosian Code, compiled by order of Theodosius II to bring coherence and chronological order to the confused mass of 4th- and early 5th-century imperial legislation. The compilers must necessarily have had to travel very widely to assemble the legislation from its scattered, often unofficial sources, and the Theodosian Code is one

of the last constructive achievements of cooperation between east and west.

The eastern court attempted to prevent the capture of Africa by the Vandals, and was compelled to recall a second expedition in order to conduct its first war against Attila. The Vandals under Geiseric built up a powerful fleet, pillaged Rome in 455 and extended their piracy to Greece and the eastern Mediterranean. In 468 a major expedition was mounted against them from the east, with support from the west, but it ended disastrously, and a further entrenchment of Vandal power resulted from its failure.

The dynasty of Theodosius petered out in the east in 450, when Theodosius II died after a riding accident and was succeeded by emperors of a more traditionally military cast: Marcian (450–57), Leo (457–74) and the Isaurian Zeno (474–91). In the west the dynasty ended with the assassination of Valentinian III (455), who was succeeded by several short-lived emperors. After the reign of Libius Severus, creature of the barbarian magister Ricimer, the eastern government of Leo was responsible for the installation in the west of Anthemius (467–72); when Anthemius and Ricimer turned to civil war against each other, Leo tried to reconcile them through the mediation of Olybrius, a western senatorial exile living at Constantinople. Anthemius was however assassinated and Olybrius made emperor in his place. Upon the death of Olybrius a few months later, the eastern government dispatched Nepos to replace his successor Glycerius, but Nepos was deposed by the general Orestes. Orestes made his own son Romulus emperor, and Romulus' removal by Odoacer in 476 can be considered to symbolize the end of the Roman Empire in the west. From 476, Italy was controlled by barbarian kings holding court at Ravenna.

Reactions to the end of the western Empire

The reactions of contemporaries to the collapse of the western Empire varied widely. One writer, a Gallic landowner, Rutilius Namatianus, returned home by sea late in 417 to meet the challenge presented by the settlement of the Visigoths in his own part of southwestern Gaul. For Rutilius, there were grounds for optimism. Despite the destruction wrought by the invasions, which was still visible in Italy in broken bridges and abandoned lodging-houses, peace had been made with the Visigoths and life at Rome was beginning to return to normal. Rutilius' was perhaps the most optimistic of contemporary reactions. Optimism of a rather different kind was provided by a younger contemporary of Rutilius, the Spanish priest Orosius. In his polemical history of Rome, *Against the Pagans*, Orosius argued with painfully monotonous documentation that the misfortunes of the Roman Empire and of his own day, including the sack of Rome, were less serious than those of the old Roman Republic. He thus countered the imputation that the fall of Rome was the direct consequence of its abandonment of the traditional gods and adoption of Christianity. But it is clear from certain passages of the history, in which he allowed his personal reactions to appear, that Orosius did not regard the contemporary situation with any genuine optimism. He had escaped from Spain, amid great dangers, to go to North Africa, and was later unable to return

Left The western emperor Honorius (395–423), on an ivory diptych issued by Probus, consul in 406 AD. Honorius appears in military dress, a symbolic rather than actual reflection of his capacities. The legend on the *labarum* or standard, "In the name of Christ may you be ever victorious," is balanced by a winged victory who might also be interpreted as an angel.

to his native province because of the ferocity of the barbarian occupation. He deplored the possibility that the barbarian peoples might succeed in establishing their kingdoms in Spain. At one point he wrote with startling bitterness of the conquest of Gaul by Julius Caesar, putting into the mouth of a personified Gaul the complaint that "so did the Romans bow me down, that I cannot rise against the Goths." Orosius' history neither carried personal conviction nor coincided honestly with his own experience, but his work became the standard medieval handbook of Roman history of the classical as well as of the Christian period.

The autobiographical reflections of another Gaul, Paulinus of Pella, in his poem the *Eucharisticon,* or *Hymn of Thanks*, give a vivid impression of the experiences of one individual dispossessed by the invasions and reduced from the standing of a wealthy landowner to that of an impoverished monk at Marseille, selling the last of his once great properties to a Gothic purchaser. A compatriot from the northeast, the priest Salvian, writing in about 440, denounced the corruption of contemporary Roman society, which he contrasted with the honest purity of the barbarian occupiers of Gaul and Africa. The surviving Gallic landowners, the *curiales* (whom it is interesting to find still in existence), he described as "tyrants" as they extracted taxation from the peasantry. The peasants themselves, he alleged, sought refuge with the barbarians or with the Bacaudae. It is not easy to determine how accurately Salvian's polemical picture reflects the facts, but his recollection of lacerated corpses lying in the streets of Trier probably owes only too much to reality. Between 400 and 440 the city was sacked no less than four times by barbarian onslaught.

By far the most far-reaching and sophisticated response to the fall of Rome was given by Augustine. In his sermons on the sack of Rome, Augustine had evoked the sufferings of Job to show that the tribulations of Christian Romans were a testing of their faith by God. But it was clear that the sack, which appeared to some to reflect Rome's abandonment of the protection of the traditional gods, required a reasoned response from the Christian point of view; in his *City of God* Augustine gave this on an immense scale. In the first 10 books, Augustine put into perspective the achievement of pre-Christian Rome, especially the early republican period which was idealized by pagan contemporaries, and then presented a reasoned case against the philosophical claims of the pagan religions: in book 10, for instance, Augustine produced an intellectually stringent critique of the Neoplatonic philosophy of Porphyry. In the second part of the *City of God*, Augustine developed the conception of the "two cities," the "city of God" (*civitas dei*) and the "city of this world" (*civitas terrena*). For Augustine, the city of God was the "community of saints," living for the time being in the society of men; their actual identity, known only to God, would be revealed in the Last Days. The Latin word *civitas* is from some points of view better translated in the sense of "citizenship" rather than "city." The member of the heavenly community was like a foreigner (*peregrinus*) living on earth and, like a foreigner in a Roman city, subject to its laws, but owing his ultimate allegiance to the city of God to

which he longed to return. For Augustine, secular society and government served certain basic material purposes in the preservation of lawful social life and the avoidance of disorder among imperfect men, but was ultimately neutral. As for the church itself, that was more like a sanatorium for the sick than a community of saints on earth; Augustine knew that his own church at Hippo contained many insincere Christians, and some whose presence within its walls was due mainly to fear of imperial legislation; these were the *ficti*, men whose conversion was "feigned" for safety and convenience, not as a matter of personal conscience. Even so, their presence in the church gave them a chance of salvation.

For modern historians as for contemporaries, the end of the Roman Empire has seemed to require explanation on the grand scale. How an empire of such resources, whose physical remains could be seen on all sides, had been brought down has preoccupied observers in most ages. In some ways, this preoccupation with the need for large-scale interpretation has hindered modern historical analysis, for its effect has been to suggest the possibility of some single interpretation which, of itself, could explain a historical transformation of immense complexity. Suggestions such as that of climatic change, and even of cumulative blood poisoning from lead piping, are only two of the more recent attempts to explain the fall of the Empire in terms of a single all-pervasive interpretation.

The solutions have often been moral, and have sometimes depended on a stated or assumed analogy between Roman society and a physical organism for which physical decline and death are a biological necessity. Voltaire, for instance, considered that the Empire had to end simply because all things must end. It is possible at once to discount the notion that the Roman Empire fell in consequence of the moral decline of its leaders. Had this been the case, the Empire would have been brought down by the Julio-Claudian emperors, or even in the late Republic, before the Empire, as we understand it, existed, for this was the heyday of Roman immorality. The emperors of the 3rd and 4th centuries were generally honest, hard-working men of great moral earnestness; one of the most striking facts about them is the almost complete absence of moral scandal attached to them by the ancient sources. The later Roman emperors and their supporters came from regions of conservative provincial virtues and were untouched by the decadence of metropolitan society.

For Gibbon, the decline of the Roman Empire was an eventual consequence of its political organization. The extent of physical coercion required to sustain the immense structure of the Empire had the effect of reducing the sense of liberty among its populations, so that when the crisis of invasion came they had lost all real interest in its preservation. At the same time, through a period (in the 2nd century) of sustained peace, the military classes lost the spirit of collective courage and the habit of obedience, while in the military crisis which followed, they were overindulged by the emperors.

The difficulty with this interpretation, as Gibbon himself conceded without pursuing its implications, is that it fails to explain how the Empire lasted so long. By a systematic increase in its exercise of power, it was able to survive the 3rd-century crisis and to enjoy a period of impressive vigor and of political, military and cultural renewal in the 4th century. The history of this immensely rich and complex period does not read as if it were faced irrevocably in the direction of decline.

The problem with Gibbon's and with other such long-term explanations is that, far from explaining the fall of the Empire, they only too easily turn into appreciations of its long survival. What is needed is something more precise and, no less important, something that will differentiate between the collapse of the western and the survival, for a further millennium, of the eastern Roman Empire.This requirement undermines the suggestion of Gibbon, developed in different terms by later historians, that the Christian church, by diverting men's ideals from civic to other-worldly aims, drew their interest away from the preservation of the Empire. Yet the influence of Christianity and of the Christian ideal was no less pervasive in the eastern Empire, which survived, than in the west, which did not. At the very least, such interpretations must be accompanied by an explanation of why the two parts responded differently to conditions that affected them both.

If we narrow the inquiry to the situation of the western government in the early 5th century, the problems of the Roman Empire are not difficult to comprehend. It is unlikely that it ever recovered from the loss of two-thirds of its eastern field army at Hadrianople (378); before this, there was the appalling waste of the unsuccessful Persian campaign of Julian and, earlier still, the civil wars of Constantius. In particular, the battle of Mursa (351), at which Constantius defeated Magnentius, was immensely destructive in manpower. When Valens agreed to the admission of the Goths to the Empire in 376, he was attracted by their potential as recruits for the Roman armies.

Shortage of military manpower was one of the basic conditions under which the Roman government was obliged to operate; it was this that compelled the Romans to accept the principle of Gothic service as federates. This solution, by creating a sort of Gothic "estate" within the Empire, made it increasingly difficult for the government to exercise a free response to external threats. During the early 5th century, the problem of relations with the Visigoths was at least as important an issue as how to deal with the external enemies of Rome, and inextricably entwined with it.

A major contribution to the weakness of the western government was the refusal of the senatorial landed class to carry its share of financial obligations. The senate of Rome was opposed to the raising of recruits from senatorial estates; it preferred instead to make a cash contribution and thus preserve intact its agricultural labor force, thereby maintaining its income. With the cash reluctantly provided by the senate, the government had to raise recruits from among barbarian peoples, and in particular to pay the subsidies demanded by Alaric. Yet at the same time the senate was opposed to the payment of these subsidies.

At a period when the imperial government was suffering from near bankruptcy, members of the Roman senatorial class continued to spend vast sums on public games, and failed to appreciate that they could not both refuse to provide recruits and object to the payment of subsidies to federate troops.

The effect of senatorial influence on the ability of the government to meet its difficulties was not only financial, but political, in that it became increasingly difficult for the government to present a unified front in its dealings with Alaric. The court behaved with an unpredictable inconsistency of which Alaric was quick to take advantage. In the eastern Empire, by contrast, although there was an assertive anti-Gothic faction and a serious Gothic rebellion (that of Gainas in 399–400), the government never depended on the Goths to the same extent as did the west in order to conduct its foreign wars. The east was comparatively free of invasion and since the eastern government retained control of the nearby recruit-producing regions of Thrace and Anatolia it never suffered from the shortages of military manpower which undermined the competence of its western counterpart. The civilization defended by east Roman policy, based on the eastern Mediterranean and its cities, coincided quite closely with the areas from which the defense was financed and mounted. In the west, on the other hand, the military resources of the Empire, in the inland provinces of the north, lay far from the regions in which most of its cultural life and financial resources lay. And finally, the eastern aristocracy, being less wealthy than that of the west and more consistently involved with the political and economic life of the imperial court, never came to form a separate estate such as was formed in the west by the senatorial class of Rome. It is in considerations like these, and not in general moral and religious reflections, that the reasons must be sought for the survival of the eastern Roman Empire while the west was weakened and dismembered.

Barbarian states in the post-Roman west

The barbarian states which established themselves in the Roman provinces of the west developed social and political characters very different from each other, some favorable to the survival of Roman manners and life-styles, other less so. In Gaul, the Visigothic regime in the southwest embarked on a process of consolidation and expansion.Theoderic died in the great war of 451 against Attila, but under his successor, Theoderic II, the Goths gained access to the Mediterranean by capturing Narbonne (462); a few years later they took Arles, the seat until then of the praetorian prefecture of the remaining Roman provinces of Gaul and a notable center of Roman culture in the west. Further up the Rhône valley lay the kingdom of the Burgundians, who settled in Savoy after a great defeat by the Huns, recorded by chronicle sources under the year 436. It is possible that this defeat is the remote historical basis for the German epic, the *Nibelungenlied*. Other barbarian enclaves, like those of the Alani near Orléans and in the region of Valence, occupied more tracts of land assigned to them from the territory of the old Roman cities. In northeastern Gaul, the forested lands beyond the Loire were controlled by the Bacaudae in what appear to have been independent principalities, governing themselves by their own laws.

The barbarian settlements in Gaul and elsewhere took place on the basis of *hospitalitas*, a sharing of

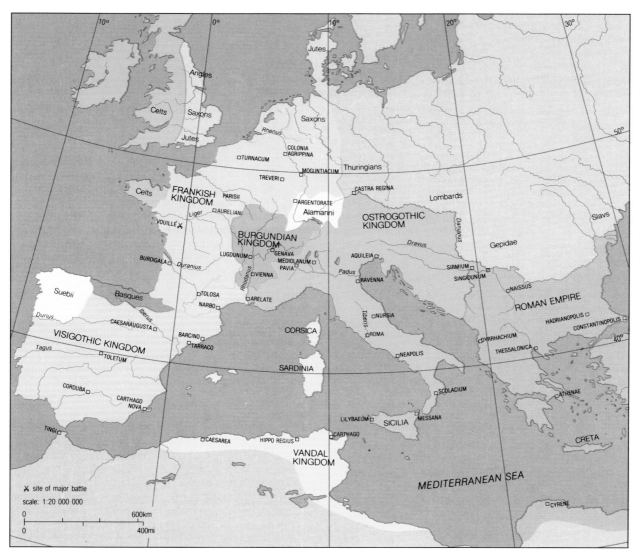

Political divisions of the Empire and barbarian occupation, 526 AD. At his death in 526, Theoderic the Ostrogoth exercised a protectorate over the Visigoths in Spain and was connected by marriage with Burgundians and with the Vandals in Africa. He had failed to prevent the expansion of the Franks under Clovis which had expelled the Visigoths from Gaul at the battle of Vouillé (507). The government of Constantinople was being drawn to reconquest by what it saw as the Arian Theoderic's persecution of his Catholic Roman subjects; but the conquest was first directed against another Arian regime. that of the Vandals, whose defeat provided a bridge with the west. In Britain it was an age of Celtic resistance to Saxons (the situation behind the original "King Arthur") and of migrations to western Gaul. The real threat to Italy came from the Lombards, and to the east from the Avars and Bulgars.

land between Roman landowner and his barbarian "guest." Unfortunately, little is known about the actual mechanics of the sharing of the land, or of the way in which the barbarian settlers were in practice distributed. Did they live in substantial barbarian enclaves – possibly on fringe land near forests – or did they scatter in smaller groups and as individual farmers on the estates and in the country-houses of Roman landowners? In the century of their occupation of Gaul before their expulsion by the Franks in the early 6th century, the Visigoths left little trace of their presence on the place-names of the region, and archaeological evidence of the Gothic settlement is scanty and indefinite. Yet the Visigothic court of Toulouse in the time of Theoderic II (453–66), which is described by a Gallic aristocratic visitor, Sidonius Apollinaris, was the scene of a colorful, opulent and in some ways quite cultured social life.

The actual manner of settlement was much less disruptive in Gaul than in Spain and Africa. The settlement of the Vandals and Suebi in Spain was attended by violence and disruption, from which little of Roman continuity appears. The fragmentary sources present none of the great landed dynastic families which are so common in 5th- and 6th-century Gaul. In Africa, the expansion of the Vandals to proconsular Africa was achieved at the cost of the widespread dispossession of Roman landowners. Many refugees found their way to the

east as victims of this dispossession and of the religious persecutions conducted by the Vandals. The discontinuity was not complete. There is evidence of the continuance to the late 5th century of traditional forms of land tenure, by the Roman *lex Manciana*, on what had once been imperial estates in a rather remote region near the borders of southern proconsular Africa with Numidia. Other Roman landowners are occasionally recorded in the sources, and the early 6th-century Vandal court of Carthage became the focus of an intellectual and cultural life of some modest sophistication, its chief representative being the Latin poet Luxorius.

It is not very clear how the barbarian peoples of the Roman west were converted to Arian Christianity. The case of the Visigoths is easiest to understand, in that their earlier relations with and admission to the Roman Empire had been in the time of Valens, an Arian emperor; further, they had been evangelized by Ulfila, an Arian Gothic missionary (and translator of the Gothic Bible). But even this case is problematical. The government of Valens had few constructive relations with the Goths in the short period between their admission to the Empire and the battle of Hadrianople, and the treaty on which their later relations with the Romans were based was made with Theodosius, a pious Catholic emperor. It remains completely obscure why the Vandals, who crossed the Rhine by invasion late in 406, should have adopted Arianism. The Suebi and

This fine mosaic, from late 5th-or 6th-century Carthage, shows a landowner in Germanic costume setting out from his villa on a hunting expedition. The portrayal, if the landowner is indeed a Vandal, suggests a certain appreciation by the barbarian settlers of at least some aspects of the civilization which they found in Roman Africa.

case of Sidonius Apollinaris at Clermont in 469, aristocrats became bishops of their cities and fulfilled urgent practical needs, securing food supplies, raising public morale in times of crisis and leading their cities against attack from the Goths. Sidonius himself was exiled and imprisoned by Euric II for his role in the resistance of Clermont in the 470s.

Sidonius' promotion as bishop after an active secular career (he had been prefect of Rome in 468) has often provoked scepticism as to the genuineness of his Christian piety, especially when combined with his obviously undiminished love of classical literature. But this would be a misconception. As we have already seen, the conversion of the Roman Empire to Christianity had taken place, despite some expressions of opposition from both sides, without the sacrifice of its classical culture. The real danger in assessing the promotion as bishop of a man like Sidonius is that of underestimating the level of genuine Christian piety which he had possessed as a layman. Like others, he made a conscientious, honest and useful bishop, whose contribution to the survival of his native city in a time of crisis was significant and admirable, and achieved not without danger to himself.

Others among Sidonius' friends made distinctive contributions to the relations of the Visigothic kingdom of Toulouse with the surviving Romano-Gallic population — men such as Leo of Narbonne, who was instrumental in devising the earliest known version of the "Roman Law of the Visigoths," an attempt to provide a simplified version of Roman law for the use of the Romans living under the Visigoths. Its successor, Alaric II's *Lex Romana Visigothorum* (506), was the chief source for knowledge of Roman law in the early medieval west. Similarly, the Burgundian law of King Gundobad, prepared in the late 5th century, was the most permanent legacy of a barbarian regime of whose internal history relatively little is known. Such achievements of Roman and barbarian collaboration in the 5th century were successful in preserving what could be preserved of Roman culture and religion without the support of Roman power, and prepared the way for the more permanent acceptance of Frankish rule by the old Roman provinces of Gaul.

Rome, Ravenna and Constantinople

In Italy, despite the loss of senatorial incomes from overseas estates, political and economic life continued very much as before, dominated by the court of Ravenna and by senatorial Rome. The sieges of Rome by Alaric had caused serious food shortages, especially when Africa too was blockaded or in rebellion, and failed to send the corn ships to Rome. On one occasion, the people assembled in the Circus Maximus had acclaimed the terrible words, "set a price on human flesh," meat being so scarce and its price so high.

Many senators with mainly provincial connections and sources of wealth must in these years have disappeared from Rome to secure what they could of their local possessions, leaving the capital and its public offices to be dominated by a small circle of clans of Italian origin, whose still great wealth derived from the possession of land retained in Italy and Sicily. Upon the initiative of these

Burgundians for some time remained pagan, while the Franks were converted directly from paganism to Catholic Christianity in the time of Clovis. There seems no reason to suppose that the barbarians were particularly attracted by the theological intricacies of Arian as opposed to orthodox Nicene doctrine. One is led to conclude that barbarian heresy had come to reflect their situation as settlers in Roman territory, their Christianity expressing shared interests with their Roman hosts, while their Arianism provided a point of distinction which limited the intimacy that could be achieved between them. Certainly, phases of more aggressively anti-Roman policy initiated by barbarian kings were expressed in persecutions of Catholics. This happened, especially, in Africa under King Huneric (477–84), and in Gaul under the aggressive Gothic regime of Euric II (466–84).

Roman continuity in Gaul was in the hands of the resident Gallo-Roman aristocracy, and their achievement was considerable. The letters of Sidonius Apollinaris, written in the second half of the 5th century, reveal an extensive network of political, cultural and theological contacts maintained among the members of this aristocracy. Some of these nobles, like Pontius Leontius of Bordeaux, preserved a Roman life-style in their villas and country-houses. The fortified country seat of Pontius, known to Sidonius as "Burgus" ("castle"; usually identified as Bourg-sur-Gironde), possessed walls and towers, porticoes with wall-paintings of Christian and classical themes, storehouses and a Christian chapel, and there are other such examples.

In Gaul the church also played a crucial role as the preserver of Roman continuity in the 5th and 6th centuries. When there was no longer an imperial court resident in Gaul, the incentive to obtain a classical education in order to secure professional advancement disappeared; with it went the motive for the cities to provide the educational facilities which they had maintained in the imperial period. The provision at least of a basic education was thus left in the hands of the church. Sometimes, as in the families, damaged parts of the city were rebuilt and public monuments, like the senate-house and the Colosseum, were restored. The Colosseum again became the scene of the elaborate hunting shows (*venationes*) put on by members of the nobility, by which they asserted their position as patrons and benefactors of the *populus Romanus*. There is evidence too that within a few years of the sack the population of Rome was again beginning to increase; refugees began to return and the public services of the city were restored.

Rome was the center of vigorous cultural and literary activity. To the third and fourth decades of the 5th century (and not, as was once thought, to the late 4th century) should be assigned the great commentary on Virgil by Servius, and the *Saturnalia* of Macrobius. To the same period belong also the *Fables* of Avienus, a Roman senator, and the preparation of the two illustrated Vatican manuscripts of Virgil's *Aeneid* known respectively as the *Virgilius Vaticanus* and the *Virgilius Romanus*. The classical revival of the time of Boethius and Cassiodorus in the early 6th century was thus the culmination of an interest in the preservation of classical learning maintained throughout the 5th century by members of the senatorial nobility and their literary clients.

The 5th century was also the time of the building of great new churches at Rome, monumental in design and decorated with elaborate mosaic sequences. Following the basilicas of the late 4th century, St Paul-outside-the-Walls and St Pudentiana, came the building of St Sabina and, shortly afterwards, of St Maria Maggiore. The dedication of the latter to the Virgin Mary reflected the support of Pope Sixtus for the Council of Ephesus (431), which confirmed her designation as Theotokos, "Mother of God."

The Christianization of the Roman aristocracy expressed itself in the 5th century in terms of an enhanced involvement in the organized life of the church of Rome. Roman senators are recorded with increasing frequency as the builders and benefactors of churches, and as participants in their regular liturgical activities. The suppression of the Pelagian heresy in 418 had put an end to a movement in which ascetic lay senators could take an independent role in dogmatic issues, and the period after this is characterized by the solidarity of the clergy of Rome with prominent lay members of the church, and of both with the Christian population of Rome.

Already in the early 5th century, the Spanish poet Prudentius had acclaimed Rome as the moral head of the Christian empire, possessing more relics of martyrs than any other city, great public processions in their honor and magnificently ornate churches. This ideal of Christian Rome was gradually deployed with increasing effectiveness by the bishops of the city in support of their claims of preeminence in the church. Pope Leo I (440–61) made notable contributions to this process in a series of sermons that presented the Roman saints, Peter and Paul, as the founders of Christian Rome, the counterparts of Romulus and Remus, and so provided an ideology appropriate for Rome's claims to be the Christian capital of the Empire. Pope Leo was also prominent politically, in particular as a member of the embassy which succeeded in averting the threatened invasion of Italy by Attila in 452.

From the very beginning of the 5th century, the imperial court lived in relative security at Ravenna; it moved there at the end of 402 in face of the threat posed by Alaric's first invasion of Italy, when Milan was actually besieged by the Visigoths. Ravenna was one of a sequence of great maritime cities at the head of the Adriatic. Its predecessor was Aquileia, which by the 5th century was a neglected commercial site with a silted harbor but still, as Attila found, a considerable fortress. Ravenna's successors were medieval and Renaissance Venice and, in recent times, Trieste. For the emperors of the 5th century, the attraction of Ravenna lay in its defensive security; it was situated among marshes and lagoons, and only accessible from the landward side by a causeway. When the generals of Theodosius II took the place from the usurper Johannes in 425, their success was attributed to the help of an angel disguised as a shepherd, who showed them the way through the marshes.

Behind its natural and artificial defenses, 5th-century Ravenna became a great center of Christian culture. The churches of St John the Evangelist, attributed to the munificence of Galla Placidia, and the baptistery of Bishop Neon (otherwise known as the Baptistery of the Orthodox), with its mosaics symbolizing the rite of baptism, were constructed in the middle years of the 5th century. Other mosaics from the imperial palace, now lost, showed the marriage of Valentinian III with Licinia Eudoxia in 437. The so-called Mausoleum of Galla Placidia is probably not to be associated with her, but the building is of 5th-century date and its splendid mosaics have major iconographical significance. The most resplendent of the churches of Ravenna belong to the time of the Byzantine reconquest, but the town's origins as a center of Christian culture are to be sought in the 5th century.

The political relations between Constantinople and the west in the 5th century have already been described. The eastern Empire was free from major invasion, although Isaurian raids and incursions of desert peoples into Cyrenaica and southern Egypt caused great local difficulty and ultimately raised the question of Constantinople's ability to defend its more distant provinces. The philosopher and rhetorician Synesius of Cyrene was made bishop of Ptolemais in 411, having as local landowner been prominent in leading armed resistance to the incursions. The rebellion of the Goth Gainas was suppressed with some difficulty, and Theodosius' wars against Persia over the Armenian situation were resolved by diplomacy to enable him to meet the threat of the Huns, who in 422 ravaged Thrace. It was probably against the Hunnish threat that the new land walls of Constantinople had been completed in 413. The subsidies paid to the Huns under treaty were a relatively serious financial burden, but by no means as crippling as some have believed.

With such exceptions, the 5th century was a time of continued prosperity in the eastern Empire. Sardis in Asia Minor now entered a period of commercial and monumental expansion. Antioch also, on the evidence of the mosaics from its villas, continued prosperous, and imperial and private interest in the Holy Land led to a period of growing economic vigor based on the importation of capital from outside by pious pilgrims and tourists. After

Top The illustrated manuscript known as the *Virgilius Vaticanus* (Cod. Lat. 3225) is an outstanding monument of the interest in classical culture sustained in 5th-century Rome. Illustrated here is one of the most pathetic scenes in the *Aeneid*, Dido's preparation for suicide. With a knife in her hand, she reclines on the funeral pyre which, by a strange convention, seems to be indoors.

Above The church, monastery and pilgrimage center of St Simeon Stylites at Qalet Sem'an in Syria was built in the late 5th century around the pillar which until his death in 459 the stylite saint had occupied for 30 years, receiving visitors, offering advice to those who came for it, and undertaking prayer and meditation. The pillar on which the performance had taken place was enclosed in an octagonal open courtyard. The shrine was equipped with a guest house for visitors as well as the monastery and basilica illustrated here.

her political disgrace in 443, the empress Eudocia, wife of Theodosius II, lived in Jerusalem until her death in 460. She was responsible for many benefactions and ecclesiastical and monastic foundations in the Holy Land, and had also built a church at Constantinople. Athens, where Eudocia was born as Athenais, the daughter of a pagan sophist, was in the 5th century the center of the famous Neoplatonic school of Syrianus and Proclus, owing its allegiance to the theurgical tradition established by Iamblichus (see above, p. 177). After the sack of Athens by Alaric in 396, an attempt was made, especially by the praetorian prefect of Illyricum, Herculius (407–12), to repair and put in order some of its public buildings, including the Library of Hadrian.

Eudocia's supporter at Constantinople, the praetorian prefect Cyrus, was, like the empress, a classical poet of some reputation, and passionately devoted to Greek culture; John the Lydian, writing under Justinian, attributed to Cyrus the responsibility for abandoning Latin as the official language of the eastern administration – a significant step in the slow transition from the late Roman to a Greek Byzantine empire. Cyrus was also responsible for extending the new city walls of Constantinople to defend the sea frontage against the threat of Vandal piracy.

After Cyrus' loss of office in 441, probably because of his excessive popularity at Constantinople, he was consecrated bishop of a town in Phrygia, where he no doubt surprised his congregation by delivering what is probably the shortest, though perhaps not the least controversial, sermon on record: "Brethren, let the birth of our Savior Jesus Christ be honored in silence, because the Word of God was conceived in the Holy Virgin through hearing alone. Amen." Despite this splendidly contemptuous gesture, and despite the accusation of paganism leveled at him, as at Eudocia, at the time of his fall from power, Cyrus, on leaving his bishopric, returned to Constantinople and became famous there for his works of charity and for his support of the stylite saint, Daniel. The combination of classical literary and Christian religious tastes was a fundamental feature of Byzantine, as of late Roman, culture.

The most intractable, and in some ways most damaging problem to face the eastern Empire in this period was that of religious unity. The Arian heresy had been effectively suppressed by Theodosius I by the councils of Constantinople held in the early 380s, but its natural successors, the Nestorian and monophysite controversies, proved still more difficult to resolve. Nestorius, patriarch of Constantinople from 428, argued that of the two natures of Christ, divine and human, only the human was incarnate and suffered on the Cross. In consequence, the Virgin Mary, the mother of the human Christ, was not the mother of God, and Nestorius denied her the epithet Theotokos by which this concept was expressed. The doctrines of Nestorius were opposed with particular force by Cyril, patriarch of Alexandria. The imperial court was divided, but Nestorius was condemned and deposed at the Council of Ephesus in 431. After an unsuccessful attempt by Theodosius to reconcile the parties, Nestorius was exiled and his writings burned.

Over the next few years, the eastern church, under the influence of the Alexandrians, was drawn more strongly towards the so-called "monophysite" position, which, at the other extreme from Nestorianism, asserted the single indivisible nature of Christ, divine as well as human. The monophysite position was upheld by the Council of Ephesus in 449, called by Pope Leo the "robber council" (*latrocinium*) because his own views were ignored. Leo denounced the council to Valentinian III, and with his support complained to Theodosius. Only after Theodosius's death in 450 was any action taken.

The Council of Chalcedon in 451, held under the eye of the imperial court, was not allowed to develop with the same spontaneity as the two councils of Ephesus. Imperial commissioners presided over the sessions and imperial secretaries took down the proceedings. The "robber council" was denounced, the Alexandrians rejected and the so-called "Tome of Leo," presented to the council by papal legates, made the basis (or one of the bases) of the Creed of Chalcedon. At the same time the eastern bishops evaded the possible implications of their acceptance of the formula of Leo by explicitly defining the see of Constantinople as equal with that of Rome. Despite the objections of the papal legates and subsequently of Leo himself, the relevant canon (number 28) remained in force in the eastern church, thus denying the bishop of Rome's claim to supremacy.

The details of the disputes in the eastern church in this period are neither simple nor edifying. The intensity of the theological struggle cannot be explained without reference to personal rivalries and to the struggles of certain sees – Constantinople, Antioch and Alexandria – for preeminence. The patriarchs of Alexandria in particular conducted themselves with a domineering ruthlessness and lack of scruple fully worthy of the traditions of their see; Cyril of Alexandria carried his opinion against Nestorius at the first Council of Ephesus, partly by presents to various officials at the imperial court so lavish that he had to borrow 1500 pounds of gold to finance them. This was more than four times the annual subsidy first agreed between the government of Constantinople and the Huns in around 435.

The Council of Chalcedon was not successful in suppressing the theological divisions of opinion so powerfully held. The danger to the emperor lay in his failure to secure through it the religious unity to which he had so openly committed himself. Monophysitism, supported by an increasingly aggressive monastic movement, became entrenched in Coptic-speaking Egypt, in the Syriac-speaking churches of Palestine and Syria and in the Armenian church, while the Christian church in Persian Mesopotamia adopted Nestorianism. The combination of theological dissension and vernacular cultures in these regions makes one wonder whether there was a real possibility of an alliance between cultural and religious allegiances to produce a form of nationalistic sentiment against the government of Constantinople. The extent to which this created a weakness in the structure of the early Byzantine empire is debated, but the possibility of such a development clearly sets a question against the political integrity of an empire to which the enforcement of religious unity was so important.

Courtly Munificence at Ravenna

Below A detail from a mosaic in St Vitale showing Justinian and his courtiers, in an image corresponding to that of Theodora and her attendants shown *opposite*. Members of the household guard are seen, one of them with resplendent monogrammed shield.

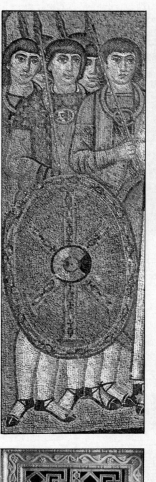

Ravenna had from the time of Augustus been the headquarters of one of the imperial fleets of Italy (the other was at Misenum), and had from then enjoyed a modestly flourishing life as a naval base. Though somewhat overshadowed as a commercial center by Aquileia, it was of obvious importance at such times as the civil wars of 68–70 AD.

The occupation of Ravenna as imperial capital can be dated precisely to 402 AD, after the siege of Milan which had exposed that city to the barbarian invasion of north Italy. Ravenna, tucked away among flats and marshes, surrounded by branches of the Po and linked to the mainland proper by a raised causeway, was nearly impregnable; it was taken only rarely, and then usually by treachery or collusion. For Sidonius Apollinaris it was a perverse city, in which the laws of nature had been reversed, where "walls fall flat and waters stand, towers float and ships are seated," while croaking frogs were citizens. More seriously, based on his security there, and on the direct sea link to Constantinople which always figured large in the advantages of Ravenna, Honorius was able to sit it out and defy Alaric when the latter's control of Italy seemed otherwise complete (see p. 209). The city was an equally secure refuge for the barbarian kings of Italy, and, after its capture in 540 by the armies of Justinian, for the Byzantine governors, or "exarchs" of the conquered province.

Throughout this time Ravenna witnessed a typically vigorous social and cultural life (not to mention periodic political violence) based on the presence of royal and imperial courts. Circus races there are described by Sidonius; the city received constant visitors; and its intellectual life is suggested by, among other evidence, the manuscripts known to have been revised there.

The churches of Ravenna span the times of the 5th-century emperors, the barbarian kings and the Byzantine reconquest, though the Byzantines did what they could to efface the memory, and the visual images, of their immediate predecessors.

The church of St Apollinare Nuovo (*above center*), originally the palace church of Theoderic, was decorated with mosaic scenes of Ravenna which give some idea of its monumental grandeur. Here are (*left*) the harbor of Classis (Classe di Ravenna) and (*far right*) the palace of Theoderic, of which the facade may still be extant in the building known as the "palace of the exarchs" near the church. In the delicately carved balustrades from St Apollinare Nuovo (*above*) the peacocks and vine tendrils are symbols of eternal life. Also shown (*top*) is the elaborate marble throne of Bishop Maximianus (546–54).

The church of St Vitale, seen by the 9th-century chronicler Agnellus as beyond comparison in Italy, was begun at about the time of the death of Theoderic but dedicated in 547 or 548, after the reconquest of Italy by Justinian's generals. *Below* is shown Justinian's wife Theodora with her attendants, in an image symbolizing her generosity to the new church. The empress bears a golden chalice as her gift to the church, and on the rim of her robe appear the three wise men bearing gifts, in an allusion to Christian munificence. The scene is visualized as a procession from right to left across the narthex of the church, the end wall, with apse, and sides of the narthex being seen as if opened out. Theodora's head, with nimbus, appears almost, but not quite, in the center of the apse, as if it were itself a mosaic image there. The progress of the group is suggested by the gently increasing sway of the figures, by the curtain held aside by an attendant and, in a touch of brilliant imagination, by the sudden implied movement of the fountain.

The Ostrogothic King Theoderic rested after his death in 526 in the still standing mausoleum (*far left*) outside the walls of Ravenna. The immense size of the monolithic roof – 300 tons of Istrian stone – is remarked on by a contemporary source. The handles by which it was maneuvered into position can be seen around the rim. The palace of Theoderic is seen (*left*) in a mosaic from St Apollinare Nuovo. The figures of Theoderic and his court, removed after the Justinianic reconquest, can still be seen in outline.

219

THE OSTROGOTHIC KINGDOM
AND THE BYZANTINE RECONQUEST

From 476, Italy was governed by Germanic kings, with their court at Ravenna. Odoacer, who had supplanted Romulus Augustulus, was himself defeated and killed by Theoderic the Ostrogoth after a long siege in which Ravenna was taken by treachery (493). Both kings ruled with consideration for the Italian peoples under their government, showing every sign of respect for the great Empire of whose impressive remains they found themselves masters. Senatorial life at Rome continued as before, the great urban offices being filled by members of the city aristocracy. The Colosseum was restored under Odoacer; entertainments and hunting displays were provided there, with chariot races in the Circus. These events are frequently illustrated on the ivory diptychs distributed by senators to commemorate the occasion. The involvement of the senate in the ecclesiastical politics of Rome grew ever more intense, as seen particularly in the disorders surrounding the election of Pope Symmachus against the claims of Laurentius (498) and in the diplomatic and theological negotiations attending the rapprochement with the eastern church which reached fruition after the emperor Justin's accession in 519.

Theoderic deserves his reputation as a humane and sympathetic ruler. He is compared by a contemporary source with the emperors Trajan and Valentinian – comparisons justified by his building restorations, in which, again, he encouraged and collaborated with members of the Roman nobility, and by his careful, restrained management of Rome and Italy. The key-word of the regime, *civilitas*, means the preservation of proper individual liberties under the protection of law. The senator Cassiodorus, a member of a line of imperial administrators, was employed by Theoderic to present his policies to the Roman public in official letters written in a highly wrought, metaphorical and, to modern eyes, extraordinarily affected style, which was nevertheless effective in maintaining an image of the regime as solicitous of the highest civilized values. From another point of view, the letters are the culmination of a long evolution of increasingly elaborate Roman "bureaucratese" which had been given its decisive impulse in the 4th century.

The reign of Theoderic also saw the preeminence of the philosopher Boethius, whose phenomenal achievement in the fields of theology, science and music, as well as in traditional philosophy, establishes him as one of the greatest minds ever produced by the ancient world, as well as a dominating influence in the Middle Ages. The fall of Boethius, described rather indirectly in his most famous work, *The Consolation of Philosophy*, was also a tragedy for Theoderic, whose reign ended in rancor and conflict between him and the senate. It is a misjudgment to regard the *Consolation* simply as a reversion by Boethius to traditional paganism; an examination of preoccupations about human fortune and the omniscience of God in the light of

"I, who once made poems in strength and hope, alas, now weeping must start sad songs." Boethius wrote his *Consolation* as a dialogue in prose and verse between himself and the lady Philosophy, who appears to him in prison. Here he is (*below*) as seen by a 12th-century illuminator of the opening page of the book, seated in his prison with a pair of writing tablets open before him.

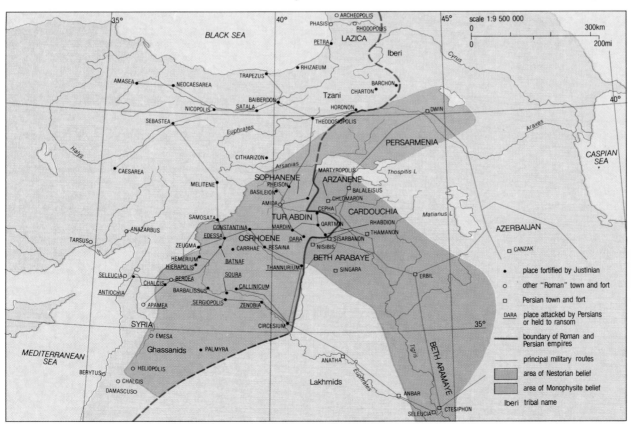

Left: Persia in the time of Justinian. For much of Justinian's reign the eastern Roman provinces had to withstand attacks by the Sasanians under their aggressive and successful Khusro I (531–79 AD). In the south limited Roman forces occupied a few strong points, while the Ghassanid Arab federation policed the desert approaches against raids by the Persian Lakhmid Arabs. In the center, the fortress of Dara, supported by the major military bases of Amida and Constantina and by the fortified salient of the Tur Abdin, opposed the Persian frontier city of Nisibis; yet the permanent garrisons were rarely sufficient to prevent Persian invasions, and the wealthy cities of Osrhoene and Syria were frequently threatened. Further north, the frontier bastions of Martyropolis, Citharizon and Theodosiopolis faced Arzanene and Persarmenia, and Justinian eventually established Roman control over the Tzani and Lazica, strategically important areas that could block nomad raids from across the Caucasus, and prevent Persian access to the Black Sea.

Above The diptych of Boethius' father Flavius Narius (?) Manlius Boethius, consul in 487. Upon his parents' early death, the young Boethius had been brought up in the family of Symmachus, consul in 485, whose daughter Rusticiana he married. After the execution of her husband, and shortly after that of Symmachus, Rusticiana devoted herself to charitable works.

Far right The diptych of Rufius Gennadius Probus Orestes, consul in 530 (the name Orestes also appears in the monogram). He sits enthroned in full consular dress, flanked by Rome and Constantinople. Below are symbols of largesse and, above the consul, the Ostrogothic King Athalaric and his mother Amalasuntha. The diptych illustrates both the favor of the later Ostrogothic regime to senatorial Rome, and the theme of east–west harmony – an association of ideas soon to be shattered by the Byzantine reconquest of Italy.

the near certainty of its author's approaching execution, the work is a masterpiece of philosophical humanism.

The conflict between Theoderic and the senate was caused by a shift of ecclesiastical policy in the east, where the monophysite preferences of the old emperor Anastasius were replaced, on the accession of Justin I (519), by an aggressively "orthodox" policy which encouraged the previously estranged churches of the west to move closer to their eastern counterparts. This policy, encouraged with still greater energy by Justin's nephew and envisaged successor, Justinian, tended to ally senatorial Christian Rome with the Byzantine court, to the obvious unease of the Arian Theoderic. The diplomatic and other relations between east and west came, only too easily, to suggest political intrigue directed against the barbarian court of Ravenna by the Christian capitals of the Empire. It was Boethius' spirited defense of a senator accused of conspiracy with the east that led to his arrest and brutal execution by Theoderic in 523. In the previous year he had been given the post of *magister officiorum* at Ravenna and his sons made joint consuls, in an obvious and perhaps desperate attempt by Theoderic to maintain good relations between Ravenna and Rome in the face of overtures to Rome from Constantinople.

In the last year of his reign, Theoderic, in the hope of moderating the ecclesiastical policies of the eastern court, allowed Pope John I to visit Constantinople, but the visit, the first ever made by a pope of Rome to the eastern capital, was greeted there with terrific enthusiasm which further emphasized Theoderic's growing isolation from his Roman subjects. When John returned he was put under house arrest at Ravenna, and his death in confinement was closely followed by that of Theoderic himself (526).

In the west, Theoderic had confirmed his position by alliances and connections by marriage with the barbarian kings of Gaul, Spain and Africa. His attempts to unite the rulers of Gaul against the increasing threat of the Franks under Clovis failed. The Visigoths were heavily defeated by Clovis at the battle of Vouillé in southwestern Gaul (507). They were reduced to their territories in Spain, and the establishment of the Frankish kingdom in the old Roman provinces of Gaul was complete.

The successors of Theoderic maintained his sympathetic policies towards the city of Rome, but suffered from increasing conflict within the dynasty. The death of the young king Athalaric in 534, and the murder of his mother (and Theoderic's daughter) Amalasuntha by Theodahad, heralded the end of Visigothic rule. By 535 Justinian's general, Belisarius, was leading the campaigns of reconquest against the west.

Cassiodorus, having served both Athalaric and Theodahad as praetorian prefect, retired from political life in 537 and, after a possibly prolonged visit to Constantinople, returned to Italy to pursue the religious activities which have earned him a less ambiguous reputation than have his political commitments to barbarian kings. His earlier attempt to found a school of Christian learning at Rome having failed on account of the surrounding unrest of the wars of reconquest, Cassiodorus returned in advanced years to his family estates at Squillace in

Calabria and founded there his famous monastic settlement of Vivarium. Here the essentials of classical learning were preserved alongside and as an integral part of the pursuit of a Christian holy life, a pattern of immense importance for the future of classical culture in medieval Europe.

The political history of the eastern Empire of the 6th century begins with the caution and stability of the reign of Anastasius, who administered the economy with such success and thrift as to leave a massive surplus on his death in 519. The reign of

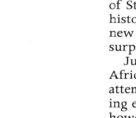

A contemporary source alleges that Theoderic was illiterate and traced his name through a brass template. It seems certain that this is a misrepresentation, based on Theoderic's use of a template to draw the complicated monogram which appears on his coinage (*above*). Also shown (*below*) is the monogram of Odoacer.

Justin I was notable for its abandonment of Anastasius' monophysite tendencies, with the consequences described above, and for the increasing influence of Justinian. Justinian's accession on his uncle's death in 527 initiated an explosion of energetic activity. Almost immediately after becoming emperor, he set in train the reorganization and codification of Roman law which remains as one of the Roman Empire's most imposing legacies as well as, in the *Digest*, a fundamental source of evidence for the social history of the classical Roman Empire itself. Justinian also turned his attention to the Persians, over whom Belisarius won a great victory in 530. In 532 the Romans and Persians signed an agreement known, with transparent optimism, as the "eternal peace." War broke out again later, and Justinian embarked on the building of a series of elaborate fortification works in northern Mesopotamia.

The reign of Justinian was almost cut short in 532 by riots of factions of circus supporters, directed initially against his unpopular ministers, especially the praetorian prefect and the quaestor Tribonian, a distinguished lawyer who had taken a leading role in the codification of the law. In the insurrection, known as the "Nika" ("Conquer!") riots from the chant of the crowds, another emperor was proclaimed, and Justinian was only saved by the determination of his wife Theodora, a former actress whom he had married years before he became emperor, and by his generals, Belisarius and Mundus, who led the troops under their command in an assault on the rioting crowds. Thousands of citizens were killed in the repression, and large parts of Constantinople burned. As in the burning of Rome under Nero, the damage provided the opportunity for magnificent rebuilding; Justinian's greatest work was the reconstruction of the church of St Sophia, described with such wonder by the historian Procopius. On seeing the interior of his new church Justinian exclaimed "Solomon, I have surpassed you!"

Justinian's reconquest of the west began with Africa, which, considering the fate of previous attempts, was taken from the Vandals with surprising ease in 533. The problem of Moorish rebellion, however, proved more intractable and took several more years to overcome. The murder of Amalasuntha by Theodahad provided a justification for extending the reconquest to Italy; in addition, the diplomatic traffic of recent years had established contacts between western senators and the eastern court, and there was also among the Latin-speaking community of Constantinople a group of senatorial exiles from the west, well placed to make contact with diplomatic visitors and to exert pressure on the eastern government.

The reconquest of Italy was much more difficult and laborious than that of Africa, and was attended by destruction and violence which cast the greatest doubt on the value, to the Italians themselves, of their incorporation into the Byzantine state. Justinian's general, Narses, eventually completed the reconquest in 553 by defeating King Teias, and the government of Italy was organized by the so-called "Pragmatic Sanction" of 554. The senatorial class of Rome, which had survived the 5th-century invasions and the establishment of the barbarian kingdom of Ravenna, makes no further appearance in history after the Byzantine reconquest. The resplendent greatness of Byzantine Ravenna, which became the seat of the new government, or "Exarchate," was achieved at the price of the impoverishment of Italy, and of Rome itself, which marks the end of the classical world. Little could be done to prevent the rapid occupation of Italy by the Lombards in the later 560s.

Justinian died in 565, the effective ruler of more traditionally Roman territory than any of his predecessors since the early 5th century. Yet the reality of his achievement is questionable. The costs of reconquest fell heavily on eastern resources, diverting armies from the Danubian and Persian fronts where their presence was more immediately necessary; moreover, the conquest itself was not in the best interests of the western provinces. The Byzantine Empire can be left to speak for itself in its survival for a further 900 years after the death of Justinian. As for Rome and Italy, where this book began, it is an irony that their latest period of prosperity, under the favorable eye of Germanic kings, was ended by a Byzantine court's repossession of them as impoverished provinces of a Roman Empire now governed from Constantinople.

The Roman Legacy

For Gibbon, the fall of the Roman Empire was "a revolution which will ever be remembered, and is still felt by the nations of the earth." At any moment until the rise of the modern industrial age, and in important respects beyond it, both parts of this statement were self-evidently true. Until quite recently "Tully's Offices" – the *De Officiis* of Cicero – could have been described as one of the most influential books in western culture, and it is still not unusual for a British civil servant, as was once normal for politicians, to know more about the history of the Roman world than about his own. That this can hardly be said to be a good thing is not the point: until the modern age its propriety would never have been questioned.

Even on a narrow understanding of what is meant by "Roman," the legacy of the Roman world to the languages, literary culture, architecture, government and religious life of medieval and modern Europe has been immense. On a broader view, comprising Roman influence as mediated through the Christian Greek world of Byzantium, its impact is even greater.

These two pages do not attempt to summarize the book which could be written on the Roman legacy in all its complexity: rather, they isolate particular examples, and suggest by implication where more may be found. The examples chosen are not unremittingly solemn. Awareness of a culture can, and should, reside in the trivial as well as the portentous, in the bizarre as well as ideal, not least in the affectionate as well as the forbidding.

Ancient mythological and literary scenes in idealized landscapes were a frequent subject of classical painters, especially of the French school, as in this painting (*top*) of Aeneas at Delos by Claude (1600–82), in which the human figures do little more than provide the scale for a study of architectural forms in their landscape. The building in the middle distance bears some resemblance to Hadrian's Pantheon at Rome (p. 104). The engraving by Piranesi (*opposite top*), of two Roman roads flanked by funerary monuments piled up in an architectural extravaganza of obsessive profusion, reflects the renewed interest of the artist's time with the physical remains of Roman power. Its date, c. 1756, is close to that of Gibbon's musings on the Capitol which first moved his mind towards the writing of a history of Rome. The inscription in modern Rome (*above*) reproduces ancient Roman practice towards disgraced emperors: the name of Mussolini has been erased. An earlier and more sinister reminder of the reactionary tendencies of Rome in the 1920s is given by the group of proto-Fascists dressed up as legionary standard bearers (*left*). The publication in 1753 of Wood and Dawkins's *Ruins of Palmyra* made available to designers the immensely rich resources of this great eastern city. Here (*below*), in attenuated but unmistakable form, is Wood's engraving of a ceiling from the temple of Bel (cf. p. 158), as adapted for use in the dining room of Stratfield Saye House, Berkshire.

The triumphal arch, a universally acknowledged symbol of war and victory adopted from the Romans, here seen (*left*) in its French imperial version at Place Charles de Gaulle, Paris. On a less elevated level, manhole covers in Rome (*bottom left*) are still cast with the traditional legend SPQR: "Senatus Populusque Romanus." One particularly pervasive legacy of the Romans, the Julian calendar, is illustrated (*left*) in the so-called "Calendar of the Year 354" (see also p. 207), here seen at October with its list of public games and festivals and the image of Scorpio; the Zodiac itself is, through the Romans, a legacy of ancient Mesopotamia to the modern world. The last word goes to the Gauls, Astérix and Obélix, complaining during a journey to Lutetia Parisiorum of the damaging effects of Roman construction on the landscape. The village from which they came, near the garrison town of Laudanum in northern Gaul, is so far unexcavated though its life is well known from literary sources.

LIST OF ILLUSTRATIONS

Abbreviations: t = top, tl = top left, tr = top right,
c = center, b = bottom etc.

All maps by Lovell Johns, Oxford.

All site plans by John Brennan, Oxford.

*End Papers: Celeberrimae urbis (Romae) antiquae
fidelissima topographia* by Mario Cartaro, 1579: British
Library, London
page

BIBLIOGRAPHY

The bibliography is from various points of view selective. It includes only books and not articles in learned journals, and with a very few exceptions mentions work written only in English. Even within these limitations, it expresses the authors' own choice of what seems to them especially important in a vastly more extensive field, concentrating first on the fundamental, and secondly on the most recent and (we hope) most accessible work. We hope nevertheless that it will provide a guide to more specialized work to those who need it, and to the general reader a way of following up topics which especially interest him.

Geography

As far as we know this is the first Atlas of the Roman world to be published, at least in English. But the Roman world is naturally covered in older historical and classical atlases, many of which are excellent and have been extensively used by us. These include H. Kiepert, *Atlas Antiquus* (Berlin 1882), A. A. M. van der Heyden and H. H. Scullard, *Atlas of the Classical World* (London 1959), G. Westermann, *Grosser Atlas zur Weltgeschichte* (Brunswick 1976), and C. McEvedy, *Penguin Atlas of Ancient History* (Harmondsworth 1967). There is no fully satisfactory treatment in English of the geography of ancient Italy and the Mediterranean. The best available is probably M. Cary, *The Geographic Background of Greek and Roman History* (Oxford 1949). The antiquated work of H. Nissen, *Italische Landeskunde*, 2 vols. (Berlin 1883–1902), is still useful in parts. The reconstruction of ancient landscape from field archaeology and air photography is the theme of J. Bradford's *Ancient Landscapes* (London 1957), which deals with Italy in particular. A very good selection of air photographs can be found in G. Schmidt, *Atlante aerofotografico delle sedi umani in Italia*, 2 vols. (Florence 1966–70). C. Delano Smith, *Western Mediterranean Europe* (London 1979), is a modern account of the historical geography of the area since the Neolithic age. The best general introduction to Mediterranean geography is probably M. and R. Beckinsale, *Southern Europe: the Mediterranean and Alpine Lands* (London 1975); the older work of E. C. Semple, *The Geography of the Mediterranean Region* (New York 1931), is still worth consulting. The most detailed account of Italian geography is the handbook published by the Admiralty, *Italy* (Naval Intelligence Division, Geographical Handbooks), 3 vols. (London 1944). The classic account of the historical role of

the Mediterranean environment is F. Braudel, *The Mediterranean and the Mediterranean World in the Age of Philip II*, English trans. (London 1972).

Sources

The Loeb Classical Library includes the works of most classical and later authors, with text and parallel English translation. Several important texts, mainly of writers of the classical period, are also available in translation in the Penguin Classics series. Useful anthologies of translated texts and documents include N. Lewis and M. Reinhold, *Roman Civilisation*, 2 vols. (rev. ed., New York 1966), and A. H. M. Jones, *A History of Rome through the Fifth Century*, 2 vols. (London 1968). For a selection of documents on the early Christian church see J. Stevenson, *A New Eusebius: Documents Illustrative of the History of the Church to AD 337* (London 1957; often reprinted). Texts which bear on economic history are assembled and translated in T. Frank, *An Economic Survey of Ancient Rome*, vol. I (Baltimore, Md., 1927). Discussion of the value and reliability of the sources can be found in most textbooks on Roman history. On particular writers of the earlier period see P. G. Walsh, *Livy* (Cambridge 1961), F. W. Walbank, *Polybius* (Berkeley, Calif., 1972), and R. Syme, *Sallust* (Berkeley, Calif., 1968); for work on later writers see below. A. Momigliano, *Essays on Ancient and Modern Historiography* (Oxford 1977), contains some important studies of the sources for early Roman history; also useful is T. A. Dorey (ed.), *Latin Historians* (London 1966). On the interpretation of numismatic and papyrological evidence, especially, but by no means exclusively, important for the time of the Empire, see E. G. Turner, *Greek Papyri* (Oxford 1968), and J. P. C. Kent, B. Overbeck, A. U. Stylow, *Roman Coins* (London 1978).

General

The classic histories of Rome to the end of the Republic are T. Mommsen, *History of Rome*, trans. W. P. Dickson, 4 vols. (London 1861), G. De Sanctis, *Storia dei Romani*, 4 vols. (Turin/Florence 1907–53), and the collective *Cambridge Ancient History*, vols. VII–IX (Cambridge 1928–32). There are convenient one-volume histories of the entire period by A. Piganiol, *La Conquête romaine* (Paris 1927), A. E. R. Boak and W. G. Sinnigen, *History of Rome to AD 565*, 6th ed. (New York 1977), M. Cary and H. H. Scullard, *History of Rome*, rev. ed. (London 1975), and M. Grant,

History of Rome (London 1979). The *Oxford Classical Dictionary*, 2nd ed. (Oxford 1970), is an invaluable work of reference.

Early Rome

The most up-to-date account in English is H. H. Scullard, *History of the Roman World 753–146 BC*, 4th ed. (London 1981). E. Gjerstad, *Early Rome*, 6 vols. (Lund 1953–75), presents all the archaeological evidence, but is unreliable in matters of interpretation. Specialized studies of early Italian archaeology (including Rome) are contained in D. and F. R. Ridgway (eds.), *Italy before the Romans* (London 1979); J. Reich, *Italy before Rome* (Oxford 1979), is a concise popular account. Also useful on early Rome: J. Heurgon, *The Rise of Rome to 264 BC* (London 1973), and R. M. Ogilvie, *Early Rome and the Etruscans* (London 1976). On the Etruscans there are good books by M. Pallottino, *The Etruscans*, 2nd ed. (London 1974), M. Cristofani, *The Etruscans* (London 1979), F. Coarelli (ed.), *Etruscan Cities* (London 1975), and M. Grant, *The Etruscans* (London 1980). E. Pulgram, *The Tongues of Italy* (Cambridge, Mass., 1958), has a good account of the languages of pre-Roman Italy.

The Republic

The best general account is M. Crawford, *The Roman Republic* (London 1978); see also A. H. McDonald, *Republican Rome* (London 1966). A. J. Toynbee, *Hannibal's Legacy*, 2 vols. (London 1966), is a wide ranging study of Roman society in the middle Republic. C. Nicolet, *Rome et la conquête du monde méditerranéen*, 2 vols. (Paris 1977–78), is the fullest modern account of the period 264–27 BC. On the fall of the Republic see R. Syme's classic, *The Roman Revolution* (Oxford 1939); also E. S. Gruen, *The Last Generation of the Roman Republic* (Berkeley, Calif., 1974), and, on the formation and attitudes of the nobility, M. Gelzer, *The Roman Nobility*, trans. R. Seager (Oxford 1975). For a clear and fully documented narrative of events see H. H. Scullard, *From the Gracchi to Nero*, 4th ed. (London 1976). Rome's conquest of Italy is seen from a regional point of view by E. T. Salmon, *Samnium and the Samnites* (Cambridge 1968), and W. V. Harris, *Rome in Etruria and Umbria* (Oxford 1971). E. T. Salmon, *Roman Colonisation under the Republic* (London 1969), is a good discussion of its subject. Juridical aspects of the conquest (and other matters) are treated in

A. N. Sherwin-White, *The Roman Citizenship*, 2nd ed. (Oxford 1973). The state of the Roman economy at the time of the Italian conquest is examined by C. G. Starr, *The Beginnings of Imperial Rome* (Ann Arbor, Mich., 1980).

On the Punic Wars see T. A. Dorey and D. R. Dudley, *Rome against Carthage* (London 1971), J. F. Lazenby, *Hannibal's War* (Warminster 1978), and B. Caven, *The Punic Wars* (London 1980). The growth of the Roman empire and the problem of Roman imperialism are dealt with by E. Badian, *Foreign Clientelae* (Oxford 1958), and *Roman Imperialism in the Late Republic* (Oxford 1968); W. V. Harris, *War and Imperialism in Republican Rome* (Oxford 1979). Notice also T. Frank, *Roman Imperialism* (New York 1914). For a clear account of the events see R. M. Errington, *The Dawn of Empire* (London 1971).

The social and economic consequences of empire are analyzed by P. A. Brunt, *Social Conflicts in the Roman Republic* (London 1971), and M. K. Hopkins, *Conquerors and Slaves* (Cambridge 1978). On the Gracchi see D. Stockton, *The Gracchi* (Oxford 1979), and A. H. Bernstein, *Tiberius Sempronius Gracchus* (Ithaca, N.Y., 1978). On the subject of slavery see M. I. Finley, *The Ancient Economy* (London 1973); J. Vogt, *Ancient Slavery and the Ideal of Man* (Oxford 1974: chapter 3 deals with the slave wars). T. Wiedemann, *Greek and Roman Slavery* (London 1981), is a collection of texts and documents in translation. The changing role of the army in the social structure of the Republic is discussed by E. Gabba, *Republican Rome: the Army and the Allies* (Oxford 1976). For a study of population figures, and of their importance for the social history of the Republic, see P. A. Brunt, *Italian Manpower 225 BC–AD 14* (Oxford 1971).

There are many good biographies of leading persons in the drama of republican history; only a selection can be given here: H. H. Scullard, *Scipio Africanus, Soldier and Politician* (London 1970); A. E. Astin, *Cato the Censor* (Oxford 1978), *Scipio Aemilianus* (Oxford 1967); P. A. L. Greenhalgh, *Pompey*, 2 vols. (London 1980–81); M. Gelzer, *Caesar* (Oxford 1969); M. Grant, *Julius Caesar* (London 1967), *Cleopatra* (London 1972); E. Rawson, *Cicero: a Portrait* (London 1975); D. R. Shackleton Bailey, *Cicero* (London 1971); W. K. Lacey, *Cicero and the End of the Roman Republic* (London 1978).

Aspects of Roman political thought and practice

C. Nicolet, *The World of the Citizen in Republican Rome* (London 1980); E. S. Staveley, *Greek and Roman Voting and Elections* (London 1972); L. R. Taylor, *Roman Voting Assemblies* (Ann Arbor, Mich., 1966); D. C. Earl, *The Moral and Political Tradition of Rome* (London 1967); C. Wirszubski, *Libertas as a Political Idea at Rome* (Cambridge 1950); E. Badian, *Publicans and Sinners* (Oxford 1972); L. R. Taylor, *Party Politics in the Age of Caesar* (Berkeley, Calif., 1966); A. W. Lintott, *Violence in Republican Rome* (Oxford 1968); J. A. Crook, *Law and Life of Rome* (London 1966); J. M. Kelly, *Roman Litigation* (Oxford 1966).

Roman society and culture

Intellectual life: R. M. Ogilvie, *Roman Literature and Society* (Harmondsworth 1980); T. Frank, *Life and Literature in the Roman Republic* (Berkeley, Calif., 1930); S. F. Bonner, *Education in Ancient Rome* (London 1977); H. I. Marrou, *A History of Education in Antiquity* (London 1956). Art and architecture: R. Bianchi Bandinelli, *Rome, the Centre of Power* (London 1970); G. M. A. Hanfmann, *Roman Art* (London 1964); D. Strong, *Roman Art* (London 1976); A. Boëthius, *Etruscan and Early Roman Architecture*, 2nd ed. (Harmondsworth 1978). Religion: R. M. Ogilvie, *The Romans and Their Gods* (London 1969); W. Warde Fowler, *The Religious Experience of the Roman People* (London 1911); H. H. Scullard, *Festivals and Ceremonies of the Roman Republic* (London 1981). The countryside: K. D. White, *Roman Farming* (London 1970); J. M. Frayn, *Subsistence Farming in Roman Italy* (Fontwell 1979); T. W. Potter, *The Changing Landscape of South Etruria* (London 1979); T. Ashby, *The Roman Campagna in Classical Times* (London 1927). The City: W. Warde Fowler, *Social Life at Rome in the Age of Cicero* (London 1922); U. E. Paoli, *Rome, Its People, Life and Customs* (New York 1963); J. Carcopino, *Daily Life in Ancient Rome* (London 1941); M. Grant, *The Roman Forum* (London 1970); S. B. Platner, T. Ashby, *A Topographical Dictionary of Ancient Rome* (Oxford 1929); E. Nash, *Pictorial Dictionary of Ancient Rome*, 2 vols., 2nd ed. (London 1968). Ostia: R. Meiggs, *Roman Ostia*, 2nd ed. (Oxford 1973); Pompeii: J. B. Ward Perkins and A. Claridge, *Pompeii AD 79* (New York 1978); M. Grant, *Cities of Vesuvius* (London 1971).

Augustus and the Julio-Claudians

The most convenient brief study of Augustus is by A. H. M. Jones, *Augustus* (London 1970); compare the more specialized discussions in his *Studies in Roman Government and Law* (Oxford 1960). Augustus' *Res Gestae* are translated and fully commented on by P. A. Brunt and J. M. Moore, *Res Gestae Divi Augusti: the Achievements of the Divine Augustus* (Oxford 1967). On Augustus' Julio-Claudian successors see B. M. Levick, *Tiberius the Politician* (London 1976), R. Seager, *Tiberius* (London 1972), A. Momigliano, *Claudius: the Emperor and His Achievement* (1934; reprinted with revised bibliography to 1959, Cambridge 1961), and B. H. Warmington, *Nero: Reality and Legend* (London 1969). Z. Yavetz, *Plebs and Princeps* (Oxford 1969), traces the political and social role of the people of Rome from late Republic to early principate. G. W. Bowersock, *Augustus and the Greek World* (Oxford 1965), studies the social, diplomatic and cultural relations of the new regime with the Greek east – compare also Fergus Millar, *The Emperor in the Roman World*, mentioned below – and Colin Wells, *The German Policy of Augustus: an Examination of the Archaeological Evidence* (Oxford 1972), its military policy on the Rhine frontier. On the literature and moral climate of Augustan Rome see Gordon Williams, *Tradition and Originality in Roman Poetry* (Oxford 1968). Miriam Griffin, *Seneca: a Philosopher in Politics* (Oxford 1976), is the best study of the problems of conscience raised by autocratic government; compare the work of Wirszubski, *Libertas* (mentioned above). Syme's *Roman Revolution* is as fundamental for the understanding of the early principate as it is for the fall of the Republic, and his marvelous *Tacitus*, 2 vols. (Oxford 1958), describes in rich detail the period covered by Tacitus – from the death of Augustus – as well as the historian's own milieu and time of writing in the Flavio-Trajanic age.

The Roman Empire, 70–306 AD

For the general history of the Empire from the Flavians to Constantine there is no real successor to H. H. Scullard's *From the Gracchi to Nero*, mentioned above. A. Garzetti, *From Tiberius to the Antonines* (Engl. ed. London 1974), covers in detail the period 14 to 192 AD, and H. M. D. Parker, *A History of the Roman World, AD 138 to 337* (2nd ed. London 1958), reaches the death of Constantine, but necessarily without reflecting recent advances in research. (It is worth noting that the familiar but now rather dated Methuen Roman histories will over the next few years be replaced by a series of new books.) The civil wars are described by K. Wellesley, *The Long Year, AD 69* (London 1975). A. R. Birley, *Septimius Severus, the African Emperor* (London 1971), is far more than a political study and also covers effectively much of the 2nd-century background. On the political and cultural history of the Flavio-Trajanic period Syme's *Tacitus* is in all ways fundamental, as, still, are his chapters on military history in the *Cambridge Ancient History*, vols. X and XI (1934 and 1936). On Trajan's wars L. Rossi, *Trajan's Column and the Dacian Wars* (London 1971), is full and most informative but with sometimes mediocre photographs. For the history and culture of Rome's eastern neighbor see R. Ghirshman, *Iran, from the Earliest Times to the Islamic Conquest* (Harmondsworth 1954) and *Iran: Parthians and Sassanians* (London 1962), and for Rome's eastern relations in their geographical and social context Freya Stark, *Rome on the Euphrates: the Story of a Frontier* (London 1966). The "anarchy" of the 3rd century is discussed in various works, notably the major books of Rostovtzeff and A. H. M. Jones mentioned below, and by R. MacMullen, *Roman Government's Response to Crisis, AD 235–337* (New Haven, Conn., and London 1976), and by Syme, *Emperors and Biography* (Oxford 1971).

On the role of the emperor in government and the development of governmental institutions and administrative hierarchies, see especially Fergus Millar, *The Emperor in the Roman World, 31 BC–AD 337* (London 1977). Millar may overstate the continuity of the conduct of the imperial office over this period and understate the impact of changing military needs on the emperors' role, on which see the absorbing study of E. N. Luttwak, *The Grand Strategy of the Roman Empire, from the First Century AD to the Third* (Baltimore, Md., and London 1976), and the very different perspective of R. MacMullen, *Soldier and Civilian in the Later Roman Empire* (Cambridge, Mass., 1963).

On the provincial prosperity of the Empire Gibbon's *Decline and Fall*, Chap. II, is still remarkable for its perceptiveness, and for its appreciation of the potential of archaeological and epigraphic evidence. The revolution in historical method made possible by the systematic study of material remains was essentially the work of Mommsen, substantial extracts from whose *Provinces of the Roman Empire* of 1885 are available in paperback with a useful introduction by T. R. S. Broughton (Chicago, Ill., and London 1968). Also fundamental, and incorporating a still wider range of material evidence, is M. Rostovtzeff, *The Social and Economic History of the Roman Empire* (2nd ed. by P. M. Fraser, Oxford 1957). The work of Mommsen is well appreciated by G. P. Gooch in *History and Historians in the Nineteenth Century* (2nd ed. London 1952), Chap. XXIV, and that of Rostovtzeff by A. Momigliano in his *Studies in Historiography* (London 1966), Chap. 5. For a comprehensive account of the regions of the Empire, with much citation of ancient sources, see Tenney Frank and others, *An Economic Survey of Ancient Rome*, 5 vols. (Baltimore, Md., 1933–40), and for a brief survey of its institutions and provincial diversities, Fergus Millar, *The Roman Empire and Its Neighbours* (2nd ed. London 1981). M. P. Charlesworth, *The Roman Empire* (Oxford 1951, reprinted with new bibliography, Oxford 1968), is also useful. The opportunities for economic and cultural life provided by the Roman pacification of the Mediterranean, and also the physical limitations imposed by natural conditions, are treated by L. Casson, *Ships and Seamanship in the Ancient World* (Princeton, N.J., 1971) and *Travel in the Ancient World* (London 1974); and the conditions of agricultural production by K. D. White in *Roman Farming* (London 1970), *Agricultural Implements of the Roman World* (Cambridge 1967) and *Farm Equipment of the Roman World* (Cambridge 1975). See also the *Oxford History of Technology*, Vol. II, edited by Charles Singer and others (Oxford 1956).

The changing nature of legal privilege in the context of the extension of the citizenship is studied by Peter Garnsey, *Social Status and Legal Privilege in the Roman Empire* (Oxford 1970), and by A. N. Sherwin-White, *The Roman Citizenship* (2nd ed. Oxford 1973); see also J. A. Crook, *Law and Life of Rome* (London 1967). R. Duncan-Jones, *The Economy of the Roman Empire: Quantitative Studies* (Cambridge 1974), provides excellent discussions of many aspects of civic munificence, especially on the cost of public works, and many useful papers by A. H. M. Jones are collected in his *The Roman Economy*, ed. P. A. Brunt (Oxford 1974). Syme's *Tacitus* (see above) is particularly good on the enlargement of the Roman governing class by provincial recruitment; see also his *Colonial Elites: Rome, Spain and the Americas* (London 1958).

On the prestige of rhetoric and its role in public communications, three recent books are especially notable: G. W. Bowersock, *Greek Sophists in the Roman Empire* (Oxford 1969); T. D. Barnes, *Tertullian: a Historical and Literary Study* (Oxford 1971); and E. Champlin, *Fronto and Antonine Rome* (Princeton, N.J., 1980). The attitudes of educated Greeks under Roman rule are discussed by C. P. Jones in *Plutarch and Rome* (Oxford 1971) and *The Roman World of Dio Chrysostom* (Cambridge, Mass., and London 1978), and by Fergus Millar, *A Study of Cassius Dio* (Oxford 1964).

On the huge topic of religious change and the rise of Christianity, a brief selection must suffice to convey the essentials. A. D. Nock, *Conversion: the Old and the New in Religion, from Alexander the Great to Augustine of Hippo* (Oxford 1933 and 1952), provides an introduction to new forms of religious experience, and F. Cumont, *Oriental Religions in Roman Paganism* (1911; reprinted New York 1956) and *The Mysteries of Mithras* (1903; reprinted New York 1956), still provides perhaps the most authoritative general treatment, despite recent criticism of some of his theories. See also E. R. Dodds, *Pagan and Christian in an Age of Anxiety* (Cambridge 1965), discussed, with the book of Frend mentioned below, by Peter Brown, *Religion and Society in the Age of St Augustine* (London 1972). Peter Brown's own *The Making of Late Antiquity* (Cambridge, Mass., and London 1978) tends, like much other recent work, to seek the origins of the new religious developments in the 2nd rather than in the 3rd century. J. H. W. G. Liebeschuetz, *Continuity and Change in Roman Religion* (Oxford 1979), is immensely rewarding for its care and thoughtfulness over a full four centuries of Roman religious experience. The best general description of the theory and practice of theurgy is by E. R. Dodds in his *The Greeks and the Irrational* (Berkeley, Calif., and London 1968), Appendix II.

On the rise of Christianity, W. H. C. Frend, *Martyrdom and Persecution in the Early Church* (Oxford 1965), is one of the most stimulating of all discussions of the subject, and H. Chadwick, *The Early Church* (Harmondsworth 1967), is clear, comprehensive and broad in scope. The two chapters of Gibbon, *Decline and Fall*, Chaps. XV and XVI, have survived the years marvelously well, and still make a fine introduction whose main lines are inherent in modern study. T. D. Barnes's *Tertullian*, mentioned above, is not only learned and precise but very vigorous and stimulating on the broader issues.

The Provinces of the Empire

On the provinces of the Empire, general surveys are provided by the works of Mommsen, Rostovtzeff, Millar and Tenney Frank mentioned above under "provincial prosperity of the Empire." For reference on individual sites, particularly useful are the *Princeton Encyclopaedia of Classical Sites*, ed. R. Stilwell and others (Princeton, N. J., 1976), and *Atlas of Classical Archaeology*, ed. M. I. Finley (London 1977). Both works contain bibliographical references and the latter has site plans and photographs.

As to books on individual provinces it is worth mentioning the series *Provinces of the Roman Empire* under the general editorship of S. S. Frere. This includes to date J. J. Wilkes, *Dalmatia* (London 1969), A. Mócsy, *Pannonia and Upper Moesia; a History of the Middle Danubian Provinces of the Roman Empire* (London 1974), G. Alföldy, *Noricum* (London 1974), and Sheppard Frere, *Britannia* (rev. ed. London 1978). See in addition C. H. V. Sutherland, *The Romans in Spain* (London 1939); Olwen Brogan, *Roman Gaul* (London 1963); Peter Salway, *Roman Britain* (Oxford 1981), and – among many other histories of Roman Britain – A. L. F. Rivet, *Town and Country in Roman Britain* (London 1958, reprinted 1966); P. Oliva, *Pannonia and the Onset of Crisis in the Roman Empire* (Prague 1962); R. F. Hoddinott, *Bulgaria in Antiquity: an Archaeological Introduction* (London 1975). On the eastern provinces: A. H. M. Jones, *The Greek City, from Alexander to Justinian* (rev. ed. Oxford 1966), and *The Cities of the Eastern Roman Provinces* (2nd ed. Oxford 1971); B. M. Levick, *Roman Colonies in Southern Asia Minor* (Oxford 1967); and various books by George Bean: *Aegean Turkey: an Archaeological Guide* (2nd ed. London 1979), *Turkey beyond the Maeander* (2nd ed. London 1980), *Lycian Turkey* (London 1978) and *Turkey's Southern Shore* (2nd ed. London 1979). J. H. W. G. Liebeschuetz, *Antioch: City and Imperial Administration in the Later Roman Empire* (Oxford 1972), has much also on the Syrian background. On Egypt, as well as the excellent chapter in Jones's *Cities of the Eastern Roman Provinces*, there is the brief account of H. Idris Bell, *Egypt, from Alexander the Great to the Arab Conquest: a Study in the Diffusion and Decay of Hellenism* (Oxford 1948).

The following are a selection of some of the more accessible works on the sites featured in the Atlas, arranged in the order of their appearance: D. E. L. Haynes, *The Antiquities of Tripolitania* (London 1955); R. Bianchi Bandinelli and others, *The Buried City: Excavations at Lepcis Magna* (Eng. trans. London 1970); E. M. Wightman, *Trier and the Treveri* (London 1970); G. C. Boon, *Silchester; the Roman Town of Calleva* (rev. ed. Newton Abbott 1974); B. Cunliffe, *Fishbourne: a Roman Palace and its Gardens* (London 1971); E. Vorbeck, L. Beckel, *Carnuntum: Rom an der Donau* (Salzburg 1973; in German, but with splendid aerial photographs, of which one is shown above, p. 143); J. and T. Marasović, *Diocletian Palace at Split* (Zagreb 1968); J. Travlos, *Pictorial Dictionary of Ancient Athens* (London and New York 1971); R. Day, *An Economic History of Athens under Roman Domination* (New York 1942). Research on the site of Ephesus is conducted by an Austrian school and the literature is almost all in German, but two books are worth recommending to English readers for their fine illustrations: W. Alzinger, *Die Ruine von Ephesos* (Berlin and Vienna 1972), and E. Lessing, W. Oberleitner, *Ephesos, Weltstadt der Antike* (Vienna and Heidelberg 1978). There is, however, a study of late Roman and Byzantine Ephesus in English: Clive Foss, *Ephesus after Antiquity: a Late Antique, Byzantine and Turkish City* (Cambridge 1979).

On the cities of the Orient: K. Michałowski, *Palmyra* (Eng. trans. London 1970); Iain Browning, *Palmyra* (London 1979); M. A. R. Colledge, *The Art of Palmyra* (London 1976). Robert Wood's *The Ruins of Palmyra, otherwise Tedmor, in the Desart*, of 1753, has been reproduced photographically (Farnborough 1971). See also J. Jeremias, *Jerusalem in the Time of Jesus* (Eng. trans. London 1969); Y. Yadin, *Masada: Herod's Fortress and the Zealots' Last Stand* (London 1966); M. Rostovtzeff, *Dura-Europos and Its Art* (Oxford 1938); A. Perkins, *The Art of Dura-Europos* (Oxford 1973); Clark Hopkins, *The Discovery of Dura-Europos* (New Haven, Conn., and London 1979); F. Ragette, *Baalbeck* (London 1980); N. Jidejian, *Baalbek: Heliopolis, "City of the Sun"* (Beirut 1975); Iain Browning, *Petra* (London 1973); and R. G. Goodchild, *Cyrene and Apollonia* (London 1963).

The Late Empire: Constantine to Justinian

There is no really good modern concise account of this period in English. Apart from the incomparable narrative presentation of Gibbon – abridged by D. M. Low (London 1960) – the best of the older accounts is perhaps that of J. B. Bury, *History of the Later Roman Empire, from the Death of Theodosius I to the Death of Justinian (AD 395 to 565)*, 2 vols. (London 1923, reprinted New York 1958). By far the best modern account of the 4th century is that of André Piganiol, *L'Empire chrétien* (2nd ed. by A. Chastagnol, Paris 1972), and of the 5th and 6th centuries the very good, though rather austere, work of E. Stein, *Histoire du bas-empire* (2nd ed. and trans. by J.-R. Palanque, Paris and Bruges 1959; reprinted Amsterdam 1968). The massive work of A. H. M. Jones, *The Later Roman Empire 284–602; a Social, Economic and Administrative Survey*, 3 vols. and maps (Oxford 1964; reprinted in 2 vols., Oxford 1973), is presented in abbreviated form in *The Decline of the Ancient World* (London 1966; reprinted 1975). Jones's work is notable above all for its appreciation of the bureaucratic nature of the late Roman state and also of the limitations of its power, and for his cool assessment of the reasons for its decline. In a totally different style, Peter Brown, *The World of Late Antiquity, from Marcus Aurelius to Muhammad* (London 1971), is a particularly challenging thematic study, skillfully illustrated.

Of individual emperors in this period, Constantine, Julian and Justinian have naturally attracted most attention: see on Constantine N. H. Baynes, *Constantine the Great and the Christian Church* (London 1931; reprinted with preface and bibliography by Henry Chadwick, Oxford 1972); A. H. M. Jones, *Constantine and the Conversion of Europe* (London 1948); R. MacMullen, *Constantine* (London 1970); A. Alföldi, *The Conversion of Constantine and Pagan Rome* (Oxford 1948, reprinted 1969). On Julian, recent biographies include those of R. Browning, *The Emperor Julian* (London 1975), and, with emphasis on Julian's character, G. W. Bowersock, *Julian the Apostate* (London 1978); though J. Bidez's *L'Empereur Julien* (Paris 1930; reprinted 1965) remains the most economically penetrating of studies, especially strong on the intellectual and religious background of Julian. On Justinian, R. Browning, *Justinian and Theodora* (London 1971).

Other works on the political and social history of the age include A. Alföldi, *A Conflict of Ideas in the Late Roman Empire: the Clash between the Senate and Valentinian I* (Oxford 1952) – extremely vivid, especially on the atmosphere of "terrorism" of late Roman government, though in some ways unreliable in its judgments – and John Matthews, *Western Aristocracies and Imperial Court, AD 364–425* (Oxford 1975). This is a study of the social context of the politics of the period but presents the narrative background and touches various other aspects of the age, especially the issue of Christianization (see below).

The literary and religious history of late antiquity is studied in several recent works, notably Peter Brown's wonderful *Augustine of Hippo* (London 1967), Alan Cameron's *Claudian: Poetry and Propaganda at the Court of Honorius* (Oxford 1970) and J. N. D. Kelly, *Jerome: His Life, Writings and Controversies* (London 1975). M. W. Binns (ed.), *Latin Literature of the Fourth Century* (London and Boston, Mass., 1974), contains chapters by different authors on Ausonius, Symmachus, Paulinus of Nola, Claudian and Prudentius, and on the religious and cultural background of their work. R. Syme, *Ammianus and the Historia Augusta* (Oxford 1968), ranges widely and to great effect among the varied literary products of the late 4th century. N. K. Chadwick, *Poetry and Letters in Early Christian Gaul* (London 1955), presents accounts of later 4th- and 5th-century writers, and the 5th-century poet and bishop, Sidonius Apollinaris, is the subject of C. E. Stevens's *Sidonius Apollinaris and His Age* (Oxford 1933). The Latin writers of the early 6th century have received recent attention from J. J. O'Donnell, *Cassiodorus* (Berkeley, Calif., and London 1979), Henry Chadwick, *Boethius: the Consolations of Music, Logic, Theology and Philosophy* (Oxford 1981), and in the symposium edited by Margaret Gibson, *Boethius: His Life, Thought and Influence* (Oxford 1981). Despite much specialized work, there are still in English no substantial general studies of writers as important as Ammianus Marcellinus and Procopius; on the first of these, however, E. A. Thompson, *The Historical Work of Ammianus Marcellinus* (Cambridge 1947), is one of the essential foundations for such study.

On late Roman art and ceremonial and responses to it, see the varying approaches and interpretations of H. P. L'Orange, *Art Forms and Civic Life in the Late Roman Empire* (Eng. trans. Princeton, N.J., 1965), R. Bianchi Bandinelli, *Rome: the Late Empire. Roman Art AD 200–400* (London 1971) – lavishly illustrated; S. MacCormack, *Art and Ceremony in Late Antiquity* (Berkeley, Calif., and London 1981); A. Grabar, *The Beginnings of Christian Art* (London 1967) and *Christian Iconography: a Study of Its Origins* (London 1969); and Gervase Mathew, *Byzantine Aesthetics* (London 1963).

The theme of the Christianization of the Empire is developed by F. van der Meer and Christine Mohrmann, *Atlas of the Early Christian World* (Eng. trans. London 1966), and by Diana Bowder, *The Age of Constantine and Julian* (London 1978), a useful introduction to the visual and archaeological evidence for the religious changes of the 4th century. A. Momigliano (ed.), *The Conflict between Paganism and Christianity in the Fourth Century* (Oxford 1963), contains some excellent papers on various aspects of this theme, as, still more so, does Peter Brown, *Religion and Society in the Age of St Augustine* (London 1972), a collection of the author's learned but vividly readable articles spanning the years 1961–70.

In the absence of any modern study of comparable scope, the classic of J. Geffcken, *The Last Days of Greco-Roman Paganism* (trans. S. MacCormack, Amsterdam, New York and Oxford 1978), remains fundamental; see also R. MacMullen, *Paganism in the Roman Empire* (New Haven, Conn., and London 1981). Though its central thesis has been challenged – though not abandoned by its author – W. H. C. Frend's *The Donatist Church: a Movement of Protest in Roman North Africa* (Oxford 1952; reprinted with additional bibliography 1971) remains a fine description of the effects of Christianization on the morale and integrity of an established church in its relations with a schismatic sect. On the duties and preoccupations of a bishop, F. van der Meer, *Augustine the Bishop* (Eng. trans. London 1961; reprinted 1978), is full and circumstantial, and on the ascetic movement Philip Rousseau, *Ascetics, Authority and the Church in the Age of Jerome and Cassian* (Oxford 1978), is a book which repays the closest attention and reflection. On the actual modes of the ascetic life, see for Egypt D. Chitty, *The Desert a City* (Oxford 1966), and for Syria A. Vööbus, *A History of Asceticism in the Syrian Orient*, Vol. II (Louvain 1960). Peter Brown's *The Cult of the Saints: Its Use and Function in Latin Christianity* (London 1981), is, as always, an arresting and profound, if at times rather intangible, treatment. One particularly interesting facet of Christianization, pilgrimage, is described and put into its cultural context by E. D. Hunt, *Holy Land Pilgrimage in the Later Roman Empire AD 312–460* (Oxford 1982).

For late imperial and early Christian Rome see R. Krautheimer, *Rome: Profile of a City 312–1308* (Princeton, N.J., 1980), and in general his *Early Christian and Byzantine Architecture* (3rd ed. Harmondsworth 1979); W. Oakeshott, *The Mosaics of Rome, from the Third to the Fourteenth Centuries* (London 1967). The fullest historical account of early Christian Rome is in French, by Ch. Piétri, *Roma Christiana: recherches sur l'Église de Rome, son organisation, sa politique, son idéologie, de Miltiade à Sixte II (311–440)*, 2 vols. (Paris and Rome 1978). On Ravenna, L. von Matt, *Ravenna* (Cologne 1971), with text, in German, by S. Bovini, but with splendid photographs. For Christianity and paganism in the life of 4th-century Antioch (and many other aspects of urban life) J. H. W. G. Liebeschuetz, *Antioch: City and Imperial Administration in the Later Roman Empire* (Oxford 1972), and for the life of a rapidly Christianized city J. B. Segal, *Edessa: the "Blessed City"* (Oxford 1970). Late Roman Jerusalem is described by Ch. Couäsnon, O.P., *The Church of the Holy Sepulchre in Jerusalem* (London 1974), and by J. Wilkinson, *Egeria's Travels: Newly Translated with Supporting Documents and Notes* (London 1971). The social life of Constantinople is explored by G. Downey, *Constantinople in the Age of Justinian* (London 1964), and by Alan Cameron, *Porphyrius the Charioteer* (Oxford 1971); cf. his *Circus Factions: Blues and Greens at Rome and Byzantium* (Oxford 1976).

On the barbarian invaders of the Roman Empire there are three especially illuminating books by E. A. Thompson: *A History of Attila and the Huns* (Oxford 1948), *The Visigoths in the Time of Ulfila* (Oxford 1966) and *The Goths in Spain* (Oxford 1969). Fifth-century relations between Rome and Constantinople are the theme of W. E. Kaegi, *Byzantium and the Decline of Rome* (Princeton, N.J., 1968); the background to the 6th-century reconquest is described in the books on Boethius and Cassiodorus mentioned above. For the barbarian settlements and the formation of the early medieval west see J. M. Wallace-Hadrill, *The Barbarian West 400–1000* (rev. ed. London 1967), and the various papers in his *The Long-Haired Kings* (London 1962); and W. Goffart, *Barbarians and Romans, AD 418–584: the Techniques of Accommodation* (Princeton, N.J., 1980).

GAZETTEER

Aalen (W. Germany), 48°50′N, 10°07′E, 108
Aballava (U.K.), (Burgh by Sands), 54°56′N 3°03′W, 135
Aballo (France), (Avallon), 47°30′N 3°54′E, 129
Abdera (Greece), 40°56′N 24°59′E, 146
Abdera (Spain), (Adra), 36°45′N 3°01′W, 124
Abella 40°59′N 14°37′E, 67
Abellinum (Avellino), 40°49′N 14°47′E, 41, 46, 62, 67
Abira (Syria), 34°11′N 37°36′E, 174
Abonuteichus (Turkey), (Inebolu), 41°57′N 33°45′E, 150
Abrittus (Bulgaria), 43°31′N 26°33′E, 140, 171
Abudiacum (W. Germany), (Epfach), 47°57′N 10°37′E, 140
Abusina (W. Germany), (Eining), 48°51′N 11°47′E, 108, 140
Abydus (Turkey), 40°08′N 26°25′E, 150
Acadama (Syria), 35°06′N 38°26′E, 174
Acanthus (Greece), 40°22′N 23°52′E, 146
Acci (Spain), (Guadix), 37°19′N 3°08′E, 72, 124
Acerrae 45°13′N 9°42′E, 62
Achaiacala (Iraq), (Al Hadithah), 34°09′N 42°22′E, 191
Acidava (Romania), 44°32′N 24°14′E, 140
Acquacetosa Laurentina 41°46′N 12°30′E, 30
Acquarossa 42°31′N 12°05′E, 21
Acrae (Sicily), (Palazzolo Acreide), 37°04′N 14°54′E, 23, 45
Acraephia (Greece), 38°27′N 23°13′E, 146
Acruvium (Yugoslavia), 42°27′N 18°46′E, 72, 140
Actium, C (Greece), 38°56′N 20°46′E, 146
Adada (Syria), 35°08′N 39°03′E, 174
Adana (Turkey), (Ataniya), 37°00′N 35°19′E, 150
Ad Aras (Spain), 38°44′N 0°39′W, 124
Adda R *see* Addua R
Addua R (Adda R), 10, 29
Adige R, 10, 140
Ad Maiores (Tunisia), 34°23′N 7°54′E, 118
Ad Mediam (Romania), (Mehadia), 44°53′N 22°20′E, 140
Adour R (France), 129
Ad Pontem (Austria), (Lind), 46°47′N 13°22′E, 140
Adraa (Syria), (Dera), 32°37′N 36°06′E, 157
Adramyttium (Turkey), (Edremit), 39°34′N 27°01′E, 150
Adria 45°03′N 12°04′E, 21
Adys *see* Uthina
Aecae 41°21′N 15°20′E, 40, 46
Aeclanum 41°04′N 14°57′E, 41, 62
Aedepsus (Euboea Isl), (Greece), 38°53′N 23°03′E, 146
Aefula (Monte Sant'Angelo), 41°56′N 12°49′E, 27, 30
Aegae (Turkey), 38°54′N 27°13′E, 150
Aegina (Aegina Isl), (Greece), 37°45′N 23°26′E, 47
Aegina (Isl), (Greece), 37°43′N 23°30′E, 146
Aegium (Greece), (Aigion), 38°15′N 22°05′E, 146
Aegyssus (Romania), 45°09′N 28°50′E, 140
Aelia Capitolina *see* Hierosolyma
Aeminium (Portugal), (Coimbra), 40°12′N 8°25′W, 124
Aenona (Yugoslavia), 44°13′N 15°10′E, 72, 140
Aenus (Turkey), (Enez), 40°44′N 26°05′E, 140
Aequum (Yugoslavia), 43°47′N 16°49′E, 140
Aequum Tuticum 41°15′N 15°05′E, 62
Aesernia 41°35′N 14°14′E, 35, 41, 46, 62
Aesica (U.K.), (Great Chesters), 55°03′N 2°06′W, 135
Aesium 43°38′N 13°24′E, 35
Aeso (Spain), (Avella), 42°02′N 1°07′E, 124
Aezani (Turkey), 39°12′N 29°28′E, 150
Agathe (France), (Agde), 43°19′N 3°29′E, 23, 129
Agedincum (France), (Senones), (Sens), 48°12′N 3°18′E, 70, 129, 192
Aginnum (France), (Agen), 44°12′N 0°38′E, 129
Agri R, 10
Agrigentum (Sicily), (Agrigento), 37°19′N 13°35′E, 23, 45, 47, 57, 72
Aguntum (Austria), 46°51′N 12°51′E, 140
Aila (Israel), (Elat), 29°33′N 34°57′E, 157, 164
Aisne R (France), 129
Ajaccio (Corsica), 41°55′N 8°43′E, 10, 12
Akheloos R (Greece), 146
Alabanda (Turkey), 37°40′N 27°55′E, 150
Alalia *see* Aleria
Alauna (U.K.), (Maryport), 54°43′N 3°30′W, 135
Alba (France), (Aps), 44°15′N 4°30′E, 129
Alba Fucens 42°03′N 13°27′E, 35, 38, 40, 47, 62
Alba Longa (Castel Gandolfo), 41°45′N 12°38′E, 27, 30, 200
Albitimilium (Ventimiglia), 43°47′N 7°37′E, 129
Albucciu (Sardinia), 41°03′N 9°25′E, 20
Alburnus Maior (Romania), 46°16′N 23°05′E, 140
Alcantara (Spain), 39°44′N 6°53′W, 124
Alcester (U.K.), 52°13′N 1°52′W, 135
Alchester (U.K.), 51°55′N 1°07′W, 135
Aleria (Corsica), (Alalia), 42°05′N 9°30′E, 23, 39, 47, 72, 107
Alesia (France), (Alise), 47°33′N 4°30′E, 70, 129
Aletrium (Alatri), 41°44′N 13°21′E, 30, 35, 40, 62
Aletum (France), 48°42′N 1°52′W, 199
Alexander ad Issum (Turkey), (Iskenderun), 36°37′N 36°08′E, 157
Alexandria (Egypt), 31°13′N 29°55′E, 60, 70, 75, 84, 107, 111, 164, 171, 173, 179, 199
Alexandria Troas (Turkey), 39°31′N 26°08′E, 72, 150
Alfios R (Greece), 146
Algido 41°48′N 12°46′E, 30
Aliakmon R (Greece), 146
Alinda (Turkey), (Karpuzlu), 37°35′N 27°49′E, 150
Allier R (France), 129
Allifae (Alife), 41°20′N 14°20′E, 62, 67, 200
Alsium (Palo), 41°54′N 12°06′E, 35
Altava (Algeria), 34°43′N 0°55′W, 118
Althiburus (Tunisia), 35°51′N 8°40′E, 118
Altinum 45°33′N 12°24′E, 38
Altrip (W. Germany), 49°28′N 8°26′E, 192
Alvona (Yugoslavia), 45°05′N 14°11′E, 140
Alzey (W. Germany), 49°44′N 8°07′E, 192
Amaro, Mt 42°05′N 14°06′E, 10
Amasea (Turkey), (Amasya), 40°37′N 35°50′E, 60, 150, 220
Amastris (Turkey), 41°44′N 32°24′E, 107, 150
Amathus (Cyprus), 34°42′N 33°09′E, 150
Ambracia (Yugoslavia), 39°10′N 20°59′E 146
Amiata, Mt 42°53′N 11°57′E, 10
Amida (Turkey), (Diyarbakir), 37°55′N 40°14′E, 150, 220
Amisus (Turkey), (Samsun), 41°17′N 36°22′E, 150
Amiternum 42°20′N 13°24′E, 38, 40, 62
Ammaedara (Tunisia), (Haidra), 35°32′N 8°25′E, 118
Amorgos (Isl), (Greece), 36°49′N 25°54′E, 150
Amorium (Turkey), 38°58′N 31°12′E, 150
Ampelum (Romania), 46°08′N 23°13′E, 140
Amphipolis (Greece), 40°48′N 23°52′E, 146
Amphissa (Greece), 38°32′N 22°22′E, 146
Ampurias *see* Emporiae
Anagnia 41°44′N 13°10′E, 30, 35, 40, 62
Anas R (Portugal/Spain), (Guadiana R), 47, 72, 75, 124, 173, 208
Anatha (Iraq), (Anah), 34°29′N 41°57′E, 191, 220
Anazarbus (Turkey), 37°09′N 35°46′E, 150, 220
Anchialus (Bulgaria), (Pomorie), 42°43′N 27°39′E, 140
Ancona 43°37′N 13°31′E, 10, 12, 20, 38, 41, 67
Ancyra (Turkey), (Ankara), 39°55′N 32°50′E, 75, 107, 150
Andautonia (Yugoslavia), (Scitarjevo), 45°49′N 16°13′E, 140
Andematunnum (France), (Langres), 47°53′N 5°20′E, 129
Anderita (U.K.), (Pevensey), 50°47′N 0°20′E, 135, 171
Anderitum (France), (Javols), 44°43′N 3°17′E, 129
Andetrium (Yugoslavia), 43°46′N 16°39′E, 140
Andros (Isl), (Greece), 37°49′N 24°54′E, 146
Anemurium (Turkey), (Anamur), 36°06′N 32°49′E, 150
Angustia (Romania), 46°03′N 26°19′E, 140
Anio R, 27, 30
Annesoi (Turkey), 40°15′N 35°37′E, 199
Antaeopolis (Egypt), 26°54′N 31°31′E, 164
Antaradus (Syria), 34°55′N 35°52′E, 157
Antemnae 41°54′N 12°30′E, 27, 30
Anthedon (Greece), 38°29′N 23°28′E, 146
Anticaria (Spain), (Antequera), 37°01′N 4°34′W, 124
Antinonopolis (Turkey), (Constantina), 37°19′N 39°26′E, 157, 220
Antinoopolis (Egypt), 27°49′N 30°53′E, 164
Antiochia (Turkey), 38°18′N 31°09′E, 72, 150
Antiochia (Turkey), (Antakya), 36°12′N 36°10′E, 60, 70, 75, 84, 107, 111, 150, 157, 171, 173, 174, 179, 220
Antipolis (France), (Antibes), 43°35′N 7°07′E, 129
Antium (Anzio), 41°27′N 12°38′E, 27, 30, 35, 200
Antunnacum (W. Germany), (Andernach), 50°26′N 7°24′E, 108, 129, 192
Apamea (Syria), 35°31′N 36°23′E, 157, 174, 220
Apamea (Turkey), 40°24′N 28°46′E, 72
Apamea (Turkey), (Birecik), 37°03′N 37°59′E, 150, 157
Aphrodisias (Turkey), 40°39′N 26°53′E, 140
Aphrodisias (Turkey), 37°43′N 28°50′E, 150
Apollinopolis Magna (Egypt), 24°59′N 32°52′E, 164
Apollonia (Albania), 40°40′N 19°28′E, 70, 146
Apollonia (Bulgaria), (Sozopol), 42°23′N 27°42′E, 47, 140
Apollonia (Israel), 32°13′N 34°49′E, 157
Apollonia (Libya), (Marsa Susah), 32°52′N 21°59′E, 164
Apollonia (Turkey), 39°07′N 27°31′E, 150
Apri (Turkey), (Theodosiopolis), 40°57′N 27°04′E, 140
Apsorus (Yugoslavia), 44°41′N 14°29′E, 140
Apulum (Romania), (Alba Iulia), 46°04′N 23°33′E, 140
Aquae (W. Germany), (Baden Baden), 48°45′N 8°15′E, 108, 129
Aquae Arnemetiae (U.K.), (Buxton), 53°15′N 1°55′W, 135
Aquae Calidae (Algeria), 36°24′N 2°14′E, 72, 118
Aquae Convenarum (France), (Bagnères-de-Bigorre), 43°04′N 0°09′E, 129
Aquae Flaviae (Portugal), (Chaves), 41°44′N 7°28′W, 124
Aquae Mattiacae (W. Germany), (Wiesbaden), 50°05′N 8°15′E, 108, 129, 192
Aquae Neri (France), (Néris-les-Bains), 46°18′N 2°38′E, 129
Aquae Regiae (Tunisia), 35°42′N 9°58′E, 118
Aquae S . . . (Yugoslavia), 43°40′N 18°17′E, 140
Aquae Sextiae (France), (Aix-en-Provence), 43°31′N 5°27′E, 60, 129
Aquae Sulis (U.K.), (Bath), 51°23′N 2°22′W, 135
Aquae Tarbellicae (France), (Dax), 43°43′N 1°03′W, 129
Aquileia 45°47′N 13°22′E, 29, 38, 47, 49, 60, 75, 84, 107, 171, 173, 179, 199, 208, 214
Aquileia (W. Germany), (Heidenheim), 48°41′N 10°10′E, 108
Aquilonia 40°59′N 15°30′E, 35, 62
Aquincum (Hungary), (Budapest), 47°30′N 19°03′E, 107, 140
Aquinum (Aquino), 41°27′N 13°42′E, 40, 67
Arabissus (Turkey), 38°12′N 36°54′E, 150
Arabona (Hungary), (Gyor), 47°41′N 17°40′E, 140
Araceli (Spain), (Araquil), 42°58′N 2°10′W, 124
Arae Flaviae (W. Germany), (Rottweil), 48°10′N 8°38′E, 108, 129
Arapus R (Sicily), 45
Arar R (France), (Saône R), 129, 192
ad Aras (Spain), 38°44′N 0°39′W, 124
Arausio (France), (Orange), 44°08′N 4°48′E, 47, 60, 72, 129
Araxes R (U.S.S.R./Turkey), 220
Arba (Yugoslavia), 44°46′N 14°47′E, 72, 140
Arbor Felix (Switzerland), (Arbon), 47°31′N 9°27′E, 140
Archeopolis (U.S.S.R.), 42°20′N 41°53′E, 220
Arcidava (Romania), (Varadia), 45°02′N 21°43′E, 140
Arcobriga (Spain), (Arixa) 41°09′N 2°26′W, 124
Ardea 41°36′N 12°33′E, 27, 30, 35, 67, 200
Arelate (France), (Arles), 43°41′N 4°38′E, 70, 72, 129, 171, 173, 179, 199, 208, 214
Arethusa (Syria), 34°56′N 36°47′E, 157
Arezzo *see* Arretium
Argentomagus (France), (Argenton), 48°32′N 4°45′W, 129
Argentorate (France), (Strasbourg), 48°35′N 7°45′E, 108, 129, 192, 214
Argos (Greece), 37°38′N 22°42′E, 146
Argyruntum 44°18′N 15°21′E, 140
Aricia (Ariccia), 41°43′N 12°41′E, 27, 30
Arienzo 41°02′N 14°30′E, 57
Ariminum (Rimini), 44°03′N 12°34′E, 10, 29, 35, 38, 41, 67, 70
Arno R *see* Arnus R
Arnus R (Arno R), 10, 14, 20, 21, 23, 29, 35, 49, 57, 67
Arpi 41°34′N 15°32′E, 35, 40, 41, 46, 62
Arpinum (Arpino), 41°38′N 13°37′E, 40, 62
Arretium (Arezzo), 43°28′N 11°53′E, 10, 21, 29, 35, 38, 41, 62, 67, 70
Arsanias R (Turkey), 220
Arsenaria (Algeria), 36°25′N 0°37′E, 118
Arsinoe (Cyprus), 34°55′N 32°26′E, 150
Arsinoe (Egypt), 29°19′N 30°50′E, 164
Aruccis (Spain), (Aroche), 37°56′N 6°57′W, 124
Arunda (Spain), (Ronda), 36°45′N 5°10′W, 124
Arycanda (Turkey), 36°33′N 30°01′E, 150
Arzen (Turkey), 38°00′N 41°47′E, 150
Ascalon (Israel), 31°39′N 34°35′E, 157
Asculum (Ascoli Piceno), 42°52′N 13°35′E, 38, 41, 62, 67
Asemus (Bulgaria), 43°38′N 24°55′E, 140
Ashtishat (Turkey), 38°45′N 41°26′E, 199
Asido (Spain), 36°28′N 5°55′W, 72
Asine (Greece), (Koroni), 36°48′N 21°57′E, 146
Asisium (Assisi), 43°04′N 12°37′E, 41
Asopus (Greece), 36°40′N 22°51′E, 146
Aspalathos (Yugoslavia), (Split), 43°31′N 16°28′E, 10, 140
Aspendus (Turkey), (Serik), 36°55′N 31°06′E, 150
Asperden (W. Germany), 51°45′N 6°09′E, 192
Asseria (Yugoslavia), 44°02′N 15°40′E, 140
Assuras (Tunisia), 36°00′N 9°03′E, 72
Assus (Turkey), 39°32′N 26°21′E, 150
Astigi (Spain), (Ecija), 37°33′N 5°04′W, 72, 124
Astura (Austria), (Zeiselmauer), 48°20′N 16°05′E, 140
Astura 41°24′N 12°42′E, 30
Asturica Augusta (Spain), (Astorga), 42°27′N 6°04′W, 124
Astypalaea (Isl), (Greece), 36°32′N 26°23′E, 150
Atella 40°56′N 14°13′E, 46, 62
Aternus R, 35, 40, 41, 200
Ateste (Este), 45°13′N 11°40′E, 20, 29, 67
Athenae (Greece), (Athens), 38°00′N 23°44′E, 47, 60, 70, 75, 84, 111, 146, 171, 179, 208, 214
Athribis (Egypt), 30°25′N 31°11′E, 164
Atina (Atena), 40°27′N 15°33′E, 46, 62
Atrans (Yugoslavia), 46°10′N 15°02′E, 140
Atrax (Greece), 39°39′N 22°16′E, 146
Attaleia (Turkey), (Antalya), 36°53′N 30°42′E, 150
Atuatuca (Belgium), (Tungri), (Tongeren), 50°47′N 5°28′E, 129, 192
Aufidena (Alfedena), 41°44′N 14°02′E, 46, 62
Augusta Praetoria (Aosta), 45°43′N 7°19′E, 67, 129
Augusta Rauricorum (Switzerland), (Rauraci), (Augst/Kaiseraugst), 47°32′N 7°44′E, 108, 129, 140, 192
Augusta Taurinorum (Taurasia), (Turin), 45°04′N 7°40′E, 10, 12, 13, 47, 67, 129
Augusta Treverorum (W. Germany), (Treveri), (Trier), 49°45′N 6°39′E, 75, 84, 129, 171, 173, 179, 208, 214
Augusta Vindelicorum (W. Germany), (Augsburg), 48°21′N 10°54′E, 75, 107, 108, 140
Augusta Viromanduorum (France), (Vermand), 49°52′N 3°09′E, 129
Augustiana (Austria), (Traismauer), 48°22′N 15°46′E, 140
Augustobona (France), (Tricasini), (Troyes), 48°18′N 4°05′E, 129, 192
Augustobriga (Spain), 41°47′N 1°59′W, 124
Augustobriga (Spain), (Talavera la Vieja), 39°48′N 5°13′W, 124
Augustodunum (France), (Autun), 46°58′N 4°18′E, 129, 192
Augustodurum (France), (Bayeux), 49°16′N 0°42′W, 129
Augustomagus (France), (Senlis), 49°12′N 2°35′E, 129
Augustonemetum (France), (Clermont-Ferrand), 45°47′N 3°05′E, 129
Augustoritum (France), (Limoges), 45°50′N 1°15′E, 129
Aureliana (Yugoslavia), (Kostol), 43°54′N 22°15′E, 140
Aureliani *see* Cenabum
Aureus Mons (Yugoslavia), 44°37′N 20°49′E, 140
Ausa (Spain), (Vich), 41°56′N 2°16′E, 124
Ausculum (Ascoli Satriano), 41°13′N 15°34′E, 35, 41, 46, 62
Ausum (Algeria), (Sadouri), 34°48′N 4°59′E, 118
Autessiodurum (France), (Auxerre), 47°48′N 3°35′E, 129, 192, 199
Autricum (France), (Chartres), 48°27′N 1°30′E, 129
Auximum (Osimo), 43°28′N 13°29′E, 49, 70
Auzia (Algeria), 36°12′N 3°43′E, 118
Avaricum (France), (Bourges), 47°05′N 2°23′E, 70, 129
Avela (Spain), (Avila), 40°39′N 4°42′W, 124
Avennio (France), (Avignon), 43°56′N 4°48′E, 129
Aventicum (Switzerland), (Avenches), 46°53′N 7°03′E, 129
Avon R (U.K.), 135
Axima (France), (Aime), 45°33′N 6°40′E, 107, 129
Axios R (Yugoslavia/Greece), 146

Babba (Morocco), 34°41′N 5°39′W, 72
Babylon (Egypt), 30°00′N 31°14′E, 164
Babylon (Iraq), 32°33′N 44°25′E, 75
Badias (Algeria), 34°49′N 6°50′E, 118
Baecula (Spain), 38°23′N 3°28′W, 47
Baesippo (Spain), (Barbate), 36°12′N 5°55′W, 124
Baeterrae (France), (Béziers), 43°21′N 3°13′E, 72, 129
Baetis (Spain), 37°30′N 5°54′W, 47
Baetis R (Spain), (Guadalquivir), 23, 47, 124
Baetulo (Spain), (Badalona), 41°27′N 2°15′E, 72, 124
Bagacum (France), (Bavai), 50°12′N 3°36′E, 129
Bagradas R (Tunisia), 45
Baiberdon (Turkey), 40°12′N 40°02′E, 220
Baie Herculane (Romania), 44°53′N 22°22′E, 140
Balaleisus (Turkey), 38°17′N 42°02′E, 220
Balaton, L (Hungary), 46°50′N 17°50′E, 10, 140
Balbura (Turkey), 36°59′N 29°32′E, 150
Baleares (Isl), (Spain), (Balearic Isl), 47, 60, 75, 124
Balestra (Corsica), 41°48′N 9°01′E, 20
Banasa (Morocco), 34°29′N 6°08′W, 72, 118
Bangor Iscoed (U.K.), 53°00′N 2°55′W, 199
Bantia (Banzi), 40°52′N 16°02′E, 62
Barbalissus (Syria), (Mesken), 36°02′N 38°04′E, 157, 174, 220
Barca (Libya), 32°30′N 20°50′E, 164
Barche di Solferino 45°16′N 10°34′E, 20
Barchon (Turkey), 40°37′N 43°30′E, 220
Barcino (Spain), (Barcelona), 41°25′N 2°10′E, 72, 124, 208, 214
Bardsey (U.K.), 52°46′N 4°48′W, 199
Bari *see* Barium
Barium (Bari), 41°07′N 16°52′E, 10, 12, 38, 41, 46, 62
Barra 40°42′N 17°58′E, 57
Barumini (Sardinia), 39°43′N 9°01′E, 20
Basel (Switzerland), 47°33′N 7°36′E, 108
Basento R, 10
Basi (Corsica), 41°45′N 8°48′E, 20
Basileion (Turkey), 38°16′N 40°02′E, 220
Bassiana (Yugoslavia), (Petrovci), 44°57′N 20°06′E, 140
Basti (Spain), (Baza), 37°30′N 2°45′W, 124
Bastia (Corsica), 42°41′N 9°26′E, 10
Batnae (Turkey), 36°49′N 38°36′E, 157, 220
Bedaium (W. Germany), (Seebruck), 47°56′N 12°29′E, 140
Bedriacum (Cividale), 45°09′N 10°28′E, 84
Begastrum (Spain), (Cehegin), 38°06′N 1°48′W, 124
Beht R (Morocco), 118
Bellamonte 46°19′N 11°39′E, 20
Belverde 42°54′N 11°58′E, 20
Beneventum (Malventum), (Benevento), 41°08′N 14°46′E, 35, 38, 41, 46, 62, 67
Bergamo *see* Bergomum
Bergidum (Spain), 42°36′N 6°48′W, 124
Bergomum (Bergamo), 45°42′N 9°40′E, 10, 29
Berne (Switzerland), 46°57′N 7°26′E, 10
Bernesga R (Spain), 124
Beroe (Bulgaria), (Augusta Traiana), (Stara Zagora), 42°25′N 25°37′E, 140
Beroea (Greece), (Veroia), 40°32′N 22°11′E, 140, 146
Beroea (Syria), (Aleppo), 36°14′N 37°10′E, 150, 157, 174, 220
Berosaba (Israel), (Beersheba), 31°15′N 34°47′E, 157
Berytus (Lebanon), (Beirut), 35°52′N 35°30′E, 72, 111, 157, 220
Berzobis (Romania), (Reşiţa), 45°16′N 21°55′E, 140
Besanduce (Jordan), 31°36′N 35°09′E, 199
Besontio (France), (Besançon), 47°14′N 6°02′E, 84, 129, 192
Besouchis (Iraq), (Be'Saukhe), 33°03′N 44°26′E, 191
Bethlehem (Jordan), 31°42′N 35°12′E, 157, 199
Beysehir Gölü (Turkey), 37°40′N 31°30′E, 150
Bezabde (Turkey), 37°23′N 41°12′E, 157
Bezereos (Tunisia), 33°37′N 9°54′E, 118

INDEX